STORMRIDER
Surf Stories
INDONESIA

Stormrider Surf Stories Indonesia

First published in 2014 by Low Pressure Ltd ©
Tel/Fax +33 (0)5 58 77 76 85   enquiries@lowpressure.co.uk

Creation of all maps, graphic arrangement and text
© Low Pressure Ltd 2014

A catalogue reference for this book can be obtained from
the British Library. ISBN Softback: 978-1-908520-34-0

Printed by Hong Kong Graphics and Printing using
100% chlorine-free paper stock from managed forests.

The representation in this guide of a road is no proof of the existence of a right of way; likewise the frontiers shown do not imply any recognition or official acceptance on the part of the publishers. Surfing is a dangerous and addictive activity. The authors and publishers take no responsibility for accident or injury as a result of using information contained within this guide.

Low-end luxury charter, Panaitan Island, Java.

STORMRIDER
Surf Stories

INDONESIA

LOW PRESSURE

Contributors

Publishers
Bruce Sutherland, Dan Haylock, Ollie Fitzjones

Editor-In-Chief Alex Dick-Read

Publishing Editor Bruce Sutherland

Design and Production Dan Haylock

Everything Else Ollie Fitzjones

Accounts Andrea Fitzjones

Cover photos: Lagundri Bay by Brent Bielmann;
Bali Rice Paddies by Marko5/Shutterstock

This page: Purple dawn reef trek with a
pre-surf buzz, Bali.

Special thanks
To all the authors for permission to reprint their
work, to all the photographers who supplied us
with images, and to all these people whose help,
above and beyond, made this book something
more than it might have been:
Gra Murdoch and Craig Simms at Morrison Media,
Scott Hulet at *The Surfer's Journal*, Gerry Lopez
for carte blanche on his amazing Indo tales,
Brett Archibald for surviving and helping us
re-tell his awesome story, Kevin Lovett for some
seriously great pieces and for facilitating others,
Matt George just because, Kathryn Bonella and
Quercus Publishing, Chris Goodnow for sharing
his untold story of the discovery of Macaronis.

Authors

Tim Baker	Alex Dick-Read	Yasha Hetzel	Hanabeth Luke
Steve Barilotti	Mike Dugerian	Gary John	Leo Maxam
Chris Binns	Matt George	Stephen Jones	John McGroder
Kathryn Bonella	Chris Goodnow	Paul Kennedy	Jess Ponting
Emiliano Cataldi	Phil Goodrich	Richard E. Lewis	Matt Pruett
Susan Chaplin	DC Green	Gerry Lopez	Ketut Sarjana Putra
Antony 'Yep' Colas	Fabian Haegele	Kevin Lovett	Bruce Sutherland

Photographers

			Illustrators
Klaus Baumgartner	Jeff Divine	Nate Lawrence	Sandow Birk
David Badalec	Tony Fitzpatrick	Brad Masters	Phil Goodrich
Brent Bielmann	Pete Frieden	Dan Merkel	Anna Millais
John Callahan	Fabian Haegele	Jason Murray	
Jason Childs	Yasha Hetzel	Roger Sharp	
Riley Cooney	Emma Lee Lovett	Andrew Shield	
Mick Curley	Kevin Lovett	Billy Watts	

MICK CURLEY

Foreword

WELCOME TO INDONESIA! Welcome to a country so rich and radical that you'll have a story worth telling before your first day is done.

Everyone on Earth has a story, and surfers more than most. Surfers who've travelled through the world's largest archipelago, no matter where they come from, will have had their eyes opened and minds blown many, many times. All of which throws up the question: how can we do justice to that? How can we build an anthology of stories from somewhere so utterly overflowing with them?

We had to get picky, so we went for what's already out there (mostly), and of that, we went for the best. Then we took some out because the real world of book publishing and free-market economics kept snarling at us, like a mangey *anjing*.

But then we said 'screw it!', and put them back in again because, well, we want to give our readers some meat. Something to get stuck into, whether you're travelling in Indonesia or dreaming from afar.

So, yes, we know that in the grand scheme this compilation represents just a few ingots hewn from a hugely rich seam. But we think you'll find that's plenty of gold.

Inside you'll find a collection of random stories, many of them entirely disconnected. Different authors, places, time periods and experiences. Put them all together and you have a collection of wild diversity, but you also have something new.

Bali's Garut Widiarta momentarily in perfect synch with all the forces of the universe, Scar Reef.

In weaving these tales together, many of them tales of discovery, we now have a tapestry showing a much broader picture, one that, in effect, charts the history of surfing's invasion of Indonesia. It's not a chronological, linear history. It's history by snapshot. Take it a step further and there's something else. Lessons to be learned. Lessons from how the Nias experience went after June 1975; the much-changed flavour of Macaronis from 1980 until now; Bali's arc from ignorant bliss to overkill, traffic jams and bombs – and so on. Turns out this compendium of boy's own adventure stories (it was usually, though not always, boys), pokes a stick at some profound and often troubling questions. Questions about our impact. And as such, it contains some useful food for thought on the future.

We didn't intend this book, nor the ones still to come in this series, to work like that. But it's a reminder that surfers, seeking the most frivolous of thrills, have profound and powerful impacts. That surfers need to travel is not in doubt. It's hardwired into our addiction. But that we, as surfers, need to be mindful as we tread, is clearly inescapable.

So wherever you're reading this, we hope you enjoy all the radical, hilarious, scary-as-hell fun and adventure. And wherever you go, go well.

Alex Dick-Read, Editor-In-Chief

Contents

ACEH

Simeulue
Banyak Islands

NIAS
BATU ISLANDS

Siberut

Sipura
Pagai Utara
MENTAWAI   Pagai Selatan
ISLANDS

SUMATRA MAP 16

Enggar

SUMATRA

JAVA AND BALI

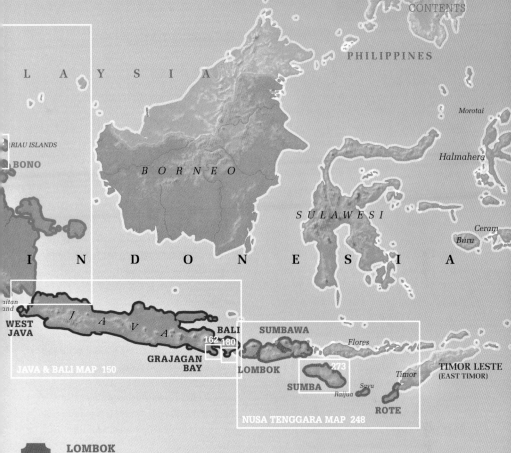

NUSA TENGGARA

Authors

Stephen Jones specialises in wetland rehabilitation and re-vegetation projects. He also was the director of the acclaimed El Mar, Mi Alma (2011), a film about surf and coastal issues in Chile. Stephen and his family live, surf, fish, dream and love in Lennox Head, Australia.

Kevin Lovett has spent 40 years in the world's largest archipelago and, he says, "only recently I've felt a sense of belonging. Caucasians rarely connect innately to the land as tribal communities do, so this continues to be an evolving experience for me. Living in Sulawesi, I remain hopeful that humanity will prosecute the powerful, paedophile, banker groups that control the world's political processes. Resist Fascism."

Emiliano Cataldi is a pro surfer and traveller who originally hails from Italy though now he lives in Byron Bay on the East Coast of Australia. Emi is a founding member of the Surf Explore collective so he spends his time travelling the lesser known corners of the surfing world, as well as writing, filming and of course, getting barrelled.

Phil Goodrich is an artist based in South Carolina. His wood-panel oil paintings are distinguished by vibrant colors and the natural wood grain that seems to guide the movement of the subject. Phil's art is influenced by his extensive traveling and search for perfect waves. His work has been featured in *The Surfer's Journal*, *The Surfer's Path*, *The Inertia* and *Soggybones* magazine.

Professor Chris Goodnow is NHMRC Australia Fellow and Distinguished Professor of Immunology at the Australian National University, Fellow of the Australian Academy of Science, Fellow of the Royal Society, and Member of the US National Academy of Sciences. Chris has been an avid surfer since his teenage years, and enjoys spending time with his family, surfing around Bawley Point, NSW.

Leo Maxam is a native of San Francisco, CA. He is co-creator and managing editor of *Bali Belly* magazine. A former Associated Press award-winning reporter and columnist at the *Santa Cruz Sentinel*, Leo is a regular contributor to publications across the globe, including *Surfing Magazine*, and *The Surfer's Journal*. He prefers a nomadic existence, but when pressed, identifies San Francisco as home.

Tim Baker is the best-selling author of numerous books on surfing, including *Bustin' Down The Door*, *High Surf* and *Occy*. He is a former editor of *Tracks* and *Surfing Life* magazines, and former editorial director of Morrison Media Services. He has won the Surfing Australia Hall of Fame Culture Award three times and been nominated for the CUB Australian Sports Writing Awards. His work has appeared in *Rolling Stone*, the *Sydney Morning Herald*, *Playboy*, *GQ*, *The Surfers Journal*, *The Surfer's Path* and numerous other surfing and mainstream magazines worldwide. At 47, he has also surfed and travelled throughout the world, and now lives in Currumbin, Queensland, with his wife and two children.

Fabian Haegele grew up landlocked in southern Germany and it wasn't until the age of 16 that he discovered his love of the ocean and surf travel. He has spent the past decade immersing himself in foreign cultures and chasing waves around the globe, visiting the Indonesian archipelago six times since 2005. These days he makes a living selling wine and banging nails in Margaret River, WA.

Alex Dick-Read is a freelance writer based in the Caribbean. He was Founding Editor of *The Surfer's Path* magazine (1996-2013) and before that worked as a news reporter for Reuters and Associated Press. His work has appeared in numerous magazines and newspapers including the *Guardian*, *Independent*, *High Life*, *ID*, *Index on Censorship*, and he has worked as a contributor and editor on books for Dorling Kindersley, Schiffer Publishing and Low Pressure publishing. He surfs most days, travels when he can and is always trying to figure out a way to get back to Indo.

Steve Barilotti a Californian photojournalist has spent many years as *Surfer* magazine's globe-roaming editor-at-large. His writing has also appeared in numerous books including *The Perfect Day*, *Best of Surfer Magazine* and biographies of renowned surf photographers Art Brewer, Ted Grambeau and the bestselling *LeRoy Grannis – Birth Of A Culture*. He has also screen-written and produced several cause-based documentaries, including *Wave of Compassion*, *Minds In The Water*, *180 South* and the Emmy-winning *Kokua*.

John McGroder, together with his wife, Belinda and his two sons, has been running the Mentawai charter boat *Barrenjoey* for the past 12 years. His calling as a surf charter skipper began in 1995 aboard Nusa Dewata off the coasts of Timor and since then he has skippered several other boats including *Indies Trader 1* and *2*. John is fluent in Bahasa Indonesian and has a reputation as one of the most experienced and friendly operators in the Mentawais.

Chris Binns is now a freelance writer after logging more than six years at *Surfing Life* magazine, including three as editor. The West Aussie moved to Bali in 2013, and now writes for *Red Bull Surfing*, the ASP and a host of surfing publications, as well as editing Sally Fitzgibbons' website, occasional commentary duties, and general mainstream copywriting for The Man.

Antony 'Yep' Colas is a surfer, writer, explorer, businessman and certified bore-surfing obsessive from the Côte Basque, France. He is author of the *World Stormrider Guides*, having surfed in over 55 countries, as well as writing for numerous global surf magazines. Antony has discovered and pioneered the Bono and Benak river bores, and has ridden many others across the world.

Bruce Sutherland is the publishing editor of *The Stormrider Guides* and has been surfing in Indonesia, on and off, since 1987.

Gary John is a hardcore surfer from Australia who regularly travels to Indonesia in search of perfect waves. Gary is also an expert at making life-saving compasses out of coconuts when lost at sea.

Yasha Hetzel graduated from UC Santa Barbara in his home state of California with a degree in geography and backside speed runs at Rincon. He spent much of the following decade documenting his search for hollow lefts in South America, Indonesia, Australia and beyond. This brought him to Western Australia were he completed his PhD in oceanography. He currently works as a scientist and continues to write, photograph, and chase swells in his spare time.

Gerry Lopez s one of surfing's best-known names and is legitimately described as 'a legend' of the sport. Surfing started for Lopez in 1960s Hawaii, when he mastered Oahu's 'Town' waves, before becoming known as 'Mr. Pipeline' for his pioneering shaping and riding techniques that put him deep inside the world's deadliest tube – with style. He was also co-founder of the ubiquitous 1970s Lightning Bolt brand. Lopez is author of an autobiography, *Surf is Where You Find It*, and is an active ambassador for Patagonia outdoor wear. He lives in Bend, Oregon where he shapes surfboards, writes, teaches yoga and healthy living, as well as enjoying deep-powder snowboarding and cold-water surfing.

DC Green is an award-winning fiction and non-fiction writer of children's books and surf journalism. He has written over 2,000 articles for 50 plus magazines and newspapers around the world, an adult graphic novel (*Lash Clone Returns to Vortex*) and contributed to a dozen anthologies. Green is widely respected as a surf writer who pioneered the 'gonzo surf journalism' style through his articles in *Tracks* magazine and Operation TubeQuest in *Surfing Life* magazine. He lives on the NSW South Coast

with one slightly crazy daughter and three very crazy cats. He continues to surf with high zeal and low skill.

Richard E. Lewis's parents were American missionaries to Indonesia, where he was born and raised. In 1965, as a nine-year old boy living in Bali, he was an eye-witness to the madness that swept over the country after Communists killed six army generals. Tens of thousands of innocent people were slaughtered. He attended college in the US and "then bailed out of a marine geology PhD program due to technical difficulties with my soul, which did not want to be shackled to a career". Lewis ended up back in Bali, writing and surfing. He is best known for his novel *The Killing Sea*, about the Asian tsunami, and he recently published *Bones of the Dark Moon*, a contemporary novel exploring the massacres of 1965. Find out more at: www. richardlewisauthor.com

Hanabeth Luke was born in the UK and spent her childhood between the Cornish village of St. Agnes and Byron Bay in Australia. In 2002 on a stop over in Bali, she and her boyfriend Marc went out for a night at the Sari Club. Then the bombs went off. Hanabeth survived but tragically Marc did not. This horrific experience led Hanabeth in two directions. One was to write down her story, published in her book *Shock Waves*. The second was to campaign for peace and against the War on Terror – which culminated in a powerful confrontation with UK Prime Minister Tony Blair on live TV. These days she lives just south of Byron Bay, teaches science at the local university and has found new love. She and her partner Kieran have a baby on the way.

Matt George is a former pro surfer, a writer, editor, model, film-maker and much more besides. His surf writing has appeared in *Surfer* and *Surfing Magazine* for over thirty years, as well as *The Surfer's Path*, *Stab* and *The Surfer's Journal*. George also wrote, directed and acted in the surf film *In God's Hands* and, in real life, worked as a first responder in major crises like the 2004 Asian Tsunami, Hurricane Katrina and the Pakistani Earthquake. George has surfed all over the world and explored Indonesia's waves for over four decades. He now lives in Bali where he runs SERF Academy and edits *Surftime* magazine.

Kathryn Bonella graduated in Melbourne and moved to London where she worked as a journalist in television and print. In 2000 she returned to Sydney to work as a producer for Australian *60 Minutes*. In 2004 she co-produced the first exclusive interview with Australian, Schapelle Corby, arrested in Bali with 4.2 kilos of marijuana in her board bag. A year later she quit *60 Minutes*, moved to Bali and co-wrote the no.1 best selling autobiography *Schapelle Corby My Story*, retitled *No More Tomorrows* overseas. Kathryn spent hundreds of hours inside Bali's Kerobokan Prison, and seeing the bizarre life up close decided the jail itself was worth a book, which became *Hotel Kerobokan*. She gained unprecedented access to Bali's biggest drug bosses and wrote the explosive best-seller *Snowing In Bali*, which looks at foreigners, many of them surfers, involved in the island's hugely profitable drug trade.

Matt Pruett is the former editor of *Eastern Surf Magazine*, and has co-authored the book *Wavescape: Portraits Of The Planet's Best Surf Spots*, directed and co-produced the surf movie *Always Right* and serves as an assignment writer for every major American surf magazine. His work has been featured in *Surfing Magazine, Surfer, ESM, Transworld Surf, Stab, Japan Surfin' Life, Surf Europe, Carve* and *The Surfer's Journal*. Currently working for Surfline.com as a senior editor from his home base on the Outer Banks of North Carolina, Pruett is best known for waving the East Coast flag in the face of a California-based surf industry.

Paul Kennedy is a freelance photographer and videographer originally from New Zealand. His photographic and written work has appeared in numerous surf and mainstream publications around the world. Kennedy is a perpetual traveller whose curiosity and work keep him moving between some of the world's most wild and beautiful places.

Susan Chaplin sold her house in California in 1991 and set off alone on a worldwide surf trip. She surfed in 20 tropical countries and traveled for three years. Returning home to San Diego, she disliked the cold, gray ocean...so she moved to the Caribbean. Based in the British Virgin Islands, she surfs clear aquamarine waves. When not surfing or writing, she paddles inter island on her paddleboard. She is first to prone paddle the Windward and Leeward Caribbean island chain. She has accomplished many other first-time long distance paddles.

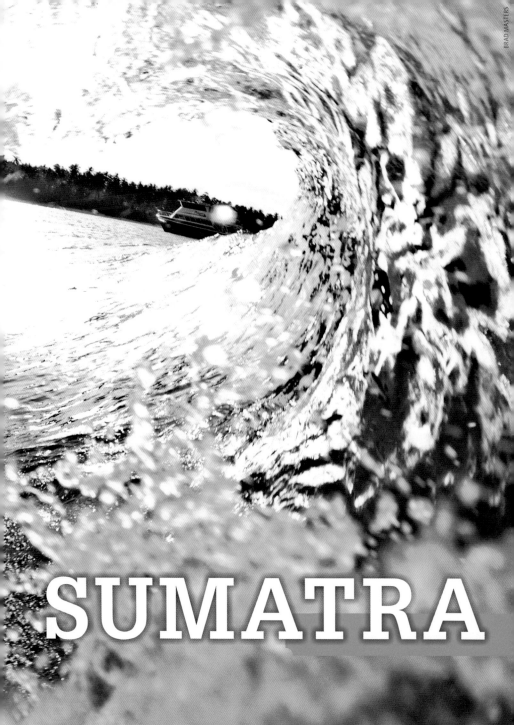

SUMATRA

Katiet kid, golden opportunity.

SUMATRA

THAILAND

Gulf
of
Thailand

MALAYSIA

Sabang
Banda Aceh

Penang

ACEH
Langsa
Pangkalanbrandan
Belawan
Medan
Tebingtinggi
SUMATERA
UTARA
Simeulue
Lake Toba
Banyak Islands
Tarutung
Sibolga

SINGAPORE
Batam
Bintan
RIAU ISLANDS

Padangsidempuan
Pekanbaru
RIAU

Nias 22
Nias

EQUATOR
Tanahmasa
Pini

132 **Bono River Bore**

BATU ISLANDS
Tanahbala
Bukittinggi
Pajakumbuh
Rengat
Kepulauan Lingga
Singkep

Padang
Solok

MENTAWAI
ISLANDS
Siberut
SUMATERA
BARAT
Jambi
JAMBI
PULAU
BANGKA
BELITUN
Pangkalpin

Sipura
Sungaipenuh
Mentok
SUMATERA
SELATAN
Tanjungpandan

Pagai Utara
Pagai Selatan
Palembang

The Mentawai Islands 70
Lubuklinggau
Perabumulih

Bengkulu
BENGKULU

Baturaja
LAMPUNG

Enggano
Telukbetung
Jakar
Bogor
JA
BA

INDIAN OCEAN
Panaitan
Bandun

| 0 | 100 | 200 | 300 | 400 | 500 Miles |
| 0 | 100 | 200 | 300 | 400 | 500km |

16

Finding Shelter

Five years after the 2004 'Boxing Day Tsunami' ravaged the coast of Aceh, local surfer Yudi Andika talks about his family's remarkable ordeal.

STEPHEN JONES

O N THE 26TH of December 2004, a magnitude 9.3 earthquake struck off the coast of Aceh at the northernmost tip of Sumatra. The devastating and unrelenting tsunami that followed caused unprecedented death and destruction throughout Southeast Asia, particularly to the "special territory" of Aceh. Of the 5,000 inhabitants of the village where Yudi Andika lives, the tsunami spared only 500, who escaped with only the clothes they wore...and each other. Yudi and his family were among the lucky survivors on a coastline completely ravaged by the waves.

As a young boy living on the coast, Yudi recalls spending a great deal of time at the beach, playing in the water almost every day. He grew accustomed to the ocean and to life by the sea. The doors of the family home were open to the beach and also to the small number of surfers that trickled through these parts in the early '80s.

"A couple of surfers came here when I was very little," Yudi recalls. "As I grew up I knew about surfing from them." Yudi tried it for the first time in the early '90s when he was 10. "A couple of surfers ask me to come to the beachbreak. They push me on a bodyboard the first time...the second time they ask me to go with my younger brother and together we surfed the beachbreak." That beachbreak was where Yudi's surfing really developed.

During much of Yudi's life, Aceh was largely isolated from the rest of the world. The people lived amidst conflict and tension. It was an unstable political period thanks to a prolonged and bloody civil war between the separatist Free Aceh Movement (GAM) and the central government of Indonesia. The war threatened a bleak future for the people of Aceh, as Yudi remembers: "It was very frightening for the civilians...people were threatened and interrogated...many questions, many questions…very dangerous because everyone was carrying guns." According to Yudi, the mountains nearby his village were a GAM stronghold, and also near the village was an Indonesian army base. "Very scary," says Yudi. "Sometimes we didn't know where the gunshots and bombings were coming from."

It was a war over land, resources, and economic profit, perhaps also fuelled by a very conservative form of Islam more prevalent in Aceh than the rest of Indonesia. It was this war that was disrupted – literally out of the blue – by a far-reaching and massively ruinous force of nature.

Yudi had returned that morning from an earlier party on the beach and was sharing breakfast at home with his family. It was all very relaxed until tremors from the earthquake began at around 8:20a.m. Although earthquakes are common to the region, this earthquake was different.

"For around 15 minutes it did not stop," says Yudi. "At first it was small, and then bigger, bigger, bigger. Sometimes, before, we had earthquakes, but not really strong and long like this."

Yudi and his family evacuated the house and gathered outside to watch the house moving from side to side. A little while later Yudi recalls hearing what he thought was an airplane, but when he looked to the sky, there was no visible sign. Turning to his mother, Yudi read her mind and within moments others were running up from the beach, shouting, "Big wave coming soon!"

Against his mother's wish Yudi took off to see for himself. "There were people on the beach, some running, some not," he recalls. "The water was shallow and drawing out to sea. Some were collecting fish off the reef, but far away, looking like an oil slick in the distance, a wave was coming."

Yudi ran swiftly back to his family and told them of the approaching danger, but the key to the family's second motorbike was missing and panic set in as Yudi, his mother, and sister all desperately searched for the key to their escape. Yudi's father was on the street with others from the neighbourhood. Distraught, Yudi told his mother to take his sister on the one motorbike, promising that he would run on foot, but his mother refused.

"If we die, we die together," she said. Just then, Yudi's mother remembered the spare key in the cupboard and for a moment the panic stopped. Yudi's father appeared as they climbed on the bikes and together they fled the family home – Yudi and his sister on one bike, his father and mother on the other.

Amidst the panic and chaos they were separated within a short distance of leaving the house. Yudi and his sister went one way, his father and mother went another. Yudi motored towards Banda Aceh in an attempt to escape the full thrust of the tsunami. "In the rice field to the west I could see this big, black monster – like 60 or 80 feet tall – just coming through the field…standing up like a cobra. It stood up like that," he says, still mystified as he shows the shape with his hand. "Maybe there were people in there mixing with wood, sand, trees…everything mixing in there."

But as they fled towards Banda Aceh, Yudi and his sister suddenly faced essentially the same wave, which had wrapped around the tip of Sumatra and was making its way back toward them through the city of Banda Aceh.

"A big swell was coming from the other direction. I was only about 100 metres from this thing when I saw it hit a roof. I swerved to the right and went faster and faster with my bike. We go very far away...far away past the wave." Yudi and his sister escaped. They sat with others, perched on a mountainside, overlooking the devastation below.

Worried for his parents he left his sister with the others and went searching. He walked the muddy roads, amidst the horror of the devastation. "There was wood and trees on the street and then I see like thousands and thousands of bodies, dead bodies." Yudi is amazed and astonished still by the memory. After walking not so far, he met a guy he knew from his own village, who was able to point him to the area to which his parents had fled. Yudi was reunited with his mother and father, who had also remarkably survived after losing their motorbike and running the last 200 metres to safety.

Hardship prevailed in the days that followed. Masses of displaced inhabitants sheltered together in makeshift tents and camps in areas free from wreckage. Shop owners gave what they had to the hungry, and people did what they could to help each other survive.

On the second day, Yudi and two others decided to return to see the remains of their beachside village. But they only made it so far through the ruins by bike before coming to an area of water that they were forced to swim across. "There were lots of bodies still floating there," Yudi says with dismay. "As we were swimming across, the bodies were under us. Some people had put a rope across there as the current was strong, and we just swim along the rope." Yudi's hand movements recollect the ordeal. "The water was strong, and the bodies ... so many. We had to swim through all of this to the village."

Arriving at their decimated village, Yudi discovered one of his best friends, who he had been with the night before the tsunami. Because Yudi's home was so close to the beach, the friend assumed he had been killed.

"He think I die already!" Yudi exclaims. "When we see each other we were so happy!" He says it with a big smile, nodding his head.

But most of Yudi´s friends were killed. Only a couple survived. Many of his relatives were also lost. "My father come from here and have lots of distant family here," Yudi explains. "Lots of them – maybe like 100 or 120 in the village – they all die." He pauses and drops his head. "Of my close family, one auntie and one cousin die...I miss them."

In the village, everyone lost loved ones, and they grieved as a village. Some whole families were lost. Many children were left without parents; many parents were left without their children. It was common for a family of six or seven to live together in one house, and now it was equally common that only one or two of them survived.

For the survivors, the first two weeks were extremely difficult. Apart from the horror and hurt of losing their homes and loved ones, there was not enough medical help for the sick and injured. There was insufficient hygiene and a lack of food and water, too, however Yudi recalls helicopter food drops to the area early in the aftermath. "Four days after the tsunami they just drop the food anywhere they want. The roads were cut, so distribution was by helicopter."

The clearing of dead bodies began almost immediately and was undertaken for the most part by the community itself. To begin with, bodies were being buried anywhere. Then a more organised system of collection by truck began, a difficult and enormously wretched task. Between a hundred and a thousand bodies were collected at a time and buried in mass graves. "It was very sad," explains Yudi. "Sometimes the families wanted to find a body, but they could not find the body amongst it all."

As the NGOs arrived during the first month, a system of food and water distribution, hygiene, medical care, and basic accommodation for the thousands of homeless was developed. For the next 12 months, Yudi's family lived in a large makeshift camp.

Within a few weeks, Yudi was employed by an NGO and was sent by boat to take food, water, mosquito nets and blankets to a heavily damaged location down the coast. On arrival, Yudi met with a doctor and immediately began work helping with everything he could as they set up a mobile clinic. "It was very hard," Yudi conveys, "a very busy job there…very ugly…because everybody get hurt by the tsunami, and they all need medical treatment. We not sleep until late at night and then get up very early to do everything we can do."

In the months that followed, Yudi continued his work. As time went on, rebuilding began and Yudi gained experience and became involved with developing community projects. He was able to work with the village firsthand. "I set up a project making boats, helping the women's group, helping the fishermen, carpenter, baker." Yudi proudly points out that, "the people were happy because when we come, we help them get their business or career going again."

Around one year after the disaster struck, people began moving back into Yudi's village. With the help of foreign aid, communities rebuilt their homes. Back on their land, Yudi's family stayed in a tent while they constructed a temporary dwelling. "It was hot…like a desert," he recalls. "There were no trees. We had just a tent…and then the temporary house," he says, chuckling as he points to the shack he and his mother and father still live in, while his father works to complete the new family home.

The 2004 tsunami brought an abrupt and complete stop to all human activity in the areas affected. Yet it was this single day of unimaginable human suffering that suspended one of Asia's longest-running wars and led to the opening of Aceh to the international community and a flood of aid from around the world. This shift in momentum led to the signing of a peace agreement between the separatist movement GAM and the Indonesian Army on August 15th 2005. To this day, the peace continues to prevail.

As I write, four years after the earth shook, the landscape still bears the wounds of nature's attack. A 30-metre-high scar marks the hills on the west-facing coast, recalling the height and force of the waves that hit these shores. Large ocean vessels rest in random locations kilometres from the sea. The few large trees on a once-forested line of dunes stand branchless up to 25 metres. A once-shaded coastline no longer boasts a palm-fringed setting, but instead a landscape regenerating. On the weekends a new generation of beachgoers leave Banda Aceh for the coast.

As for Yudi, he just walks to the end of the street. The beach there is his life and life goes on. He often thinks of how it was to be with friends and family in the times before the tsunami. It's a new village now, and there are new challenges. Although the tsunami changed so many things, some things remain the same.

Yudi, a talented surfer, can be found clocking up plenty of tube time at one of his local breaks. Many of his new friends have followed his path and taken to surfing to find peace and joy, riding waves on a reborn coast.

On the flats just back from the beach, my bungalow shakes with earthly vibrations. It's first light and I wake to turbulence, an emergent deep rumble and – in a moment of recognition – fear. I picture a larger-than-life sized wave, unimaginable amounts of water, uncompromising and headed for my bungalow. I launch from bed and run outside, climbing into some shorts along the way. Like me, others have fled their dwellings, and we group outside. In all of 30 seconds, the tremors stop. Yudi calmly heads to the beach to survey the ocean. He soon returns.

"No problem," he declares. "The wind is offshore. Let's go surfing."

This article was published in *The Surfer's Path* magazine, Issue 71, March/April 2009.

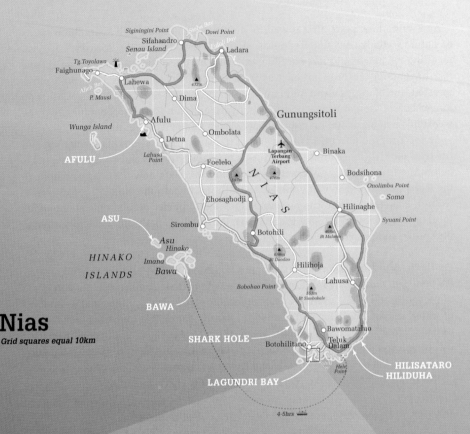

Sarangbaung Island

Siginingini Point
Sifahandro   Dowi Point
Senau Island
Siuba Bay
Eafeki Bay
Ladara

Tg. Toyolawa
Faighunago
Lahewa
Aleu Bay
P. Mausi
Dima   472m

Wunga Island
Afulu
Detna   Ombolata

Gunungsitoli

Lahusa Point
Foelelo
Lapangan Terbang Airport   Binaka

Bodsihona

Onolimbu Point

AFULU
557m
N I A S
476m

Soma

Ehosaghodji   Hilinaghe

ASU   Syuani Point

Sirombu   Botohili   498m
Bt Malana

Asu
Hinako
Imana   630m
Bt Daodao

**HINAKO
ISLANDS**   Bawa
Hilihoja
Lahusa
352m
Bt Siaobale

BAWA   Bobohao Point

Nias
Grid squares equal 10km   **SHARK HOLE**

Bawomataluo
Botohilitano   Teluk Dalam

HILISATARO
LAGUNDRI BAY   **HILIDUHA**

Hele Point

4-5hrs

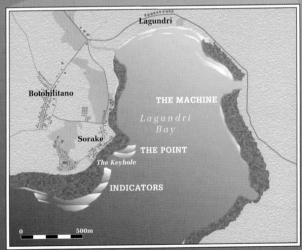

Lagundri

Botohilitano

THE MACHINE

*Lagundri
Bay*

Sorake   **THE POINT**

The Keyhole

INDICATORS

0   500m

The Surfer's Dream

An Introduction to Custodians of the Point

KEVIN LOVETT

T HE DREAM STATE is where we go to meet the future, rehabilitate the past and apparently where we make sense of our waking state, but what if that waking state is the moment when rider, board and wave melt into that singular, seamless experience of universality? How do we then convert the results of this sublime activity performed in real time when the self dissolves momentarily thus allowing a glimpse of other peoples' struggle for existence to arise into an altruistic force supporting positive change?

Surfing at best remains a hedonistic pursuit that represents one of the most self-gratifying of all activities, yet on a daily basis it continues to offer us up endless opportunities to release ourselves into the innermost essence of the vast expanse and thereby the chance to make a difference. Trying to remember dreams is not easy, trying to spin yourself a great one is challenging. Ruminate therefore on Larry Yates' zen like articulation of his Santosha dream: "its not just a place, more like a state of mind...a forgotten state of mind".

The so called 'Surfer's Dream' was essentially created in the Indonesian archipelago, it has been massively oversold in the international arena and the maintenance of a 'business as usual' attitude towards the promotion of 'The Dream' presumably cannot continue at its current exponential and unsustainable rate.

Some of the surfing related companies that comodified 'The Dream' via saturated advertising (flogged in decades-long campaigns like 'The Search' and 'The Crossing') transformed their businesses on the back of such promotion into large international corporations. Many of them now appear to be crumbling, but 'The Dream' seems to live on endlessly in the minds of the masses.

We've had close to 40 years of grassroots surf travel through the Indonesian archipelago and the results are clear to be seen by all that are interested in surf ecology. We now have festering surf slums that ulcerate the archipelago in most of the original centres of surfer traveller settlement. Admittedly we didn't know then what we know now, therefore I feel in Indonesia particularly, that we are now at a critical juncture, and we need to start changing our group modus operandi, pronto.

Surfers are predominantly self obsessed and largely ignorant of the impact that they have on fragile communities and the physical environments within those communities. However, that isn't to say that as a group we can't become more aware of others' needs, and by making subtle changes to our own behaviour begin to transform the scene around us wherever we pitch our tents or laydown our backpacks.

In terms of 'sustainable tourism' it seems the current rhetoric is framed within the phrase "acceptable limits of change". Obviously no one could see that coming when John Geisel and I showed up at Lagundri 37 years ago. But that same quandary is still occurring all over the archipelago and the limits of acceptable change will be severely challenged in the communities of all of these semi-remote locations in the near future.

Recurring patterns of behavior become apparent when one researches the history of the archipelago. We find a litany of conflicts and dispossession. The colonial attitude towards the locals was "gives us your spice, or we'll blow you out of the water". Latterly it became: "I ignorantly wish to keep you trapped in a poverty cycle because I want to sample your excellent waves on my smell-of-an-oil-rag travel budget". Basically it's a classic case of mutually dependent stakeholders clashing heads as one party's needs are met at the expense of the other.

The thing is that a local family living at subsistence level in semi remote Indonesia, in a location that has valuable, sustainable, economic assets like quality waves, is not going to be able to extricate themselves from the poverty cycle unless greater economic opportunity occurs. For so long it has all been about us getting our waves. The primary focus in the past has unequivocally been on travelling surfers having their needs met with everything else coming a distant second. Maybe now is the time to tread a little lighter, consider the whole as opposed to just one's own 'needs', and perhaps attempt to contribute something from the knowledge-base that the travelling surfer is coming from – something that will lead to a better long-term outcome for not only the environment that the wave is located in, but also the disadvantaged community that those waves support.

Lets face it, surf travel these days is a numbers game, and I feel it has reached a tipping point where innovation and forward thinking need to be actively pursued in order for 'The Dream' to stay alive.

John and I had the great good fortune of sharing the delights of "The Point' with Peter Troy in June, 1975. The doyen of traveller/surfers adds some much needed clarity to the dilemma of the ever-changing dreamscape; "It really is hard to realize that our paradises just can't be kept. I expect that's the way life is, and what for me is important is to know it and not be disturbed by what the progress of time does, for somebody already knew it for something else before oneself experienced it."

Custodians of the Point

The story of Lagundri Bay, Nias

KEVIN LOVETT

A S I LOOKED down at the newsstand and saw the April cover of *Surfer* magazine in 1974, little did I realize that this was then to become a significant moment in my journey. In fact, I didn't even know I was involved in a journey. The images captured on the cover entitled 'The Forgotten Island of Santosha' set my heart and mind racing. The overwhelming sense of adventure. The allure of the unknown. The ecstasy of riding perfect, uncrowded waves: these feelings were to crystallize in the proceeding months into a thought, which became the nucleus of our dream. The Surfer's Dream.

Recurring images of pristine tropical environments, swaying palm trees and perfect surf seemed to fill my every waking moment from the time I read this article. The author, Larry Yates, however, drew a red herring across the trail to the site of his experience by describing "Santosha" as not really a place, but a state of mind. Actually a forgotten state of mind."

What a curious quote. Was the Surfer's Dream just a state of mind? Was there no physical basis for its existence? My friend John Geisel and I were determined to prove that Santosha was a hoax and that somewhere out there The Dream burned brightly and we were a part of it.

This was the Cyclone season of '74. John and I lived in Gladstone in central Queensland, Australia. We would make the weekend migration to the idyllic Agnes Waters, a location with a coastal environment similar to Noosa. There we camped out with friends, explored mind and body and occasionally surfed. The frustration of constantly putting ourselves through a punishing road trip only to be denied good waves, reached a climax which resembled something akin to the blinding flash on the road to Damascus. A major blowout of a tire on my Holden station wagon after careening along on an empty, unpaved, pot-holed, dirt road caused a major rearrangement of our immediate priorties. We resolved at this point to throw it all in and search for our dream – but where? Then came the lightning flash. We agreed almost simultaneously it had to be Indonesia. A whole archipelago of approximately 13,000 islands stretched out to the north of Australia. *Morning of the Earth* had firmly established Bali as the major Indonesian surf destination. Reports in *Tracks*, the Australian surfer's bible, confirmed what we suspected, that the so-called "Island of the Gods" was getting crowded. But what did we know? We had my school atlas and a dream, fueled by a naive sense of adventure. But what was obvious to us was that if Bali was blessed with so many great waves, then the possibilities that existed in Sumatra must be endless. Sumatra then became our focus. It conjured up all the images of dense tropical jungles, white sand beaches, wild animals and an indigenous population to match. All the ingredients of a *Tarzan* movie. The only question was, who was going to play the role of Cheetah?

I bought a Super 8 camera with interchangeable lenses. John bought a two-man tent.

We left Gladstone with no guidebooks and little fanfare. Along the way we bought a map of Southeast Asia. We were to discover that journeys are rarely in straight lines, and that digressions occur for the most sublime reasons. That fresh-faced feeling of traveling for the first time, experiencing life moment by moment, the realization of being a part of a bigger whole, never leaves you.

We arrived in Kuala Lumpur on March 23, 1975, with three surfboards and two backpacks, 1,000 miles from the nearest known surf. It seemed an unusual call in hindsight, since we had no idea of which season provided the best opportunities for swell, prevailing wind conditions or visa applications. Ours was to become a voyage of discovery in the deepest sense of the word.

By the time we reached Penang, we had assumed the full novelty value of being traveling surfers in a land that had no surf.

The boards always became a focus of other people's attention. The more we spoke about seeking out and exploring for waves in Sumatra, the more we convinced ourselves we were actually on a mission. We lucked out in a coffee shop in Penang, coming in contact with an Australian surfer who had actually spent time in Sumatra travelling down the east coast of the island of Nias by boat. While he did not have a board, he had seen the backs of breaking waves around the southeast corner of the island and suggested we try there. Somehow, we felt we were being lured in a particular direction, but it was difficult to say where that was taking us. This was Penang in 1975. Georgetown, Batu Feringi, Teluk Bahang. The island was a major way-station along the overland hippie trail from Bali to Kathmandu. Freaks, travelers and a colorful array of local people created an eclectic consommé of humanity. The Chinese operated opium dens that flourished with police immunity. Haunched skeletal figures tended to their clients who sought comfort through a heated-up clay bowl on the end of a carved ivory pipe while reclining on a wooden pillow. Colorful identities like Jimmy the Buddha, Mr 0 and Mr High added a new dimension to our quest. In fact, the quest was starting to turn into something more like the Magical Mystery Tour. Boundaries were beginning to be pushed outward in every direction as we exercised our consciousness for what seemed like the first time ever. I guess there was a point at Mrs. Lee's bungalows at Teluk Bahang, while spending another day marveling at cloud formations, that we concluded we were in danger of losing the plot and needed to re-focus on The Dream. But the travel fever had hit, every day was a new adventure. We had heard tales of Luang Prabang, the mystical Royal Palace in Northern Laos. The Pathet Lao were slowly closing off as Laos was becoming embroiled in a civil war. Vietnam of course was in its death-throes. Angkor Wat had been overrun by the Khmer Rouge in Cambodia. History was occurring daily. We felt swept up in the crucible of change that was engulfing Southeast Asia. We figured that June would be a good time to hit Sumatra, which meant that we had enough time to head for Vientiane in Laos, the French colonial city on the banks of the Mekong River. All we had to do was survive the journey through Thailand, and in particular, Bangkok.

Leaving the boards in storage, we pushed on into the Kingdom of Siam arriving in the capital after a bone-jarring 27-hour rail journey aboard the Butterworth Express to Bangkok, the overnight excursion turning into a nightmarish scene of sleep and sensory deprivation – complete with the occasional bouts of out-of-body experience. Only the road-weaned warriors and those on restricted budgets (which seemed like everyone), travelled third-class with the chickens, ducks and pigs. Shoulder-to-shoulder, we slouched on upright wooden benches, the putrid odors filling our breathing space.

The Hotel Malaysia came with a high recommendation. In later years, when I saw that bar scene in Star Wars, I immediately flashed on "the Malaysia". There was a lot of violence in the air. The city was teeming with GIs on R&R from 'Nam. The interaction with the local heavies seemed to create a feeling that was the antithesis to what you believed would exist in the Kingdom of the Buddha. We pushed north through Undon Thani crossing the Mekong at Nong Kai and entering Vientiane on the day before the start of the Water Festival. The placid nature of the Lao people immediately became apparent. The Water Festival was held at the end of the dry season, and was meant to herald the arrival of steady, soaking rains. It amazed us to witness this genuine outpouring of joy by the people in the various festivities while seemingly oblivious to the fighting between the government troops and the Pathet Lao raging just 15kms outside of town. Tucked away in "The Bungalows" in the seedy old French quarter, we could hear cannon fire at night. The Water Festival worked on the precept that because you are coming out of a drought and water is still scarce, you should really throw it around because you know that the "wet" is imminent. It was hilarious. You would be walking down a street heading for breakfast when a child would race up and completely surprise you by dousing you with a bucket of water. So, of course, you get in on the act and retaliate. The daylight hours were just one long water fight. Vientiane was a charming. vibrant, colonial city with the largest market in Southeast Asia, selling everything from grass to grandmothers.

It was also on the verge of shutting itself off from the West for approximately 18 years. This was April, 1975. The CIA and the Soviets were involved in their useless charades using human pawns to achieve myopic supremacy as they watched Laos, Cambodia and Vietnam bleed to death. On the 25th we arrived back at the Malaysia. We heard that the last chopper had left the U.S. Embassy. The war was effectively over. One epoch was in its denouement – a new one was just beginning.

Exiting Thailand, our focus now shifted back onto The Dream. Lake Toba in north Sumatra was our next destination. Nestled in the highlands, the ancient caldera once formed the base of the largest volcano on the planet. Samosir Island was a jewel, which sparkled in the blue-green water of the lake, which in some parts they had yet to find bottom. Samosir was also home to several Batak tribes, and unbeknownst to us, it was to provide a crucial piece of information. Maungaloi was a tall man with broad shoulders. He was the chief of Tomok, the Batak village on Lake Samosir. He carried the authority of a leader with assuredness. Showing us into the restaurant under his traditional house overlooking the lake, we were transfixed by what we saw on the wall. There before us was a roughly hand-drawn map of Nias. In the Southwest corner of the map we could see a long bay called Lagundri that had surf potential written all over it. We suddenly had a destination, the focus tightened. We were pumped.

Toba was another big transit room, being a focal point on the overland trail from Bali to Bangkok. The invigorating climate, the stunning scenery and great food made it a very attractive watering hole. We had not had our boards in the water for $2^1/_2$ months so the idea of organizing a ferry-boat to try some skurfing on the lake was appealing. It was outrageous to say the least. This big old boat belched out diesel smoke while John skipped across the stern wake from one side to the other. Passengers cheered from the top deck as John entertained them while being dragged around the picturesque lake.

When we packed up and headed for Sibolga it was as if we were on a date with destiny. We felt that Lagundri would produce the wave we were searching for. Overnight in Sibolga was a little hazardous, as it was a military town and they always seemed to have a way of doing things differently.

The boat left for Teluk Dalam on the evening tide. We got down to the dock to be greeted by two other people, a tall, rangy man with a well-travelled face and an equally tall woman who introduced themselves as Peter and Wendy. Peter was very interested in John's two boards. They quickly fell into an expansive conversation as we pulled away from the dock and headed for Nias. While I spoke to Wendy, I couldn't help but overhear what Peter was saying. Some of the details of his travels sounded fascinating. During a break in conversation I pulled John aside and asked him who this guy was. John had been surfing for a lot longer and was much more experienced than I. He had a good grip on surfing history and knew of the exploits of our distinguished fellow traveller, the legendary Peter Troy.

Well this was going to be a real expedition. We made good time under the cool star-filled evening sky and our anticipation was building. However, sometime during the middle of the night, the motor stopped and we drifted away from Nias. It was one of those boats on one of those trips. We kept breaking down, but managed to limp into Teluk Dalam harbour at approximately 3pm, Saturday the 7th of June 1975.

We had entered the bay just after a rainstorm. The sun was filtering through and I had never seen so many shades of green. It was a breathtaking vision – all so lush and tropical. Just the stuff of dreams. The swell was pumping. Over to our left was a silver cylinder spinning off in the distance, breaking about 8'. To our right was a righthander going off in the 5' range. It was too good to be true. First impressions always linger longest. We quickly located the only *losmen*, grabbed our boards and hit the beach. We were immediately engulfed by large numbers of kids of all sizes following us along the sand around to the silver cylinder. It was a big bay and a very long walk, but we immediately learned something invaluable from Peter. He told us not to walk in the wet tidal surge on the sand, as your feet could get nicked by chunks of coral and rock, thus causing little cuts and scrapes and eventually, if unattended, sea ulcers. These would keep you out of the water reducing your surf time. It was a great tip that we adhered to. The Silver cylinder turned out to be a righthander breaking on dry reef. John was tired, so he paddled in while Peter talked me into paddling across the bay to the other wave we saw. This was about 1/2 km paddle, which was exhausting considering I hadn't been in the water for nearly three months. We surfed a couple of waves each, which was similar to a Kirra-style righthander. It had a gnarly end section onto bare reef, so as the sunset was already starting to fade, we turned for home, which was now an unbelievable 4-5km paddle away. If Peter hadn't been there counting out the strokes I don't know what I would have done to overcome my exhaustion. Here we were, bobbing up and down in the middle of a huge bay in complete darkness, paddling towards a little red light on the end of Teluk Dalam's jetty. It's amazing what you can pack into a few hours. Peter and I finally hauled ourselves up the wharf like a couple of bedraggled water rats.

Sunday and Monday were spent exploring. John and I headed out with our boards and canteens full of water to find what we had come for. We headed back overland to the southeast head of the bay where Peter and I had surfed the right. It had a very sharp rock and coral-strewn beach attached to the headland, which was difficult to traverse. Getting out there was relatively easy. Heading back, we tried to create a shortcut. There were no paths over terrain that featured 8' high *alang alang* grass and tropical rainforest. We made a decision to paddle across a bright green colored stream that was barely moving, full of debris and overhung with vines. I half expected Tarzan to come swinging across overhead with a deep throated yodel and hoped that crocodiles didnt exist in this part of Nias. Needless to say, it was a very quick paddle. John had a wonderful sense of direction, even standing in the overhead grass he knew the right way to go. But how do you move through a razor-sharp *alang alang* grass field without a machete?

Since he was leading, John would take a running leap and dive out onto his board flattening a section of grass, ahead. I tramped along behind. This was great, as school days spent dreaming of adventure finally took on a reality.

We crossed the southeast side of Teluk Dalam bay off the list, and on Monday spent the day heading to a bay on the southwest side. Peter was in holiday mode with his girlfriend so we headed out walking, carrying our boards alone. This didn't last too long as we attracted a tribe of kids who were very amusing. Heading towards the beach through a large coconut plantation, we started the chant "surfboard, surfboard". By this stage we had off-loaded our boards for the kids to carry on their heads. It was a wonderful scene to be caught up in, this procession of chanting, laughing, happy kids. We slipped easily into our newfound celebrity status.

Another bay and another unsurfable wave. We paddled out, but both of us ended up being caught on bare reef screaming for our mothers. During the trudge back to the losmen, it started to dawn on us just how fickle it was to find a surfable wave and what a unique combination of conditions it took to create one. We had looked at all of the possibilities, but still hadn't found what we were looking for. Back on the verandah of Menanti, we put our feet up and tried to figure out what was going wrong with the search. We took out the map and it was obvious everything pointed to Lagundri. Asking around, everyone said Lagundri "*ombak besar*" but they also had said that about Teluk Dalam. The swell was still running on the outside reefs. We decided that Tuesday we would head for Lagundri but it was supposedly 15km away with no direct transport bus or bemo available. We organized two pushbikes, leaving our boards behind. With our canteens full and a supply of Ibu's little *roti kelapa* (coconut bread rolls), we headed out to reconnoiter Lagundri Bay.

The rutted bitumen road ran out after about 6 or 7 kms. We then headed off on a rock-pitted track towards Lagundri. Travel was slow as we had to push our bikes for the most part in the steamy conditions. The track was bordered by forest so that it was difficult to see what lay beyond and where exactly we were heading. About 2pm we finally came through a clearing and saw a magnificent gold sandy beach with huge coconut trees fringing a spectacular looking bay. We made our way to the beach and stood in the middle of the large horseshoe bay, dumbstruck at the sight. The shorebreak was pounding and to our left was a set-up churning out spitting barrels. This spot eventually became known as "The Machine".

Our gaze stretched further out towards the southwest part of the bay and there we saw it. The most amazing sight of a set of waves peeling around the palm-tree covered headland. The waves were large because we were at least 4km away and the sets just seemed to produce a continuous line of almond eye barrels as they marched around the point and into the bay. Across on the opposite headland was a giant lefthander that seemed a little out of control, but an equally majestic sight.

We fell back onto the sand laughing our heads off before grabbing the bikes and heading off around the bay to the point.

As we got back on the path, we entered a small fishing village where we were greeted by lots of startled locals. At this stage we had been travelling just inland off the beach, but the bay was still clearly visible. However, we were persuaded by the crowd forming around us to leave the bikes and follow them up a large steep hill. By now we had a crowd of about 100 people all around us. The mood was friendly, but we were staggered by the scene that confronted us upon reaching the top of the hill. We climbed a flight of large stone stairs, and then before us was a large stone paved courtyard that extended some 200 meters by 30 meters lined with wooden houses on stilts linked together in the shape of an old boat. This was the Stone Age. This was Botohilitano Village.

As we strode down the middle of the courtyard, people and kids raced out from the houses forming an aisleway to walk through. We stole a glance at the over-sized stone chairs and tables. Situated in the middle of the village there were stone carved crocodiles and a 2-meter high jumping stone. It felt very wild. The looks on some of the faces of the people around us confirmed this: wild-eyed stares with the betel nut dribble, tobacco-stained teeth, set in chiseled features, tough looking bodies and that was just the women. I turned to John and said, "It feels like we're Livingstone and Stanley". We could see into the houses through the slatted stern section overlooking the courtyard. If you caught someone staring they would quickly turn away. We also caught sight of some amazing looking spears and lots of traditional swords.

The chief village leader came out, and we exchanged pleasantries. We had only been in Indonesia for two weeks, and could barely stumble through some simple phrases. At this stage we had to ask, "But where are the waves?" "*Di mana ombak?*"

This was one phrase we could get out. The procession then moved out of the western end of the courtyard down a narrow path. We were desperate to get to the beach and confirm what we had seen from the middle of the bay. The path wound down through thick jungle until we finally came onto flat land in a magnificent coconut plantation. We could see the reef. The sound of the pumping waves was deafening.

Impossible looking waves with truly smoking sections, broke just 75 metres out in front of us. For a few moments, confusion reigned supreme. Had we come all this way here to ride the wave that later would become known as Indicator? The swell was big. Further around to the west, 10' plus waves were cornering off the reef. It was then we finally realized we had come down from the village on the western side of the point. Walking back then towards the point, we could see a stupendous sight – 6-8' waves of almost perfect shape, funnelling around the point. It was late afternoon and the rich equatorial lines in the sky cast an ethereal appearance over the bay. We stood on the point marveling at both the magnificence of the wave, and also the incredible beauty of the backdrop which featured lush green covered hills with a golden sandy beach, fringed by incredibly tall coconut trees, front-lit by the sunset hues. Continuous sets kept marching in and while the waves appeared demanding they also looked perfect. The search was over. We burnt offerings to Buddha to celebrate the joy of life.

The Dream was for real

Time was getting away from us. We now had to get back to our pushbikes and Teluk Dalam to load up for our return the following day. The adrenaline surge from our discovery made us as high as kites. The 15km return journey in the dark was a mere formality.

Getting back at about 8.30pm we excitedly told Peter. Pumped up at the prospect of perfect surf, he went out to organize transport while we ate. We planned a crack of dawn departure, but sleeping wasn't easy. I spent a restless night wondering whether I had what it would take to surf the point. Riding a kneeboard, I was conscious of the Greenough factor. Peter had spent time with George and had related stories about their shared surfing experiences. I wanted to surf well for a number of reasons. John and I had scored a week of great surf at Kirra in March before our departure. I had replayed one particular tube ride constantly in my mind since then, and, of course, it was what I referred to now. We were on our way early. Peter had scored an old Toyota Land Cruiser with no roof, but a frame to carry the boards on. The scene had surfing written all over it. We piled in with our backpacks, as John and I were planning to stay. I plugged Santana's "Black Magic Woman" into my mind, the staccato cries of his wailing guitar causing my anticipation to build.

We finally arrived in Lagundri village about 8.30am on Wednesday, June 11th, and then made the journey along the beach out to the point. There had been light showers falling and the point was shrouded in mist. We were all spellbound at the natural beauty of the environment. At the time, John and I were jointly reading Tolkien's *Lord of the Rings*. It was his book, but he kindly shared it with me by reading a chapter then tearing it out for me to eagerly absorb. Peter reminded me of "Strider" the guardian, a character in the book. It was the way he carried himself, the experience he drew upon from his travels. He looked as though he had stepped straight out of the book. It's an image I've always kept of him.

The swell was very consistent, pumping at 6-8' foot. Not a breath of wind. The mist just hung like a cloudy apparition over the crashing waves. We once again burnt an offering to Buddha and paddled out into the most significant session of our lives.

I had picked off a smaller one on the inside and was paddling back out, when I saw John drop into a 6-7' wall that just stood up and pitched straight over him. Not a drop of water out of place. The moment crystallized. I was spellbound. It was all happening in slow motion. As he cruised by I stared in amazement at the ecstatic look on his face – water droplets hanging in his beard, totally immersed in the experience. Peter borrowed John's 7'4" yellow pintail, single fin, while John rode his 6'6" swallow-tail with the drawing of the Buddha embedded in the glass on the deck. He called it his favorite board, his "Buddha stick". Peter took a bigger one from out on the peak, and with a classic laid over bottom turn, projected further out onto the wall to stand proud in the mouth of a gaping barrel. The quality of the waves was mind-blowing. We were in a trance. The sets were continuous. I paddled into perfection with four easy strokes, slid over the ledge and leaned forward during the freefall to connect halfway down the face. Looking up, I felt the adrenaline surge as a feeling of calmness enveloped me. The dark green cylindrical womb kept extending out in front. I could see Peter up ahead on the face, preparing to duck dive. Thinking I was going to hit him as he pushed through. However, it seemed to take ages for me to go past him. Choosing the high line through the bowl, sunlight came streaming in and a flash of the trees across the bay. Upon making my exit, the red steeple of the church atop the bay came into view. One of the amazing aspects of the surfing experience is the view of life looking out from inside a breaking wave. These unique, intense, timeless moments help shape consciousness and are carried with you forever. We came in, saturated by the experience. After something to eat and rest, we surfed again. The sets were relentless. The wave shape was of the highest quality, with every wave tubing in its entirety.

Peter paddled up to check out Indicator, which was pumping its heart out. He noted the keyhole crack in the reef, which offered a perfect entry into the water by padding around the back of the breaking waves on the point. Later in the afternoon, we returned to the village and Peter's helped organize a house for us to stay in with a local family. He also left me with a phrase book on Bahasa, which was most helpful. We said our goodbyes to our friends and they wished us well before driving off, leaving us all alone.

John Geisel realizing the dream, June 30th, 1975. This discovery not only fuelled the dreams of other surfers worldwide, it also changed the future of Nias' Lagundri Bay community.

KEVIN LOVETT

KEVIN LOVETT

Surfing's first foothold in Nias, established 1975 – Taninjin's shelter on the point right in front of Indicator.

Our living quarters were cramped to say the least, but we were on an incredible high from surfing. The house was really just a hut with rough slabs of timber for walls and a thatched roof. It had a couple of rooms, but we were allowed to place our sleeping bags up in a loft, which was situated above the kitchen. Little did we know that next morning the old *ibu* (mother) would smoke us out with her fire, for as we discovered, the hut had no chimney. The following days were spent out on the point in two or three sessions a day. The swell stayed in the 6-8' range. It just seemed endless. We were having trouble organizing meals. It seemed that while we were novelties in Lagundri, we were also untouchables. Prices offered for meals were exorbitant; the smoky loft was giving us black faces and the bananas and coconuts were starting to lose their appeal.

John was turning 23 the next day, so we decided we'd walk into Teluk Dalam to celebrate by fuelling up with a good meal at Sabar Menanu, and bring back a supply of Ibu's famous *roti kelapas*. We sat on the beach soaking up the sunset and vowed to hang in and live The Dream for as long as possible. A quick check on finances, however, revealed a small amount of cash and a $50 traveler's check between us. We eventually stretched it out for 6¹/₂ weeks, and still managed to have enough left for transport back to Toba.

Our final decision was to move out onto the point and pitch John's tent in the little thatched roof shelter we had seen on that first day. This was going to send out a strong message to the locals that we were very committed to what we had come to do – surf! The owner of the hut was a young man named Taninjin. He said it was okay to stay there, and seemed proud that we had chosen this spot, in front of the thundering Indicator.

It was a wonderful setting; paradise with an ocean view. The two-man tent fit snugly under the thatched roof. We took our sleeping bag covers and collected some thick shell grit and covered the ground surrounding the campsite; we were styling.

Not having to make the long walk to and from Lagundri each day saved energy. The food situation still hadn't improved, and this was already about a week after our arrival. Something was obviously in the air, but we didn't know what.

Our celebrity status had grown to the stage where people were traveling from Gunung Sitoli in the north, a nightmarish eight-hour bus ride away, to come out to see us. Everyday we had inquiring faces appearing out of the jungle and from behind coconut trees to watch our every move. We were starting to feel like goldfish. On occasion, some very heavy looking characters visited and hung out with us. Men that looked like they were from another world. We communicated in sign language, explaining we were surfers with few possessions and little money. The food issue finally came to a head. We needed to resupply. We took Taninjin with us and headed up to Botihli. The elders assembled in Taninjin's father's house, the oldest standing structure in the village, over 200 years old.

It was a magnificent example of traditional architecture incorporating large teak slabs and beams polished by continuous human contact over the years. The women were herded out and it was left to the men to decide our fate. Buddha's offering was passed around the gathering with the elders inhaling deeply. Within moments, the tension of the past ten days dissolved into fits of laughter as huge grins broke out over these Stone Age faces. Laughter filled the house as we were finally accepted for who we were. Magically, the women then filed back in carrying trays of food for an impromptu celebration. It wasn't a roast turkey dinner but was one of the best meals of my life.

Following this incident, we organized a late afternoon meal in Lagundri village at the home of Pringitan and his wife Norhyat. These people we grew to love. We would walk in around sunset time and return in the dark carrying our canteens full of tea and water with some fruit for the next day. The one meal a day regimen fit into our budget. At night we read by torchlight, however, during the lead up to and immediately after the full moon, we could easily read outside as the moonlight flooded the coconut grove with light.

We were stunned one evening upon arriving at Norhyat's for tea to find letters and a package waiting for us. We had organized for mail to be collected from Poste Restante in Sibolga and be hand carried over to Teluk Dalam. We had not expected it to happen but here it was, news from home, which seemed like a world away. The big surprise was that my mother had sent me one of her traditional fruitcakes (my favorite) to celebrate my 21st birthday on the 30th of June. It had arrived a week early; we laughed until it hurt. The nightly ritual of a slice of fruitcake with a cup of tea and a fresh installment of *Lord of the Rings* just made The Dream seem all the more vivid.

From our first sight of the point, the waves continued for two weeks in a constant range of 6-8'. On Saturday the 21st we walked into Teluk Dalam for Ibu's *roti kelapas* and a change of cooking. On the journey back, we saw the full moon rising, which heralded the summer equinox. A new swell had kicked in during our absence and on Sunday the bay was flooded with swell on the high tide with 10ft sets marching in. It must have been 20ft plus on the big left out the back. Just before my birthday, a guy walked around the point and into our camp. John was stunned to immediately recognize him as Steve, a friend of his from the Gold Coast. Steve had been in Toba recovering from a bout of malaria and had met up with Peter Troy who had explained about our set-up and that one guy had two boards. Steve thought he would come and check out the surf. He stayed and surfed for over a week before returning to Sibolga and continuing his journey. What a detour.

The swell started to become inconsistent as July began. It was at this stage we hurriedly realized that we should start using the camera equipment that we had lugged around. The weather patterns changed. The wind came up. We ventured around to the west looking for other possibilities, but to no avail. The $50 had finally dwindled after $6^1/_2$ weeks, forcing our departure. In retrospect, it was the best $50 I've ever spent in my life. John and I scratched our initials into the tree – JG, KL, 1975. We lit a fire in the campsite and bade farewell to Ma-ur and his stepson Sifarma, our neighbors on the point. It was an emotional farewell from Lagundri.

After approximately one month in Toba, we found ourselves sleeping on a boat in Padang, the capital of West Sumatra. We had booked a passage out to the Mentawai group of islands believing that what we had experienced at Lagundri was just the tip of the iceberg. However, during the morning of the first day of the trip, we both found ourselves overcome by the most intense illness either of us had ever experienced. We had wrapped ourselves up in everything we would find and laid under a tarp on the deck in the bow of the copra trader, our jaws chattering uncontrollably. Fortunately we managed to get the captain to change direction and head south to Bengkulu, a couple of days away. We didn't realize it, but we were both in death's grip. I was to have a running battle with malaria over the next year and a half. For John, it was to kill him within nine months. By the time we departed Sumatra, we had spent $3^1/_2$ months journeying along the road less travelled.

We were greeted with great, consistent surf on our arrival back in Bali in September. Kuta Reef with two guys out most days. Our first venture out to Uluwatu one Saturday morning saw us witness some inspirational surfing by Gerry Lopez and Roy Mesker. Out alone and carving up 8ft long walls from way out beyond the peak, down through the inside, kicking out in front of the big rock. The first and only time I've ever seen that done.

John was coming down with more attacks. I tried to talk him into returning to Australia with me, however he had money sent to him in Bangkok. His goal was to head overland to Europe. At the significant moment of our parting I had just met a girl who was to become my wife. As it transpired, one major role player in my life was exiting as a new one appeared. I never saw John again.

I returned to Australia and made my way around to Perth to meet up with Jan. It was then, in February '76, that I received a letter from my mother. Upon opening it, a tiny newspaper clipping fell out of the envelope and onto the ground. I picked it up with utter amazement and welling emotion, trying to comprehend the enormity of what I was reading. It was John's death notice. I sat down and cried. I had recently received a letter from him in Tehran, Iran where he was holed up because of a severe winter storm. He had bought a kombi in Kathmandu and traveled with friends across the top of India, Pakistan, Afghanistan and into Iran to be halted by blizzards and freezing temperatures. He had been ill with malaria in Kathmandu at Christmas, so it was obviously still in his system. He was in a weakened state. In Tehran, the temperatures dropped to below -20°. He succumbed to double pneumonia, but it was the malaria that killed him. I suddenly found myself cast adrift. We had shared so many remarkable experiences together that it seemed incomprehensible that he was gone, and that I had no one to recount and reminisce with.

Jan was one of triplets, and, together with her sister Judy and brother Bugs, we made the journey back to Lagundri, arriving almost exactly a year after John and I had walked in. I felt that I had to share the experience with someone who was living. Upon arriving, I couldn't believe it, there was another guy staying in the village.

It was obviously going to be different this time around. We immediately moved around to Taninjin's hut and set up camp with three tents. The locals greeted us with glee. The news of John's death, however, shocked them. We were intent on being self-sufficient. Jan and Judy shared a very similar appearance, blonde haired, they charmed the locals in every way. They together with Bugs, the eldest by ten minutes, were very astute at camping. We carried water from Ma-ur's well, who greeted us as distant relatives. The girls would walk up to Botohilitano and buy vegetables and fruit on a daily basis. I remember we bought a bunch of 300 bananas for 300 rupiah and ate them as they opened. We organized the fish man to come by with his catch and carried in rice from Teluk Dalam.

The surf pumped. Bugs was in his element. The other surfer left and we had it to ourselves. Days were spent keeping the camp running smoothly and maintaining harmony. Self-sufficiency is a wonderful expression, but it requires a lot of hard work. The weather pattern seemed different to the year before. There was more wind in mid-June and darkening skies threatened rain, which came with a vengeance.

Seven days and nights of torrential downpours with wind gusts that drove the rain at an angle parallel to the land.

Huddled in our tents at night under the thatched hut, it seemed like everything could go at any time. The noise of coconuts falling were like small bombs going off. The trees themselves were bent over at seemingly impossible angles by the ferocity of the wind. At various times during the day, we would scout about for semi-dry kindling for the fire. I walked into town one day when it had partially cleared up to buy some antibiotics for a leg infection that Jan had. Coming home, I was held up in Lagundri as night fell by another raging storm. I finally made it around the point expecting everyone to be tucked in, but there to my surprise was Bugs huddled over the campfire, semi-protected by his makeshift shelter. He cried out "The *nasi goreng's* ready, come and get it". In the middle of this gale, he had achieved the impossible. We were ecstatic at the simplicity of the moment. But the deluge had come at a price. Up on Botohilitano, the pig troughs had overflowed into the wells causing an outbreak of cholera. Eleven people died in the week following the rain. For us it was malaria. I obviously was in a weakened state, and became quickly engulfed yet again by the disease. It felt like it had a mortgage on my life. Jan and Bugs also came down with it, only Judy was spared. This now really started to worry me as it is one thing to put up with hardship and sickness to live your own dream, but it's another thing to have that impact on others. Jan and I had the same symptoms, while Bugs' attacks came on a different time frame. He would usually kick off with a fever around 5p.m. and then be horizontal for three or four days. Jan and I shared a tent. The heat from our rising temperature would cause condensation to form on the roof of the tent and drip back down on top of us. After four or five days, you would be feeling like death warmed over. We now started to relate to the lethargy that also overwhelmed the locals. For my companions, the dream burned as brightly as ever, but for me it was somehow starting to fade. In the weeks following the storms, we were greeted by consistent swells and picture perfect conditions. Bugs and I shared a memorable 10' day with the swell peaking on low tide with the afternoon glass off. It was a watershed in his surfing experience; just as it had been for me the year before. Bugs recently recounted his feelings, "The whole Nias experience changed my life, in some ways forever. It is impossible to explain to people who have never shared an experience like that. To live on the edge of civilization with a dream to find perfect uncrowded surf and to forgo the daily comforts for not just a day or two, but for three months. However, in that abstinence, finding harmony and clarity that borders on the spiritual cannot be translated easily, nor should it be. It is for the individual to keep in a place inside himself and to savor the memory."

We caught sight of two Westerners one day approaching our camp. As it turned out, it was a guy I had met in Perth and had briefly mentioned that I was returning to Nias. He decided to join us with his girlfriend, who was of Indian descent born in Perth. This upset the harmony of our camp, much to our annoyance, but being peace-loving hippies, we let them stay.

Within a short time, Stuart had flipped out and had assumed the persona of a modern day Rambo. Ingrid, his girlfriend, was suffering from neglect. They had attracted a lot of strange looking locals to the camp. As time wore on, we gave them the adopted names "stupid and ignorant," because when you are out there on the edge just existing, you can't hide anything. All is revealed. Stuart became more one-dimensional and eventually left the camp and left Ingrid behind. She had by now also become very ill with incredible stabbing pains in her kidneys. We looked after her, however, it was difficult to know what she was suffering from as she displayed no chills or fever. We had been there ten weeks when Jan and I had our third attack.

It lasted approximately five days. Bugs enticed me out for a surf in prime conditions, but I felt like I was on another planet. From out in the line-up, we watched one of the girls walk down to the point. Halfway along the beach she collapsed, and it looked as though she was lying down. What had happened in reality was that Jan had fainted. We immediately came in.

Upon learning of Jan's fainting spells, I packed a small bag and decided to evacuate her to Teluk Dalam. There had been more rain and the conditions were wearing to say the least.

Ingrid's condition had also worsened. However, there were these local guys, her "friends" paying a lot of attention to her. We also thought she had to go, as well. Jan and I struggled out and onto a copra truck heading into Teluk Dalam. By great fortune there was a travelling medical orderly staying at Sabar Menanti who gave Jan heart stabilizers to stop her heart from fibrillating (beating too fast). Her fainting spells had signified that she had entered into a very vulnerable phase of the disease. After taking the medication, she immediately began showing improvement. I returned to camp the next day to pack the remainder of our belongings and to check in with Judy and Bugs. The heavy overnight rain and high tide meant the river in Lagundri was flooded. It was a hair-raising crossing. I relayed the news of Jan to a relieved brother and sister, then we set about packing up the camp. I left late in the afternoon, while Judy and Bugs would follow in a couple of days.

Returning to the rivermouth, I noticed a great commotion occurring as Ingrid was in the throes of being evacuated to a hospital at a German mission up in the highlands. Here were the same guys that used to hang around her and go for walks with her, now crowded around lifting her into an old rusted utility vehicle, which had been brought down onto the beach. I also noticed Pringuan, the Lagundri Village headman and lots of locals standing by and looking very agitated. The whole scene had a very strange vibe. I threw our packs into the back and climbed on board. The sunset colors were starting to fade as the truck headed out to Teluk Dalam. I stole a glance over my shoulder at the bay and the point, and sighed. The dream, as far as I was concerned, had turned into a nightmare. I felt overwhelming feelings of death and sickness. I never wanted to see the place again. And I didn't for twenty years. John and I had made a pact that neither of us would expose the place unless we were both in agreement. With his death, I had lost interest.

Time is a great healer. I had answered a letter in *Tracks* for information regarding the two surfers who accompanied Peter Troy to Lagundri in '75. As it transpired, the woman had written a synopsis for a documentary for broadcast on SBS, the multicultural television channel in Australia. They planned to shoot the documentary during the WQS event in June '96.

The minivan deposited me at the back of the point in the middle of the night. It seemed like somewhere in the back of beyond. It was in fact, almost twenty years to the day that John and I had stumbled into the bay. If I was disorientated in the dark, I was downright lost when daylight revealed my complete surroundings. Yes, the other side of the bay was still there, untouched in its pristine glory, however, the point had been raped beyond belief. The coconut grove had been decimated to create stumps to sit the little stilt houses on. The resulting feeling was "funky jungle" without the jungle.

Why build right on the high tide mark? It's coral reef. The only constant with a fringing reef is that it is constantly changing. Where was the beach? Where was The Point? It was apparent that a good 25-30 metres had actually disappeared during the building program. After a quick surf, I realized that some things don't change. A couple of 4-5ft waves were fun with the promise of more to come. If I had planned a return to Lagundri, I would not have chosen it to coincide with a WQS event. I thought 'great, how many more surfers will there be in the water?' Sure enough, the swell did not build until the day before the event, which was already a week after my arrival. I surfed that morning in a pack of about 25 of the contestants. It was a furious battle for the sets. I was content to watch and try for the crumbs. Halfway through the session, some 6ft-plus sets started appearing. Joel Fitzgerald paddled up to Indicator and provided me with a sight I had never seen before. Taking off on a bomb from way over, he rode it all the way through the perilous inside section. It was a majestic sight, looking up from the line-up on the point I had watched countless, perfectly formed waves break at Indicator and never before seen one ridden.

Perhaps Lagundri was going to share some more secrets with me. The following day I was to be impressed yet again. While taking an early morning stroll on the beach past the hotel, I caught sight of a group of pros with their boards tearing up the beach ahead of me. I pondered as they watched the lumbering righthander funnel around to the west, open its jaws and spit out a big plume of spray. With growing disbelief, I sat and watched them paddle out to this wave which must have been breaking in the 8-10ft range, and take it apart. Of course, the spoils were shared evenly at the end of the session, as shredded skin and broken boards were tallied against outrageous barrels and adrenaline-charged rides. Later in the afternoon, Lee Winkler and Koby Abberton took on the "Indicator" in a hell session. I wondered why it all looked so different. It was, of course, because I was about 10-12ft up above the ground on a verandah, viewing the action from on high. The curvature of the reef was so apparent. This was truly a magnificent set up, with outside Indicator wrapping into Indicator, the gap at the key-hole and then the wrap around The Point into Kiddieland.

What kind of forces had conspired to construct this unique wave-riding location? After taking into account the hazardous physical conditions involved in surfing those other breaks, The Point itself in comparison rated five stars in terms of safety! I was privileged to witness some outstanding surfing during the three-day event. Mick Lowe and Beau Emerton charged in their semis, pulling big floaters and riding the pocket when they couldn't find the tube. I would've given Tony Ray a "12" for effort in a memorable display. He scored a 10, but lost in his heat. Margo, however, impressed in every heat, his fluid, radical, bold, hard driving maneuvers, blending beautifully with Lagundri's long, languid walls. He was a very popular winner and accepted the kudos of his peers in his typically understated manner.

After two days cooped up in my little box overlooking the point, I had moved west to greener pastures. Almost on the border of the hotel, I found Losmen Simson. It was very relaxing. The palm trees in front and the roar of Indicator out front soothed me to sleep at night. In an emotional meeting with Taninjin, we walked over to our original campsite. It was in fact now a rubbish dump. The coconut tree John and I had scrawled our initials in had blown over the year before. The path up to Botohili Village had disappeared. Familiar faces who recognized me started filing out of the woodwork to come and chat. There were some touching scenes as I met 30-year old men who were mere 10-year-olds, little boys who helped carry Jan and Judy's shopping down from the village. They told me how lucky they felt meeting us, the girls having given them their first rice meal. I really started to settle in. Walking past the hotel about 800m around to the west from the point, I was confronted by the fact that the beach was deserted and that development had not encroached beyond the hotel's boundary. The dense foliage on the edge of the beach reminded me of what the point was really like. Why then couldn't the point be re-landscaped if there was a coastal management plan in place, and if the locals were committed to improving and protecting their environment? Perhaps the point could recover a little of its natural beauty. It was food for thought...

The day after the contest finished, the point was like a ghost town. The place just emptied out in record time. The swell hit at 2am the next morning. The sunrise session revealed some eight-footers coming through, but the force of the running tide and a light church wind was messing it up. At Lagundri you still measure quality in degrees of perfection. The low tide, late afternoon session was going to be my date with destiny. I had spent $2^1/_2$ weeks hanging out for real surf. I was becoming desperate to confirm the memories I had been carrying for the last twenty years. Were the waves really as good as I had experienced and remembered? Or was it all something that I had dreamed up during a malarial nightmare? Conditions were glassy when I joined the pack of ten guys out the back. Ani Devine and Koby Abberton were charging the sets, which had become very consistent. This was thrilling, this was how it always was. Pick your wave, three or four strokes into a smooth-as-silk take-off, over the ledge, adjust your line on the free fall and lean forward as an impossibly long section in front of you goes vertical and cylindrical all around you. There was always lots of room in the 8ft wombs. The recurring image is always of the feeling of timelessness spent inside the Lagundri vortex. Time travel still occurs on The Point in more ways than one. It was an emotional session, the adrenaline releasing a lot of tension that I had been carrying. I could now leave a happy man, having tapped back into the fabled portal of power.

It's amazing what you can learn over a *kopi-susu* and a couple of *roti kelapas* first thing in the morning. I had met with Sifarma just after my arrival nearly three weeks previously. Whenever I cruised past his losmen cafe called Hatu Gala, he would always call out. When he knew I was preparing to depart, he said make sure I come to see him because he had something to tell me. He also wanted to show me Ma-ur's grave, his uncle, who along with his wife and Sifarma were the only locals living on the point and surrounding areas back in '75-'76. They became our friends.

The morning before my departure, I strolled down to Hatu Gala and Sifarma proceeded to shock me to my core! Sifarma, at 45, is salt of the earth, and not prone to flights of fancy. He is also a direct descendant of the original inhabitant of the point the legendary Sar San Gaila. He proceeded to relate exactly what had happened around us during our '75-'76 trips. It all centered on a man, a shaman by the name of Nadea who was also known as the *Pemburung* (Hornbill Man). Sifarma, who was approximately 25 at the time when John and I showed up, had been up in Hilismantano in the market when he heard the gossip that the *Pemburung* from Sosro Gamung was on a mission to cast out the *bules* (Westerners) who were living on the point at Jamburae (Lagundri). He also received some backyard information concerning the fact that the *Pemburung* was searching for a skull to place in the foundation of the bridge at Sorso Gamung, 7kms from Hilismantano. The bridge, built by the Japanese during the war, had fallen into disrepair and was being given an overhaul. The 75m suspension bridge spanned the I Dano Ho River and Nadea had to consecrate the spirits in the area by burying a skull in the foundation. By the time Sifarma had made it back to the point, everyone walking the track leading into and out of Lagundri and Botohili were warned to look out for the headhunters. Everyone that is except John and myself. Sifarma told me that when he first caught sight of Nadea, he almost crapped his pants. Sifarma was drawing water from the well about 25m into the jungle off The Point. Nadea had appeared on the beach from out of nowhere with an accomplice. Sifarma hid behind a tree shaking and watched as the two men walked up to our camp. Sifarma quickly told Ma-ur, and together they crept through the coconut plantation until they got right up behind our tent under the little thatched hut. There they hid and looked and listened to what transpired. Nadea had agreed that John and I were perfect specimens. They then proceeded to sit, talk and interact with us for over two hours. During this time, we must have burned more Buddha offerings because somehow we disarmed their initial intentions.

As they checked out our boards, we tried to explain what surfing was all about in a game of Stone Age charades. Somehow the "natural persuader" had yet again saved the day and more importantly our heads. Sifarma could read their lips. There was something mentioned about them actually needing a woman. In our blissfully ignorant state we waved them on their way and returned to the hobbits in *Lord of the Rings*. Sifarma and Ma-ur, however, had run back to their huts on the point and intercepted the two men on the beach. Nadea put the fear of god into Sifarma. The shaman was described as being approximately 40, medium height, of stocky build with longish hair. His eyes were blood red, which signified that he was a practitioner of red magic. He was a major evil force. His form of magic had originated in the Aceh of north Sumatra. He roamed the whole of southern Nias on hunting raids for various ceremonies or whenever he received a calling. It was understood that a shaman with his powers could kill by using his thoughts, or just by touching a certain area of a person's body. They used sickness as a conduit to transmit their evil intentions. He could communicate telepathically and more than likely possessed the ability to fly. After all he was called the *Pemburung*, the Birdman.

Ma-ur asked why did they want us. We spent all of our time in the ocean riding those boards. The two men joked and said they were really after a woman, but they still didn't want Westerners living on the point. With that they disappeared.

Three weeks after we left, they returned. All the local people were very frightened. They quizzed Ma-ur and Sifarma about our disappearance. They were very upset. They desperately wanted our heads. They returned every 2-3 weeks for the next year until I returned in June '76 with Jan, Judy and Bugs. Within five days, Nadea showed up, this time with three others who were not Niasan, but more likely from the Aceh. They were also described as looking like they had just crawled out of the jungle. It was explained to me that the constant appearance of Nadea in the Lagundri and Botohili area had completely freaked out the locals. The locals apparently directed an overwhelming feeling of compassion towards us in our predicament. Yet no one could tell us what was happening.

I asked this question several times. Sifarma said they were just getting to know us and didn't want to chase us away. They were intrigued by our presence and wanted to learn from us through our surfing experience. Sifarma anchored himself behind a coconut tree and shouted out to Nadea and his henchmen. What did the shaman want. Nadea's reply was, "I really need them". He was ready to take one, two, three or all four of us. It was obvious to Sifarma that Nadea was now fully committed to his task and he exuded a feeling of gross intensity. Sifarma was filled with a sense of dread. The locals had received news of John's death with blank faces of disbelief. I had returned with another male, but more importantly, two attractive blonde females.

Sifarma and Ma-ur yet again took up their listening posts behind the tents and watched the proceedings. It was obvious Nadea was in the grip of blood lust. Nadea asked me why had I returned. He still had a problem understanding the surfing experience. He was completely enraptured with the appearance of the two girls. The head-hunting party then began discussing the strategy of killing each of us and making a successful get away. Bugs and I were tall and solidly built, we would put up a struggle. But it was the escape route that created the most concern. Also, on this particular day five Botohili villagers were working in the plantation, up trees collecting coconuts. They had a very good vantage point to watch what was happening to us. All of these men were armed with traditional swords and spears.

Sifarma had alerted them to remain in the plantation for protection. Nadea and his assistants debated the possibilities for some five to six hours, hanging around the campsite and also returning to the beach. The problem was they were becoming very frustrated. The locals were aware of the shaman's intentions, and the only escape route was back around the beach to Lagundri. The only other track through the dense jungle was the one beside our hut, which led up to Botohili.

If they attempted to murder us, they feared that they then could be hunted and killed during their escape. The frustration increased until they abandoned their plan and disappeared in disgust. Sifarma, who still believed in the traditional ways, had also converted to Christianity, as had many others in the village. He told me at the sight of Nadea's departure he fell to his knees and profusely thanked Jesus for our salvation. It's amazing isn't it, when you consider how naive you can be about events that happen in your life. Sifarma, with perfect recall had given me a first person account of the proceedings. I listened in awe. In June '76, while perfect surf pumped around the palm-lined point, for all intents and purposes, we believed we were experiencing heaven on earth. In actual fact, the locals saw us in a transitory stage of passing through hell. What is this thing called reality? It's all either illusion or delusion, we can only find what is real by first finding ourselves.

The story of the Birdman didn't end there. He became a figure who loomed large in our lives and who I now believe directly contributed to the sickness which eventually engulfed the camp. Ingrid and Stuart the mismatched couple showed up several weeks later. Nadea was back immediately. He had now found exactly what he was looking for. Ingrid was an attractive, 19-20-year-old of Indian descent. Unbeknown to her and us, she was to become Nadea's black magic woman. As Stuart dealt with his disintegrating personality, Ingrid became the center of attention for these heavy looking guys. They were always hanging around her. We recognized them from past experiences, but had absolutely no idea of their real intentions. They would take her away for walks. We remarked to each other that there was a strange vibe in the air. It was tough on Ingrid, because she had never traveled before, and she found herself dumped in a remote location by a boyfriend who had run off to play Jungle Jim. We cared for her as best we could when her sickness developed. As she entered the downward spiral of her illness, Sifarma became very concerned with the continued appearance of Nadea and the obvious influence he had over her. On the day of her evacuation, Sifarma could not believe his eyes as the party moved off from the camp carrying Ingrid on a roughed-out stretcher. Her kidneys were so inflamed and painful that she could not put weight on her feet.

Sifarma recounted that as the party walked around the point, he threw himself down on his knees and prayed desperately to Jesus for Ingrid's protection from the headhunters. He never saw or heard of Ingrid again, and it was the question he had waited twenty years to ask me. Well, I was reeling from his account of this separate reality of events, which had occurred so long ago. We were unwittingly cast as the main protagonists in the unfolding drama, which was witnessed and understood by all the inhabitants of both villages. Sifarma finished up by saying that the locals always considered that one or all of us would die. Ma-ur, his uncle, had always wondered when we would come back. He had recognized that somehow we had broken through the taboo that had been imposed on the point by Nadea the birdman.

The bridge was finally consecrated in 1976 with a skull neatly placed under the foundation stone. For twenty years Sifarma wondered if it had been Ingrid's.

I had to move. I needed air. A breeze on my face. I needed confirmation of this story from someone else. I borrowed a bike and rode around to Lagundri Village to my friends, Pringitan and Norhyat, at Losmen Aman. I walked in and Pringitan knew exactly what I had come for. The first thing he asked me was, "Kevin, what happened to the *orang Indian*?" What happened to Ingrid? I then asked him about the headhunters, if it was true.

"Of course," he said, all the locals liked us. They didn't want us to leave. That's why they didn't tell us. I was dumbfounded. It was a classic piece of Indonesian reasoning. He then filled me in further. When Ingrid had been brought across the flooded rivermouth, the locals became very heated and agitated as to what was going to be her likely fate. Pringitan, who was *kepala desa* (headman) of Lagundri at the time, vehemently warned Nadea that if Ingrid died, he (Pringitan) would alert the government authorities in Teluk Dalam, and they would hunt him down and kill him. Ingrid disappeared in the back of the rusted out ute headed for the decaying German mission hospital outside Hilismantano. The Germans had apparently run off years ago and the hospital had been partially reclaimed by the jungle. Pringitan had also wondered for twenty years what had happened to Ingrid. Well, so it was all true. The thing about Niasans is that they do have incredible memories. As for Ingrid, what was her fate? I don't know. Maybe someone reading this account can verify her continued good health. I would very much appreciate it.

As Norhyat brought the food to the table, Pringitan reappeared accompanied by a tall, proud looking old man wearing a traditional black Muslim cap. He introduced him as Damrah, his 74-year-old uncle, who he said was the oldest living descendent of the first inhabitant of the point. Pak Damrah was also the aural historian of Lagundri. He could recall names, places, dates and times from yesterday to 250 years previous and beyond. I pushed the food away and listened as he told me about the life of the son of the warrior chief, the man known as Sar San Gaila. The constraints of time melted as the events of a bygone era were recounted with vivid imagery. Mysteriously, Sifarma reappeared as we were drawing to a close. He wanted to take me to Sar San Gaila's grave, nestled in a little hook in the bay just off the beach between the village and the point. Pak Damrah explained the line of descendents, originating from Sar San Gaila. Ma-ur and Sifarma were the only inhabitants on the point when we arrived. They were of course directly related, as was Pringitan. Interestingly, it was these two families that we were drawn towards. It was with these two groups that we had the most interaction.

As Sifarma cleared some undergrowth away from the headstone, a feeling of strength and resilience emanated from the site. The great man and his wife's grave lay side by side. Kanowi, the shaman, who preceeded his master as the spiritual convener of Jamburae, lay a short distance away. My mind harked back to the many times I had passed this site just off the beach. I remembered sticking my head in once to check it out. Little did I realize the significance of what I was viewing.

The bus would come for me in the middle of the night for the return journey to Gunung Sitoli. It meant I had enough time during my last day to accompany Sifarma on my motorbike to the bridge over the I Dano Ho River some 25kms from Lagundri. It was a magnificent ride. Upon seeing the decaying remains of the bridge, and the large teak bearers still lying in place, I was overcome by a vision. I sat down on the foundation stone that Nadea had consecrated so long ago.

Lagundri should have a museum dedicated to the preservation of its natural history. It would also provide a focal point for the establishment of a coastal management plan that is so desperately needed for the area. Wastewater treatment and the removal of all buildings back from the high tide mark are two issues currently being discussed by the local community. Government bodies are in consultation, but of course, time drags on. This is an open invitation for any interested individuals or outside bodies to offer assistance in the establishment of the museum.

Lagundri has now become a way-station for forays into other more remote areas. We've had twenty-two years experience of interaction and development between the surfing tribe and a megalithic Stone Age culture. We can learn from the mistakes to ensure other fragile environments don't suffer the same fate.

Our covenant with the creator to draw breath in this life is made on the assumption that by helping ourselves we also help each other. We also must protect, maintain and restore that which has been given to us. We are all custodians of The Point wherever that point may be.

On the bone-jarring journey north to Gunung Sitoli, I wrestled with discomfort in the front of the bus as we plunged on relentlessly through the cool dawn mist of another Niasan day. In a semi-dream state, I reflected on Larry Yates' curious quote, "It really isn't a place, it's a state of mind," the now and zen of it all, I concluded, was that the experience had transcended into a "state of being". We had lived out a myth at Lagundri, and our lives had been transformed forever. It was a different time; it was a different place.

Custodians of the Point/Ode to John first published in *The Surfer's Journal* Volume 7 No. 1

KEVIN LOVETT

In 1975, after their first stay in Lagundri, the author Kevin Lovett's best friend and co-explorer John Geisel headed on to Europe overland. Some months later, in a van in the mountains of Iran, he succumbed to malaria and died.

An Ode to John

"A change of reality and the impossible becomes serene."
JOHN GEISEL, 1975

The difference between life and death is breath. When we breathe we live in this world, with our last exhalation we exist in another. John was a very warm and loving person who turned 23 in Lagundri on 12/6/75. He had grown up in the Broadbeach area of Queensland's Gold Coast. In 1965, when he was 13, he won the Surfers Paradise Boardriders trophy for "Most improved". The club boasted a very competitive membership during the mid-to-late-'60s – illustrious names such as Rick and Paul Neilsen or Peter and Tony Drouyn, to name a few. After graduating from Miami High School, John expressed his radical bent in the halcyon days of Queensland University in the early '70s. He eventually graduated as an upper level, high school science and maths teacher.

Being a goofy foot on the Gold Coast, he had to hunt further south to sate his passion for lefts. He had a special affinity with the sacred site of Black Rock in Jervis Bay. He recounted vividly to me the timelessness he felt inside "the pipe".

John Geisel's early death was not the waste of a good life. It was the celebration of the principle that "life is for living!" He used his surfing experience to explore philosophical tangents. The knowledge gained became his spirit boat, which he traveled on through the void into another world. I know he died a happy man. He had meshed with his spirit. Saying goodbye to all his family and friends, he would have felt the warm embryonic embrace of the cascading curtain of translucent water as he drifted through the green cathedral, onwards, towards the light.

Spirit Of Place

The legend of Sar San Gaila as told to Kevin Lovett by Bapak Damrah, the oral historian of Lagundri village.

KEVIN LOVETT

T HE HUNTING PARTY rose well before dawn. They would use the cool mist-laden air of the early morning to create distance between their village of Hilimeta in the south and their final destination, the Raja's village in the Gomo River region of central Nias. Farewells were brief. Sar San Gaila, five years old at the time, felt the warm breath of his father's words caress his face as the warrior chief clutched his son to his chest. Their bond, eternal and undeniable, Sar San Gaila stood shivering and watched his father disappear out of the courtyard and out of his life forever. The party of ten warriors was also accompanied by a shaman, the navigator of the other worlds.

He would communicate with Lovalani, the sprit of the heavens, the god of the upper world who presided over the sun and air, the mountains, gold and birds, light and the life force. The opposing ruler of the underworld was Lovalani's brother Latura Dano, the god of darkness, earth, the moon and the snake. The constant struggle to maintain balance between the forces of good and evil was left to the shaman who would confer with the ancestor spirits and the Chief to chart a course through the hazardous rainforest. All types of terrain lay before them from fast-flowing mountain streams in steep ravines to crocodile-infested swamps teeming with malaria bearing mosquitoes.

The atmosphere in the hunting party was buoyant. While they took every precaution to ensure their own security as they traveled, they were in fact quite relaxed. This was not a war party seeking heads, they were actually seeking peace; it was a journey of appeasement. The father of Sar San Gaila had led his village successfully through fire, famine and war.

But it was an ongoing demarcation dispute over land, slaves and the taking of heads, with the chiefdom of Gomo that forced him to initiate peace talks with the Gomo village leader. It was the classic struggle between opposing Niasan villages fighting for power and prestige. He had agreed to the Raja's invitation to a meeting in Gomo to settle all outstanding debts in a peaceful resolution to their hostility.

The light rations that the party carried would sustain them during the four-day journey to Gomo. The Raja's invitation had made much of the celebration of the peace accord with the corresponding ritual feast. The red-orange color of the sirih nut dribbled down the lips of the warriors as they fell into a light trance state while picking their way along the thin path. The sun was, in some cases, completely blotted out from view by the canopy of the primordial teak forest. This was their homeland where they interacted directly with their ancestral spirits in the most sublime manner. At night, the glow of the waxing moon and the Milky Way allowed them to continue. It was a celestial river of souls that carried them onwards to their destiny.

On the third night, the party camped alongside the swift-flowing Gomo River just outside the village of Sifalago, an area that held great spiritual importance for all Niasans. The village was also known as Boro Nadu, which means "the beginning of ancestor images". This was where the Niha culture was conceived. Hia, the patriarch of the Niha, which means "man of Nias" is said to have descended from the upper world. His son Sadawa Molo had five sons who fathered the clans that inhabited the entire island. Hia had planted the sacred fosi tree in the center of the megalithic courtyard of Boro Nadu. Legend has it that the tree grew directly out of Hia's heart. Anyone approaching the tree, other than a priest, suffered dire consequences.

The sacred spirit of Hia filled the peace party with a sense of atonement. Late the following afternoon, the party arrived on the outskirts of the chiefdom of Gomo.

The Raja's representatives met with the father of Sar San Gaila who was persuaded to accompany them alone to meet their chief. It was to be one on one. Despite the protestations of the Hilimeta warriors who were commanded to stay outside the village, the warrior chief consented. After all, he had come seeking peace; to fear peace was to fear the life force itself. The father of Sar San Gaila was led through the magnificent courtyard of the Gomo village past the large carved stone spirit boats called *daro-daro*. On each side stood the stone representations of the Nias Cosmos, large oval and rectangular platforms with carved reliefs of crocodiles and hornbills adorning the sides.

The Raja invited the Hilimeta warrior chief to sit on a sacred *lasara* chair. The large basalt carved chairs were presided over by the lasara, the mythical being which linked the upper and lower worlds in one to represent the universe. Only on symbolic occasions when tribal nobility met was anyone allowed to occupy these chairs.

As the full moon rose in the east, the ritual feast to consecrate the peace pact got under way. Women adorned in elaborate gold headdresses wearing traditional ikat fabrics carried gifts and gold to Sar San Gaila's father. Many pigs were slaughtered in a show of respect for the warrior chief. The journey had been exhausting and a combination of the festivities and the food and drink caused him to retire early. The terms of the agreement would be brokered tomorrow.

But for the father of Sar San Gaila, there would be no tomorrow. The Hilimeta warrior chief was led to his room in the Raja's house. The five-meter high teak panelled walls were decorated with elaborately carved ancestor images. The altar was perched high on the wall above a massive horizontal beam called a *lago-lago*. From where he was lying, looking upwards, the man forever more known only as the "father of Sar San Gaila" could see fresh offerings on the altar.

While he slept heavily, at some point in the stillness of the night, the massive tropical hardwood beam was released from its resting place. Silently plummeting downwards, it crushed the living spirit out of the Hilimeta chief. The Gomo warriors quickly entered the room, and in the splintered light of the full moon, one of them took out his sword and in a single blow, severed the cerebellum cortex of the shattered corpse. Dancing with glee, they charged out into the courtyard singing the praises of their Raja. In the aggressive and violent backdrop of traditional Niasan culture, justice, whether right or wrong, was always swift and severe. The head of the father of Sar San Gaila was then thrown into the turbulent waters of the surging Gomo River. However, the karmic forces of retribution had immediately come into play. The village of Gomo would forever remember this day with dread. The murder of a warrior chief was the ultimate insult, for that person would forever lose the right to have his full name mentioned.

There was also the possibility that this person would become a *bechu*, an evil ancestral spirit. For Sar San Gaila, who was but five years old, he had lost his father and was *sakit hati* (broken-hearted) that he could not honor him with the burial ceremony befitting a man of his stature.

The resultant ignominy would live with him every moment of his life until he could avenge his father's death. An old Niasan proverb "*mati sebelum malu*" (death before disgrace) was to stick in his gut for thirty years. The year was 1805, and Sar San Gaila's journey was only just beginning. At this time, Nias was in constant turmoil. The Dutch had involved themselves in the slave trade and had become major players in purchasing and poaching low caste Niasans for sale and distribution in Sumatra and then on to Batavia. The Dutch with their jackboot mentality had been involving themselves in Niasan affairs for some 140 years. The English and Portuguese had also established trading relations with local people at Gunung Sitoli in the north. The Portuguese had a friendlier disposition in their interaction with the traditional Niasan culture. However, this was only to disguise their real intentions of establishing a business and military network through the islands.

By now, Sar San Gaila's family had moved to a new village called "Hilizondigeasi" which means "village near the waves." It was situated not far from the present site of the village in Lagundri Bay. One day during a chance meeting with a group of Portuguese traders on the beach near his village, Sar San Gaila seized an opportunity that was to change his life forever. Through an interpreter, it was explained to his mother that the traders were offering to take Sar San Gaila with them to Sumatra to educate him in the ways of the world, and it was agreed that he would go. Standing on board the brig, the little boy with the big heart waved goodbye to his mother and family. He was only eight years old, yet he carried the hopes of the village on his shoulders. Deep within, he also knew that this was a path towards his destiny of honoring his father's demise.

His early schooling was conducted within the Portuguese community in Padang on the west coast of Sumatra. Sometime later he entered a Dutch military school in preparation for life in the armed forces. The youthful Sar San Gaila was to complete his military training fully adept in the art of killing. For a number of years, he performed as an infantryman in the Dutch corps during their attempts to quell the fierce tribes in Aceh, located in the deep north of Sumatra. It was during this time in Aceh that he was introduced to the shamanic culture of the Acehnese, who were, and still are, the most feared practitioners of this archaic tradition in the Indonesian archipelago. He became initiated into the ways of *limu* an Acehnese form of magic, which also incorporated a series of self-defense techniques similar to silat. Magical powers were adopted in his rites of passage; he became empowered, and therefore, could not sustain an injury by use of a knife, and a bullet aimed at his body was always destined to miss its target.

In undergoing this spiritual transformation, he had become fearless in the face of death. He had also converted to Islam.

Meanwhile, back on Nias, not much had changed. The Dutch had stepped up their quota of slaves. Records showed some 1500 people's lives being traded in a year as the Dutch military warred incessantly with the Acehnese pirates for control of the Niasan slave trade. However, a major turnaround occurred in approximately 1835 when the Dutch bowed to international pressure by the anti-slavery movement to halt their trade. But instead, they cunningly used this scenario to mount a full-scale military campaign to take control of the island. Sar San Gaila had by now become a military commander, and at the age of 30, he returned to his homeland on assignment for the first time since leaving some twenty-two years ago. Because of his Niasan heritage and communication skills, it was his responsibility to recruit and organize groups of mercenaries from opposing tribes in the north. This meant for the Dutch that they could conscript these local warriors who relished the idea of settling past injustices with each other, but in doing so, they allowed the Dutch to subjugate their people. For the Dutch, they were simply introducing "divide and rule" tactics that had worked so successfully for them in their other colonial experiences. They were smart enough not to arm these Niasan conscripts with rifles, as they feared for their safety in the event of reprisals. The marauding bands of mercenaries laid waste to village after village in the north, which had already suffered brutally at the hand of the slavers. Looting of the revered gold jewelry became the major incentive in these rape and pillage campaigns. Suddenly the focus shifted to the Gomo River region in the center of the island. The Gomo warriors had barricaded themselves in their uniquely designed stone boat houses, which offered protection and the ability to retaliate while under siege conditions.

However, nothing could have prepared them for the ferocity that descended upon the village in the shape of the son of the Hilimeta chief. Sar San Gaila had dispensed with his army uniform. He wore instead a warrior's jacket or cuirass made of thick leather and six long iron flaps, which protected the shoulders. The metal strips and leather were fastened together by rattan string. The back was reinforced with a broad rectangular sheet of metal bordered on either side by a row of sharp metal teeth. This strip extended high up to protect the back of his neck. His helmet was composed of sheet iron cobbled together with brass wire. A large plume extended upwards from the front made of tassels of red and yellow cloth and a branch of *lagene* tree. It was said that evil spirits adorned themselves with the branches of this tree, so that when a person displayed such a branch, the spirits would be confused and believe the person to be one of their own, thus providing protection. In the roll of the ikat *lap-lap* that he wore, Sar San Gaila had stuffed the petals of the *soma-soma* flower. This also had the magical properties of providing a connection to and a line between the living and the dead. His sword sheathed at his side had been empowered in a ceremonial communion with Lowalani and Laturo Dano. The 75cm steel blade was attached to a cast brass hilt in the shape of a stylized lasara head. Large boar tusks were attached to the wooden sheath, protecting a small cocoon-type rattan basket filled with shark's teeth, a fossil stone and an ancestor figure. Sar San Gaila was going to expunge the dishonor of his father's murder by the complete desecration and destruction of Gomo village and its inhabitants. In the dawn's early light, he strode into the courtyard brandishing a Dutch-made gatling style machine gun. With a soldier assisting him by feeding the ammunition belts, he commenced strafing the houses and occupants with continual raking gunfire, which lasted for hours on end. The Gomo was awash with blood and bobbing heads when the killing finally ceased late that afternoon.

At some point after this incident, after a period of quiet reflection and contemplation, he resigned his position with the Dutch army and headed south to the village near the waves to an emotional homecoming.

By 1844, Sar San Gaila was nearing the middle stage of his life. Like his father before him, he was seeking the solace of peace. While the battle with his demons had been laid to rest in Gomo, the war with the Dutch raged on. Now it was the Niasan tribes from the south that were under threat. The battle-hardened warrior used his experience gained in guerilla warfare to organize hit-and-run operations against the Dutch expeditionary forces to the south. Using firearms captured from these raids, and also munitions acquired during the slave trade, the tribes in the south were able to repel the Dutch who were again frustrated in their attempts to achieve complete domination of the island. For many years, these skirmishes continued between the Dutch colonial government in the north and the fierce chiefdoms of the south. But finally, Sar San Gaila had finished with war. He had taken a wife and was the father of

EMMA LEE LOVETT

Ancient Niasan warrior-spirit traditions remained intact until relatively recently. Even today they are central to the islanders' cultural identity and important bloodlines like those of Sar San Gaila are highly respected. Ceremony at Bawomotaluwo, Village of the Sun.

two girls and a son. In his search for solitude, he moved his family from the "village near the waves" to a house beside the waves. In the intervening years since returning to his village, he had spent much time on the southwest point of the bay called Lagundri. There he meditated and practiced his shamanic rituals communicating with animal and ancestral spirits and traveling in the "other" worlds. Although the village of Botohilitano had been established on the 200-meter high hill above the point some one hundred years earlier, none of the villagers dared live in the pristine natural environment of the point because of its strong spiritual portent. Sar San Gaila built a house at Jamburae on the point, named for his jambu (fruit) crops, and fished the surrounding waters raising his children in the traditional manner. But in 1856, the silence of Lagundri Bay was shattered with the arrival of a Dutch brigantine carrying cannons.

The landing party had made its intentions clear by commencing immediately with the construction of a fortress and jetty facilities off the beach in the middle of the bay. In the face of this threat, the shaman of the point sent his wife and children north to her family's home. Their security was utmost in his mind. With the garrison nearing completion and the arrival of more troops, anything could happen. And it did. A year later, the earth cracked open consuming the garrison and its occupants in a powerful display of retribution. The effects of the severe earthquake caused a re-think of Dutch military plans and a complete relocation back to Padang in Sumatra.

Peace had finally been achieved in Sar San Gaila's life. It is said that he possessed an affinity with the power that was situated on the point; he was drawn to it by its magic. The thundering detonations of wave after wave, when the big swells were running, provided the trance music by which he relaxed into old age. He had entered the final stage of his life in this natural bardo by achieving complete harmony with the lush tropical surroundings of Lagundri point and his shamanic traditions.

The son of the Hilimeta warrior chief had been a witness to much change throughout his life. His respect for the power of the natural world was immense. But what he experienced on that day in August 1883, was to leave him spellbound. The lead up to the cataclysmic event had begun three days earlier. The ocean had suddenly begun to surge up the beach and back out in a continuous motion. The warning signals were obvious. Impending destruction was at hand. Sar San Gaila, at this stage, a spry 83 years of age, along with most other residents of the Muslim village in Lagundri, evacuated themselves and their belongings up to Botohilitano, the village on the hill behind the point. And there they waited. During the evening of the 26th and 27th, it finally came; the resultant volcanic eruption of the Island of Krakatau in the Sunda Straits off the west coast of Java produced one of the loudest noises in the planet's recorded history. The massive bang shattered the calm resolve of the villagers sending them into a frenzy. Then came the rumbling of the ocean. The explosion of Krakatau was accompanied by a submarine earthquake of such epic proportions that the ensuing tidal waves were eventually felt in the Thames River in London. But at the epicenter, 50' high walls of water caused death and destruction as they impacted along the coasts of Java and Sumatra. In Teluk Lampung, in south Sumatra, it was reported that a tidal surge had measured 15' in height, 30 miles inland. In Lagundri, in the early hours before dawn, the rumbling grew louder, as the tsunami, while smaller in volume and height offshore, grew tremendously, rising to some 25' as it surged over the remnants of the old Dutch garrison and carried all before it. The tidal wave was still 10' high when it was finally halted by the escarpment at the back of Lagundri village, some 1 1/2km inland. As dawn broke, the devastation was revealed in its entirety. Fortunately, there had been minimal loss of life, and in a miraculous effort, a 70 year-old woman by the name of Tanomi survived the full impact of the surges by climbing a huge kapok tree to escape. The sky remained clouded in dust, blotting out the sun for three days.

Sar San Gaila lived out his days on the point in the company of his remaining family. His constant aide through the latter years was a shaman by the name of Kanowi, an Acehnese possessing deep magical powers to communicate with the upper and lower worlds. Kanowi assisted his mentor to prepare for his new journey. His incantations were rhythmic and spoken with compassion directly to the guides.

The son of the warrior chief of Hilimeta, the custodian of the point, was now ready, and Sar San Gaila gently exhaled for the last time, as Kanowi helped the shaman's soul climb aboard his ancestor spirit boat and watched in awe as he paddled into the light.

This story appeared as part of Kevin Lovett's 'Custodians of the Point' story in *The Surfer's Journal* Volume 7 No. 1

Generation Nias

In a perpetual cycle of upheaval and shape-shifting, Lagundri struggles to find its way in the surfing world

EMILIANO CATALDI

THE YEAR WAS 1975, and the two Australian surfers who were travelling through the Indonesian archipelago had no idea of what lay ahead of them while crossing a large island off the coast of Sumatra. Riding along the tortuous road that led through a thick rainforest, past muddy rivers, endless rice fields and tiny Christian villages, these contemporary explorers were chasing a dream in true romantic fashion. At that point in time the word "Nias" didn't ring a bell yet in surfers' imagination, but thanks to Kevin Lovett and John Geisel, plus Peter Troy who they bumped into by chance on the ferry from Sumatra, things were about to change.

It was at the very end of that muddy road that the two mates first laid their eyes on something that would change their lives forever and redefine the concept of tropical perfection for many generations of surfers to come. There it was, peaking, barrelling and peeling along the western edge of a large bay – emerald wall after emerald wall of raw Indian Ocean energy coming out of a deep trench, climbing the slope in the reef and turning into the most stunning wave ever witnessed by a surfer. That was the end of the road, both physically and metaphorically: they had found what they were looking for. They had arrived at the bay of Lagundri.

They invited Peter Troy to share their first proper session but for the rest of that season they had those waves all to themselves. And the next summer, after John Geisel had died of malaria, Lovett was back at Lagundri again, surfing the wave alone but for his one travel companion, his brother in-law to be.

They didn't just find their own tropical getaway; what they found was the first world-class righthander in a land mainly known for its dreamy lefts like Uluwatu, Padang Padang and G-Land.

The equatorial latitude of Nias, at 2° South, guarantees shelter from the south-easterly trade winds that blow in Bali, Java and the Nusa Tenggara islands during the dry season. On one hand this seasonal wind adds the magic touch of offshore winds to the world-class lefthanders of G-Land and the Bukit Peninsula, while on the other, the same winds blow onshore at virtually every righthand setup in the region. The light winds in the equatorial area of Indonesia left Mother Nature free to play with every bend in the coast and each bit of exposed reef, and it didn't take long for surfers to figure this out. Quite predictably, word of a dreamy righthander somewhere in Indonesia spread far beyond the close circle of friends of Troy and Lovett, so much so that by the early '80s the village of Sorake, a tiny hamlet of fishermen and rice farmers in front of the spot, was already one of the most visited surfing destinations in all of Indonesia.

Driving along the same ramshackle road and chasing the same dream 33 years later, I can't help but wonder how much of what I'm seeing out of the minivan window has changed since Lovett and Geisel were here in 1975. At first glance, it doesn't seem to be much: the air is still steamy, the jungle is still thick and hostile, the road is scattered with muddy potholes, the bridges are still precarious and the village kids that chase our van as we drive by still have that timeless, astonished look in their eyes. As island life flows by in slow motion like frames of a faded Super 8 film, I realise that it might be 2008 for us, but it could still be 1975 out there.

Getting to Nias was a hell of a mission back then and it still is. My journey from Bali consists of almost 20 hours of absolute chaos amidst delayed flights, a missing boardbag, a few dozen frantic phone calls and a thick wad of rupiah for the ubiquitous fixer to ensure my boards make it to Medan on time to get on the next flight. They don't, but somehow they materialise in Gunung Sitoli a couple of hours later, and with a 6-8ft swell on the rise, a 17 second swell period and an ideal 203-degree SSW angle, I consider that as a sign of good things to come.

Even if the assignment for this trip is try to understand how three decades of surf tourism, two major earthquakes and a tsunami have changed one of the most iconic waves in the world and affected the lives of those who shape their existence around it, my own personal aim is to contract the Nias bug, get barrelled and live to tell the tale. It seems like even the original dream, like most things on this island, hasn't changed a bit in the last 33 years. I wonder whether the small village of Sorake is any different now from how it was portrayed back in the early '80s in surf magazine articles: a modest village of fishermen and farmers, crossed by a single road, devoid of electricity, running water or any other modern day comfort. Photographer John Callahan, whose first trip here dates back to 1981, doesn't notice many differences as we approach the village on the single-lane road. "The only difference I can see," he comments from the front seat, "is that now all the houses have been rebuilt with concrete after the earthquakes, but everything else is just like I remember".

Although nowadays most of the local families rely on seasonal surf tourism as their main source of income, the lifestyle and overall vibe of Sorake remains pretty constant. Tourists and locals alike wake up with the roosters at dawn, take care of business during the daylight hours and go to sleep shortly after sunset. As simple as it sounds, that's the power of having no power. The surf, and evening Bintangs and chat on the porch, are still the only entertainment available, but surfers seem to adapt well to this lifestyle and the absence of the comforts of modern surf travel. A mosquito net and a fan are still considered the height of luxury in most guesthouses, while air conditioning, satellite television, and internet access belong to a world literally light years away.

The way this place has evolved after the advent of surf tourism is interesting to say the least: its development over the years has followed a path that's antithetical to the rest of the Indonesian surf destinations. While most areas frequented by surfers have seen increasing coastal development (just think of the exploitation of the Bukit Peninsula in Bali or the flourish of luxury surf resorts in the neighbouring Mentawai Islands), Sorake never experienced such a destiny. For some reason Nias had the misfortune, or the fortune, of being in the media spotlight ahead of time and consequently has been able to dodge the seemly unavoidable and unconditional exploitation of its resources. Even at the apex of its popularity during the '80s and early '90s, the island remained an outpost that was too difficult to reach and too challenging to deal with, mostly luring hardcore surfers of the extremely adventurous kind.

John Geisel himself, one of the original party with Lovett and Troy and perhaps the first surfer ever to slip into one of these beautiful green tubes, had a thirst for surf exploration, but he paid for it with his life. Having contracted malaria on that first trip to Nias, he died from it nine months later in Iran while en route overland to London. Then, when high-end surf tourism took off in Indonesia around the late '90s, the aura of Nias was overshadowed by the flashy discoveries and media saturation of the nearby Mentawais, leaving the village of Sorake in a state of picturesque but poor isolation.

Rumours of frequent petty theft, violent crime and increasing tension in the line-up between local surfers and visitors, turned travelling surfers away from Nias and onto boat charters in the Mentawais. There was a new breed of surf travellers that seemed to think: "Who needs Nias anymore, now that we have Lance's Right?" As the new archetype of tropical perfection shifted from Lagundri to Lance's, on Sipura Island in the Mentawais, so did the media spotlight. Hordes of surfers followed, leaving the rustic huts of Sorake empty. It was as if the island's own peculiarities and limitations conspired to protect the village and the line-up, from the new wave of globalised exploitation.

By then most of the surfers who were filling line-ups in the Mentawais were 'surf tourists' rather than 'surf travellers', and their demands for instant surf gratification by moving the boat to any spot with a surfable wave didn't chime well with Lagundri's fickle nature. Before the March 2005 earthquake raised the whole island by an estimated one metre, the wave only broke on south-angle swells bigger than 4ft and couldn't compete in consistency with the multitude of waves in the Mentawais.

That factor alone meant that a high-end surf resort at Nias wasn't an option – after all, who would spend 250 hard-earned dollars a day just to sit and wait, often in the pouring rain, with no internet and nothing to do, for the swell to get big enough from the correct angle to make a world-class wave? Nias required a courtship longer than two weeks to get to know her intimately, let alone be conquered, and by the late 1990s surfers simply didn't have that kind of patience.

The Nias previously known by surfers finally ruptured on the night of March 8th, 2005 when a powerful earthquake shook the island, leaving death and destruction in its wake. It was a tough blow for the island's inhabitants, occurring just a few months after the devastating tsunami of December 2004, which taxed the disaster response ability of the Indonesian government to the limit. The March earthquake could easily have been the death sentence for Nias surf tourism, but a lucky rise in the sea floor as a result of it meant the wave actually got better than it was before – more consistent, a lot more hollow on the peak and the inside section, and less tide-affected.

Before the good news spread, however, rumours circulated that the village had been wiped out and the wave wasn't breaking at all anymore. Ironically, that summer, instead of celebrating the 30th anniversary since the first wave was ridden in Nias, the locals were left wondering if Sorake's luck had finally run out.

"2005 was a terrible year for our economy," explains Avenus Zagoto, one of the most respected local surfers. "Hardly any visiting surfers came that whole season. Many of them avoided Nias after they heard all those made-up stories about the tsunami and earthquake. They were scared by all the rumours of destruction, epidemics and theft. The truth is that the wave improved after the earthquake and we rebuilt the few damaged guesthouses almost immediately. But still, for a couple of years we basically had the spot to ourselves. It was paradoxical: some of us had lost everything on land, but we were surfing the best waves of our lives right here in front…"

Most of the local boys had to leave Sorake to seek a better life or simply to find a job. Some got seasonal jobs as chefs, deckhands, or drivers on surf charter boats in the Mentawais, some worked hard construction labour in Medan or Jakarta, while others travelled all the way to Bali to try their luck with the holiday makers. In Bali, they got exposed to the opulence of mass tourism and it didn't take much for reality to kick in hard.

"The feeling among the locals is that we've been really unlucky compared to other parts of Indonesia," continues Avenus. And he's right: the Nias people felt like they were in the right place at the wrong time, at least over the last three decades. And this brings us to yet another Nias paradox: Sorake is the only major surf spot in Indonesia where the wave quality has actually improved, but the development on land and the quality of life of the locals has remained unchanged.

The local surfers, as a result, have had surfing paths that took the opposite course from many of their Indonesian peers. While tourism and media attention has opened the doors of international stardom and sponsor endorsements for the Balinese and

Javanese surfers, the kids of Sorake haven't shared the same fortune. Despite being as good and progressive surfers as their Balinese peers, most of the local surfers still ride broken boards left behind by visitors and share shorts and t-shirts for months on end. Understandably, they're hungry to finally grasp some of that good life: most visitors, myself included, tend to confuse their attitude with arrogance or insolence, but it's actually their way to vent and express motivation to get a share of the pie.

The sun has yet to rise when, early the next morning, for the first time I find myself face to face with the primary element of this story: the fabled righthander. As I try to rub some stiffness out of my back by stretching on the balcony of our guesthouse, I can already see six or seven guys sitting in the predawn line-up. A smaller set peels down the edge of a huge reef that's completely exposed despite the high tide, awkwardly sticking out of the ocean. "The reef didn't look anything like this back in 1981," says Callahan, "even at low tide it was always covered by some water". We turn towards the top of the point, a mysto reef called Indicator, as a solid set jacks right on the edge of the reef and turns into a backless drainer, flawless but crazy shallow. Mind-surfing the wave, it feels a bit like flirting with death, even from the reassuring safety of the porch. They say it's rideable sometimes, and if it's true then it has to be the shallowest wave on earth, no doubt about it.

Back out on the main peak, The first wave of the set ends its crazy run in the deep-water channel in front of the keyhole, and seems to vanish into thin air as if swallowed by the depth of the ocean; meanwhile the surfers on the peak start to paddle hastily, deeper and deeper, fighting for position. For a few seconds the approaching set remains almost imperceptible, before the waves pop up again as dark, intimidating walls when they hit a massive step in the seabed. It looks more like perfect Off the Wall than Nias, but that doesn't seem to stop the boys in the line-up from sitting impossibly deep and battling for position. You can almost smell the testosterone and bravado from up here.

They all freeze for a split second before the wave stalls and starts throwing its glassy lip, then one of the boys turns around and, with two casual strokes, commits to the latest possible take-off: the inner rail of his board and two fins are his only footing as he slides sideways across the 6ft wall. The thing is about to swallow him alive in a big closed-out wall, but with a naïve spontaneity he sets the rail at the bottom, over-extends his thin body into a contemporary soul arch and pulls into the daunting barrel. He disappears under the curtain for four, five, six seconds – not a chance he can backdoor that first heaving section, we think – and to our amazement emerges in a cloud of spray. He lays into a high-speed roundhouse cutback before pulling into the second section. Now I see what Avenus was talking about; that second section is the one that went through the most radical change. Before the earthquake it was known as a soft, picturesque shoulder, but now it generates a brand-new barrel section a dozen metres long, reminiscent of a Velzyland inside bowl. The surfer negotiates the second pit as if he's taking a walk in the park, and as he reaches the exit the clock reads 6:14am. Just another new day for Justin Buulolo.

Nineteen years old and a Sorake native, Justin is, on any given day, one of the best surfers in the line-up, regardless of how many pros or psycho-chargers crowd the peak. The way he surfs his home spot and the lines he draws are simply amazing: every gesture looks so instinctive and every pose is so natural one gets the feeling that the wave adapts to his needs rather than vice versa. Although Justin and his peers get any wave they want and absolutely dominate one of the most competitive line-ups in Indonesia, back on the beach things don't look so bright for them.

The isolation and the lack of any kind of infrastructure in the village is a real threat that stands in the way of their ambitions. Justin's peers, such as Serius and Rahiel Wau, Avenus and Saldin Zagoto, Alex Buulolo and Sesuaican Dachi, are the third generation of local surfers. They dream of a chance to make it into the Indonesian surfing scene and regard sponsorship and competition as a goal, but isolation and prejudice seem to be killing their aspirations.

Nias is not Bali. There are no surf shops packed to the ceiling with brand new boards, clothes, and accessories, nor the visitors that buy them. There are no team managers for international labels eager to sponsor and spoil the best surfers, let alone photographers that can ensure them the required dose of international media coverage a sponsorship demands. And so, despite their surfing being right up there with the best of their Indonesian, Australian or American peers, they struggle to make a living and can only dream of riding a new stick, let alone owning one.

But it's not just a matter of boards and shorts, the competitive surf scene as a whole is virtually non-existent in Nias. Any career ambition for these kids depends on whether or not they can prove themselves on the regional big stage of Bali and, as absurd as it sounds, most of them can't afford the trip. Avenus is one of the lucky few that, after many sacrifices, finally managed to raise the money he needed to get to Bali by local ferry and long bus trips and enter a six star ISC (Indonesia Surfing Championship) contest. His dreams of glory sunk in the first heat, held in disappointing 1ft Kuta Beach close-outs.

For someone raised on rice, fish and gaping barrels, it's hard to mind-surf those racy close-outs, let alone find the motivation to stand out among such fierce competition. If the mind-blowing surfing achieved by the local Balinese surfers isn't intimidating enough, another major obstacle that the rest of Indonesian surfers have to face is prejudice.

As tolerant and open as the Balinese society may look from the outside, the rigid Hindu caste system and the general mistrust of fellow Indonesians (mostly Muslims and Christians from other islands) still plays a tremendous role in reducing career opportunities for the up-and-coming surfers of Nias. The Balinese take care of their own first, with non-Balinese a distant second, and confronted with this harsh reality, many talented Indonesian surfers end up returning to their villages from Bali, broke and disillusioned.

"The tourism industry in Nias is something we can't really rely on yet," continues Avenus. "Most travellers still tend to avoid the islands around Sumatra because of

BRAD MASTERS

Lagundri Bay – The Point   LAT. 0.568591° LONG. 97.733914°

It's been called many things including Nias, Lagundri, Sorake and most often just The Point, but whatever name is used, it always ends up in the world's top 10 waves. Here's why; the paddle out through the keyhole is dry-hair simplicity, the take-off is predictable, the barrel is a flawless almond shape that peels with precision at the perfect speed for up to 10 seconds, the reef is well covered, even though the recent up-thrust has made it barrel harder from waist-high up to double overhead and beyond, plus the light seaward current from the channel deposits you nicely back at the peak, ironing out any shoulder bump on the way. It's all tides, all (light) winds, all year (with luck) and all too easy to stay encamped in one of the many losmens or hotels that line Sorake Beach. Negatives include the crowd, some localism, flying boards, sea-lice, the crowd.... Losers in the new reef levels include Kiddieland, which has been replaced by a softer inside section of the point and The Machine, an ultra hollow left that now needs spring high tides and a macking swell.

the lack of infrastructure, malaria, or ethnic clashes in areas such as Banda Aceh. Yet our island has everything to rival the rest of the country, both in natural beauty, cultural traditions and overall safety".

But Nias never strove mindlessly after the Balinese tourist utopia.

"The people of Nias carry a cultural and historical heritage that dates back hundreds of years, but few of the visitors show any interest in it. All they want to do is surf, and even when it's flat they never leave the village to experience some of the local culture. There are so many interesting things to see, like the Lompat Batu (a traditional exhibition in which the warriors test their courage and skills jumping over a stone wall) and it should attract more visitors". Listening to his words, I find it interesting that he points to history and culture rather than nightclubs and bars. It's as if they're not ready to trade in their identity and traditions in the name of business at any cost.

The world around Sorake is moving fast though. Nias is, after all, just an hour and a half from Singapore. Rumours of a new airport planned in the town of Teluk Dalam have further fuelled the hopes of the locals. Residents of Sorake believe that the distance from Gunung Sitoli airport keeps most tourists from visiting the south side of the island. Truth to be told, it's arguably the unreliability and difficulty of the domestic air links with mainland Sumatra that keeps tourists from the island, definitely not the three-hour bemo ride down to Sorake.

But the fact is, with each passing season more and more travelling surfers flock to Lagundri Bay and that's despite the immense and largely unexplored wave potential of the rest of the island. In fact, the vast majority of surfers ignore the entire east coast of Nias and still gather on the main peak of Sorake. So, despite all the isolation and the struggles of its residents, its line-up is still one of the busiest in the whole Indian Ocean, even 33 years after its discovery. Thirty hungry surfers in the line-up are the norm nowadays, and it's not rare to feel some tension on the peak, especially on the smaller or less consistent days.

Now that the wave is hollower and more intense than in the past, it appeals to a different group of hardcore tube chargers – surfers who spend whole months out there doing what it takes to claim their spot in the strict pecking order.

Young Australian pros, brave Brazilian tube riders, feral slab hunters and underground chargers keep the testosterone level in the line-up always high, fighting with a knife between their teeth for every set wave as if it could be their last. Thirty-three years have passed, but the place is still as intense as it gets. "The more things change, the more they stay the same" – jokes a smiley Avenus as he waxes his beaten up 6'3" round pin.

Many things, including the waves, have changed in the last 33 years. Others, like the fact that all the guesthouses and warungs are still owned and operated by local families, have stayed the same. Judging by the amount of waves that the locals get during each session though, the place is in good hands.

First published in *The Surfer's Path* magazine, Issue 71, March/April, 2009.

Durian Point

On an island like Nias, a wave is never just a wave. This is an island where convoluted local politics merges with murky mysticism. Quasi-fictional memories from a long-term, ground-level surf tripper.

PHIL GOODRICH

HE CHIEF OF the village was drunk when he took me to the tomb of the Queen of Nias Island. High on a hill above the coconut palms was the fantastic monument with finely carved dragons writhing around its pillars. It was from the balcony of the Queen's tomb that I first saw the wave wrapping into a small bay. I asked the chief about it, but he quickly changed the subject. He just wanted me to play a song. "Rock Star!" he slurred.

"What should I play?" I said.

"Elvis" said the chief.

I really didn't know any Elvis songs. In fact, I still don't know a complete song from start to finish from anyone, just riffs and pieces from lots of songs, but definitely no Elvis...so we settled on Led Zeppelin. This seemed to make him happy, and when we returned to the subject of the wave, he explained that because he was the chief, that he got to name the wave, and it was called, "ROCK STAR!"

I've always hated that name for the wave, and adamantly refuse to call it that, so I call it by the name of the village, which is Hilifalawo, or sometimes Durian Point, because I like that better. Durian, which is the king of all fruit, when it ripens, emits an odor so pungent, that it attracts the ghosts of blues singers from the exact opposite side of the globe – deep in the American South. By the time the odor reaches that side of the globe, the smell is just faint enough to be sweet; some people even describe it as sexual. The lonely ghosts of blues musicians Robert Johnson, Bukka White, Blind Willie McTell, Lightning Hopkins, and Lead Belly have all made the ghost pilgrimage to the tiny village called Hilifalawo, home of a wave shrouded in mystery and tragedy – obscure and mythical as the ghosts that wander through the village, drawn to the smell of their last sexual encounters on earth.

EMI SAX, OIL ON WOOD 18" X 24" BY PHIL GOODRICH

At sunset, the drunken chief and I walked through the village in order to find a papaya stem (makes a great pipe), and a better view of the wave. An old man sputtered something to me in Nias language. This is quite different from standard Indonesian. I asked the boy who was following us and serving as a translator what the old man said.

"He says that you wear your pants too low." said the boy.

The chief only laughed and shouted, "Rock Star!" with a rolling 'r'.

At that moment, a faint voice drifted into our midst. It was blues music mixed with the sound of snorting pigs, bleating goats and pounding surf. This was music in a language that I recognized that carried the same loneliness that I felt. I took a hit from my papaya pipe and closed my eyes to follow the sound to the front of a tiny bungalow that looked like all the others along the road except for the enormous pile of durian skin outside. Durian is spiked and has an ominous look, like a medieval torture device.

We pushed open the door and there in the shadows sat the ghost of Bukka White who paused in the middle of singing when he heard us come in. He shot us a look then continued his singing. It was a warning about women. There was pure and beautiful agony in his words. He explained that when you give your woman everything she wants at one time, she'll leave you. Materialistic jealousy, envy and drunkenness were other things his song warned against. The unmistakable smell of ripe durian was overpowering as Bukka continued to explain that true bluesmen were not concerned with money. It was the love for music and travelling that completed their souls. Getting paid just enough to "go big" for one night and then move on to the next town was their goal.

His scratchy voice vibrated off my skin and I realized that the wave I was chasing, and the paintings I recently finished, were my blues song. My lyrics were what I was willing to cast aside to arrive at this moment. I began to realize that few people really care about some lethal wave on a tiny island in the middle of the Indian Ocean. They may seem amused at the time of the story, but will never fully understand how riding a wave can affect your life.

The presence of Bukka White faded with the ending of his song, and as I scanned the room I noticed a window onto the ocean. A wave peaked quickly and snapped out of view, which stole my attention. I rushed forward to watch its progress and my heart started to pulse. The wave zipped along, gaining speed as it warped and peeled through three different sections, squaring off at the end as if to take a bow, and then rudely spitting at the audience. Hidden from the road's view and cut off on both ends by a series of bridges that were nothing but rotten planks and slippery steel, this village wave was a true secret spot. An hour away is the famous Lagundri Bay, which long ago sold out to the whims of international travelers seeking to digest their piece of surfing's mythical Mecca. The beauty of this secret was that it was shrouded in a tall tale based on a real two-fold tragedy.

The Feud

In 1998 a feud between neighbouring villages was born out of a classic plot between a young virgin girl from Teluk Dalam and her involvement with the son of a prominent durian farmer from Hilifalawo. The durian farmer was a drunkard, but was rich for the standards of the village. He had delusional expectations for his son to attend university somewhere in Jakarta, which seemed like another planet to his son, who was content with the simplest pleasures in life and wanted nothing more than to settle down in the village and build a life with his young girlfriend Yusnidar. She was the daughter of a Teluk Dalam fisherman, poor as the day is long, but extremely beautiful in a plain, lazy-eyed, gap-toothed, unique sort of way.

The durian farmer loathed Yusnidar, because when he became drunk (every evening) Yusnidar transformed into his estranged wife. She had long ago run off with his former durian agent in Jakarta. The farmer's delusions would cause him to verbally abuse Yusnidar because he truly saw all of the best qualities of his wife in her, and he hated himself for having driven her away. His own expectations to reclaim his wife were pinned on his son, who had no interest at all in attending university on planet Jakarta, where Muslims bombed Christians and Christians sold out to big businesses to bring western decadence that fueled the Muslim hate.

For his son's 20th birthday party, the farmer organized a banquet where three pigs would be slaughtered for the occasion. The parents of Yusnidar would attend, along with about 100 people from the neighbouring villages. At the height of the celebration, which coincided with the height of the farmer's drunkenness, a song by bluesman Robert Johnson limped from the battered speakers, "I've got a kind-hearted woman, she studies evil all the time!".

Indonesians are fond of their karaoke, and the farmer began to call attention to himself by singing along to one of his favorite blues songs of all time. He could really identify with the painful falsetto crescendos of Johnson's voice, and he felt his own voice was quite the match. His painful rage began to bubble as he spotted Yusnidar and reminders of his tragedy magnified when he saw the way Yusnidar looked at his son. It was a look of total devotion that seemed to make a mockery of his own sad loss. He began to direct the song to his son's love interest, which drew a crowd of smirking villagers, who knew from experience and rumor what was going down. Virginity is a commodity in the animistic society of Nias, and a high price is paid in the form of a dowry even in this modern age. As the farmer's voice became louder and more overpowering than the whole commotion of the banquet, he decided to freestyle some lyrics of his own. These lyrics were about as offensive as you can get, severely questioning the validity of Yusnidar's virginity.

> So high the price of a pure gal these days,
> How low we men go,
> The deeper the jungle, the cheaper the prize,
> A man can sell his daughter's rights,
> Just rewrap the goods, 'cause her beautiful face
> can slip past the blame!

A look of utter shock first crept into Yusnidar's face and then onto her proud, poor-fisherman father's, followed by the oldest brother, and her cousin (who had a secret crush on Yusnidar and was considering hiring a local witchdoctor to inflict a painful death on the farmer's son). Virtually the whole village of Teluk Dalam was swept into the fire of rage by the pathetic, blundering lyrics and pseudo-Elvis gyrations of the foolish durian farmer from Hilifalawo.

In a society where two generations prior the people were hunting each other's heads, cooking and eating each other's flesh to gain strength, and praying to animal spirits was normal, this very public attack against Yusnidar's honour quickly escalated into a William Wallace-style war. Depending on whom you asked, arms were severed, skulls were mashed like watermelons, and fires were strategically set to the soundtrack of steady blues music. After the skirmishes at the banquet, travel and commerce between the two villages became impossible. Teluk Dalam (a large village near the port) and Hilifalawo (a much smaller village, but in control of all the durian fruit trade) were inconsolable.

Simple business transactions became covert revenge operations. Travel and communications via minibus and motorbike along the tattered jungle roads became less and less safe.

A few weeks later the chaos seemed to settle. The son of the durian farmer made his way cautiously into Teluk Dalam, with an apology speech prepared and a pocketful of money with the intention of paying the dowry for his love, Yusnidar. When he arrived at the bungalow of Yusnidar's father, who had yet to return from his daily fishing trip, Yusnidar's oldest brother and jealous cousin were sitting playing cards and drinking asoka (local rice vodka). His greeting of "*Ya'ahowu*" received nothing but a bloodshot stare and a jealous glare. The durian farmer's son decided to wait for Yusnidar's father on the beach as it was nearing dark. As he sat on the sand and watched the octopus hunters pick through the reef, he could make out the outline of his love's father's boat bobbing through the shorebreak. It reminded him of the countless times he would rush down to help the old man drag his outrigger canoe back up the beach and under the mango tree. The young man was not a fisherman, but loved to hear the old man's stories, and he loved the sight of a boat full of shiny fish. As he approached the old man and his canoe, he noticed the scowl on the man's face and was taken aback.

"I can do it myself!" the old man sputtered. He watched the old man's rippled and gnarled arms straining under the tension of pulling a canoe full of water and fish. It was all he could do to hold back from helping as the veins and tendons struggled pathetically. He began to follow the old man up under the tree and started into his well-practiced speech. The old man snapped at him again.

"Save your breath!"

It was hard to hold his tongue, considering how much time and respect he had paid this man over the three years that he had courted Yusnidar.

The farmer's son realized the futility of his efforts and decided to change his approach. He would try reasoning with Yusnidar's mother. He could see his love and her agile, protective mother (who would never leave them completely alone) across the road hanging laundry.

The sight of Yusnidar, in the purple-orange sunset light refracting off the white laundry fluttering in the breeze, sent him in a trance of love. She had never looked more beautiful to him than at that moment.

Had he not been so caught up with the sight of her, he would have noticed Yusnidar's brother and jealous cousin crouching behind some palm trees – one with a gasoline can and the other with a torn fishing net. As he reached the trees he was met with the sound of metal colliding with skull.

When he awoke, the farmer's son could smell gasoline and taste the metallic tinge of blood in his mouth. He could feel something gouging into the delicate skin between his lips and nose, but he could not remove the torn fishing net, which he was now tangled in.

Everything slowed down as he heard the click of the lighter, and saw the look of helpless horror on Yusnidar's face. The heat raced over him in a breeze and the smell of his own flesh burning overcame him.

The Tragedy

July 2002 – I had a connection with her. I felt it. But at that moment, with the time delay on the phone and the realization that my girlfriend had caught me cheating, my head was spinning.

"I fuckin' hate you!" she screamed (muffled with static)

What could I say? Halfway around the world on an island in the Indian Ocean I couldn't do a damn thing except watch the waves pound the reef, and trust in my intuition that I was doing the right thing. We had both hurt each other so many times so, in a way, her finding those pictures on my laptop was a necessary evil. Something to get off my chest. There is no denying photographic proof of Indonesian conquests complete with accidental self-portraits in the hotel mirror behind a young "model" in various sexual positions.

Needless to say, I was up for anything (expecting the worst at home) when the drunk American Tim virtually offered me a map to a secret wave a few hours to the north. He began to describe 17-second righthand barrels, ten-dollar ounces of weed, civil war so harsh that weeks before he had spoken with a village girl who watched with her own eyes as soldiers chopped her father and brother into pieces, starting with the arms and legs. There were people fighting for independence to control a province that holds close to 85% of the region's cash-yielding natural resources (oil, natural gas, ganja, durian), a province still torn by a feud between two families over the tragic end of a durian farmer's son, and the soiled reputation of a young virgin beauty named Yusnidar.

This sounded like my kind of risk. My mind was swimming and scheming and plotting, but mostly I just wanted to figure out a way to stay right there in Indonesia for the whole season, and then the next...

What did I need to go back to? A girl who hated me? My job serving coffee, and surfing closed out west-facing beachbreaks overcrowded with mtvspringbreakextremexgame-generation San Diego kids?

Early the next morning I sat with Big Mike watching clean 6ft bombs pump into Lagundri Bay. We were sharing a few papaya stem bongs when we spotted "LA Tim", my new friend from the night before, silently pushing a motor bike under the losmen so as not to wake anyone who might follow him to his secret wave. We began stirring him up, saying that we were bringing six French bodyboarders, two chicks and a handful of photographers to his new spot. He gave us a maniac smile, behind a middle finger, and sped off down the road.

Little did we realize it would be the last we would ever see of him.

It was the amount of blood that was most shocking to the local people of Hilifalawo. It flowed past Tim's desperate fingers, down his leg and onto the sand, and then into the reef. Absurd amounts of blood – a small lagoon of blood mixed in pools between the rocks. The children of the village wondered silently if all bule (foreigners) bleed this much. An argument broke out between the villagers. Half of them wanted to take him to the local witch doctor, who would prepare a salve of mud and leaves to clog the wound, the other half wanted to take Tim to the modern doctor Ima Restu, who worked in Teluk Dalam (40 minutes away if the bridge wasn't washed out.) No one wanted to drive Tim's motorbike into Teluk Dalam because the embers of the feud between the villages were a wisp of wind away from igniting again. Despite Tim's desperate pleas for medical attention and his aversion to seeing a witch doctor, his life expired before a decision could be made. His last words were whispered because Tim could feel the cold chill running through his body.

"Tell my mother I love her!" he gasped.

But the local villager who was holding his hand heard his final words to be,

"Tell Yusnidar I love her." He believed it to be the restless ghost of the durian farmer's son, which only furthered the belief that the village of Hilifalawo is overrun with lonely ghosts and the wave is a cursed and dangerous entity.

A shockwave rippled through Lagundri Bay. The news of a fellow surfer bleeding to death travels like a gasoline fire through a tight-knit United Nations of exotic surfing characters. Tall tales were speculated on just what caused the laceration on Tim's inner thigh, which had severed his femoral artery. Was it his fin, the reef, the nose of his board? Was the wave too dangerous to surf? Too shallow? The rumors gained momentum, and curiosity got the best of me, which is how I found myself alone in the room with a view of the lethal wave, the smell of durians and the echo of Bukka White, Robert Johnson, and Lead Belly.

I entered the line-up cautiously, unable to get the mental picture of Tim's bleeding to flee from my mind. My first few waves were a blur, but the amount of time spent inside the tube mixed with the uncertainty of what would happen after falling off, combined to make it a truly exhilarating experience.

July 2005 – The village wave is not so secret any longer. Not crowded, just not secret – still a bit tricky to find – and the road to get there sucks. To surf the wave is still a unique experience, and I swear if you find yourself surfing there alone, just close your eyes and you can hear the sound of blues music rustling through the palm trees, and if the wind is offshore you can smell the sexual odor of the durian. It's an emotional experience – one that can leave you wondering if westerners were ever actually meant to be traveling in this remote village on a cursed, fatalistic, headhunting, war-torn island in the Indian Ocean.

First published in *The Surfer's Path* Issue 81, December, 2010

✈ Padan

Mentawai Islands

Grid squares equal 10km

○ Muarasaibi

Sakubo ○

PULAU
○ Maurasiberut
SIBERUT

Taileleu ○
Nyang
Nyang
Mainu

E-BAY
NO-KANDUI
Karangmajet
Selat Siberut
RIFLES
Simakaka
Pototogat
ICELAND
TELESCOPES → ○ Tua Pejat
SCARECROWS ✈ ○ Rokot
7 PALMS Pitojat ○ Siberimanua
○ Sioban
○ Sibetumonga
PULAU
SIPURA
○ Sigici
LANCE'S RIGHT
Teluk Pasir
Siduamata Bosua
○ Katiet
LANCE'S LEFT
Selat Sipura

Tg Sumiayu
PULAU
Simaganjo ○
PAGAI
UTARA
Tg Simatobe

CHARTER BOAT
TRAVELLING TIMES

Boat Cruising Speed	Distance covered in 1hr (km)
	• 5
5 knots	• 10
	• 15
10 knots	• 20
	• 25
15 knots	• 30
	• 35
20 knots	• 40

Sikakap ○
Selat Sikakap
MACARONIS → Betamonga ○ Seai
For detailed map
see page 75
P. Siruso
○ Mapooepooe

PULAU
Pitojet
THUNDERS
PAGAI
Sibigau
SELATAN

○ Tiop

Pulau Sibarubaru

Padong to Mentawai passenger ferry 14hrs

Finding Macaronis

A 1980 Expedition to the Mentawai Islands

CHRIS GOODNOW

First Attempt, July, 1978

GRAJAGAN, G-LAND, IS an amazing sight, especially when you know you have it all to yourself for the next five days.

I was staying in what were the beginnings of the world's first commercial surf camp, then an exclusive arrangement of uncertain legal basis between Californian Mike Boyum and the Chief of Police in Banyuwangi, the nearest Javanese city, otherwise known only for its notorious jail. Aside from my sister and I, there were no other 'guests' that season because Mike had allegedly abandoned the project for the hills of Thailand, pursued by US narcotics agents.

There was, however, evidence of at least one famous guest who'd stayed there before us – several of Gerry Lopez' Lightning Bolt boards were stored in the rafters of our hut.

Ironically, my trip to G-land to surf its semi-known wave was simply the back-up for failing to achieve my primary goal – to fulfil the surfer's dream by finding perfect, unridden waves in remote parts of Indonesia. My Java exploration had included getting permits from the Indonesian National Parks Office in Bogor to stay in Plengkung (G-Land), from where I planned to search unexplored surfing territory in Ujung Kulon and the island of Panaitan at the other end of Java. I only got as close as the nearest port to Panaitan, where my $5-a-day budget was not remotely close to covering the quotes for a boat charter.

But Java itself was only a back-up plan that kicked in after an arduous and unsuccessful attempt to fulfil the dream over five weeks exploring, on my own, way off the beaten path in Sumatra. I'd had OK surf at Lhoknga near Aceh in the north, and a wild trip on public buses along the Trans-Sumatran Highway down the west coast to Meulaboh; then sleeping on ferry-decks along the island chain, starting at Simeleue and heading south towards Nias. It was obviously rich with potential for surf, and nowadays that potential has almost all been revealed in all its glory. But to get to those waves in 1978 – on the other side of islands with jungles and no roads, a long way from the main ports – you needed more planning and resources than I had come with.

A storm and a fever of unknown origin had aborted my ferry trip towards Lagundri Bay on Nias, where it was already known there was some kind of a wave. The discovery of waves in Nias back in 1974 had spread by word of mouth in the cliff-top warungs at Uluwatu, and surfing at Lagundri was even mentioned in the Lonely Planet guide in 1978, but no photographic evidence had leaked out. What I'd missed out on only became clear the following year, when *Surfer* magazine published on its cover Erik Aeder's classic shot of the emerald, then-empty Lagundri righthander, complete with palm-ringed bay.

If there were good waves in Nias, I'd reasoned, there had to be good waves in the Mentawai Island chain to the south. On the way back from Sumatra to Java I took a steamer from Padang to Jakarta past the southern Mentawai Islands, the ship rolling in a 10ft Indian Ocean groundswell. Out on the horizon, those islands gnawed at me as we steamed on by. Out there lay some unfinished business.

Second Time Lucky, May, 1980

Back in Sydney, I was now in the second year of Veterinary Medicine and Surgery at university, but was determined to fulfil the dream by returning to Indonesia, this time much better equipped and organized for the challenge of exploring the Mentawai islands.

From the middle of 1979, I began developing the plans together with Scott Wakefield, who was studying Economics at Sydney Uni. It became our obsession. Weekends digging through the Mitchell Library for anthropological accounts of the Mentawai revealed there was no cash economy and the only currency was bartering slabs of tobacco. Our information proved to be several decades out of date – rupiah were king and the kilos of tobacco we lugged around were only good as paperweights. We scouted through ship-merchants for high quality British Admiralty and Dutch East Indies maps of the islands and reefs. Survival handbooks were memorized, and pages of lists assembled detailing essential supplies for surviving weeks in the jungle.

We knew the Southern hemisphere autumn and winter is peak swell season for Indonesia, but there was zero information on winds and climate in the Mentawai. This was the era before satellite imagery and computer modelling. We chose May to coincide with a between-term university break of three weeks. It was clear we needed at least four weeks, so I took the calculated risk that by missing a genetics exam worth 30% I could still pass if I did well enough in the end-of-year exam. To finance the trip Scott was packing supermarket shelves at Woolies, and I was making backyard surfboards.

As plans developed, my cousin Tony Fitzpatrick joined the team. He had finished two years of studying medicine, but was planning to take a year off and travel. With the over-confidence of youth, we reasoned that two years of medical textbook knowledge was as good as having an emergency trauma surgeon on the expedition. Luckily none of us tested that assumption.

We set off from Sydney Airport on 26th April with two single-fins each and a mountain of medical and survival supplies packed into our backpacks. First we overnighted at the Jalan Jaksa youth hostel in Jakarta and then in Padang at the old Tiga Tiga hotel. Dressed in our Sunday best, sweltering but trying to stay cool, we went around in circles between the Padang offices of the army, navy and police: they were all very suspicious about why Australians would ever want to go to the Mentawai islands. When we initially tried to describe our plans to ride pieces of fibreglass on large waves over coral reefs, this was viewed as definitely something they couldn't approve and would need to be referred to Jakarta. The solution turned out to be to say we only wished to *"jalan jalan, lihat lihat"* – to go sightseeing – which reassured them we weren't spies but just crazy westerners.

The following extracts are taken from my diary of the trip that followed.

Monday, 28th April, 1980 – Padang, Sumatra: Staying in Tiga-Tiga Hotel, got up at 7am and caught bemo to Teluk Bayur. Find out there's a boat to Sikakap, Sioban and Sikabaluan leaving tonight.

Back in Padang, we change into good clothes and go to Police Headquarters to get a permit to travel around Sipura/Sipora (both spellings are used). They want to know why we're going to the Mentawais on a business visa. We tell them about surfing. They don't know what surfing is but they decide that we ought to get permission from Kantor Gub Autorita Mentawai up the road.

They in turn also don't want to risk granting permission, and reckon we've got to have written permission from Jakarta – the Institute of Science, Head of Police, and Home Minister.

We go back to the police, who tell us we only need our passports to go there.

Three hours left. A mad dash to change $200 in travellers cheques, post letters and buy a million things. Charter a minibus to Teluk Bayur for 1500rp, unloading all our stuff onto the dock.

The *Balam* (Prentiss Lines) looks like a refugee boat, overflowing with people and belongings. We rent a room from Indra, a crewmember, but only 2 beds. Tony cheats in picking straws, and I have to sleep on the floor. Scott cheated too.

Tuesday, 29th April, 1980 – Sikakap, Pagai Utara: Arrive at Sikakap, Pagai Utara about 8am. We make a quick decision to get off here if we can charter a boat. We quickly do – from a guy named Asril, for 15,000rp a day. So we spend the day walking from office to office, getting signatures for our form from the Kantor Wali Negeri. We also meet the pastor of the Catholic church, who lends us a mask and snorkel.

We stay the night at Asril's house where we have an unreal traditional Minangkebau meal with rice, fish, chilli sauce, eggs, spicy vegetables and mango. After dinner we relax with Asril's family and friends and have a cup of coffee.

Rainy at dawn, then thunderstorms, then clear arvo with west winds.

Wednesday, 30th April, 1980 – Sikakap to Sabeugukgung: We head out before dawn in a setting full moon. Asril's worried that the waves are big. Pick up Rasid, who we find out later was told we were only going for two days, and head off downstream.

The day is clear and the wind light NE. Pass Pulau Siruso, our first perfect left pointbreak – it looks about 6-8ft and barrelling. The coast to Sabeugukgung is protected by funny reefs with shifting waves.

[Author's note: I have no recollection why we didn't head straight for the 6-8ft left pointbreak. This is not a generally surfed spot nowadays, so perhaps it wasn't as "perfect" as the diary records.]

Come ashore at the house of Tuan Tambak. The *kepala kampung* (village head) doesn't really seem to know what our form is for. After lunch, which Asril and Rasid cook, we go walkabout around the point looking for perfect righthanders, through swamp and across reef, only to be stopped by a razor-sharp reef. Scott would have kept going, but Tony and I turn back.

The wind switches from S to N as a thunderstorm hits, then glassy and calm all afternoon. Asril takes us around the bay looking at waves. He really seems to be coming to the conclusion that we're lunatics. So on returning from our fruitless search, Scott and I go surfing on the beachbreak to show them how it's done.

[Author's note: Ironically, during this "fruitless search" we spent a little while watching and even photographing a shallow left reefbreak in this bay that was too small on the day. That break is now known to be legendary with a big S swell, and goes by the name of "Greenbush".]

Thursday, 1st May, 1980 – Sabeugukgung to Betumonga and Silabu: Set off at dawn for Betumonga. Rounding the last point, Tanjung Toitet, we're looking into an unreal but sectioning 4-6 foot lefthander. The day's clear and the wind light ENE. We jump off and surf the 4th bowl.

Scott surfs with typical zongo wave judgement and breaks his legrope. Then we paddle up to the 3rd bowl for a few larger and faster waves. Wind comes up light southerly, so we head back to the boat.

Travel up the coast to Teluk Pasongan. The left point looks promising – glassy, spiralling tubes – but we're not so sure it's rideable. The right point, Tanjung Sinjai, looks like an OK wave.

[Author's note: Interesting that we didn't immediately recognize "Macaronis" as it is now called for the perfect wave it is. On this morning it was 6-8ft, thick southwest groundswell and low tide, with the Bommie in Pasongan bay breaking consistently. As I recall we were worried about the dredging reef being too shallow, and were probably focussed on the outside sections that are unmakeably fast.]

The other side of Tanjung Sinjai is a long rolling left with some good-looking sections. The left point at the entry to Silabu looks good: an easy peeling sort of wave, 1-2ft when Betumonga is 3-4ft. A ledgy right guards the other side of the passage.

Pull up at Silabu Gedang (Besar), a beautiful lazy village. Too bad there's no surf. Spend the afternoon trying to organize a trip to Sipura. All we come up with is a one-way trip to Pulau Siduomata (off Sipura) for 20,000rp, or a 2-way trip in a small "speedboat" for 1 day at 65,000rp!

A thunderstorm comes up about 2pm, but misses us, and the wind comes from the NE. Afternoon is calm and sunny. We sleep in the house, which is also a shop, upstairs.

Friday 2nd May, 1980 – Silabu Gedang: Head to Betumonga Pt at dawn. Surf's 3-4ft and peeling. Everyone gets plenty of waves. Scott uses zongo judgement and takes the first set he sees halfway between bowl 4 and bowl 3, breaks his legrope, and has to swim all the way around the reef. The wind, which was light E, comes up from the S and we paddle back to the boat.

Decide to stay at Betumonga, in the little shop at the rivermouth there. Nice beach, lefthander at 'Monga Pt looks good: a short peeling section into a nice shoulder for a cutback. Only 1-2ft today.

Eat lunch, give Paludrine pills to the mother with malaria, sit around during thunderstorm at midday, when wind temporarily switches northerly.

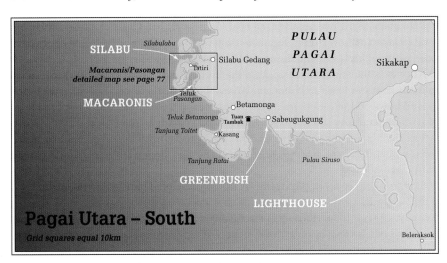

Outside the boat shed at Betumonga rivermouth, about 4km southeast of Pasongan Bay.

Afternoon we go to the Betumonga village to show our permit to the kepala kampung and give him ¼ slab of tobacco. Boat trip up the river was straight out of *Apocalypse Now*.

Load the boat in the late afternoon and head for Kasang, since there's no way Asril will take the boat out if the swell comes up.

Kasang is a cubby house in a swamp!

Saturday, 3rd May, 1980 – Kasang: Arise at dawn and head to the point, Rasid at the helm. Surf's good but swell inconsistent and more from the west so it's not lining up so good. Rasid disappears with the boat and we're left out in the middle of nowhere in the heaviest bloody rainstorm. Start paddling back into the bay.

Rain stops, Asril returns with the boat, and we all head back for lunch. Rice and TVP (Sanitarium's Textured Vegetable Protein) – a combo not fit for pigs but we've been eating it for lunch and dinner! Still, the coffee's good.

Afternoon the wind comes up from the north (it was pretty calm till then), so we take the boat and Rasid to Pasongan. We see the house there, and how nice the beach is, and how good the left there really is, and how if we stay here we won't have to go to church tomorrow and can surf instead. So we decide to stay here.

The right is looking good so we surf that. Cleanest, offshore, 5ft waves I've surfed for a while. Just long, fast, peeling walls. The reef slopes off very gradually, with shifty take-off spots.

Stay the night again in the swamp at Kasang. Plenty of rain during the night.

Sunday, 4th May, 1980 – Kasang to Pasongan: Partly cloudy at dawn. We load the boat and head out for Pasongan. Wind is light NNE and swell seems bigger and stronger and more from the west.

Pasongan Point is pumping. We take a few pictures from the boat, unload our stuff to the dilapidated house at Puba Ruwayat, and head out. Paddle round the point and into the most perfect 3-5ft waves. Wind blowing into the tube, but no real problem. Reminiscent of Tamarin Bay only shorter, hollower and more bowling.

Tony cuts his back on the reef.

By midday the wind is too strong from the north and too choppy. Head in and fix up house with plastic tarps for walls, fix the floor, etc. Rain all night.

[Author's note: we stayed in a day-house belonging to a man named Martin. It's a tiny hut in his coconut garden. To the east was the coconut garden and house of Seratubu, a teacher from Silabu, and his son Parmin. Martin still lives in Silabu. His children are now teachers in Silabu village, and Seratubu's daughter is headmistress.]

Monday, 5th May, 1980 – Pasongan: Wake at dawn and paddle out around the point after a cup of coffee. Wind is light offshore NE (*timur laut*), the sky is partly cloudy, and the swell up about 4-6ft with a few 7-footers. Scott and I the only ones out in perfect, barrelling waves. Unreal.

Tony walks around the point, followed by Asril. The tide is high and they're keeping near the swamp. Tony plods along with camera gear, then notices Asril heading out to sea at a rate of knots. Apparently a 6ft crocodile had come out of the swamp about 15 feet behind Tony!

Wind turns calm, then SW, then freshens NW to W making surf too choppy. Come in to yet another meal of rice and TVP, although this time also with snails.

Spend the afternoon on the beach writing a letter. Rain and wind heavy at night.

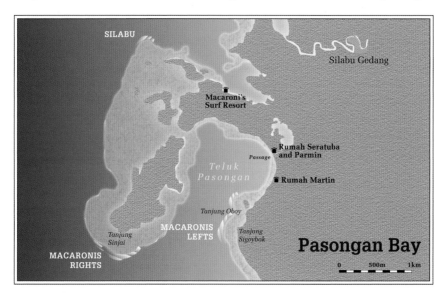

*Walking through
the swamp behind
Teluk Pasongan.
Scott, Asril and
Rasid, keeping an
eye out for crocs.*

Tuesday, 6ᵗʰ May, 1980 – Pasongan: Rain stops at dawn, but wind already blowing from NW and grey clouds scudding from W. Doesn't look too promising. But wind soon drops to light NE and we paddle out. Swell less consistent – still 4-6ft and perfect. Surf till midday, when the wind comes onshore. Go in to a nice bowl of *bubur* rice porridge (2 grated coconuts, onions and rice), biscuits and coffee.

Very long and heavy rainstorm hits for about an hour at midday. Afterwards the wind is light easterly so we eat a couple of lollies and walk around the point.

The waves are classic: 3-6ft, low-tide cylinders. Glowing aquamarine waves and white spray, against a dark grey sky to the south. If only we had a water camera. Stay out till sunset, the wind eventually swinging light SW-NW, then back to N late. So many perfect waves....

Rain heavy again at night and into next morning.

Wednesday, 7ᵗʰ May, 1980 – Pasongan: Rain in morning and heavy cloud. Wind drops at dawn to light easterly. Walk around for a surf, but the wind overnight has churned up a NW surface chop and the lefts are a bit bumpy. It looks big and mean so we decide to give it a miss. Have breakfast and sit around for a while.

Go for a surf at 10am, as the wind has now turned SSE. The waves are still a bit bumpy, but classy and bowling around the inside. Surf for a couple hours, 3-5ft, till the S wind gets a bit too strong out at the take-off.

Thursday, 8ᵗʰ May, 1980: Wake early and head around. Tony brings camera. Sky is clear and the wind is calm – maybe a breath of offshore.

Swell's a lot weaker, bit inconsistent, usually only 1 or 2 waves in a set instead of the 3-4 before. Still there are a few perfect glassy 3-5ft barrels, and we surf till the wind comes up SW-W at about 10:30 or so.

Later, at midday, Martin takes everyone on a walk to Silabu, the last leg by sampan. Wind is too strong for a surf in the arvo. A thunderstorm threatens, but nothing comes of it.

Friday, 9ᵗʰ May, 1980 – Pasongan back to Sikakap: Wind is light offshore, high cloud clearing, swell is weak 3-5ft from the south more. We leave, saying farewell to still perfect waves.

Betumonga is very small, too, and the swell irregular. Wind comes up light easterly in the straights. Heavy thunderstorm in the afternoon, which we miss by being out snorkelling with Father Pio, who gives us two rooms to stay in.

Eat that night at Asril's. His wife has made a bit of a feast, including rendang and a vegetable dish that was a scorcher: "*pedas sekali*!!!"

After dinner Asril drives us around to the Catholic school with all our stuff. An eerie night-time drive with the kero lamp hissing at the bow, nocturnal fish glinting in the sheet-of-glass water, and fleeting glimpses of small-town nightlife in Asia.

Saturday, 10ᵗʰ May, 1980 – Sikakap: Sat around most of the morning, either at the shop eating fried bananas, biscuits and milk coffee, or in our rooms writing letters.

Chopped wood for Father Pio, like true Aussie timber cutters, in the afternoon. The boredom of waiting for a boat was beginning to get to us.

Sunday, 11ᵗʰ May 1980 – Sikakap: Grabbed a few fried bananas and jumped on the pastor's boat to Beleraksok. Checked out the coast to the south. Wind light east, turned south later, and swell small with quite a surface chop. Nearly tipped over in the sampan which two girls ferried us ashore in. Went to church, introduced by Father Pio as student priests! Nearly fell asleep during the Mass: church is as boring as I remembered it. Afterwards, walked around the village, ate rice and Super-Mi, heard about run-ins between the villagers and the logging company, etc.

Probably an OK left point here when the swell is big. Today it's tiny and we don't bother surfing but go diving instead on the way back. I slept: think all the infections are taking their toll.

Eat at restaurant that night. No rain today.

Monday, 12ᵗʰ May 1980 – Sikakap: Wake after a night where I really felt a bit sick, and ate brekky at the usual coffee spot. Bought some Rinso and Tony and I washed our clothes. Scott fixed dings, spilled resin all over himself, and timed it all perfectly with the schoolkids lunch-hour, attracting a huge audience.

Ate lunch at Asril's, took photos of the family, etc. Asril's wife sure can cook!

Helped Father Pio move some huge sections of a tree at high tide. Looked totally impossible, but that guy's got a will and determination that is unbelievable. Amazingly, we got the logs out into deep water and floated them down to the church.

Tuesday, 13th May, 1980 – Pagai to Sipura: Asril drove us out to *K.M Balam* at 9:30am. Tony and I went ashore again to eat and buy food for Scott, and then we were off. Wind was light NE, then northerly later in the afternoon. Swell seemed only small, but very long period. Apparently it was big, we heard later at Bosua.

Arrived in the evening at Sioban, got ripped off severely for the boat that ferried us ashore with Ronni, to the house of the *wali negeri* (state official), who was in Padang.

Saw the pastor, Father Petrus Grappoli, who recommended we steer clear of Ronni, gave us bread (REAL bread!!), wine, cheese and salami. He tried to set us up with a boat going to Bosua the next day, finding us a place to stay for the night.

Wednesday, 14th May, 1980 – Sioban to Bosua, Island of Sipura: Had to do the rounds of reporting to all the officials again.

Basril, the guy who owned the boat, was looking impatient by the time we'd finished, and downright restless after we'd gone to a million shops for supplies. Set off finally at about 11am into a light SE wind (*tenggara*).

[Author's note: we passed Katiet at midday, and while there were small crumbly onshore waves breaking on the reef we didn't see what we might have: the legendary righthander of Lance's Right (or HT's) would not be discovered until Lance Knight arrived 10 years later. A thunderstorm was brewing and Basril wasn't up for detouring along the edge of the reefs as we rounded the SW end of Sipura. We passed straight by without seeing the excellent lefthander now known as Lance's Left. Moral of the story: discoveries aren't made when you're in a hurry.]

Arrived at Bosua just as the afternoon rain hit at 2pm Got soaked, carried our stuff to the house, had some tea. Cleared up later in the arvo, wind was light NW and swell about 6-7ft on the crummy reefs at Bosua.

Later we walked to Gobi and on to Teluk Pasir in hope of waves, through some beautiful gardens. Unreal place, perfect bays and close villages, but the reefs were all weird: submerged coast or something. Really disappointing. Wind turned W later.

[Author's note: had we continued on this path to the other end of the bay we would have seen Lance's Left, and another 1km would have brought us to the beach at Lance's Right where, by now, the wind would have swung offshore. So close yet so far.]

Ate dinner prepared by Osmar's wife, Osmar being the local *Guru Agama Katolik* (Catholic teacher). Tony wrecked his knee trying to sit cross-legged at dinner, and had cartilage damage during our little feast of biccies and Indomilk later, in the privacy of our own room.

Thursday, 15th May, 1980 – Bosua: Woke and looked at the sea. Wind was already blowing from the south and cloudy. Had breakfast (boiled bananas and coffee) and went to church. Seats were hard and too low, and the service was as boring as ever – if not more so because they're all EZONCS (Excessive Zeal Of the Newly Converted) and take it all deathly serious. Ate at Osmar's house afterwards – another great meal of rice and *keladi*, fish and vegetables. Really good. Wind blew strong S all day, cloudy too. We went for a walk while the locals sat or played volleyball.

After another good meal that night, had a good session of language swapping.

Friday, 16th May, 1980 – Bosua to Siberimanua: Left with Basril at 8am, heading north. Wind already coming up light southerly, sky clear, swell still a bit bumpy at about 5-7ft. Wind became moderate S.

Stopped for late lunch of Super-Mi, rice and bananas in Sibetumonga. Headed on again past a few likely-looking reefs after the thunderstorm. Wind was now blowing NNE. Arrived at sunset at Siberimanua, where we stayed with a family of Minang descent but now 3rd generation Mentawai.

Ate well, rice, fish, coffee and tea. Slept on the porch.

Saturday, 17th May, 1980 – Siberimanua to Sioban: Left soon after sunrise, after having to pay the lady an exorbitant 1500rp! Since they ripped us off for that, we told her brother he couldn't be a passenger in our boat. There really was no room, only now we felt we had good right to refuse.

Wind was light ESE in the morning when we jumped in the boat at about 7:30. Floating in the water wiping the kerosene off my feet, I couldn't help thinking about Asril's stories about sharks in Sipura. The waves at what is now called 7 Palms Point were good, 4-5ft, some long walls, fairly powerful, 'tho a bit inconsistent. Later the wind swings S and freshens, but the end sections still smooth and improves with the dropping tide. Good to be in the surf again!

Back on board, after two well fought-over cans of Indomilk, we go as far as an island off Tua Pejat. We stop for a surf in crummy waves, but aquarium conditions and lunch in a classic tropical coconut palm grove. Super-Mi for a main course with *kelapa muda* (young coconut) and sugar for dessert.

[Author's note: this surf spot is now called Icelands, and apparently only gets really good when huge. On the way there we also marked up on our maps a reef that had very small waves on the day, but looked like it would have Tamarin Bay-style perfection with a large west swell. That spot is now called Telescopes.]

Go straight through to Sioban after lunch, arriving at sunset. Stay at the local PPA office. Basril wasn't too happy about 30,000rp around the island! Fall asleep like a rock after a late dinner.

Sunday, 18th May, 1980 – Sioban: Slept in, picked up our passports, hung out wet clothes, and went swimming. Sorted out who owes who what. Spend the afternoon at the eating-house on the water, with *kopi susu* and super-biscuits.

Had coffee and dinner with the secretary to the *wali negeri* and his wife. Food was unreal: potatoes cooked in margarine, potato-puffs with meat, fried noodles, etc. Easily the best meal so far.

After dinner, went to wali negeri's house and watched *Voyage to the Bottom of the Sea* on the television, and talked. The wali gave us a map of Sipura: an unreal one.

Wind fresh from the south today.

Monday, 19ᵗʰ May, 1980 – Sipora to Pagai: Wind SW-S today, and half cloudy. Posted my letter after breakfast at the secretary's house (meat and eggs!).

Boat left at 12 noon. Swell large and a sea running from the south. All the women got sick when we went between the islands, and managed to spew in the most strategic places. There was spew everywhere – in the toilet, on the deck, on the stairs, and even over the railing.

Huge thunderstorm and wind hit about 2:30-3pm. Arrived in Sikakap late afternoon. Asril didn't bring his boat, but met us on deck. Stayed at Asril's that night: great meal with dishes including potatoes and little fried fish.

Went first to the timber company and saw Mr Hans, a German now resident of Australia, who works as chief mechanic there, has a "girlfriend" in Bangkok, etc. "No chance" of getting on the company plane with surfboards.

Tuesday, 20ᵗʰ May, 1980 – Sikakap: Wind fresh SE-S, no rain although cloud in arvo.

Drove Tony to the boat this morning, said farewells, etc., including making him promise not to tell a soul about Pasongan. The third horn sounded, and he was off towards the next chapter of his journey.

Scott and I were covering old ground waiting for Pak Wali to show up so we could get another letter full of stamps, etc. Didn't take so long this time, though he didn't show

The author Chris Goodnow tucking into what became their daily fare...and soon to be known as 'the world's funnest wave'. Pasongan Bay, aka Macaronis.

up for work till 10, on account of some Indonesian official parade, which gave us time to go see Father Pio. Father Pio was his usual jolly self, which caught us in the nick of time from sinking into depression. When we set off again I felt fresh and light-hearted again: essential for red-tape hassles.

With completed form, we went back to Asril's for a nice lunch. Afternoon I wrote letters, bought bananas (4.5rp each), etc. Dinner at Asril's, then slept.

Wednesday, 21st May, 1980 – Sikakap to Pasongan: Woke by alarm at 4am. Sky was dark and clear, wind light. Boat and Tiar arrived at 4:30 (rubber time) and we were off. The boat was slow, and a small SSE chop really upset Tiar, who obviously wasn't used to open ocean.

Arrived at Pasongan about 7:30. Beautiful morning with blue sky and water clear, wind light SSE, and so peaceful once the boat left. Swell unfortunately was a weak 1-3ft.

Spent the morning organizing the house and belongings, getting water, went snorkelling. Plenty of big fish straight out, too bad we don't have a speargun. Lay on the beach. We also discovered that badar kering (dried minnows) are shithouse. "Not those little fish again?!"

With only two people here – Scott and I – the local wildlife was a lot more adventurous: a lot more noises from the jungle at night, and a running battle with the squirrels, which keep stealing food at night.

Thursday, 22nd May, 1980 – Pasongan: Wind light early, waves 2-4ft and a bit weak and bumpy, but still good. Wind comes up a bit from the S at about 7am, but backs off.

We see four sharks (4ft reef sharks I assume) and paddle in. They were swimming in the face of the waves, just near the impact zone. Paddle out after half an hour: waves OK and good to be in the surf again. Surf til midday, then come in and make lunch.

Afternoon we just sit around talking, reading and drawing. Wind freshens from the south later. No rain. Tried fishing after dinner: boring.

Friday 23rd May, 1980 – Pasongan: Wind light offshore at dawn, with some fairly dense high cloud around. Surf still only 2-3-4ft, a bit lumpy, but very glassy and good fun. Wind flukes between SSE and E til 2pm, then comes moderate S. Some heavy clouds threatened to rain, but nothing comes of it. Bloody hot day.

Had more bloody little fish fried with onions and peanuts again, added to Super-Mi and Scott's *keladi* balls. Not too bad, at least this one was edible.

Washed our hair this afternoon: first time in four weeks. I also squeezed out the pus from the zillion little infected cuts and mozzie bites.

Saturday 24th May, 1980 – Pasongan: Glassy at dawn today, and swell very straight with more power. Wind stayed offshore or glassy till noon or so, and we surfed till then. Three to four foot and some perfect and very hollow waves. A good surf.

Some High cloud, wind finally came up southerly, but never got very fresh. Scott saw the sharks again, but this time the surf was too good to go in. We just didn't sit up on our boards for a while. Later, I get a wave and line up the tube. Scott's paddling out and it seems as if he's staring awfully hard at me. I keep going along in the tube and fall off just as I'm coming out. Scott's right there looking a bit worried. Apparently there was a shark skimming along inside the wave about five feet ahead of me, and when I fell off Scott thought I'd had it. Later, Scott sees a shark surface about 10 yards out the back, but it's heading out to sea, and the surf's still really good, so we stay out.

Exhausted, after lunch of noodles, fried rice and TVP, sleep on the beach having already washed and squeezed pus from the zillion cuts.

Scott is up at the swamp, standing on a log naked and brushing his teeth, when two Mentawai men from Tatiri paddle round the corner in a sampan. Scott sees them and jumps into the bushes. They see Scott, their first view of a white man, and head back out to sea at a rate of knots. God only knows what sort of ghost or spirit from the swamp they thought they'd seen, but judging from the shaky way they paddled that sampan back I'll bet there were some lively stories in Tatiri tonight.

Sunday, 25ᵗʰ May, 1980 – Pasongan: Surf was really flat today: 1-3ft and inconsistent (ie 15 minute waits or longer). Wind light offshore from the east, then glassy, then light SSE Thunderstorm at 11, glassy surf in afternoon when we went round the point to fibreglass a memento of our stay here. It read like this:

> Australian expedition to the Mentawais, first surfed here May 1980 by:
> Scott Wakefield: The surf's bloody perfect but the regular drop-ins by the sharks worried me a bit 'tho. It was no pleasure cruise.
> Tony Fitzpatrick: I didn't fancy getting chased by the crocodile from the swamp behind the point – a lot of hassle just for a surf!
> Chris Goodnow: I'm complaining to the North Pagai County Council about the shocking living conditions and lack of seating arrangements!
> All from Sydney, Australia

Then went for a nice, easy afternoon surf. Came in at sunset and got totally ravaged by clouds of little biting sandflies. Ran across the rocks and home to dinner of fried rice and *keladi* chips.

Monday, 26ᵗʰ May, 1980 – Pasongan to Sikakap: Woke to find the surf was even smaller. Didn't even bother to go surfing. Packed up, leaving wok, pots and pans, plates and cups to Martin along with a note saying thanks.

Tiar arrived soon enough with the boat, and we left as the wind began to freshen from the north. Out on the ocean the swell was larger, maybe 3-5ft. Seems it was so

Chris Goodnow (left) and Scott Wakefield checking their expedition supplies, which were basic but enough to get them through a long stint in the jungle at Pasongan Bay.

much from the west that Tanjung Sinjai was blocking it from Pasongan. Maybe we should have gone and looked at the little point at Silabu. Next time!

Betumonga had some fairly good waves breaking hard around bowl #4, which was as big as bowls 3, 2 or 1: an indication of the west in the swell.

Back in Sikakap we picked up our passports. Got a lift across to *K.V. Bella*, a huge timber cargo ship in port at the lumber company.

The captain was a jolly Israeli who thought our being "tourists in the Mentawais" was the funniest joke he'd heard in years. He gave us cold, Californian soft drinks out of the fridge, and salted almonds, and offered us a free ride to Padang.

Ate lunch (another great meal) at Asril's, gave him jerry cans and left over food, etc. Said goodbyes to all the family, and headed off to the ship.

Ate dinner on the ship: steak, tomatoes, onions, peas, bread. Unreal! Kept our heads down as all-out war erupted in the ship's mess hall between a crew of 7ft tall Nigerians who swarmed in on the cook with some complaint about the food. Next thing the Nigerians are being pursued by the little Chinese cook, waving a massive meat cleaver. We just keep eating and hope we survive the trip.

Slept that night on the floor of the officer's mess.

Tuesday, 27th May, 1980 – Padang to Jakarta: Arrived at dawn to a wet Teluk Bayur, wind from the west, fishing boats chugging and rocking to safety. Unloaded ourselves, with the Indonesian crew of stevedores, into a tiny covered boat. Got soaked by rain.

Arrived at Tabing airport smelly, wet, dirty, wearing boardshorts and raincoat. Disapproving looks from fellow travellers, but in 10 minutes we board the plane. Cloud seems heavy all along the west coast of Sumatra as we fly to Jakarta.

From 1980 to present day

When we returned to Sydney, everyone we surfed with at Manly and Curl Curl beaches knew where we'd gone and wanted to know what the surf was like. We resisted the temptation to boast and stuck to "a few waves, nothing to write home about, and shocking living conditions". This decision was made while Scott, Tony and I were in Sipura because we could not see a way to expose the region's waves for the benefit and not the harm of the wonderful people of Silabu and other villages around Macaronis.

We were acutely aware that these people had already suffered a great deal of adverse change. At the start of the 20th century Western missionaries arrived and taught them that, in addition to the hundreds of ocean and jungle deities they already feared, there was an additional almighty god whose son had died for their sins. With the formation of the Indonesian Republic, its Java-based government forced the Pagai people to live in policeable villages near the coast, and abandon a thousand-year old lifestyle that kept them deep in the jungle and safe from the region's devastating tsunamis. Once they were shifted out of the forest, the logging company had set up a factory in Sikakap and was in the midst of clear-felling the Pagai islands when we arrived in 1980. I'd seen the "gold rush" that descended on Nias after Erik Aeder's photos were published, and the last thing the Pagai people needed was the arrival of hordes of surf nazis.

There is an Indonesian saying that translates as: "To step on a man's ground, to break his twigs, you must understand his culture". We figured that if we resisted the exposure that occurred in Nias then, at least for some time, the only other surfers that walked on the twigs around Silabu would also have done their cultural homework. We told Martin, our host, that his village was sitting on a gold mine and that one day people from around the world would want to come ride its' waves, but whether or not that was a good thing would depend upon how it could be managed.

Remarkably the secret held without a leak for more than a decade. I returned to Pasongan/Macaronis for several weeks in May 1981 with Tim Annand, a fellow veterinary medicine student from Sydney. But the four of us soon became busy with other challenges, and anyway we swore we'd never go back unless it was with a boat that had a fridge!

Who was the next to arrive, and who gave Pasongan its current name of Macaronis, remains unrecorded. I've heard that a surfer, possibly Peter Reeves from Newcastle, NSW who had spent a lot of time at Lagundri in Nias in the '80s, was camping and surfing there towards the end of the decade when Martin Daly turned up in his salvage boat and asked what the spot was called. Reeves was eating a bowl of macaroni and said "Macaronis". In March 1991, Lance Knight was out surfing at Katiet in Sipura when Martin Daly arrived there, giving it the name of Lance's Right.

Rip Curl's 1992 Search video shot from Daly's boat started the gold rush of Mentawai surf-charters. I was running a research lab at Stanford University in California by that time, but while in Sydney for Christmas I dropped in at the surf shop of an old friend, Julian Taylor. Up on the screen was footage of Tommy Carroll surfing a perfect lefthander I recognized immediately. Asking Julian where it was shot he replied, "Oh you won't know, Chris, its some ultra-secret new spot". I laughed and said, "I think I do know".

Scott and I returned to Macaronis in July 1996 with a group of Sydney friends aboard the yacht *Katika*, skippered by the wise John "Bucket" McGroder. The good news was that we were out of the jungle away from the malarious mosquitoes, and we had a fridge. But by then there were usually 1 or 2 other boats anchored off the break plus a few tents in Martin's coconut garden in the bay.

Scott, Tony, Tim and I returned again with our families in 2013 as guests of Macaronis Resort on the other side of Pasongan Bay. With a swimming pool, air conditioning and a fridge (of course!), our living conditions had certainly improved. We caught up with Martin in Silabu, who like us is now in his fifties with grey hair, his kids proudly expanding the family teaching tradition. The village of Silabu has grown a little, the kids are better nourished, and there is intermittent electricity from a generator and a little income flowing from the resort.

Out in the Bay there are always between 2 and 6 surf charter boats at anchor, and the postage stamp-sized take-off spot was always packed as densely as pictures you see of the Superbank. As our teenage sons pointed out, the line-up was way more crowded than any of the waves we surf at home, and much more tense. More than 60 surf-charter boats are now heavily overfishing the wave resource at Macaronis. Some contribute a tiny mooring fee to Silabu village, but many refuse even to do that. Looking at the packed line-up of surfers and boats, Joni Mitchell's 1960's verse popped into my head: "take paradise, put up a parking lot".

The Future

On an optimistic day I can imagine Macaronis not as a parking lot, but managed as a sustainable resource: a destination that remains attractive with an openly accessible waiting list and a finite number of surfers at any one time, each paying a substantial daily fee into a trust that funds education, medical services and infrastructure for the Pagai villages. If surfers could achieve that goal we would avoid following the surfing "race to the bottom" that unfolded in Nias, or the pattern set by the logging companies in the Mentawais.

This is the first time Chris Goodnow's diary of the discovery of Macaronis has been published.

Macaroni Squeeze

When moor means less for visiting charter boats hoping to score the 'world's funnest wave'.

BY LEO MAXAM

IEHARD SURFERS NEVER abandon good waves. And they certainly never leave perfect Macaronis with just three people in the water – unless, of course, they are forced out at gunpoint. This was the scenario our group found itself in as we reluctantly vacated the Maccas line-up and paddled back to our boat, under the stern gaze of the local Mentawai police. I still couldn't believe what was happening. All seven surfers in our group were top-tier American pros earning serious coin to disassemble waves like this and capture it on film. But now we were all wilting under the pressure of our surf guide, Dale, who was leaning over the side of the dinghy, pleading with us to leave the water.

"You can stay in the water, but we can't guarantee your safety," screamed Dale. "These guys are serious, they're talking about sending the villagers out here with bows and poison arrows."

Just then a crack of thunder split the afternoon sky, adding emphasis to Dale's already panicked words. Then more screaming from the surf guide: "You guys seriously have to leave the water now!"

The day had started casually enough with an unremarkable dawn surf check at small Greenbush. From there we motored straight to Macaronis to find four boats in the channel. Two were tied up to moorings, the other two were anchored in the bay just opposite the wave. The swell was still filling in, but there were already a few overhead sets coming through.

The sight of a Macaronis wave can turn even the most jaded pro into an excited grom. Our group included four surfers on the WCT Dream Tour and another three who burn through passports like toilet paper, all in search of perfect waves. However, before we had even dropped anchor these guys were already scratching out to the line-up, frothing for their first Maccas session of the trip. Our photographer and cameraman were then ferried to shore to shoot the day's action. None of us had any idea that by anchoring our boat in the channel and paddling out for a fun morning surf, we were actually breaking the newest law of the land in this part of the Mentawais.

In 2009, two moorings were put down in the bay at Macaronis, the mechanical lefthander deemed by many surfers as "the funnest wave in the world". With the new moorings came new laws established by the local *kepala desa* (village head) and enforced by the local police. The Macaronis Resort land camp outlines the new rules on its website:

As of Tuesday, 20th April 2010, Silabu Village has introduced compulsory use of two moorings for visiting charter boats to Teluk Pasongan/Macaronis wave. Implementation of the mooring system is to prevent over-crowding in the bay and to protect the marine environment, as well as to benefit co-existence between Macaronis Resort and the charter boat fleet.

Basically, no more than two surf charter boats are allowed to be at Macaronis at any time. Throughout 2009, visiting boats were warned that the mooring system would take effect beginning the following season. At the time of writing, the charge to tie up to one of the two moorings was 300,000 Indonesian rupiah per day (about US$30). Charter groups can reserve and check the status of the moorings in advance by going online to the Macaronis Resort website.

Our captain, a frail Indonesian man who looked like he hadn't slept for days, failed to relay any of this information to us. Instead, while we were out surfing, he and the crew were walking on eggshells, anxiously awaiting a visit from the local police. Both our captain and surf guide knew the mooring rules were already in effect, but after seeing four boats in the bay they figured they could get us in the water for at least an hour.

We had only been surfing for about 30 minutes when five officials from nearby Silabu, dressed in brown and green government uniforms, motored out on the Macaronis Resort speedboat and boarded our ship. They said they represented the kepala desa and told the captain we had to leave immediately. Our captain argued that he had only anchored because he saw more than two boats in the channel and now his surfers were already out in the line-up (apparently, two of the four boats weren't surfing and were allowed to stop in order to use the land camp's facilities). His stalling was able to buy us more water time, but eventually they gave our captain an ultimatum: If we didn't leave the water in one hour, he would be taken to jail and we would be removed by force at the hands of the local villagers.

At this point, our crew – a mix of Javanese and Sumatran guys – were visibly shaken. They had heard stories about the savagery of the Mentawai people and weren't keen to find out if the old tales of cannibalism and poison arrows still held any truth. It didn't help matters that earlier in our trip the boat's first mate told everyone a story about a dispute he had witnessed at Lance's Left between a visiting surfer and local villager. According to his story, the misunderstanding resulted in the local kid returning to the beach with a bow and arrow and stalking the boat for nearly an hour trying to get a clean shot at the surfer's head.

Our crew of professional surfers, meanwhile, was incredulous. Reactions included: "Is this really happening?" "Can't we just pay them off?" and "I wonder what the guy would say if I gave him $1,000?" The swell forecast was so good that some of the guys suggested renting rooms at the land camp just so we could have access to the

JASON MURRAY/A-FRAME

Macaronis LAT. -2.78525° LONG. 99.9703°

Machine-like, fun park left with all the rides. Barrel-riding, lip-smacking, air-popping and wall-gouging are religiously practiced by the hordes who come to ride the Mentawai's most rippable and apparently the world's funnest wave. The coral platform curves alluringly into the deep bay and the speed at which Macca's peels is fairly predictable, starting with a perfect pipe section and often ending with a ruler-edge quarter-pipe wall. Jostling at the take-off is a given and it is easy to get pushed too deep when it's smaller. Looking further up the reef it sometimes looks doable and unlikely stories of pros making it right down the reef exist. The reef is sharp and shallow, but somehow less threatening than comparable depth spots. Getting caught inside will usually result in being flushed to the end if the sets are pouring through. Best at head and a half on a SW swell, mid tide and E wind, it maxes out at double overhead, when the tubes go square, but will still be fun if there is a direct onshore SW wind. There's a land camp, good anchorage, viewing tower and a constant supply of hungry surfers wanting their own plate of carbs!

waves the following day. In the end, we all succumbed to fears of restless natives armed with machetes and poisonous blow darts, and left fun Macaronis to a crowd of three Brazilian surfers who must have thought they'd won the lottery. With a bitter taste in our mouths, we traveled three hours south to surf small onshore rights at Coldsprings. The wave was productive for photos and the pros made it look like the best day of the year at Lowers, but there was no denying that the morale of the boat had suffered a serious blow.

How visiting surfers view the new rules at Macaronis will most likely depend on what side of the mooring buoy they're on. Guests of Macaronis Resort shouldn't see any problem because it essentially gives the land camp near-exclusive rights to the wave. If you're on one of the two charter boats lucky enough to snag a mooring it's a great deal – government-regulated crowd control all day. One thing is certain: if the new mooring system wasn't in place the day we arrived, there would have been seven or eight boats anchored in the bay and three times the people in the water. Crowds of fifty surfers have become a regular sight at Macaronis in recent years.

However, if you're Joe Goofyfoot who surfs religiously before work everyday and has been saving up for a Mentawai fantasy trip for over a year, you are not going to be a happy camper when some guy in a green uniform tells you that you can't surf your dream wave. We met one group of surfers who told us that during their 11-day charter they had tried on two occasions to surf at Macaronis and both times they were denied access.

"We have guests paying anywhere from US$2,000 to 4,000 for a ten-day trip to these islands," explained one concerned charter boat captain. "How are you gonna tell them they can't surf one of the best hotdog waves in the world?"

That night we anchored at Silabu. Not even charter boats with a mooring reservation are allowed to spend the night at Macaronis anymore. We decided to take a gamble and return in the early morning in hopes of snagging one of the moorings for the day. Our crew woke up at 3:30am to pull anchor and get us running towards Maccas. We arrived in the dark to find one of the moorings open, the other already claimed. Without hesitation, Adi, our speedboat driver, tore out on the dinghy into the black water and pounced on the mooring line. As our crew quickly tied us up, we could already hear by the thunder over the reef that the swell had increased overnight.

Now the mooring system worked to our benefit. The day dawned with offshore breezes grooming a pumping swell. The frequency of waves was exceeded only by their perfection. We sampled the finest delights Macaronis had to offer with just one other boat and a handful of guests from the land camp who staggered their sessions throughout the day. It was the Mentawai equivalent of an exclusive velvet rope party, and the surfers made sure none of the delicacies on the menu went to waste.

"Geez," exclaimed Dale the surf guide as he watched Pat Gudauskas pigdog through one of his thirty backside tubes of the afternoon, "how many barrels can you get in one day?"

We surfed from sunup to sundown, logging about eight hours total in the water. Videographer Mike Lopez shot over two hours of footage and photog Nathan Lawrence filled up his 32GB memory card and had to retrieve an empty one from the boat.

"Great job out there today, boys," exclaimed a surf-delirious Alex Gray, Bintang in hand as we all watched the last rays of sherbet light slip below the horizon. "Now let's just burn down the land camp and go home."

We didn't burn down the camp, but we were able to reserve the mooring again for the following day and enjoyed an instant replay of all-day perfection. We also got barred one more time when we tried to return later in our trip for an evening session.

It will be interesting to see how these developments at Macaronis play out. The West Sumatra Police, stationed in Padang, have authority over the local Silabu officials policing Macaronis. Considering the significant economic boon the surf charter boats provide the city of Padang (e.g. tax revenue, jobs, airport traffic, hotels, money spent in Padang, etc.), it would seem to be in the government's interest to keep the 35-odd boats who use their port happy. However, if the new mooring system at Macaronis continues to go unchallenged, could we see this strategy of limiting boat access in favor of land camp use spread to other premier breaks in the Mentawais?

As it stands right now, you can potentially surf the funnest wave in the world with a guaranteed manageable crowd, enforced by the local authorities. But you better wake up early to claim that mooring buoy. Otherwise, watch out for poison arrows.

First published by *Bali Belly* magazine, Issue 002, June, 2013

Lance's Luck

A fortuitous surf discovery in the Mentawais.
Make that two – Lance's Right *and* Lance's Left.

TIM BAKER

I N FEBRUARY 1991 there was little to suggest that a sea captain down on his luck was about to make the greatest surf discovery of modern times. Lance Knight had been plowing the Yamba-to-Lord Howe Island run in an old cargo ship for years off the New South Wales north coast, delivering supplies to the tiny island community and enjoying the odd sly surf during lay-overs. When he lost his job and his girlfriend in quick succession, rather than writing a plaintive country ballad, he thought he'd go to Singapore, look for a boat to buy and duck across to Nias, off the west coast of Sumatra, and try and score some surf. 'I was really stressed out, so I thought, I'm out of here,' he recalls.

Lance had met legendary surf explorer Peter Troy on a trip to Lord Howe and had been spellbound by his stories of discovering the famous righthander at Nias back in the early '70s. 'That inspired me a bit and I thought I might see if I could find my own Nias,' he says. He'd got hold of marine charts of the area and started looking at a promising island chain to the south of Nias, called the Mentawais. He flew to Sibolga in western Sumatra and, after a typically hair-raising overnight bus ride, arrived in the town of Padang. 'Almost as soon as I got off the bus in Padang, this truckload of soldiers pulled up and insisted that I jump in with them,' says Lance. 'I didn't know what they wanted, but they were very insistent, so I hopped in. I thought, Uh-oh, what's going on here?' As it turned out, Lance had arrived during Padang Tourism Week, and a gala launch had been marred somewhat by the complete absence of tourists, so the soldiers had been ordered to drive around until they found some. 'They drove me down to the beach and there was this huge reception, with dancers and politicians and dignitaries all gathered around under these big banners,' he says. 'I had to sit there, in the front row, through all these speeches and dances, as the honorary tourist.'

After this auspicious start, Lance spent the next two days walking around town, trying to find a fishing boat to take him out to the islands around 100kms off the mainland. He befriended a local rock star named Henry, and together they hit the town, where screaming girls mobbed them wherever they went. Henry introduced him to an Iranian doctor based in Padang, Dr Manoo, who had been conducting medical clinics in the Mentawai Islands for years as a one-man humanitarian mission. For $50 Lance was able to hitch a ride on Dr Manoo's next flight out to the islands. Equipped with one board, a backpack, a bag of rice and a water bottle, he found himself deposited on a grassy airstrip on the sheltered, waveless side of the island of Sipora.

'Dr Manoo went off into the village, and I was just sort of left alone,' says Lance. 'I started walking along the beach. This old guy came paddling along in a canoe and pulled into the beach. I couldn't speak Indonesian and he couldn't speak English, but we communicated by sign language, and I offered him some money to give me a ride.'

The old man transferred them to a larger boat and gave him a tour of the island, stopping to allow Lance to surf as they went and sleeping in huts on the beach. 'I only knew him as Mr Brasur. He had this old outboard, there was no cover on it, just a bit of string to pull-start this thing,' says Lance. 'And down the middle of his canoe he had all these bottles, bits of plastic, anything that could hold petrol – no caps on them – and he had a bit of garden hose. When one bottle would run out, he'd just shove it in the next bottle.'

Eventually, after a few days, they were approaching the southern end of the island when the weather turned ugly. Lance was hoping to get around the corner to a bay that he hoped would offer a wave, but his host insisted on pulling in through a gap in the reef to the little village of Katiet to take shelter. 'As we started coming in I saw all the spray coming off the back of the waves. We were looking into this incredible right-hander,' says Lance. He was surrounded by curious villagers on the beach as he pulled his board out of its cover and donned his helmet and rash vest. 'All these men came over and picked my board up, feeling it, tapping it, looking around it, running their hands over it – all the canoe builders – because they build canoes there. They couldn't believe it. The way they were looking at this thing, they'd definitely never seen a surfboard before.' Alone, in the middle of nowhere, confronted with heaving 6ft waves barrelling over shallow reef, surveying the line-up from the channel, Lance took a while to work up the nerve to take off. 'By this time there were people up in the trees. All the young guys had climbed this huge tree that used to be in the keyhole. There must have been 100 people up in this tree, screaming. Every time I got a barrel these people were screaming. It was just insane.'

After surfing for a couple of hours he returned to the beach and was taken in by a local family, who insisted he sleep in their small timber house. Lance stayed a couple of weeks, surfing the right by himself for four or five hours a day, wearing a big straw hat in the water to ward off the sun. His host, Hosen, and his family fed and housed him, refusing all offers of payment. When the wind puffed up onshore one day, Hosen led Lance to the other side of the island, where he found a perfectly offshore lefthander in the bay he'd originally been headed to – Lance's Left!

BILLY WATTS/A-FRAME

Lance's Right LAT. -6.655053° LONG. 105.171153°

Lance's Right (or HT's) is the pin-up centrefold for the Mentawai islands, bringing a new machine-like level to the word perfection. At the top of the coral platform, The Office section breathes in sharply, scooping up the next lucky expert who is hoping to be there when it exhales deeply, then launches through the Main Peak and into the inside where the shallowness of the Surgeons Table awaits. Size determines whether these 3 link and if any turns can be attempted. Perfection arrives with 6-8ft of S-SW swell, light W or no wind and at least 2hrs of tide. It's surprisingly consistent considering the swell refraction required and the afternoon land breezes can clean it up quickly. Dangers are coral heads appearing, trying to duck dive when caught inside and being pushed too deep by the entrenched crowd. Top tips: don't fall, go in over reef to deep paddling channel and surf somewhere else!

Lance had brought a first-aid kit with him. Each day he'd bring it out and the local kids would gather around as he applied antiseptic to their sores. At night, his hosts shut all the windows and doors of their hut and built a fire to ward off the malarial mosquitoes that infested the island.

Two weeks later, Lance was sitting on the beach when a large Western salvage ship, the *Indies Trader*, approached the line-up. On board, Australian skipper and salvage diver Martin Daly and his crew had been working their way through the islands, exploring for surf in between salvage jobs. 'I saw them pull up – they anchored just out in front of the keyhole – and guys were pulling boards out, and I've gone, Oh no,' Lance says. 'I grabbed my board and paddled out to them. They were pretty surprised to see me. By that stage I was ready for some company, but I was disappointed because

I knew this place was special. I felt a bit sad that word was going to probably get out.' After a surf together, Martin invited Lance on board the *Indies Trader* for a beer and a meal, and offered to give him a lift to Java. It was Martin who insisted the wave should be called Lance's Rights, as it is known today. Lance said farewell to Hosen and his family and spent three days on the Indies Trader en route to Java, then spent a couple of days in Jakarta, enjoying the charms of the big city. 'That was pretty wild. The nightlife was unbelievable,' says Lance. 'Martin had this big white Mercedes and he'd drive you around all night. I'd try to escape in a taxi. I remember one night I tried to go home about midnight. The next minute the taxi got run off the road by the white Mercedes. Martin hops out with a handful of money, throws it at the driver through the window, tells him to bugger off, grabs me, throws me in the back of his Mercedes and takes me off to this other nightclub 'til five o'clock in the morning.'

When Lance returned to Yamba, he bought a boat of his own and resumed the Yamba-to-Lord Howe run, started a family and didn't get around to returning to Katiet for more than a decade. 'Martin and I actually stood on the back of the *Indies Trader* and Martin said, "This place is unbelievable. We'll keep this a secret." We actually shook hands and agreed that this would be a special place, and if he took people back here surfing he'd never tell them where it was. But you can't keep a secret like that – it's just impossible – and I don't hold anything against Martin Daly at all.'

Inevitably, word got out. Martin invited a few friends on an informal surf charter through the islands, including pro surfer mates Tom Carroll, Martin Potter and Ross Clarke-Jones. That fateful trip they encountered huge, perfect surf – and the photos found their way into a surfing magazine. 'One day I pulled up at the point at Angourie and Grant Dwyer from Fandango surf shop in Yamba came up to me and said, "They've found your wave."' Lance recalls. 'He had this magazine article and it had this big spread on the Indies. After that, every time you opened a magazine there was a picture of Katiet.'

Surfing has impacted countless remote regions, but nowhere have the positive and negative impacts of surf colonisation been more vividly on display than in the Mentawais. The power of the modern surf media had accelerated the speed with which a new surf discovery became a household name. By the end of the decade the Mentawais was the hottest ticket in surf travel, and Martin Daly was the commander of a growing fleet of luxury surf charter boats while rival operators squabbled over wave rights. The *Indies Trader* had been given a fancy blue-and-orange, Polynesian-themed paint job and was re-badged as the Quiksilver Crossing, ferrying surf stars and film crews around the world. And a surfer-led humanitarian aid agency, Surf Aid International, had been formed to deliver much-needed medical aid to the remote islands.

First published in *Australia's Century of Surf* by Tim Baker, published by Random House.

Trashing the Place

The life of a Mentawai garbage collector is light years from the life of a surf tourist on a fantasy boat charter. The dirty truth is, one man's trash is another man's survival.

FABIAN HAEGELE

JUST LIKE EVERY morning, Un wakes up at sunrise. He gets up and makes the short walk down to the beach to see if the surf's up in front of his village, Katiet. Today it is. "HTs" or "Lance's Right", that legendary definition of Mentawai perfection featured in just about every surf video made in the past decade, is firing.

Four boats are already anchored in the channel at this early hour, so the forecast must look promising. A natural-footer takes off on a bomb and gets spat out of a gaping barrel while the rising sun paints the sky in every possible hue of orange, pink and purple. This is the surfer's ultimate Mentawai fantasy.

Of course, it isn't all like this all the time. A goofy-footer who pulls into the next wave, doesn't make it and gets nailed on the infamous coral outcrop known as the Surgeon's Table. Not a nice place to be, especially with the low tide. Un doesn't wait to see what happens to the guy. He turns around and walks back to his little shack. For him it's going to be just another busy day.

Un doesn't surf. He's never even tried it. (What a strange way to pass your time, just playing in the sea like kids and risking your life while you do it). Nevertheless his life (at least during the dry season) revolves around those often-flawless waves, which every year lure thousands of unimaginably wealthy westerners to fulfill their surfing wet dreams. Unimaginably wealthy, that is, if you think of money in Un's terms. He shares a tiny, windowless wooden hut, no larger than two by four meters, with his wife and three young children. Apart from their humble home, his family's possessions are limited to a smutty old pot, some kitchenware, a couple of sheets for the night and the ragged clothes they wear. I doubt Un has ever even had a whole bottle of Bintang to himself, let alone sampled any of the other luxuries most of us take for granted. And whenever he gets his hands on anything of any value, like a bunch of bananas, a ripe papaya, a full can of Coke, or one time, a jar of French mustard, he tries to sell it to one of the handful of visiting surfers who put up with the basic living conditions on land in order to get their slice of HT/Lance's tasty barrel pie.

Un, who moved to the Mentawais from mainland Sumatra some years ago, has never had it easy in life. It's not like he has ever done anything to deserve his fate, it was simply poor luck in the genetic lottery. When you first meet him, it's hard to look past his enormous crooked front teeth, which have quite drastically disfigured his face. Mental health problems have left his psychological capabilities underdeveloped, caused by either a birth defect or malnourishment and disease. These aren't great odds in a society where, although family bonds and support among relatives and neighbors are often a lot stronger than in our western societies, social welfare systems don't exist and survival of the fittest is still very much a reality

Un has done alright for himself, though. He gets by. In order to feed his family, to maybe make a little money, he paddles his little sampan, a traditional canoe, out to the charter boats whenever they stop at HTs. It's not to sell them anything or to conduct any other kind of business, but simply to relieve them of their trash, which, rather than taking it back to Padang where it comes from, the majority of charter boat captains dump in the very same islands they advertise in glossy ads and on fancy websites as pristine and unspoiled. Not one lousy rupiah changes hands in this shameful transaction. Garbage disposal in the Mentawais is free of charge.

The reason this happens, from Un's perspective, is that from the large plastic bags – which contain anything from plastic wrappers and empty juice boxes to kitchen scraps, empty batteries and medical waste – he can usually salvage a handful of soda and beer cans, which he can then sell on for recycling. For all the other waste, most of it non-biodegradable, there's no use, so it is either burned, or just left a stone's throw from the waterline to rust and rot and befoul the beaches.

To say this appalling example of profit-driven arrogance is a disgrace is, in my opinion, an understatement. Every time a new charter boat shows up in the channel at Lance's Right, Un and a handful of kids from the village can be seen racing their *sampans* for pole position astern of the often luxurious charter boats. For the 10-12 year-olds it's a way to earn a little pocket money. Some use it to support their family, but most often it's just spent on sweets and junk food. They come back to shore, their sampans loaded with black trash bags, and dump all the waste in the bushes just up from the beach. There they sift through the garbage with their bare hands. With rotting food scraps, maggots and even used, bloody bandages and syringes among the rubbish, you don't need a medical degree to figure out that any of the good educational work done by SurfAid International – who, among other things, is trying to build awareness about simple hygiene, the lack of which is one of the main causes of preventable diseases in the islands – is ineffective, if not futile.

The paddle race to the charter boats is also joined by other men from the village. Apart from Un and the kids, the rest of them paddle out to sell wood-carvings and other small artisan crafts to the guests on the boats. It is a lucrative source of income in an area where most families make a living by harvesting coconuts and selling the dried flesh to oil manufacturers in Padang and Medan. While many of the souvenirs sell for US$20US or more, a kilogram of coconut flesh earns the Mentawai people a mere 1000 rupiahs, currently around 10 cents. This also explains why the 5000 rupiahs (50 cents) paid per kilogram of recyclable tin cans might seem like a good deal to Un.

But in contrast to the boat captains, he and the young boys don't have the educational background to understand the implications of the deal they're making. Neither are they aware of the danger of contracting acute and chronic diseases from the trash, as well as from the smoke when they burn it. Nor do they understand that they are polluting their own back yards with hazardous and harmful materials that won't go away for generations. Of course, by doing this they undermine the potential for future land-based tourism, from which they could profit on a whole new scale. Not to mention the aesthetic aspect in its own right and the long-term health implications of more and more plastics, rusting metal cans and leaking batteries accumulating on their beaches. The fact is that their needs are so immediate that they can't afford to think of the bigger picture.

Thus, even though nobody is forcing the locals to accept the charter boats' waste, this common practice of trash disposal in the islands is yet another gross example of the exploitation of the weakest and most vulnerable members of an already poor society. This needs to stop. Idreal, Jormin, Hidel, Daniel and Alpon – the young boys who collect the trash – are all smart kids as well as avid, talented and fearless surfers. They should spend their time in school studying and having fun in the waves when they have time off, not digging through white man's trash for a few rupiah. Un, on the other hand, really does profit from the little money he makes out of recycled cans. It helps make his life a little easier. So why not separate the cans from all the other trash on board the boats and hook him up with what he can use? Keep the rest and take it back to Padang and in the process keep the Mentawais the beautiful place they truly are. Without doubt, space is limited onboard most boats, but to accommodate one extra bin for cans shouldn't be impossible, even on the smallest vessel.

Long gone are the days when the Mentawai Islands' crystal-clear and mechanical barrels and palm tree backdrops were the exclusive realm of an intrepid few adventurers. The surf charter industry is a reality in today's surfing world, where not only fully committed dropouts, but also doctors, lawyers and investment bankers (and of course people with every job description in between) are capable of and willing to surf the shallow and often unforgiving reefs. Consequently this article is by no means meant as a general attack on, or a damnation of, the surf charter industry in the Mentawais, or anywhere else for that matter. On the contrary, if managed and run responsibly and intelligently, I'm convinced surf tourism can contribute to the welfare of remote areas such as the Mentawais and be both ecologically and socially sustainable.

Neither am I claiming that every single boat operating in the Mentawais is involved in littering in the islands, although sadly over the three month period I spent at Katiet this past year, I have seen the majority of surf charter boats dumping their trash there at least once.

Nevertheless, while the sheer magnitude and complexity of many of the ecological predicaments we face nowadays can be daunting, I believe there is justified hope that the problem of waste disposal in the Mentawais can be solved both quickly and completely. It is the simplicity and the overwhelming one-sidedness of the argument – the obvious fact that dumping waste from a commercial enterprise in an unspoiled environment is utterly unjustifiable – that gives rise to my optimism. Some parts of the surf industry are starting to care more about their impact on the environment, or at least trying to portray a greener image to their customers and the public. So maybe the big companies, some of whom financially support organizations like SurfAid International, can put pressure on the charter industry to stop this dirty practice. Besides, isn't it nice to believe that despite our often horrific carbon footprints, surfers as a community are generally an environmentally conscious people, that we do care at least a little bit about the impact we have on the ecosystems surrounding us, and the people and societies we touch when we travel in search of waves?

First and foremost, this is of course an appeal to all boat owners and captains to stop their unnecessary pollution of the Mentawai Islands. It is irresponsible and inexcusable. Also, surf guides, photographers and crew members – go ahead and ask uncomfortable questions if you find your boat involved in this. And last but not least, guests, travelling surfers – whether you work for one of the industry's giants and are sending a team of pros on a luxury photo trip, or if you're an Average Joe getting away and surfing your brains out with your mates for a couple of weeks – enquire about what happens to your boat's trash before you book your trip, and again when you're out there enjoying the good life. Experience shows that consumer-driven change is always fastest and most effective. And these are changes that can make the lives of people like Un quite a bit better, with very little inconvenience to the businesses involved. Let's get some common sense and common decency in the garbage department. Just make it happen!

This story was first published in *The Surfer's Path* Issue 81 December, 2010

Wandering Eye

Field-note observations on chasing bombs – and dodging them – in the Mentawai Islands

ALEX DICK-READ

THANKS TO THE internet, surf magazine editors don't, technically, *need* to go anywhere these days. We generally stay where we belong, behind a computer, all day, every day. But while we may be pale skinned and unused to sunlight, deep down in our DNA we are hunting, roaming animals. And, of course, we're professionals, so we need to cast a professional eye over our subject of enquiry.

In this case the subject was perfect waves, and the roaming and hunting took place in Bali and on a small island in the Mentawai chain. Perfect waves aren't hard to find in either of these places, so the research went fairly well. In fact, we snagged quite a few, taming some and getting mauled by others. Overall a successful research trip. Here are some observations from along the way:

- Picture-perfect waves can be mean. Waves don't break hollow unless its shallow, so in general the prettier the wave, the nastier the consequences. Kandui waves are really pretty. When we arrived my friend Ian Battrick, a professional barrel-rider and Indo adoptee, had a big, fresh claw mark down his back. "Aw," he said, "it's a just a tickle."

- Surfers are generally an alright bunch once you get past the crackly exterior. We seem a bit like dogs sniffing each others' arses when we meet out there on the road, but like dogs, we quickly figure out a hierarchy and slot in. Thereafter we can act like normal human beings, or dogs, or whatever we really are.

- Most of us don't go on surf trips very often. We save, slowly usually, for that one trip a year, or every two years, or not at all. One life-long friend of mine, longtime surfer, expert sailor and all round ocean man said to me when I got back: "A trip entirely dedicated to surfing? Interesting. I've never done that before."

- The best surf moments usually happen when you don't think they're going to. When you do think they're going to, they usually don't.

The coral reefs around the Playgrounds area were much more alive and vibrant than when I was there eight years ago. This may be because there's less bomb fishing going on. Our friend Jordan Heuer, who has lived on Kandui Island for over a decade, told us a story about a time he saw a group of boats bomb-fishing out by Rifles (literally throwing small, home-made explosive devices into the sea to kill the fish).

He jumped in his boat and went out to harass them. Jordan and his crew, who included Scott Bass of *Surfer* magazine, got close in to the bomb boats and started taking photos, then noticed someone lighting a fuse on a bomb and getting ready to throw it. They hit the throttle just in time and it exploded a few feet behind in their wake.

Jordan radioed his buddy to tell him to call the police boat and tell them illegal bomb fishermen had just thrown a bomb at him. The buddy did this, but also called the US Consulate, who transferred on a message to Washington and Langley and where ever else, that a US national had 'been bombed' in Indonesia. This set off all the security alarms in the western world, shut down airports, marshalled troops and caused serious issues between Washington and Jakarta. Immediately afterwards Jordan got a phone call from the US National Security Agency (spooks). They wanted him to tell them exactly what happened so he explained that it wasn't a terrorist bomb, it was a fishing bomb. The NSA guys wanted him to say he'd been the victim of a terrorist incident, but he couldn't because he hadn't. They called him three times to try and get him to say it. In the end he told them to fuck off.

Of course, Jordan took a bit of heat from the local police, who themselves took heat that had travelled down the chain all the way from a pissed off Jakarta government.

But one good thing did happen: the bomb-fishing ring that operated around that area of the Mentawai Islands – a big-ish operation based near Padang – was busted. There's been very little bomb fishing ever since. And it looks to me like the reefs are more alive.

[Author's Note: In 2013 there were reports that bomb fishing has once again been taking place in the Playgrounds area.]

- Last time I went to Indonesia – eight years ago – I swore I'd return every year for the rest of my life. This time I mean it.

First published in *The Surfer's Path* magazine Issue 81, December, 2010

The Jungle is Looking Back

At the end of the world, deep in a malarial jungle, a small crew of barefoot surfing doctors just might help to save the world...and surfing's lost soul

STEVE BARILOTTI

"This is Taileleu village, it is the rainy season. Many children are sick, they get the fever, shakes and sweats that can last 2-3 weeks. It causes them to pale and affects their schooling and some may die."

DARI KITA UNTUK KITA (FROM US, FOR US), A MALARIA-CONTROL PLAY
BY DAVE JENKINS, MD.

T HE JUICE STINGS. The juice burns. The juice melts the gloves and gets on the skin and up the nose and it makes you feel like hell. Its Thailand-based manufacturers assert in small red type that the juice is safe when used in its diluted form but strongly recommend wearing thick rubber gloves when handling the concentrate. The juice has the insulting aroma of cheap third-world roach poison.

But the milky, bad-smelling juice of the *Doktors Ombak* kills mosquitoes, keeps them from buzzing in the ears of the villagers at night, piercing them with the Evil Sweat Spirit that lets the soul go wandering and makes the children shiver and die.

Unable to endure the searing equatorial sun any longer, I stagger into the stifling shade of the Taileleu village hall. Thick fluffy fumes of juice from the drying nets rise up to the hardwood rafters. I use my sodden t-shirt as a stopgap filter. Village workers – skinny Mentawai and Minangkabau men smoking sweet clove kretaks – periodically bring in dripping mosquito nets and hang them on plastic lines strung from side to side across the cavernous wooden hall. They see me hunched over and panting, expressing large beads of chili-flavored sweat from my forehead. They smile through cigarette-stained teeth and give me a big thumbs-up.

The juice is permethrin, a military-grade insecticide used for impregnating clothing and mosquito nets, thereby tripling their effectiveness against the female anopheles mosquito that transmits the malaria parasite. The US Marines use it for jungle warfare, which is close to how Dr. Dave Jenkins – part-time surfer and full-time medical director for Surf Aid International – describes his hut-to-hut guerilla ops against tropical disease here.

"It's simple mathematics," asserts Jenkins, a lumbering 43-year-old New Zealander who speaks in a nasal Kiwi drawl that turns "nets" into "nits". "If I can get 90% of the people sleeping under nets, we halve the malaria transmission rate of this village within months. Less infected people means less infected mosquitoes. It's the cheapest, most effective way to break the malaria cycle. For a seven-dollar net a kid gets a good night's sleep and doesn't have to die. Simple."

Jenkins has seen a lot of dead children out here. He's held their small, fever-racked bodies, felt their pint-sized death tremors as their brains seized up under a fatal stroke brought on by cerebral blood clots. He's seen kids dying of common childhood diseases – measles, diphtheria, chicken pox – that could have been prevented with a course of commonplace vaccines costing less than a surf leash.

Outside in the mucky 90-degree heat, Jenkins cajoles and coaxes his small squad of doctors, nurses and village volunteers to not slacken the pace. Half of the 300 new nylon nets have been dipped since 10am, and if they don't break for lunch they can finish by this afternoon, have a nap and sign off with a sunset surf session at ER's.

The Surf Aid platoon sweats on. Ollie dips, Amanda wrings, Ben shuttles the nets inside. Liz fits the village workers with latex gloves and translates Bahasa to English for Dave with a French accent.

The local people seem to enjoy Dave's latest attraction. Last month he invited a pair of tattooed Mentawai shamans, clad in traditional kerei beads and loincloths, to come down from their river village to bless a new microscope. His school play last March – a live-action malarial infomercial where small children dressed in black swarm in as mosquitoes and bite an unprotected sleeping man – was a huge hit among the entertainment-starved villagers.

When Jenkins first arrived in Taileleu two years ago most of the villagers assumed he was another Christian missionary – a label Jenkins resents.

By now, however, they're convinced Dave is either a government doctor or just a slightly crazed tourist who likes to surf and help the children. They don't know much else about Dave since Dave's command of Indonesian is limited to the "Me-David-where-sick?" level. These days he is simply known as Doktor Ombak, the wave doctor.

Today Dave is fighting a cold. He bellows like a wounded mud buffalo, blowing an angered red nose into a rolled up wad of napkins. Jenkin's normally florid face is pale and clammy; cheeks hollowed out by weeks of eating a monotonous diet of small fried fish, boiled jungle ferns and rice.

Jenkins is also working with the village nurse Erfina to take blood samples and test for malaria and other infectious diseases. Today Erfina is looking a bit under-the-gun as Liz translates and Dave scrutinizes her malaria logs. She's been charged with taking blood samples and examining them for the malaria parasite. Although Erfina is diligent, her note keeping is not up to Dave's exacting first-world standards.

These mundane questionnaires, however, are the key to Surf Aid International's future financial survival. The arcane disease data Surf Aid is collecting on this fringe of the developing world – where jet-setting surfers might possibly be the Patient Zeros of infectious tropical disease – is invaluable to a deep-pocket's health watchdog like the World Health Organization or CARE.

As the world heats up and sea levels rise, tropical disease is bouncing back in regions once eradicated of such exotic plagues as malaria and dengue fever. Low-lying populated coastal regions such as Florida and Australia's Queensland coast are especially susceptible. As recently as last year, a rare but disturbing outbreak of malaria was reported near London's Heathrow airport. The Mentawais, which are sinking at an alarming rate of 2-3cm a year, provide a textbook lab control for studying the effects of global warming and disease.

A reliable malaria vaccine – the Holy Grail of epidemiology akin to finding the cure for AIDS – has eluded researchers since the Middle Ages. Dave and the others just may hold the missing pieces to the puzzle. By accident or design, Jenkin's barefoot crew of surfing do-gooders has found themselves unexpectedly on the cutting edge of global disease research.

Finally the last of the nets have been dipped and hung. Dave gathers up his medical kit and motions for his crew to head for the motor canoes. It's a half hour crossing via Evinrude to the Surf Aid camp on Nyang Nyang, a small crescent-shaped island just off Siberut's southern end.

Our hand-hewn longboat, named "Muttara Bunda", is driven by a gregarious chainsmoking young Minangkabau man named Feri. It makes good time across the ten-mile channel. A powerful rhythmic groundswell lifts us auspiciously. The Indonesian sunset is a lurid, psychedelic swirl of carmine and rose. We arrive at the camp with just enough light to wash off the sweat and insecticide.

Jenkins, who'd been dozing under an umbrella, revives as the canoe ground itself on the white coral sand beach

"My God!" he proclaims to the hushed drooping palms. "Isn't this just too freaking surreal?"

"The world is a giant gecko, blindly devouring the most beautiful butterflies of intentions." – DEWI CHANTIK

The camp children are bright, affectionate, filthy, and most likely diseased. Little Mual, 4, named for Emmanuel, is hot and squirming in my arms. He smiles up at me and

A Mentawai shaman, or sikerei, who blessed the microscope first, looks in to see the evidence of malaria firsthand. SurfAid's founder Dr. Dave Jenkins and a local assistant, Erfina look on.

snuggles close to play with my camera. I am alternatingly charmed and repulsed – as if handling a cute but rabid rabbit. He is a child, he craves knowledge and love. I am an adult, fearful of lice and malaria. I'm revolted by my uncharitable thoughts. But they're there.

Later, the children sing to me. Their voices clear, unaffected and full of strange, doomed hope, nearly bring me to tears. These children have no sense of how they appear outside of their jungle home. They are not afraid to laugh or cry or sing loud and lustily without a parent moderating or feeding them camera cues. They are completely without self-perception. Strum of guitar, wail of harmonica, the distant putter of a generator. A single yellow light illuminates the main hut, drawing an entomologist's motherlode of tropical flying insects, including mosquitoes. For the last week the Surf Aid crew has been pitched up in a half-built surf camp sited a stone's throw from E-Bay, a treacherously shallow but photogenic left featured in a dozen surf videos to date.

The camp, which was being built by Padang boat-charter baron Rick Cameron as a hedge against the future, was abruptly stalled by the September 11th attacks in 2001. In lieu of paying customers, Cameron, who has supported Surf Aid since their inception, allows Jenkins and the others to use the camp as an R&R base. Dave sprawls on the verandah of the central hut blowing a mean blues riff on his harp. He used to front a popular frat-house band during his med school days in Dunedin, New Zealand. Dave's ankles are covered with infected reef cuts and swollen insect bites. I asked if he's ever had malaria. He said he wouldn't know – he's never been tested.

Three years ago Dave was living and working in Singapore, making $150,000 a year crunching actuarial numbers for a multinational health organisation. He played his sax, drank imported New Zealand chardonnays and entertained lavishly at his $5,000-a-month hillside home. He decided to take a surfing vacation to the Mentawais with his surf buddy Andy Lucas and brought his medical bag as an afterthought in case he or any of the other surfers got injured or ill.

One afternoon after a surf session at Lance's Right, Jenkins and Lucas went ashore to the village of Katiet for diversion. As soon as word got out there was a doctor in town they were deluged with the walking wounded. Jenkins saw a constant parade of ulcerated sores and malnutrition. From dank little huts crawled the walking dead – wasted wretches left to die in torpid agony from malaria, diphtheria and typhoid fever. A woman dying from TB was carted up to Dave in a wheelbarrow. Suddenly he was Jesus among the lepers – disgusted, saddened, petrified.

"I knew right then that I had to do something. But I didn't have a clue what that would be."

A few months later Jenkins came back came to Indonesia and founded Surf Aid International. He and Lucas opened a storefront office in a rundown hotel in central Padang that would transform into a tourist brothel each night. He sold his house and poured his savings into his fledgling NGO. A year later, Andrew Griffiths, an Aukland-born investment banker, quit his high-paying London job to become Surf Aid's admin man.

Dave draws no salary, nor does Andy or any of the other doctors. Only the office staff back in Padang receives a wage. His two teenage daughters from a previous marriage attend a public university on a poverty scholarship. "We get paid in waves," he quips.

For six months last year Dave and Andy slept on the floor of a small house in Taileleu while they set up their immunization and education program. They lost weight and became listless, ground down by the sheer bottomless need of the people here.

"It's not all beer and skittles out here, mate," says Jenkins, who divides his time equally between fieldwork in the villages and office duties back in Padang. "This is a harsh environment for white people. There's no privacy and everything you do is under scrutiny. The heat is draining; the lethargy relentless. There's not a lot of stroking here; no "thank you doctor". They are, in many respects, a very fatalistic people. Good health is not high on their list of priorities."

A good portion of the village doesn't believe Surf Aid will last. Over the last 30 years since Taileleu was established they've seen a host of missionaries and foreign aid workers come, then succumb, to the heat, disease, burnout and sheer despair. Dave relates how the UNESCO guys, both highly committed aid professionals, ended up in intensive care last year from stress and disease. What makes the difference for him and the others, he says, is getting stoked together on a regular basis.

"If we didn't surf, doing this work would dry us up like that (snaps his fingers). Surfing re-energizes us. Not just the surfing but the chance to appreciate the beauty of the area – the sunsets and big sky. It's so easy to miss that when your nose is up against the wall all the time. If you don't take time for yourself in this business, you're doomed."

The Surf Aid crew is forced to work within the consensual hallucination that is post-Suharto Indonesia – a fragile cobbled-together democracy riddled with corruption, tribal hierarchies and a near-fatal language gap. They are running across diseases and weird skin-burrowing parasites only found in obscure medical texts written by 19th-century missionary doctors. Without telephone or short-wave radio they live as self-exiled Robinson Crusoes. Out here, nothing ever dries out, everything rots and communications revert to smudged pen and paper messages ferried hand-to-hand via dugout canoes. They are exposing themselves to life-threatening diseases on a daily basis. And they are surfing perfect empty waves and having the time of their lives.

Ben Gordon, 33, a Perth-born GP is newly arrived from Ireland with his fetching Chinese-Australian wife Amanda. Ben and Amanda deplaned in Padang seven weeks ago after quitting good-paying government jobs in Ireland. Neither of them spoke a word of Indonesian or Mentawai but they are tutoring themselves at night with books and tapes. Both are from comfortable middle-class upbringings so the culture shock is palpable. But so is the excitement of living overseas doing frontline work.

Ollie Jenkins (no relation to Dave), 22, is a fifth-year med student finishing his doctor's training at Southhampton University in the UK. As Surf Aid's medical grommet, he volunteers on summer holiday as part of his practical studies. Garrulous, laughing and characteristically Welsh, Ollie speaks in a rapid-fire Welsh brogue peppered with fashionable Cockney slang and surfisms. He studies for his upcoming exams listening to thumping hip-hop house beats through a pair of muff-sized earphones. In two weeks he will return to the UK to deliver his first baby.

Liz Henderson is a pretty 28-year-old French surfer nomad who has worked as a Mentawai boat cook for two seasons now. Originally trained as an import/export agent in Strasbourg, she chucked in her career six years ago to follow her dream of world travel. She started surfing in Australia and it quickly became her life's passion and compass. Within two years she'd surf-trekked to Western Oz, South Africa, Morocco, Reunion, and Baja.

Liz eventually drifted in the global surf trades to the Mentawais. She established herself in Padang, learned Bahasa Indonesian, and ingratiated herself with the Padang academic community teaching French between boat trips at the local university.

By the end of her first season, however, she had become quite cynical about surfers and disillusioned with the whole commercialized surfing culture. It manifested itself in the empty Surf Aid donation boxes.

Between cooking gourmet meals for the ever-starving hordes of international surfers that came aboard her boats, Liz would gamely try to get the guys interested in the plight of the Mentawai villagers. After dinner she would put on the Surf Aid video and encourage the guys – many of them famous pros making six-figure salaries

– to drop their pocket change into the collection boxes. Most just feigned interest, though a few seem genuinely concerned.

But after each trip when the surfers had left, Liz shook the poor box hopefully… and heard nothing. Not even a few thousand rupiah, less than a dollar US. Nothing. Just bags and bags of empty beer cans on the deck. It angered, then saddened her. Ultimately it forced her to radically alter her surfing belief system – and to question what had happened to the soul of surfing she'd revered for so long.

"I keep thinking that the next boat will be different, that someone on the boat will have a clue," reflects Liz flatly. "But they don't. I used to have such a huge spark for surfing and surfers, but somewhere it went out. I think forever."

"If filthy barrels were mosquito nets we wouldn't have a problem."
SURF AID AD IN *NEW ZEALAND SURFING MAGAZINE*

At the end of good day of waves, the surfers on the great white boats, surfed out and full-bellied, lie under gently flapping tarpaulins sipping a cold Bintang. It's then, often in bored moments of introspection, they might contemplate what lies behind the mute, unbroken wall of primeval jungle barricading the islands less than 100 feet away.

What they don't realize is that the jungle is looking back.

Over 60,000 people live on the Mentawais, an archipelago of four main islands lining the southern half of Sumatra. Despite their close proximity to Sumatra, the Mentawais have existed in relative isolation. Although the Dutch colonialists used the islands for copra plantations, they contain some of the most primitive and pristine regions of Indonesia.

The Mentawai islanders are for the most part a melange of races made up mostly of indigenous Mentawai tribesmen and transplanted villagers from overcrowded islands like Sumatra and Java. A smattering of Chinese traders and European missionaries also live on the islands. Small pockets of stone-age tribes still exist in isolated pockets up river, living an ancient, animistic way of life that up to now has sidestepped the disastrous cultural and environmental impacts of colonialism.

However, it's the end of the line for Mentawai's native people and for much of the island itself. The Mentawais are under assault from multinational logging companies and palm-oil corporations who see the islands as a cheap source of rare hardwoods and unskilled labor. The Indonesian government continues its policy of cultural genocide against the Mentawai people by transmigration schemes and forbidding traditional Mentawai rituals such as tattooing and teeth filing. Both bans are based on Islamic tenets, not health issues.

Democracy has done little to improve their lot. Under post-Suharto autonomy, the Mentawais have been given two years to develop their own economy or face intervention from Jakarta. The pressure to exploit the last of the old-growth forests is irresistible. Although the western half of Siberut was declared a World Heritage biosphere in 1981, less than 60% of the 160 million hectares of Siberut rainforest remain. To build logging roads on the soggy, low-lying islands, the surrounding reefs are blown to rubble for road fill. Runoff and sewage chokes what's left. Factory fishing boats from Taiwan and Japan hoovered up the fish years ago. An ancient forest culture that possesses plant cures for everything from snakebite to hookworms is being mowed down with the trees.

And while the island dies, surfers from around world use the ravaged reefs offshore as their playground and photo studio. The juxtaposition of the richest and poorest cultures of the world is akin to something out of a Josef Conrad novel. This is where the worried well meet the happily doomed.

A decade ago Indo pioneer Martin Daly began taking the first surf charters out the Mentawais. Boat trips allowed maximum access to the surf breaks while minimizing the exposure to malaria and other tropical diseases rife on the islands. The trips, although pricey by surfer standards, were an instant success. They represented the ultimate surfer fantasy of perfect, uncrowded and warm waves but without the infamous disease-plagued hell trips experienced by the early Indo surf explorers.

The Mentawai mystique sells well in the malls. Photos and film footage generated from various Mentawai boat trips are used in countless ads and editorial each year to promote the surfers sponsored by multimillion-dollar surfwear companies.

But the surf industry had been way behind the curve with support to the Mentawai people themselves. Few Mentawai people are employed on the boats and little, if any, of the charter money makes it way out to the islands. To date total contributions to Surf Aid from the surf industry – whose combined international income topped US$4 billion last year – has been less than $8000. The combined income from the donation boxes aboard the boats totaled less than $200. Most of Surf Aid's money has come from outside the surf industry, most notably from *Lonely Planet* publications.

Jenkins has a civil but increasingly strained relationship with the surf-charter operators. Many are sympathetic but stop short of soliciting donations among the surfers for Surf Aid. Others offer Dave and his doctors free lifts to and from the Mentawais. But most keep Dave at arms length. Some are outright hostile to the whole concept of trying to help the islanders for fear of breeding native-born surfers. One uncharitable skipper refused to let his clients leave broken boards with the island kids.

"The last thing we need is for these fucking islanders is to learn how to surf," he said. "We don't want another Nias."

Surfing is a young adolescent culture. Being completely insular and hedonistic, it comes as no surprise that it has no tradition of philanthropy. Surfer altruism is rare and can evaporate overnight in the face of cynicism, misplaced ideals, or the realities of living in the mud outside the western materialist media bubble.

After a feature article critical of the surf industry (*Surf Inc. Invades an Island Paradise*, June 22, 2002) came out in *Sydney's Daily Telegraph* last June, Surf Aid's

marketing man Andrew Griffiths said he could hear wallets snapping shut across the surf industry.

But Surf Aid has proven irresistible to the mainstream media, who love the idea of a bunch of high-spirited surfing doctors practicing MASH-style preventive health care in the jungle. Australia's "Foreign Correspondent" recently aired a Surf Aid segment showing the docs in a remote Siburut jungle highland village treating a young Mentawai mother dying of TB and sending her at their expense via motor-canoe to a government clinic in Muara Siburut. The show, which was broadcast nationally, brought a surge of small donations from little old ladies and various non-surf businesses.

Yanto is a half-Mentawai, half-Japanese surfer who runs "cultural tours" up to the traditional Mentawai villages. Under Yanto's guidance adventuresome western tourists can sleep in the thatched umas at night and watch shamans do the "Dance of No Meaning" for their benefit. Yanto learned English from backpackers passing through Sumatra ten years ago when Sumatra was still on the must-see list for dirtbag travelers. He was born in Maura Siberut in 1969 before there was electricity or even a cash economy. He has stopped by the Surf Aid camp enroute to catching a ferry back to Padang.

His feelings for the Mentawais are ambivalent. A modern man with a tailored haircut and a house in Padang, he receives many of his clients via email on the net. He has no desire to grovel in the mud and return to the demon-filled night forest. He does not hear the calling to become a shaman.

Still, this is his home. He can see the changes civilization is bringing, or inflicting, on these people. He knows there's no going back. The only thing he might be able to change is change.

He tells me that the villagers see the surfers as rich. Through satellite TV they realize they are poor. They want the toys. They want the TV's and Discmans and the jetskis. They want electricity and flush toilets and air conditioning. And good health. It's hard to go back to sweating in the malarial dark once you've had night lighting at the touch of a switch.

He lights a Marlboro…

"The Mentawai people do not want just money. They need education and medicine. But they need a plan right from the beginning or you will have another Bali or Nias. What they see right now is a lot of money for the boats, but none to cure malaria. They are beginning to question what surfing is doing for them. Everyone comes to the Mentawais to take, not to give."

Some of the kids are learning to surf and they're getting good quickly. As the surf scene develops, Yanto says, they don't want to be just cooks and boat drivers. They want to be part of it.

"If they're not, there could be problems", he adds ominously.

He tells me that the boats from Malaysia came over a few years ago and dynamited the reefs. The logging companies buy off the village honchos with outboard motors and the promise of work.

During the week I spent at Nyang Nyang a haggard-looking timber freighter hovered like a rusty vulture off a nearby islet, gobbling freshly felled hardwood logs into its hold. As we cruised by to have a look, a scared crew of smoking, bare-chested Laskar deckhands cast straight out of a Sinbad matinee shooed us away yelling "no cameras!"

"The villagers only think for today," says Yanto. "The challenge is to give them a tomorrow."

"Making money is like drinking salt water. The more you drink the thirstier you become. Love is like fresh water for the soul."
SONY, MENTAWAI-BORN COOK ABOARD THE *SANTA LUSIA*, MENTAWAI SURF-CHARTER

From the bow of the *Muttara Bunda* I see Liz, Ben, Ollie and Dave hassling for the third wave of an overhead set out at ERs. Dave is in position but Liz is a goofyfooter, more experienced and more likely to make the fast crumbling lefts of ER (Emergency Rooms). But she pulls back to let him have it. He staggers to his feet, sticks out his ass, draws a line and draws a strict no-nonsense course to the shoulder. He paddles back looking pleased with himself.

ER, despite it's foreboding name, is actually a fairly benign and predictable wave, perfectly suited for the middling surf skills of the surf docs.

Of all the Surf Aid docs, young Ollie is the most accomplished. He came from a surfing family in Wales and has spent a lot of summers surfing in France and Spain. Ben, from western Oz, is keen and competent but a bit rusty after a year's layoff in Ireland. Dave's surfing prowess could be diplomatically described as: "he goes hard and he has a lot of fun". After the airing of Foreign Correspondent, which showed Dave wobbling backhand into an anemic four footer, he received an e-mail from an admirer: "Love your work but your roundhouse sucks."

Ironically, Dave and the others surf much less than if they lived and worked 'real' jobs back in their respective home countries. In Ben and Amanda's case, they live and work on the wave-less east side of Siberut. It's a half-day's canoe journey through a leech-infested mangrove swamp to the nearest surf break and Ben is loath to expend precious time and fuel on a surf check unless he can tie it in with some medical work along the way.

But you can tell they love their work. Most doctors will never have a chance to meld all their healing skills with their deepest human values. And in such freewheeling fashion. This is third-world medicine, improvised guerilla immunology done with bamboo and washtubs. In a sense, they're artists.

Dave has a fondness for reciting the apocalyptic, sexually charged lyrics of Leonard Cohen and loves shouting them at full volume out in the line-up. "As I knelt at the delta...of her Alpha...and Omega," he booms at me.

Dave and Andrew's latest scheme to raise money from within the surf community is the proposed "Mentawai Charity Challenge". Modeled on the OP Boat Challenge, the contest-cum-expression session would involve a handpicked celebrity roster and surf, drugs and rock and roll – the drugs being disease vaccines.

They're angling for an angel, hopefully, but not limited to, the surf industry. Their pitch, under the guise of cause marketing, is that it would be great for a savvy surfwear company to do something that really benefits children and in the process make their employees proud of what their company does. That a surf logo could actually stand for something real.

"I know I'm dreaming," he sighs. "But then again, the world was never changed by a reasonable man. I think the time's ripe for a new legacy for surfing'

Jenkins scans the horizon, takes a beat, then retrieves his loopy leer.

"Besides, it's been proven that philanthropy stimulates endorphins. It's just good physiology – by far the best drug there is. So the proposition I put out there is: 'just how good do you want to feel?'"

Dave takes in the sunset, where pink rain-fecund clouds drag themselves like recalcitrant pachyderms across the flat graveyard horizon

"My God...can you believe this place?

He spots a set and paddles off. I sit, gazing back at the palms, contemplating the end of the world.

And from somewhere deep in the jungle I hear children singing.

[Since this article was published in 2002, SurfAid has grown into one of the most respected and recognised NGOs in the region, with branches appearing in NZ, USA and Australia. Earthquakes and tsunamis have dictated that they add Emergency Response and Disaster Risk Reduction to their wide-ranging remit of community development and education programs that are central to their mission statement "...to improve the health, wellbeing and self-reliance of people living in isolated regions connected to us through surfing". The surfing industry has gradually come to the party with more corporate donations, including major support from Billabong, Quiksilver, SIMA and others.

Resort and charter boat operators are compelled by law to collect a daily tax from each visiting surfer on behalf of the Mentawai Regency Government.]

First published in *Surfer* magazine, November, 2002, Volume 43 No.12

Sensory Overload

The 2009 Padang earthquake.

FABIAN HAEGELE

I SHOULD HAVE COME home one week earlier. If I had, my only stories would have been of beautiful, crystal-clear, warm water; flawless turquoise barrels and palm-fringed, white sandy beaches. Maybe add in a couple of grueling ferry rides, the never-ending search for nutritious food on the islands, a few festering reef cuts here and there, the two weeks of constant rain in August, the rats, the mosquitoes, Californian charger Tyler Rootlieb – without ever asking any money – just giving me one of his nearly brand new boards when I had nothing left to ride; the time we put a crab in my German neighbor's tent – which unintentionally resulted in him being eaten alive by sand flies all night – that flat and lazy Sunday afternoon when we all got on it, not caring that the Bintangs were about as warm when we drank them as they were when they left our bodies …

But I hadn't left early. I changed plans and stayed until the bitter end, unwilling to swap this Indonesian island surf fantasy for a new life of university education. Higher education, jobs and a proper career could wait yet another year. Little had I known, that the final week of my prolonged mission would give me a story I won't forget for as long as I walk this precious, beautiful and sometimes angry, Earth.

At the time things were looking great. One week to go, with a solid south swell forecast for the last few days. After this I'd have to spend two days in Padang before flying out, which I was actually looking forward to after so long enduring the most basic of living conditions.

I had met a distinguished crew of guys, all hardcore solo travelers, who were keen to charter a local dugout and go camping on an uninhabited island in the northern Mentawais for a few days. It was a daring and challenging mission, which would prove to be the icing on the cake for an already memorable journey. Apart from some minor difficulties, the types of things that always seem to go wrong on these kinds of endeavors, it all seemed to be going our way.

First we got a teaser of the prime righthander in the area – some long round barrels over very shallow reef that unfortunately weren't always makeable that day. Aussie

Chad paid the price when the razor sharp coral claimed a good chunk out of the ball of his right hand. The next morning the swell had come up even more and the wind had shifted. One of the lefts was offshore and pumping, and the high tide made the racy tubes reasonably approachable, which meant we had to share the goods with surfers from a couple of charter boats. When we returned from a lengthy lunch-break back at camp, however, only one boat remained in the channel. It was glassy by now, breaking top to bottom and, incredibly, there was nobody out.

We couldn't believe our luck...until we saw the reason why it was empty – intimidating boils everywhere and parts of the amazingly alive reef sticking out of the water only meters from where chunky lips were impacting in the flats. With waves like this going by unridden though, no one out of our select bunch could justify any further hesitation, so we soon found ourselves trading waves and pushing each other deeper as the session unfolded, hearts in mouths every time a new set showed on the horizon. Pure magic!

Then, perhaps an hour and a half into our surf, I noticed something happening on the ridiculously shallow inside, which we had previously named the Pinball Section. Rod, nicknamed the "big friendly giant" for his towering height and close to 100 kilos, as well as his ever-lasting good mood and the perpetual smirk on his face, was lying on his board at the edge of the impact zone, limp, like a sack of rice. Marco, who had taken to shooting photos after a scary wipeout earlier in the session, had jumped out of the boat and was frantically swimming towards him. The tender from the last charter boat remaining in the channel, was also trying to get to Rod without getting caught by a set.

Clearly Rob had done some damage. He was having serious trouble moving and was unable to get himself out of further harm's way. We later learned that Rod had pulled into a barrel and eventually got sucked over the falls. The lip had driven him into the reef, where he'd landed on his butt. Apart from numerous cuts to his body's best cushioned parts and his feet, the impact had done something to his spine about halfway up his back, which left him in excruciating pain, not feeling his legs and barely able to breathe or move his upper body at all.

Now what to do? Here we were with a potentially major spinal injury, stranded in the middle of nowhere in a tiny dugout canoe, probably days from the nearest x-ray machine and professional medical help. At the best of times we were crammed into our trusty hollowed-out tree like sardines in a can. Finding enough room to lay Rod down while getting him back to the ferry port, from where transport back to Padang could be organized, was out of the question. We needed to find an alternative, some way to get him out of there and back to civilization, laying down flat to prevent any further spinal damage.

As luck would have it, a 30ft fishing boat was anchored up in the bay nearby, preparing for a night's work at sea. When he saw our predicament the boat's captain, a heavy-set friendly fellow with a weathered face, immediately agreed to sail three

hours to the nearest ferry port. Ignoring work commitments, he dropped everything
to help us out, and all for a very fair price, barely enough to cover the cost of fuel.

A lot of things, large and small, have gone wrong during my five trips to Indonesia,
close to a year spent there altogether. Again and again, though, I have encountered this
unconditional readiness to help; in fact it has been a recurring experience. Indonesia
is a crazy, far-out country. The ubiquitous chaos, anarchy and public mayhem can be
mind-blowing for first-time visitors and even for well-seasoned travelers. Everyday
situations can become demanding adventures in the blink of an eye. Often it feels
like the next scam or rip-off is waiting just around the corner; someone's always
trying to get a buck out of a wandering surfer, often testing the grey areas between
making an honest profit and openly robbing you. Add in fears of extremist Muslims
and terrorism fed by the western media, and the largest Muslim country in the world
can seem like a daunting place. But as any hardened Indo traveler will tell you:
despite all the disorder and negative propaganda, the vast majority of Indonesians
are genuinely good and compassionate people.

The mighty 7.6 magnitude earthquake struck West Sumatra at 5.15 in the
afternoon, three days later when Rod, Marco and I were sitting in the lounge
of Maranatha losmen back in Padang. We were each doing our own thing
– reading, writing, playing the guitar – when the earth began to tremble
violently. We looked up. Our eyes met, questioning for merely an instant. The next
moment the three of us were scrambling over each other, nearly tripping, falling,
stumbling, floundering, running out into the street. No more than three seconds later
we were in the middle of the road, sidestepping so as not to get knocked off our feet.
The noise was deafening. A thunderous roar was drowning out everything else, the
shattering of glass, people screaming in fear and panic. The ground shook ferociously,

FABIAN HAEGELE

*Moments after the
quake: once the
asphalt road had
finished undulating
like the sea, chaos
reigned. A family
home across the
street caught fire
and people headed
one way to hunt
for loved ones and
the other way to
escape a tsunami
that, thankfully,
never came.*

along some invisible axis, it felt, not in random directions. Everything I had believed to be rock solid suddenly proved to be highly elastic. Waves were rolling across the asphalt road we were standing on like it was water, only faster than ocean waves. All I registered was just peripheral vision. My eyes were fixed on a point in the street in front of me, concentrating hard on staying upright.

Rod, who had been diagnosed with a fractured L1 (lumbar) vertebrae the previous day, was struggling and calling for help. Marco and I had to brace him, which gave us all more stability.

Then suddenly it was over. The whole thing had lasted no more than 15-20 seconds – no time at all, but it had felt like an eternity.

I looked up and looked around. People were scrambling to their feet. Most had ended up on all fours. One guy had apparently got knocked off his motorbike and was licking his wounds. Rod was in pain, but said he was alright. Fiona, a Scottish girl staying at our losmen was trembling, sheer terror in her eyes. A cloud of brown dust was hanging in the air at one end of our street. The road was cracked. There was smoke coming out of the house directly opposite.

Someone muttered the word 'tsunami'. The horrifying memories from the Boxing Day Tsunami flooded in. It made sense, and if there was a tidal wave coming, time was of the essence. Tsunamis travel at great speed and with the tremors being this intense it felt like we must be close to the epicenter. I rushed inside to grab my camera, wallet and passport. The relatively new losmen building was now in a dire state. Windows were shattered, there was glass and debris everywhere, the tiled floor was heavily cracked and uneven. I had to kick in the door to my room where the back wall was now half a foot away from the structural beams and daylight was pouring in. It was cracked diagonally along its entire width. The bathroom ceiling had collapsed and water was gushing down from the first floor.

It had been less than a minute but when I came back outside the building across the street was being consumed by a raging fire, scorching flames angrily devouring what moments ago had been a family's home, thick black smoke billowing towards the overcast sky. The owners were watching helplessly. We ran. Or at least we tried to since Rod with his broken back was slowing us down considerably, limping along as best as he could. People were rushing everywhere; mothers with their children; a barefooted man with no shirt leading his wrinkled grandmother by the hand, a stern but calm look on her face; a group of girls in school uniform; worried-looking men on motorbikes.

Not everyone was heading for the hill on the other side of the river though, where masses of people were already crowding the steep slopes. Almost as many were rushing into the city center, presumably to find family members. We followed a narrow footpath and steep steps and found ourselves a spot on the patio of a private home hugging the hillside, relieved to be in relative safety. The family there welcomed us, telling us to stay, spend the night if we wanted to. Strikingly there were no men

Ambacang hotel in Padang, West Sumatra after the 2009 Sumatra earthquake.

around, only three generations of women and the children. One of them was wailing and inconsolable, it was a heartbreaking sight. Everybody else was shaken up, too, spooked by the ferocity of what just occurred. We watched in silence as the sky over Padang darkened with the smoke of numerous burning buildings. Plenty of other buildings had partially or fully collapsed. How many people were trapped under rubble at this moment? How many had lost wives, husbands, parents, children? The thought was hard to bear…

We decided to head back into the city, to check on our friends and to see what we could do to help. Most of the people we knew had already gathered at the losmen and fortunately nobody had been seriously hurt. A couple of young girls were in shock, but they were being looked after. Marco, TK and I ventured off towards the Ambacang, a large hotel where our friend Stacey had a room on the fourth floor. I wasn't really too worried about her at that point, assuming that the Ambacang, being one of the best hotels in Padang, would be one of the safer places to be during the quake. That changed quickly though when we walked past Spice Homestay, another hangout popular with surfers, where people told us that the Ambacang had collapsed. Spice, once a three-storey building, had been reduced to a pile of rubble. The only reason nobody had lost their life in there was that it was mid-afternoon and no one had been on the upper floors. What if Stacey had been in her room…? I didn't even dare to finish the thought.

When we turned the corner and saw the remains of the Ambacang my heart sank. Parts of the building's façade appeared intact but behind it the floors and ceilings from the upper floors formed a tight sandwich. It didn't allow for a very high chance of survival for anyone caught in between.

Soldiers were directing the traffic, but no emergency response teams appeared to be anywhere near. No sign of the fire brigade or even a single ambulance – just a crowd of onlookers that mostly stayed well clear of the ruins. No one knew what to do; there was desperation and despair in people's eyes. Among all this overwhelming helplessness, I then experienced one of the happiest moments of my trip. We found Stacey, well and healthy, trying to help some injured people who'd managed to escape out of the collapsing building. She had been in the lobby at the time of the quake and got outside only seconds before the ceilings caved in. Many of the 200 guests and staff inside the building were buried.

The woman Stacey was looking after had been dragged from the ruins with a mangled leg and was in a dreadful condition, pale and cold from all the blood loss, drifting in and out of consciousness from the pain, throwing up from time to time. Next to her was a beaten-up looking, heavily bruised man with a broken leg which had provisionally been fixed with a crude makeshift splint made from a piece of wood. A couple of dead bodies wrapped in tarp had been laid out on the grass seemingly carelessly only a few paces away. Nobody seemed to be paying them any attention. We stayed for a while trying to help as well as we could, which to be honest wasn't all that much due to our lack of emergency medical skills.

Then came the rain. It rained all night, pouring buckets at times, then dying off to a drizzle before increasing in intensity again. One can only imagine what some of the people trapped under merciless mountains of rubble, alive and conscious and hurt, must have gone through that night. Inconceivable. At Maranatha Losmen everybody was dealing with their demons in their own ways. Some curled up in a corner, some huddled together in small groups talking with muted voices, others were playing the guitar and singing along, drinking beer, nobody slept much. We all spent the night outside under a canopy that usually shelters the cars, so great was the fear of an aftershock during the night. The house was uninhabitable anyways.

Throughout that night, and at the airport the next day, I was lost in thought. Was it right to run like this, to just flee back to my safe little bubble in the West? Was it not my moral obligation to stay and help after what we all had just been through? Should I not at least try to support the victims of the earthquake somehow, even if my unqualified help might not really be all that useful? I have yet to find an answer to those questions, although perhaps I never will. All I know is that in the end, it sure did feel strange to be in the air, a pretty stewardess offering me a drink, while people in Padang were still fighting for their lives, and slowly starting to rebuild their homes, their shops, their neighborhoods, their city.

This story was first published in *The Surfer's Path* magazine Issue 81, December, 2010

Boat To Hell

When cheap really is nasty

LEO MAXAM

O
ON AUGUST 20TH, 2011, Jay Johnston and nine friends left their small coastal village in Sussex Inlet, Australia, bound for Indonesia's Mentawai Islands. The boys had been saving and psyching for their fantasy surf trip for six months. It would prove to be a journey they'd never forget – for all the wrong reasons. By the time they returned to port in Padang eight days later, their boat was damaged, Johnston was seriously ill, and everyone on board was thankful to be alive. Johnston, 29, returned to Indo this season for the first time since his nightmarish experience. I spoke with him and got this first-hand account of the Sussex Boys' boat trip from hell. Their story will make you think twice before booking that budget surf charter boat:

The Deal – A friend of a friend back in Oz, Andrew Burnton (not his real name), said he could get us a good deal on his boat, the *Asian Priceless* (not its real name). I think the total price came out to about $24,000 – or $2,400 a head – flights to Padang not included. So it was a pretty good deal for a boat trip to the Mentawais.

The Pickup – When we arrived at the airport in Padang around 10pm there was nobody to pick us up. After about an hour of waiting, the lights started shutting off and the place turned into a ghost town. Luckily we found this one local guy who happened to know Burnto through other people, and he made a few calls and finally we got hold of Burnto. When he pulled up at the airport he said, "I thought you guys were coming tomorrow night!"

The Hotel – We're leaving the airport and Burnto says, "Boys, I got some bad news. I got no accommodation for you because I had you down for tomorrow night." He takes us to this little hotel up a backstreet somewhere in Padang. The place is just a big dorm room with these flimsy bunk beds. By this time it's about four in the morning. We pile all our boards on one of the bottom bunks. Just as we're all drifting off to sleep, the top bunk collapses with my mate Mark in it and he goes crashing straight into all the boards below.

The Boat – The next morning Burnto picks us up and says, "I've got some bad news about the boat too." He says on their last trip the motors blew up on the *Asian Priceless* and it's going to take three more days to fix them. A few of the boys in our group suggested we just get refunded all our money and take off up to Nias or head back to Bali or something. But in the end we all decided to sit still and head out in three days' time. For three days we pretty much just went to the bars and got pissed all day. There wasn't much else to do.

The Switch – On the third day we rock up to the boat in the harbor and the motor is still sitting on the side of the road. Now all of us are really starting to get the shits. So Burnto says, "Look, I can get you guys another boat. If you all throw in another 300 bucks each, you can get on this other boat – *the Sadonya* – and leave tonight." At that point all we wanted to do was get out of Padang and get into some waves. We ended up paying another $300 per head – $3,000 total – to get on this other boat. We left Padang at midnight on the *Sadonya*, three days after we were originally scheduled to leave.

The Surf Guide – The whole time we were in Padang people were chasing Burnto for money. Long story short, Burnto had other dramas back in Padang and he couldn't be our surf guide as originally planned. He tells us, "Look, we got this other guy. His name's Eric... He's a little bit different...but he's alright. Just give him a chance." Turns out that Eric is an ex-drug addict from back in Burleigh Heads. He told us he used to be a fisherman but he had to get away from Australia. He'd been in Indo for five or six years, living out at Katiet, in the village by Lance's Right. Every day on the boat Eric would have a rollie and sprinkle crack on it. All day, every day. He kept telling us it was medicine. But it was crack.

The Disagreement – We were up in the Playgrounds area and Eric kept telling our Indonesian captain, "The boys wanna surf Lance's Right. Let's go around the east side of Sipura, it'll be faster." And the captain kept telling Eric, "No, we're not going around the east side of the island because of the wind." The wind was blowing hard from the east, onshore on that side. But Eric insisted we give it a go. As soon as we came around the corner at the northern tip of Sipura, we knew we shouldn't be on that side. It was just howling onshore, 30 knots or more. The captain said to Eric, "We can't go this way! We have to turn around and go down the other side." That's when Eric said, "No we're not!" and just pushed the captain off to the side and started driving the boat.

The Storm – Eric spent all morning and afternoon behind the wheel going full-throttle into heavy storm winds. We were taking 6 to 8-footers with whitecaps all day on the nose, breaking over the bow of the boat. We were going so slow, it was just stupid. When we finally pulled in at Lance's Right around 4pm it was howling onshore and there were no other boats to be seen. Everyone agreed, even Eric: we had to get to shelter at Lance's Left.

The Wave – To get to Lance's Left from the right, you gotta go around this big peninsula at the southern tip of Sipura island. As we rounded the peninsula, the swells started coming in from a different angle and peaking up. Me and three mates were up on the top deck of the boat surveying the situation and we're all shitting ourselves because we're not in a good position. This one wave comes and peaks up right on our boat and just lays the boat on its side – a 56ft boat! We're hanging on to the roof, trying not to go overboard. Then the boat pops back up and another wave hits us. This time the wave picks up the speed-boat we're towing and sends it straight into the back of our boat. It smashes all the fridges and the bathroom on the back deck. There's food and broken beer bottles everywhere and there's a speed-boat sitting in the back of our boat.

The Captain – I ran down to see the captain and he was pale white. He had the boat throttled as fast as it could go to try and get us out of there (by this time Eric had passed out on the ground and the captain was back behind the wheel). Our boat was getting tossed around like a bath toy. For about 30 minutes there we thought we were swimming, for sure. All of us had untied our boards from the racks and were ready to abandon ship. Somehow the captain got us to the bay at Lance's Left.

The Black Plague – At that point we were just happy to be alive. We surfed Lance's Left that morning, 4-6ft and good fun. The only one of us who wasn't surfing was my mate Woody. I figured he was seasick from the night before. I go down to check on him and he's lying in bed and looks pale white. He's wearing two jumpers and long pants and shivering like he was in the Arctic. He tells me straight faced, "Man, I'm not well. I'm dying." I get some water into him and get him to try and sleep. Then I go surfing again and start feeling really weird out in the water, weak and dizzy. By the time I get back to the boat I'm spinning out. Sure enough, I had the same thing as Woody. Then two more of us go down in the next two hours. And by that night, eight of the ten people in our group are all really sick.

The Longest Night – I had never been that sick in my life. It was next level. I started spewing up blood and shitting blood. I reckon I was on the toilet 40 times a day. I didn't sleep at all and spent the whole night spewing over the side of the boat. There were two of us at a time spewing off the back deck, just taking turns all night. The Indo crew really looked after us. They were up with us all night hosing us down.

The Doctor – Four of us had it really cruel. Hallucinations and shit. We didn't know if it was the food or what. Eric kept telling us we had heat stroke and needed to drink more water. So we were pounding water, and the more we drank the sicker we got. We headed to Tua Pejat, the main town in the islands, and got off the boat and took a taxi to the local hospital. While we were at the hospital, Eric was getting sick too and he jumped off our boat and caught the ferry back to Padang. That was the last we ever saw of him. The doctor in Tua Pejat hardly spoke any English and we couldn't speak Indonesian, so we just tried to explain what was wrong with us using sign language. He gave us some drugs and told us to get home immediately. I got on the phone with my wife and said, "I don't care what you do, just get us flights out of Padang as fast as you can." At that point it was pretty clear the trip was cursed, and everyone was ready to get out of there.

Home – When I got home to Australia I went straight to the doctor and had blood tests done, and that's when the results came back as salmonella poisoning. The doctors reckon the crew had used up all the bottled water on board and were using the desalination pump on the boat for our drinking water. It was just desalinated water out of the pipes of the boat, contaminated with this strain of salmonella bacteria. So we were basically poisoning ourselves every time we drank water. Woody lost 12 kilos. I lost 10 kilos. All of us who were sick lost between 8 and 12 kilos. My guts weren't right for a year after.

The Snake Oil Salesman – Burnto said he'd never had this happen before. We came back to port four days early, but he didn't offer us a refund or anything. I didn't care. I just wanted to get home at that point. We were more focused on getting some clean water and getting some medicine in us. But you'll love this one: months later I get an email from Burnto. He says, "There's a few spots left on the boat. If you can get me four paying customers, I'll let you on for free!" I didn't write back.

The Lesson – What I learned from that whole experience is don't be a tight-arse when it comes to a boat trip. If you're gonna do a boat trip to the Mentawais, make sure you pay good money to get looked after well. We tried to do it on the cheap and got burned. A couple of my mates went back the next year and paid more and said they got looked after like kings. Don't try and cut corners when it comes to a boat trip because you'll just end up paying for it later. What we went through, I wouldn't wish that on anybody.

First published in *Bali Belly* magazine, Issue 002, June, 2013

Man Overboard

The search for and miraculous rescue of Brett Archibald

JOHN MCGRODER

O
UR MENTAWAI SURF charter boat *Barrenjoey* is sitting in Teluk Nibung (Padang Harbour) after a cancelled trip. The crew are wafting over jobs after completing most of them during the "going off" season. We are alongside on our newly acquired family boat, *Amandla*, a 45ft power cat that frees us up from the BJ, 10 guests and crew, yet still allows us to keep an eye on business. Something different this year. Doris is on the blower, a bit stressed about his charter and new boat, *Raja Elang*.

"What's up mate?"

"Ah this shat itself, that shat itself, etc. Had to put the guests in at Wavepark for a couple of days. Promised I'd sort the boat or get another one."

"*BJ* is sitting here after a cancelled trip if you need it."

"Give me an hour, if I can't sort it, let's work something out."

"Roger"

A couple of hours later, Doris rings back.

"I've chucked in the towel. Can I take you up on that offer?"

The offer, by the way, was that "it'll work out in the wash".

BJ is ready in a few hours.

Captain Tony "Doris" Eltherington takes the helm, heads out to pick up his guests. All good. They continue on with their charter for the next week. On the last day, they are in the port of Tua Pejat, on Sipura's north coast. The weather is crap and the surf is small. Elvis, our main crewman, gets the word of a MOB from the harbourmaster. That's a Man Over Board and it's a guest from another charter boat, *Naga Laut*. They lost him during the crossing from Padang to the islands. I get a call around 11.30 am from Doris.

"A punter's gone overboard. Can you call someone there and let people know. We need to get a search party out to look for him."

I look out the window. It's raining, and blowing around 25-30 knots. It wasn't a nice night to go overboard, it's not a nice morning to be searching.

"See if you can confirm details with *Naga Laut*. Position, time, etc. I'll see what I can do from my end".

I call the agents here in Padang. Belinda gets onto the internet, Facebook, etc. She recognizes a photo on Chantal's Facebook of her guests heading out on *Naga Laut*. Chantal and Gideon are friends of ours who used to run the charter boat *Laut India* up here. Now they have their own booking company in South Africa. They've tried to raise the authorities here, but to no avail. From experience we've learnt that when shit happens among the fleet, you have to call in your mates on the other boats, and any other boats and camps willing to pitch in.

I would never normally go to sea on a day like this, but there's a bloke floating, possibly alive, and besides the *Naga Laut*, which has turned around, no-one else is looking. We have a fast boat and can be there by sunset. Doris is thinking the same thing and heads to the area in *Barrenjoey*'s fast tender. Belinda corresponds with South Africa before we lose signal, and we head into a lousy sea. I would not like to be swimming around in it.

Back in West Oz, they are burying Dave Kinder after losing his battle with cancer. Dave worked for Martin Daly for 20 years as his fleet manager. He didn't surf but he was a salvage diver and shipwright. He was the man behind the *Indies Trader* flotilla, Martin's righthand man. He fixed stuff, dealt with politics, made shit happen. His famous quote, and legacy to all those who worked under him was, "In the scheme of things: you just gotta get right on up it!"

Martin has just buried his friend when he hears the MOB news. I am with my family, getting pitched around in a horrible sea-state. Conditions are getting worse. I have no crew, as we are on a private boat. But we can be there by sunset. I notice one of the engine room bays is taking on water. My youngest son Duke is green and throwing up. Fynn my eldest, is also changing colour. B and I are silent, staring at a wild sea with hardly a vessel to be seen for miles. We are out of sight of land. We are both thinking about the guy in the water. As far as we know, only *Bynda Laut*, *Naga Laut* and *Amandla* are looking.

About now I think about Dave Kinder and I remember a moment with him. I was skippering the *Indies Trader 2*. Dave was with me, overseeing the maintenance of the charter. We were anchored at Dua Mata island during very similar conditions to what I am experiencing now, when we received a call from the *Laut India* (Chantal and Gideon's boat). They had dragged onto reef and wanted us to help drag them off. I'd started the engine. Dave looked at me intently and said, "No mate. Conditions are too rough, we'll be putting our vessel in jeopardy. Never put yourself or your vessel in jeopardy." He then put his dive gear on, dived on the *Laut India*, came back and predicted they'd be right till the next tide. He was correct.

I turn and relay this story to B. It doesn't feel right. Sign enough for us that we turn back. I lose an engine due to a fuel blockage and just want to make harbor by dark.

Martin rings me just as we return close to the coast. Martin asks for an update. I let him know what I know. I'm bummed.

"Geez mate, do you think there's a chance?" I ask.

"Of course," he responds. "It's warm water. We have to look."

He suggests I rally the other boats, and we discuss options. One option is for everyone to be floating around with lights on 'til dawn and continue the search. I tell him it's pretty shitty out here. He scoffs. He offers the *Indies Trader 3* and I agree to head back out.

Back in port, B and I are feeling lousy we can't continue our search. Then I get a phone-call from Doris. He's just returned to the *Barrenjoey* after five hours' searching in the tender and confirms that the weather has gone to shit. He's angry that no one else is looking. He agrees it's too shitty to be floating out there all night on a boat, let alone by yourself. But he holds onto the hope that there's a lot of debris floating around. The next call is from *Indies Trader 4* who are complaining about the weather. They have turned back. If the *IT4*'s copping it, you know it's bad. B is back on the internet getting as much info as she can about the MOB. Brett Archibald, 51, a fit mountain biker, father of two kids under 10. Later on, I relay this info to Doris who is angry and frustrated. "Mate, he has kids to live for. There is hope. We will rally the boats. Get some rest, we'll get him in the morning."

Before sleep, B puts this message on Facebook.

> **Hey fleet and camps.** *Naga Laut* **lost passenger around 4am this morning last known coordinates 99 degrees 55' east and 1 degree 50' south. According to Tony/Doris on** *Barrenjoey* **there is a lot of debris out there, ie. Large logs. Weather conditions horrible. We need to have every boat out there at first light. We need to form some sort of grid. We will be on** *Indies Trader 3, Indies Trader 4* **will be there, so too** *Barrenjoey,* **along with** *Kuda Laut.* **We need more. Please factor in current and strong WNW winds. Please communicate on VHF16, and HF8.179MHz. Come on surf community we have to try! Its warm water, he's a surfer, imagine if it was one of you. Team work time.**

We are halfway across the strait by dawn aboard the *IT3*. Dolphins playing under the bow. Hope again. We are in comms with *Barrenjoey, Huey, Mangalui* and *Kuda Laut.* That is the sum of the boats, as far as I know, looking for one of us. Five boats. The Aussies. No plane. No coastguard. Things move slowly over here. *Jam karat.*

We are going to find this guy. It feels right. Dave is going to find him. My boys are going to find him. Someone will.

My boys are searching. B is searching, Tim is searching, Chris is searching. I am on the blower to Albert Taylor discussing current options. Doris reckons the current is going north. Bert agrees it does this sometimes.

There is a jumbled call from *Kuda Laut*. What..."They got him! They got him! He's alive!" Unbelievable. 28 hours in the drink. He's alive.

"*BJ, BJ, IT3.*"

"*BJ* back. Yep we got him. He's alive. 100%. Got a red noggin, a couple of cuts where the seagulls got him. He is talking and thirsty." Doris. Hard nut. Hard as they get. Fucken good surfer. Real. A seaman. He got the guy. He got right on up it. *Naga Laut* finally comes up on the radio. They declare they wish to pick their guest up and so we turn the *Indies Trader 3* around, and head back to Padang into a media storm.

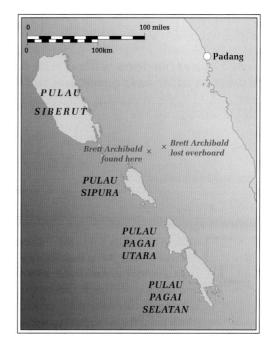

The next morning, *Barrenjoey* turns up. We are there cheering them. We are so proud of Doris cause he was the one that kept at it and used his experience to find Brett. We are also so proud of our crew, Elvis, Wilson, Anas, and Adek, because we know they had Doris's back, as well as making sure the *BJ* did what she had to. And good on the West Aussie boys. What a charter for them. Doris doesn't want to know about the media storm. He did what any real seaman would. He wants to know where all the other boats were. I tell him not to worry about that and just enjoy being famous.

Martin turns up and the morning becomes emotional. We talk about Dave Kinder, and Doris's late sister Denise playing a surreal hand in finding Brett. Doris tells us he'd talked with Denise while he was out searching, "She always comes good for me." he reckons. And we also can't help but think that Dave urged Brett to get right on up it.

And with that, Uncle Doris – accompanied by a well-deserved breakfast beer – turns his attention to the next matter at hand: the business of building rocketships with my boys.

First published in *White Horses* magazine, Issue 5

Man Back On Board

Fresh conversations with a still dripping Brett Archibald moments after being rescued in the Mentawai Straits.

CHRIS BINNS

ANTASTIC NEWS FROM Indonesia today with South African man overboard Brett Archibald found after 28 hours lost in the Mentawai Strait. Durbanite, Archibald, who was seasick as the charter boat *Nagu Laut* made an overnight crossing from Padang, fell overboard yesterday morning. His absence was not noticed until breakfast a few hours later, at which point the *Nagu Laut* turned around to retrace its path. At the same time the crew alerted Indonesian Search and Rescue and all charter boats in the area, who mobilized to join the search.

A few short hours ago Tony "Doris" Eltherington, skipper of the *Barrenjoey*, reported that they had found the stricken swimmer floating 12 miles east of the island of Sipura. Archibald is dehydrated and sunburned, and the *Barrenjoey* is now steaming to meet up with the *Nagu Laut*, to return their missing passenger and reunite him with his surfing buddies.

An incredible feat of endurance from Archibald, and an awesome show from all of the charter boats that ply the Mentawai archipelago, not least Martin Daly, who had no second thoughts about mobilizing all three of his *Indies Trader* boats and jumping straight into the rescue mission.

Update:

Less than an hour ago *Surfing Life* managed to talk to an exhausted Archibald aboard the Barrenjoey, via a terrible mobile phone line. The *Nagu Laut* arrived on the scene mid-call, reuniting their missing passenger with his friends, which led to an abrupt and understandable conclusion, but here are the words of a true ironman, still coming to terms with what he just survived. Doris, being the legend that he is, couldn't quite understand that his new passenger wasn't up to a beer yet, and gladly handed the phone to him with the line, "Bretto, the paparazzi want a piece of you already!" Cheers Doris!

Brett! Amazing. Obvious question, how are you mate?
I'm not good, hey. 28-and-a-half hours in the water – I am broken. I feel broken in half.

What happened?
We were in a bad crossing. The seas were really rough. I went up on deck to take a wee and drink some water, and then realized I was really seasick. I had two really big vomits, and then I think I blacked out while I was retching. I don't remember falling overboard or anything. If you fell, you would know. You'd try to grab a rope or something. But I woke up in the water with no lifejacket, the boat 100 metres ahead of me with no tender behind it. It was 3.15am, there was a dark storm, I'm in the middle of this nasty strait, I saw the boat sailing off and I thought it was all over. There were no islands anywhere for 15 kilometres, but I figured I just had to remain calm, and that once the boat realized I was gone they'd turn around. And they did come back, they got to within 250 metres of me, but they couldn't see me because the swell was so big, and then they kept going past me and I knew I was in real trouble. The night was carnage. I had sharks swimming past me, I got stung by every jelly fish in the ocean. Seagulls even tried to peck my eyes out, so I have big holes in my nose.

No!
It was insane, just insane. I actually gave up. I went under and said, "screw this, I can't carry on". But I couldn't swallow water, I couldn't get my lungs to take the water and I kept coming back up. So then I pulled myself together, said, "Okay, we need to keep going here", and I kept swimming and treading water. I treaded water all night, I saw a couple of islands and tried swimming to them but the current was too hectic, I wasn't able to kick, so I just floated with the current. This morning I saw a couple more islands, but again I couldn't get to them.

Did you have any driftwood or anything to help float you?
No, not a thing. I couldn't believe it. You see rubbish everywhere, and yet I didn't see a single log or branch or boogie board or anything. I did not see one single piece of litter anywhere, not even a piece of paper. I treaded water for 28-and-a-half hours.

How much longer do you think you could have lasted?
The human body is an amazing, amazing thing. I don't think I could have gone much beyond today, by the time night came I might have been cactus. I had to get my rhythm, I was treading water for five minutes, then I'd swim again. I saw land five times, but I could never get closer, the current pulled me away every time. I saw a fishing boat come out, and thought "Okay, he'll get me." He was headed straight for me then turned to port and buggered off that way, and I didn't see him again, and then the boat I'm on now, these Aussie guys, just turned up from nowhere, and they were insane. The captain, Tony (Eltherington), had already organized the whole search and rescue

Saved! The moment South African Brett Archibald waited 28 ours for after falling of a surf charter boat in the Mentawai Straits.

party, and then they were the ones who found me. I saw these masts and started swimming towards them, obviously they were trying to find me but they weren't coming straight for me, they were going to miss me by 200 metres. I couldn't whistle my mouth was so dry, so I just started hollering. Tony heard me but he couldn't see! They eventually pinpointed the noise and found me in the binoculars and came and picked me up. I tell you, I'd never been so happy to see a boat in my entire life, even if it was full of Aussies! I'm a converted Aussie, I love these guys!

When you get onboard what do you do? Drink lots of water and phone your relatives?
Thankfully there was a doctor onboard, and he was amazing. He controlled the situation from the start. He gave me plenty of water, got me warm. I could barely drink, my tongue was the size of a tennis ball. The doc really looked after me, got me on a drip, patched up all my wounds, looked after my face, glued my nose back up. It was good.

Great to hear. Where are you now?
I'm still on the *Barrenjoey*, and the boys onboard have all been surfing this perfect left while I've been asleep. My boat is coming to catch up with me now, and then we can go and carry on with our surf trip.

Your surf trip? You're not going to get checked out at a hospital or anything?
No, no. We've got a doctor here and he's really taken care of me, you know? He says it's all good, and in a day or two I should be OK. I must say, my liver and kidneys are buggered, my blood sugar levels are low, my heart rate is very slippery and not great, but I reckon I'll come right tomorrow…

...bloody hell.
They make us tough in Saffa-land, boy! We've got eight days left on our trip, I can't go to hospital, we've got to surf.

You've got to get your money's worth, too. You've paid for the trip already. No South African is going to let his coin go that easily.
Exactly! We've had a good adventure, but we've also wasted two days searching for me. And they just pulled up! I have to go and say hello to them.

Well mate we're really, really glad you made it.
Ah, thank you. And thanks a lot for the call, appreciate it. Tell everyone back home I'm okay.

Will do... (line goes dead).
Brett, we're glad you made it back in one piece mate. Your story is incredible, as is your willingness to have a phone jammed in your face so soon after you towelled off. Sounds like there's some swell headed your way, may you get what you deserve. Apologies if any of these quotes aren't quite 100%, the line was atrocious. Cheers, bru.

First published on *Surfing Life*'s website www.surfinglife.com.au.

The Bono River Bore

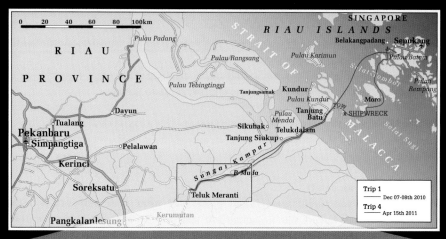

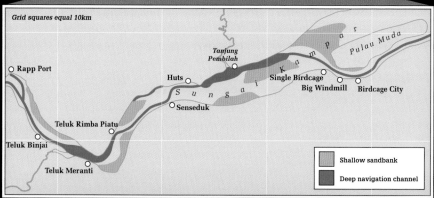

Boring Facts

River Name	KAMPAR	SEVERN	QIANTANG	ARAGUARI
Bore Name	Bono	Severn Bore	Silver Dragon	Pororoca
Bore Length	50-60km	40-50km	80-100km	80-100km
Width	1-2km	40m-500m	2-4km	1-3km
Speed – (shallow)	8-15kmh	8-13kmh	8-15kmh	8-15kmh
– (deep)	16-25kmh	16-21kmh	16-27kmh	16-30kmh
Wave Height	1-3m	1-2 m	2-4m	2-3m
Tidal Range	3-4m	9-10m	8-9m	6-7m
Days Per Year	160	260	365	200

Finding Bono

**Timeline of the discovery of the 'Bono' tidal bore on
the Kampar River, Sumatra**

ANTONY 'YEP' COLAS

01 December, 2008

'M NOT AN insomniac, but when I can't sleep, I sit in front of a computer
screen. That's how I came across a photo of people riding canoes on a river
wave and, by association, the word "Bono" which I soon discovered was a
word of some significance. A few mouse-clicks later, I found the name of the
river – the Kampar, in Sumatra – and so began a long journey that continues
to this day.

11-15 October, 2009

I go to the Malaysian tidal bore, the Benak, following a surf trip to the Mentawais.
The Benak reaches a respectable size, up to 1.5m at it's peak, and breaks for two
hours on a dozen sections. I become the first surfer to ride the Benak standing on a
board and the local authorities are super-excited. With this small triumph, I prepare
for the Bono experience in mid-September, 2010.

July, 2010

Despite extensive research, the plans are slow to advance. I have no idea if I can
hire a boat, but nor do I have a plan B other than to show up in the village of Teluk
Meranti and hope to find something solid that can handle the job. Most info from the
region centres on the filming of *Inglorious Bastards* and the fire that recently ravaged
a Greenpeace deforestation protest camp. As for the Bono itself, I found some pictures
of the wave on a website about protecting Sumatran tigers, but I can't dig up anything
on the size of the bore, propagation distance, times and types of tides. This makes it
hard to tempt others to take a gamble on what could be a myth. I manage to convince
my brother Fabrice, and Patrick Audoy, two St. Pardon *mascaret* (a river bore in
France) addicts to accompany me. And then Rip Curl propose sending Indonesian
pro Garut Widiarta and circumnavigator Teiki Balian. Teiki just happens to be visiting
France, so we meet for a training session on the Dordogne *mascaret* in mid-July.

15 August, 2010
Via Facebook, I managed to make contact with someone called Wewen of the River Defenders Association, who conducted an expedition to the Kampar River in June. We want his Zodiacs, at any price, and I finally strike an agreement that will bring us two Zodiacs from Jakarta. Clement at Thalassa had to cancel but a guy called Maxence at Eyesea Productions is now interested in shooting the expedition and our friend Bage also joins the crew.

27 August, 2010
The news is bad! After investigation, Wewen tells us that according to the villagers there will only be a "small Bono" – barely 1m high – when we're there. We finally understand...the tides are semi-diurnal mixed (two tides a day of different ranges) and there is a large height difference between the big high tide at night and the smaller high tide during the day. The villagers talk about a 1m wave, while some sources say 4 to 6m, leaving lots of room to be disappointed! I call Rip Curl and Teiki to discourage them from coming because a 1m max wave height will make shortboarding difficult to say the least. We decide to take thicker, wider, larger boards.

Trip 1

07-13 September, 2010
Day 1 – It's tiny, but we spot the potential of one particular section.
Day 2 – We awake to rain and to find our Zodiacs had been slashed during the night. A local speedboat is rented, and some small waves are ridden. Only one of the Zodiacs is repairable and is patched up with local materials.
Day 3 – It's the revelation! Long, endless walls with clean, carvable faces in the 1.5-2m range, traversing the river with lefts and rights into the channels. However, on the boat, the plywood floor collapses under the weight of five big guys and their boards. The Zodiac limps back to the village.
Day 4 – Ecstasy! No wind leaves the Kampar looking like a brown opaque mirror, as we gouge repetitive snaking signatures across the glassy surface and Bage slips into a short tube like a liquid chocolate dream.
Day 5 – Conditions are idyllic and perfect for the first ever local ride as driver Eddie surfs for five minutes on one wave at the smaller Teluk Binjai section.
Day 6 – The height drops by 20%, but the good weather and light winds continue. I surf a section of 45 minutes, but can't match Bage's hour-long ride! Mission accomplished.

In early October I share my discovery with good friend Arthur Moreno and begin planning a trip that will coincide with the "big Bono" season, between October and March. We decide that taking a jet ski from one of the established resorts on Bintan or Batam in the Riau Islands would be the easiest way to get there.

Trip 2

05-07 December, 2010

The original plan of renting jet skis in resorts proves a big disappointment. Most of the hire skis are unreliable wrecks and thirsty models with 700-800hrs on the clock and up to 7-8yrs of constant tourist abuse. A last-minute meeting with a jet ski specialist, highlighted further problems we might encounter when making a long voyage, besides the worry of driver endurance. Rinsing the pump is key to reliability, plus it was strongly recommended we only use a special, higher-octane fuel, which was unlikely to be sold in tiny Teluk Meranti, 100kms upstream. Of course, we didn't tell the owner that we were going on the River Kampar, we just talked about doing a tour of Pulau Kundur, a large island at the mouth of the Kampar. So we finally rented two unresponsive open boats; one fiberglass, 6m long hull with a 40HP outboard and a smaller, wooden, locally made boat that didn't look up to the difficult, dangerous crossing of the Straits of Malacca. We set off from Batam early in the morning hoping to make "Bono village" by nightfall and initially made good progress, cruising at 20 knots. Two hours into the trip, the wooden boat's engine overheats thanks to a plastic bag over the water inlet for cooling the engine. We transfer the luggage and leave the driver floating in the middle of nowhere, seemingly happy to repair the engine and find his way back to Batam. Progress on the bigger fiberglass boat, now overloaded with 6 people (Arthur and Geoffrey Moreno, Bruno Memvielle, Arnaud Decarne, David Badalec and me) plus the driver and all the gear is very slow... in fact too slow at 12-13 knots. Two similar speedboats divert to come our way. As they approach, we get the feeling they could be pirates, but it turns out they are police!

"What are you doing out here?"

"*Berselancar*, we are here to surf"

"OK fine, good luck"

We are not even halfway as evening closes in, a storm rages through, with strong gusts and choppy, heavy seas. Suddenly we run aground on an island in the black of night. Rain hammers down and lightning shows us an inhospitable coastline of sharp rocks with a thin coating of sticky mud. Each series of waves results in more water sloshing aboard the boat, so we scoop and bail continuously. We send David, who speaks some Indonesian, to the village lights we could see in the distance, and two hours later, he returns with a boat, just as we begin to shiver uncontrollably with serious cold. The rescue boat tows us out of the mud and escorts us for an hour to Tanjung Batu, a seaport on Pulau Kundur, where a downright friendly hotel is located, with cold beers and hot water. We set off at 9am to complete the 225km crossing with at least 130km left of mainly straight shooting down the river. After the chaos of the night before, it is an uneventful voyage to the village. That night the "little Bono" sweeps through, leaving a meter of water in the streets of Teluk Meranti.

Drenched, shivering and shipwrecked on one of the muddy islets that make the Malacca Straits so dangerous to navigate.

DAVID BADALEC

08-12 December, 2010

Unlike in September, we arrive after the peak spring tides. The maximum tidal coefficient is 88; much lower than last time, but wave height should be much larger thanks to the daytime "big Bono" factor.

Day 1 – It's big and we only start from around halfway. Soon, we lose sight of Arthur and during the desperate search in the moguls and rapids behind the bore, the boat conks out from either dirty fuel or water in the carburetor. Luckily, we get a tow back to the village, where Arthur awaits us among the crowd. He babbles about surfing an amazing righthander all the way back to the village and we couldn't see him because he had to spend some time lying down getting pounded in the whitewash as the wave rumbled through some shallow sections.

Day 2 – Because we are lacking speed and space in the boat, we draw straws to split the group and drop off three surfers at the "huts". The Moreno brothers and David become team short-straw and have the unenviable job of trying to catch the Bono from the riverbank, on a section known to be powerful and unpredictable. We motor downstream and pick the wave up at Tanjung Pembilah, allowing a few shorter sections before we approach the huts. We watch from the middle of the river as the boys time their dash into the water to nab a great glassy left peeling off the smashed jungle riverbank. Somehow, they pull it off and we all ride down into the steep, ripable righthander that Arthur scored yesterday. The Bono fades out in the deep water opposite the village as it hits a 90° bend in the river and for the first time, we chase it further upstream and discover another handful of sections. The first section is a consistent left shoulder running for 45 mins down past the next village at Teluk Binjai and on to RAPP[1] port far beyond; then a 5-10 minute righthander runs between

---

1   Riau Andalan Pulp & Paper (RAPP) runs one of the biggest pulp mills on the planet, feeding the Chinese market with over 2 million tonnes per year. They are the major employer in the area and provide infrastructure from roads to school ferries and therefore have a lot of influence over local politics and issues.

two islands before disappearing and popping up again for another 5min ride. The final section we caught was a smaller straighthander that bounced along for 10min, finishing a full 45mins upstream from RAPP Port. It took an hour and a half to motor back against the strong current that follows behind the Bono.

Day 3 – Less glassy conditions, but still a blast, especially through the "Good Rights" section on the approach to Teluk Meranti and to conserve fuel we only do a short run down the Teluk Binjai stretch.

Day 4 – It's already smaller, so longboard and SUP only, which make light work of catching, cruising and most crucially, traversing the whitewash when the wave closes out across the shallow parts of the river.

Day 5 – Very small, just a few waves so we leave first thing the next morning on the Lurah taxi-speedboat (35-40 knots) to Tanjung Batu to make the connection with the Batam speedboat and be in Singapore by 1500. Two hours later we're riding the Flow Barrel, which feels more skate than surf.

28 January, 2011
Thalassa broadcasts a 13min documentary called *Bore in Sumatra* on French TV and the program is watched by 2.5million viewers.

15 February, 2011
Arnaud who works for Rip Curl, pitches for a "Search" project to the Bono, but the Australian office doesn't really seem keen on the idea. I start up a new company called Bonosurf by convincing a dozen friends to put in 2000 Euros each so we can order special boats and set up a proper surf operation.

Trip 3
March, 2011
Two weeks before departure, the Rip Curl Search project gets the green light. I need to find boats fast because the two new Chinese ribs I ordered won't arrive in time. A team of 21 people will be in Teluk Meranti to meet the March super-moon that will produce a peak tidal range of 118 (out of 120), which only happens every 19 years! The team includes:

- 5 pro riders - Dean Brady (Aus), Oney Anwar (Ind), Bruno Santos (Brz), Tom Curren (USA), Tyler Larronde (USA)
- 2 jet ski pilots - Vincent Lartizien (Fra), Michel Larronde (Fra)
- 3 videographers - Jean-Patrick Mothes (Fra), Lachlan McKinnon (Aus), Jon Frank (Aus)
- 2 photographers - Ted Grambeau (Aus), Nathan Lawrence (USA)
- 1 sound engineer - Stéphane Queme (Fra)
- 3 organisers - Arnaud Decarne (Fra), Antony Colas (Fra), James Hendy (UK)

Whoever dubbed the Bono "Seven Ghosts" obviously didn't have this bird's-eye view.

BONOSURF.COM

growing crowd of villagers paddling across the channel to the Village Peak, but has more knowledge of the river and wave than anyone. Next up was Viqi Lestari, who watched her friend Sawal ride on the front of Bage's SUP during the first ever trip. By the time we returned, she had badgered her uncle to shape her a solid hardwood mal, copied from *Local super-grom, Viqi, emulating the T-shirt twirling, style master himself, Tom Curren.*

a fiberglass model we left behind. From the first time she stood up as a 10-year-old, we could tell she was going to be a good surfer and have always taken her out when there is room or met her at the Village Peak. Super athletic and always playing football on the pier, Viqi managed to win the *Ondines* (womens) category in the local competition, strengthening her "tomboy" label. Her parents run a little eatery next to the Mega Lestari "hotel" and she is definitely set to become one of the hardcore locals. Guys like Jon Jon mix it up by shaping home made paddles and boards, creating an indigenous SUP style and like all remote surfing locations, the villagers are always looking for secondhand equipment. It's a great vibe and hopefully it will remain that way, by maintaining that frontier feeling.

Based on an interview by Alex Dick-Read that was first published in *The Surfer's Path* Issue 85 July/August, 2011

JAVA
& BALI

Birds-eye Bukit from Uluwatu to Dreamland.

Jambi

Mentok

Pangkalpinang

Palembang

Tanjungpandan

SUMATRA

Baturaja

LAMPUNG

Telukbetung

Krakatoa Islands

Panaitan
Island

Jakarta

JAKARTA ★

Bogor

JAWA
BARAT

BANTEN

Bandung

J

A

V

A

Cirebon

Semarang

JAWA
TENGAH

Surakarta

Surabaja

Yogyakarta

YOGYAKARTA

JAWA
TIMUR

Pacitan

Malang

Pulau Merah
(Red Island)

Sumenep

BALI

Denpasar

LOMBOK

SUMB

Java Sea

BORNEO

Sukadana

Ketapang

Sampit

Buntok

Amuntai

Banjarmasin

Martapura

Samarinda

Balikpapan

0   100   200 Miles

0   100   200   300km

I N D I A N   O C E A N

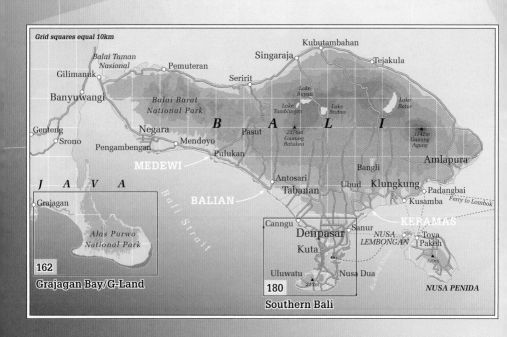

Grid squares equal 10km

Balai Taman
Nasional

Gilimanuk

Pemuteran

Singaraja

Kubutambahan

Tejakula

Banyuwangi

Balai Barat
National Park

Seririt

Lake
Buyan

Lake
Tamblingan

Lake
Bratan

Lake
Batur

Genteng

Srono

Negara

Pengambengan

Mendoyo

Pasut

B

2276m
Gunung
Batukau

A

L

I

3142m
Gunung
Agung

Pulukan

MEDEWI

J   A   V   A

Grajagan

Alas Purwo
National Park

162

Grajagan Bay/G-Land

BALIAN

Antosari

Tabanan

Bangli

Ubud

Klungkung

Amlapura

Padangbai

Kusamba

Ferry to Lombok

KERAMAS

Bali Strait

Canggu

Denpasar

Kuta

Sanur

NUSA
LEMBONGAN

Toya
Pakeh

529m

Uluwatu

213m

Nusa Dua

180

Southern Bali

NUSA PENIDA

Coconut Compass

Lost at sea off Krakatoa

GARY JOHN

W E'RE HANGING AROUND near Pelabuhan Ratu (West Java), surfing these little righthanders down there. There's the late Dave Shiller – a geologist who lives in Jakarta and works for an oil company – Robbie McIver and myself. Robbie's a bodyboarder, Dave rides a kneeboard and I ride a shortboard. We're looking for a bit of adventure and the prospect of unsurfed breaks, so we decide to go and check out Panaitan. We tee up a boat and collect our permits from the port authority at Labuhan.

The captain picks us up down the river – it's your classic, typical Indo boat. About 28ft, small wooden wheelhouse at the back with the engine in front of it, and the driver sitting on wooden slats at the back with the tiller. He has a little wooden frame up front so we buy a tarp and cover it so we can stay dry.

We steam up the river and into the Sunda Strait where we hug the coast and head towards Ujung Kulon National Park. It's like the Everglades – mangrove forests everywhere. We get to Ujung National Park and there's a ridiculously well-maintained camp there – it looks like a scout camp – beautiful manicured lawns, Indonesian flag flying, galvanised huts – completely unexpected! We stay there, get up early in the morning and the first thing I see is a bloody great monitor lizard out the front of the hut. Absolutely huge! I can't get over it.

We set off to Panaitan. There's a rangers hut near a reef pass. A left on one side and a right on the other. We surf it for a day or two. Once the wind and swell drops curiosity gets the better of us so, we ask our captain to take us around the corner – a fair drive around a very exposed headland. As we sail across the headland there are lefts breaking inside of us all along, but it looks unmakeable. At the end of the headland we enter a very deep bay. And there it is – this left just reeling down the reef, getting faster and faster as it goes. We decide to surf it. I manage to get a couple, but can't make them on my backhand and get smashed. Robbie gets a couple on his bodyboard but we decided to look further. We head deeper into the bay, spotting a left and a yacht's mast in the lagoon. We figure it's surfable and paddle out. It's big, long, and flat, soft fun.

KLAUS BAUMGARTNER

Krakatoa – a mountain that may be worth heading for, if you know where the hell you're going. If not, break out the coconuts.

The next morning we head back to look at the point we'd seen and it's different – it's bigger and breaking better. We get a couple of waves but it's incredibly intimidating. It needs a better tide. It seems to grow and get faster as you get further down the line. It's intense! Dave breaks his kneeboard so we decide to get out of there. This break is soon to be known as One Palm.

We figure there's enough swell to surf a wave on Krakatoa – apparently a left-hander. It's not far off dark when we set off. We head around the corner and back to our rangers' camp to gather our stuff and bolt. With Krakatoa ahead in the distance we sit back and try to relax.

It feels strange from the word go. The trade winds come up on dark – blowing hard. We're under the tarp, trying not to get wet, being lashed by the ocean, and wondering what the hell we're doing.

After an hour or so, it feels that the wind's changing. Something isn't right so I head down the back and find the captain, half asleep, holding the tiller arm – just sitting there. His thinking is if he keeps the boat at the same angle to the wind, he'll stay on the course he'd set visually on a distant Krakatoa on dusk.

I ask him: "Where's Krakatoa?", to which he replies confidently "dead ahead". I know the wind has changed, and ask him again and he replies, "dead ahead", but I know it's not the case.

Next question: "Where's your compass?" Of course he doesn't have one.

I return up front and tell the boys, "We're in deep shit here, old mate hasn't got a compass".

A week or so previously we'd been reading in the Jakarta Post about some European guys who'd been lost down the coast off Enggano. They were down to eating their toothpaste to keep them sustained! We're freaking. The straits here are radical and if you get lost you're in serious trouble. And it's pretty clear we're lost.

So we decide to make a compass. We have foam from Dave's snapped kneeboard and we have a medical kit. We use a torch battery to magnetise a needle from the medical kit by putting a current through it. We fill half a coconut shell with water, float the foam disc on top of it with the magnetised needle attached. The process takes forever – in the dark, getting hammered, but it works! It might not be the slickest compass ever made, but the needle seems to stay in the same direction – it looks like it's doing the job.

We have nothing to lose, so I take it down the back and we basically relieve the captain of his duties. We take it in turns, one steers the boat and another looks after the coconut compass. During the night our captain comes to us and says we can still go to Krakatoa, to which we reply "Fuck-off – we want to go home back to Carita".

So onwards we steam all through the night.

When the sun comes up we're shitting ourselves, because we can see nothing ahead but clouds on the horizon. Gradually all the clouds move except one – it reveals itself as the mountain behind Carita.

We're OK! If we'd gone with the captain's assurances we would have found ourselves out in oblivion in the Sunda Strait as sure as anything.

The fun doesn't stop there. An hour later the engine's running but we're not moving – the clutch has gone. There's a spare board, it obviously happens regularly. We throw an anchor line over the side while the captain starts ripping things apart.

We're not in the mood to be helpful, so we mope around up the front. I look down at the anchor line and it's swaying limply, this way and that. We check the admiralty charts Dave's brought with him and realise we're in a humongous depth of water, the anchor is just drifting – and so are we – back out into dire straits again.

Eventually they get the motor going again, but it's getting late in the day, the boat isn't running terribly well, and we're thinking, "Here we go again!"

This wasn't going to be good, it's getting dark again and another night with an unknown amount of fuel is not something we're looking forward to.

As if that's not enough, about 200 metres behind us a giant, twisting waterspout springs up! We go right through its path. They're serious stuff. I've never seen anything like it since.

We finally make it to the river at Carita Beach, get back to the Beach Hotel and get on the piss.

The next morning the captain's knocking on the door, repentant, cap in hand. He's shitting himself because we could have handed him in to the law. But we don't. We buy him a compass instead.

First published in *White Horses* magazine Issue 8.

The Camel Concept

He is the *orang gila* of Panaitan, the wildest cat in the G-Land tube jungle, he's got a dog-chewed, canary-yellow single fin and a menagerie of other weird hybrids. He is a mythical creature whose legendary exploits are whispered far across the archipelago. He is...Camel.

YASHA HETZEL

□

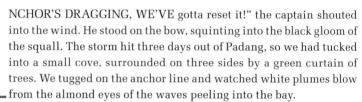

ANCHOR'S DRAGGING, WE'VE gotta reset it!" the captain shouted into the wind. He stood on the bow, squinting into the black gloom of the squall. The storm hit three days out of Padang, so we had tucked into a small cove, surrounded on three sides by a green curtain of trees. We tugged on the anchor line and watched white plumes blow from the almond eyes of the waves peeling into the bay.

"What the...there's someone out there!" the captain suddenly said as he stared towards the waves. We all looked to see a gray figure streaking through the mist into a huge, dark barrel. The wave sectioned off and all that was left was a leashless single fin twirling in the wind.

"Who was that?" the captain screamed...

With the anchor set, we watched for the mysterious surfer and expected him to re-emerge from another wave. The sets kept pouring through, but each peeled without a rider. The shadows in the trees grew darker and we wondered what had happened to the guy. Just then, we heard a knock on the hull. Over the rail, a curly blonde head bobbed in the water in a dugout canoe.

"Hi, I'm Cam," he said, "Do you have any fruits and veggies you could trade me? There's not much on this island."

He climbed aboard but didn't stay long. After a quick talk, a cup of tea, and some veggies, he was off.

"If you're ever in West Australia, look me up," he said with a wave and a smile as he hopped back into his canoe. As he paddled off to his camp on the edge of reality, the darkness closed in around him.

The Yellow Board

The brown water of the Batang Arau snaked through Padang and out to the harbor. The air stank of diesel fumes and resonated with the thumping bass of Indonesian techno. I had been walking along the curb, carrying a sack of fruit and veggies to the boat, when I gazed out into the traffic. Choking the street were dozens of loud and brightly painted disco buses. Beyond them a gleaming single fin whizzed by, sticking out of a taxi window. The board was at least eight-feet long and looked straight out of Barry Kanaiaupuni's Sunset quiver, circa 1971. I'd heard rumors that a young guy called Camel was in the area. The board looked like it could be one of his. I stood and followed along the street, as the cab weaved around bicycles and buses. Outside of a tinted-glass door painted with a sign reading "No Ecstasy," I caught up. The board and passenger were gone, but the driver pointed me to the Hotel Dipo. It was dark inside and smelled of cigarettes. A few tables with checkered tablecloths filled the space near the front window and surf photos hung on the walls. In the rear was the bar, depressingly dark and empty for that hour of the afternoon. "Why are you following me?" I heard a coarse voice say from the corner. The words came from an old salt with graying hair, a gap in his teeth, and an empty Bintang bottle that glowed in the afternoon light. On the floor was the yellow single fin, but the guy was too old to be who I was looking for.

"Sorry, I was looking for a guy called Camel," I said. The man introduced himself as Moose. As he began to speak, the wrinkles around his milky eyes deepened. He had been running surf charters out to the islands since the beginning and knew a lot about Indonesia and the people who go there. He'd bought the yellow board from Camel the last time he'd seen him. Moose started into his fourth beer and told me about that day.

"I took a charter out to One Palm at the start of the season and he was there camping in the jungle. Sad story though. He's had all the diseases – typhoid, dengue, four strains of Malaria – I think he's got a new strain now, one that might finish him off. We scored a big swell out there, one of the best in years. One Palm was perfect. Our crew surfed it alone for two days before Camel made it out, riding a bodyboard. He was too sick and weak to stand up. So he rode prone, then crawled back across the reef to his camp in the jungle. I offered him a lift back to port and hospital but he refused and said he wasn't yet finished with One Palm."

"So, that's the last you heard?"

"Yep, he crawled into the shadows and I haven't heard any more about him since. I really hope he's okay, but I don't know..."

Moose tipped the last bit of beer back in his hand. Sunlight passed through the bottle and reflected green across his face. He nodded his head and made no attempt to speak more. Standing up, I thanked him, and hurried out of the air-conditioned room, back into the warm smell of chillies and diesel.

The Cave

I found Camel 3000 miles away, on a gray, windy afternoon in Western Australia. The parking lot on the point was nearly empty, blown clean of trash and sand by a strong spring breeze. At the far end of the car park was a white Toyota van, the lone occupant shuffling a pile of surfboards under the front bumper. I climbed out of my car, zipped up my jacket, and walked up to say hello. In the rear window was a sign, crudely written with a marker advertising the sale of surfboards of "all shapes and sizes."

Rap music, loud and obnoxious, spewed from a stereo with oversized speakers. It was powered by a pair of wires that connected it to a car battery with a set of alligator clips. The wiry, curly-haired owner moved to the beat while tightening a sarong around his thin waist. His skin, though tanned from a life in the sun, still looked young and full of life. He had the kind of face that changes little as the years go on, and had pure gray-blue eyes that seemed to stare not at you, but into you. It was the man born as Geoff Goulden, but better known as Camel for his curious extended neck, long surf sessions, and determination. There was a rumor that at 8ft G-land, he slid into the tube and pulled a camera from his wettie. He snapped a shot from the inside looking out, then advanced the film and shot two more frames before re-emerging into daylight. Camel retreated back toward the rear of the van, motioning for me to follow. "Come hang out in my van and talk, it's got the best view in town," he said. I climbed inside the rear of the van that was open to the sea and padded with mattresses and blankets. There were cardboard boxes that smelled of fruit and damp wetsuits; surfboards were tied to the ceiling. Camel had created a cozy cave where he could wait in warmth until the conditions got just right.

One night, when he was 18, he and his best mate had been driving home along a narrow tree-lined road. Geoff's car was overheating and they stopped to fix it. Just as they fitted a leg rope in place of a broken belt, they were hit by another car. Both he and his friend were taken to the hospital where they cut open his leg and bolted it back together. The doctor told him he would never surf again, but within a year he was back in the water, keen to charge more big waves. However, after the accident, he found he couldn't surf as well on the new, thinner boards, so he just went back to the older ones that worked. "Also, since my leg was weak, I started trying single fins and found they went really well for me" he said, "and then I started experimenting and never went back."

For the last 10 years, he had spent almost all of his winters in Indonesia. He started out camping in the jungle at G-land until he got a job managing one of the surf camps. For a couple of seasons it was the perfect arrangement: free accommodation and lots of time to tune his barrel riding. Since then, Camel's bounced back and forth between treks into the jungle and his home in Australia. His home that summer was his car.

YASHA HETZEL

Orang Gila (crazy man)

The sky darkened while we talked of the last season in Indo. He laughed when I asked if he had been really sick. "Sick... dunno about that. I had a pretty good run of the shits at Panaitan Island, but as far as being on my deathbed – no way. I was just experimenting on the bodyboard. I really have no idea how these rumors get started," he said. We laughed at the absurdity of some of the stories I'd heard: "Camel's got cerebral malaria, he's got encephalitis and typhoid, he's paralyzed, he'll never stand again..." The truth was really that he was just surfing, alone and in the nude in Lombok.

There are many solo feral Indo travellers but none has quite the reputation of this guy, Geoff Goulden, aka Camel. His quiver can best be described as eclectic, his travel style is below the radar and his tube-riding skills are simply insane.

"October and November were really good, but strange for me," he said. "After the bomb in Bali, there were still these really nice swells but the place was empty." He'd gone to Desert Point and stayed with his Indo friends in the village, needing to be with people after the tragedies he'd witnessed in Kuta. "It was torture though, weeks on end of 6ft Deserts and no one to share it with."

"You were riding the bodyboard?" I asked.

"Nah, I had this board that Gerry Lopez gave me a few years ago. I rode it with no leggie, no helmet, and no boardies for a month," he said. The local kids started calling him "Cam, the *orang gila* who plays with no clothes."

Tied to the roof of the van was a pile of boards he'd been riding at the point. Most were at least a decade old, tossed away as obsolete by their previous owners. It was a small-time version of the quiver he'd had one year at G-land. That year he had taken 42 surfboards to the camp. Sometimes he would walk up to his boards with his eyes closed and select one without even looking. Other times, he would spend hours fine-tuning a certain board – preparing it for the perfect session. He said he'd ridden at least a thousand boards. From this he learned that "a magic board can come in any shape or size. You just have to have the right one for the conditions."

"How many boards do you have now?" I asked. He held up a sheet of paper with a list of boards, numbered to 86. "I've got heaps of these in my Mum's garage," he said. I imagined a collection of old boards in a shack covered with cobwebs – boards that reflected his unique approach.

The Proof's in the Pudding

He told me of his most extreme tail-chopping experiment, on a board he'd taken to G-land. Originally, it had been a 9'6" Rhino-chaser, given to him by Mark Heussenstam, a Californian who'd bailed to West Australia in the '70s for the big and uncrowded waves. I'd seen the board at G-land, while it was still in its original condition. It was a beast of a board, made for really big waves. It didn't quite fit the tube at Speedies, so out came the saw, and off came two-and-a-half feet of the tail. From a narrow pin to a wide, wide square tail. He says, "Wide tails work in the tube because, for example, a Boogie board has a really wide tail, and they go really well in the tube. And the proof's in the pudding, that a wide tail is good in the tube. All of them are sick tube riders, those lid riders."

Yet more proof came during a contest at 8ft Speed Reef. Camel had been surfing between heats and watching from a boat while the contestants dueled for points. Raul Garcia, from Spain, broke his board in one heat and swam over to the boat for a replacement. To Camel's surprise, he wanted to borrow "the beast." The Spaniard paddled back out on the 7' board and stroked into a set at Launching Pads. He struggled with the bottom turn, but made it under the lip. Nine seconds later, he kicked out in the channel—a perfect "10" and advancement into the next heat. Camel told the story with pride. He reckoned that the board had been in so many tubes that it knew exactly what to do. "The board steered through the tube, and the Spaniard just had to hold on for the ride!"

The Lucky Method (his first board)

By the time we had gotten near the end of the collection, the garage looked like a giant matchbox had been spilled. The single-fins had been pushed aside to make room for the channel bottoms, which were forming the base of a new pile

ANDREW SHIELD

One Palm Point   LAT. -6.655053°   LONG. 105.171153°

World-renowned left holding some of the longest barrels on Earth in a pristine wilderness setting. It is super-shallow, very dangerous and hard to get to. Low tide equals suicide for all but the pros and mere journeymen have to wait for mid tide and/or smaller swells to make it from the air drop to deeper water in the channel. Requires a fairly high line to stay out of trouble making it a real backhand challenge. Can be incredibly long when aligned on S-SW swells and any E wind. It's not always perfect by any stretch, but has rideable waves in the highly consistent bracket (7/10). Smart pig-doggers wear rubber!

of experimentals. It started with a kneeboard named "the slab" and continued with other bizarre chunks of glassed foam like the "stingray pin," or a thicky with dimensions: 7'10" x 5" x 11" x 20" x 16". These were shaped by his own hand and called "Camel Creations" or "Camel Concepts." He said he shapes his own boards because when "you shape it and it works it's an unreal feeling because you are really just believing in yourself." Many of his creations had some kind of animal logo, signed on the stringer by a guy called Alas Purwo. Geoff's favorite red hat, from the national park where G-land is found, had the same name on it. A familiar logo shined through the fiberglass on one board. It was the one from Penguin Publishers; he'd cut it from the paper bags at the bookstore. "They'll probably sue me," he said with a shrug and a laugh.

Paying little attention to the others, he dug until he came to last year's Indo travel board, shaped in his friend's factory in Bali. He pulled the odd, asymmetrical 'weapon' from the stack with the softest touch. He'd ridden it for six months without a leg rope at five of the world's best tube riding waves: God's Left in Sumba, Supersuck, G-land, Padang, and One Palm Point. He said it was the "best board ever" and related the story of a session at Padang-Padang.

"That day there was nobody out because the wind was really howling northeast and it was really choppy, but it was good and big and everyone was saying 'no you can't surf, it's blown out' But me, coming from West Australia it was like, strong wind, no one out – exxxcceeelllant. And so I went out, and got a bunch of waves really quickly and that just caused this crowd to start coming out. So they all came out, and then a water photographer came out as well, and Mikala Jones. Then I got this really good wave, it was about my seventh, and the crowd was getting thicker, and I thought, oouuuugh, I gotta get out of here, quit while you're ahead."

"And then I got this wave, pulled in and got a beautiful barrel. I was in there, real deep, and it was all dark and shady, and right in front of me was the photographer's arm just in front of me and it just disappeared with the camera. I thought – oooowww. That had to be a good photo because I was really deep. It was just a highlight session because I went in after that, and Padang's one of those spots you don't ever want to lose your board at with the cliff right there. But I didn't lose it; I was lucky. That's just how I like to surf, the 'lucky method.' Wear no leg rope and just hope for the best."

The board he'd ridden at Padang was sprayed his favorite yellow. Although it was 7½' long and 2½" thick, it had a strange pear-like shape. The tail looked as if a dog had chewed on it, but it was the final outcome of jungle modifications with a file. The center fin – created from a piece of G-land driftwood he'd glassed "as is" – was angled and offset, "for more grip in the tube." A guy on a bicycle had inspired the design.

"That's that thing, you know, the ball of your foot, the power. I was just talking to a guy, a cyclist, and he's got those shoes with the clip on it, and he's saying, well that's the part of his foot with the power. It's the same as when you are surfing this board." To compliment the center fin were two red "butterknife" side fins placed along the outside rail.

"Yeah, that's the thing," he said. "If you're going left, I believe you don't want to have all the grip on the inside. That's the whole real thing that I've worked out through bodyboarding. When you're bodyboarding and going left, you use your right leg more. Honestly, your left leg basically can trail really lightly but your right leg you stick down on the face and push hard off it into the bottom of the wave, and that's what these are, these outside fins."

The favorite board's final test had come at the end of the season in Indonesia on the small, uninhabited island where Moose had seen Camel. The island is found in a national park where access is difficult and usually only by yacht charter. He doesn't do expensive boat trips. There is no accommodation, just a few hiking tracks patrolled by some of the few remaining Javan rhinos in the world. He got dropped off on the island by a rotting boat carrying coconuts and told them not to worry. There were six surfers at the start, but after a week, it was just Camel and one other guy who was begging to leave.

"About a week into the trip, I fell off," he said, "and that's when I lost the board to the reef. I wasn't using a leg rope for the safety factor. It is so shallow there, I thought that if you were going to wipe out, it would be better not to have a board attached and it made it heaps safer. With a board, it's 100% dangerous, but if you get rid of the board, it's just you and the reef sort of thing. That place, along with a secret reef in Oz that I surf, is the sketchiest wave. All I know is that I paddled for a wave that was about 7ft. I pulled back and noticed my heart was beating very loudly – boom, boom, boom. Since I hadn't felt that since Australia, I knew it was the second scariest spot I'd seen. But it's one of the world's best waves."

They were without help and without a boat when he'd wiped out and lost his favorite board to the reef.

"But you had food, right?" I asked.

"Yeah, at first, then we had to fully go feral and eat leaves; that sort of thing."

He was boardless, but still in his element. He wasn't worried at all about food or the board that had taken him so far. He said he "… just like, let it all go." He had learned that all special boards have a life of glory but eventually just get put away.

This story was first published in *The Surfer's Journal* Issue 12 No.4

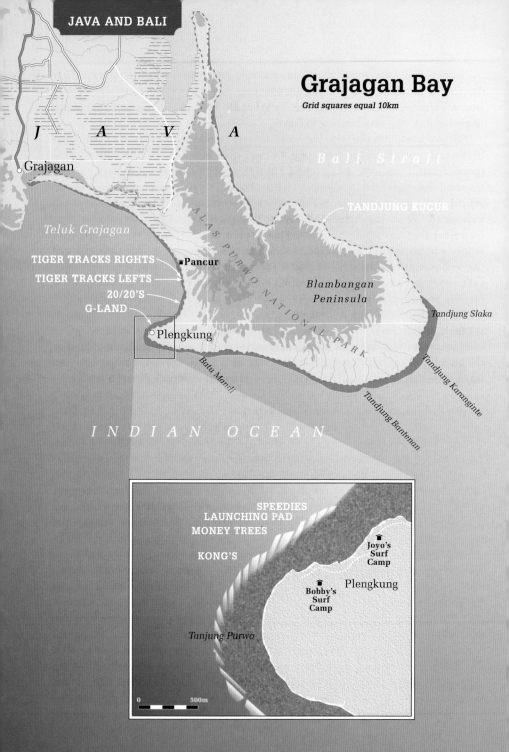

Grajagan Bay

Grid squares equal 10km

J A V A

Grajagan

Bali Strait

TANDJUNG KUCUR

Teluk Grajagan

TIGER TRACKS RIGHTS
TIGER TRACKS LEFTS
20/20'S
G-LAND

Pancur

Blambangan Peninsula

ALAS PURWO NATIONAL PARK

Tandjung Slaka

Plengkung

Batu Mandi

Tandjung Karanginte

Tandjung Bantenan

I N D I A N   O C E A N

SPEEDIES
LAUNCHING PAD
MONEY TREES

KONG'S

Joyo's
Surf
Camp

Bobby's
Surf
Camp

Plengkung

Tanjung Purwo

0   500m

The Edge of Panic

Cracking the code of the coral kilometre at G-Land

GERRY LOPEZ

□

MANY OF THE close encounters with my inner self while surfing have taken place at the surf spots I like and frequent the most. G-Land is one of my very favorite places. Every time I return, I can feel a very definite warm feeling permeating my entire being the moment I set foot ashore. This feeling is hard to describe. It's like a coming-home feeling but I never feel it as intensely when I go back to my real home. This unique feeling seems to say, this is where I should be, this where I belong.

But as familiar and comfortable as G-Land feels when I first get there, there is another feeling that I must deal with every time I paddle out on a big day. It is a feeling of trepidation and great apprehension. Much more than the line-up or the waves when they are big, it is the getting-there part that can be the most difficult. The paddle out at G-Land is a tricky and sometimes treacherous process that requires perfect timing, strong paddling ability and often a bit of luck.

The way G-Land is set up to receive the swell is a miracle in itself. The beach looking out to the surf faces straight west. This is truly a wonderful direction at the end of the day. The spectacular sunsets in Indonesia are some of the best in the world. The easterly flank of Grajagan Bay rolls around to become the southeastern tip of Java. It is ideally situated to catch the southerly swells as they march in. A submarine canyon lying just offshore further assists the waves. This undersea trench is only one of many that abound in the area. Some, like the Lombok Trench and the Java Trench, are among the deepest in the world. These underwater canyons allow the swell to expand its energy in the deep water. When it exits the trench, the energy is compressed as the swell moves into the shallower water near the shoreline. This has the effect of magnifying the power and the size of surf. There are always bigger, stronger and more consistent waves in G-Land compared to Uluwatu and the Bukit on Bali just 60 miles to the east. This is an interesting phenomenon as the West-facing aspects of both spots are the same and only a short distance apart yet the surf at G-Land is always larger. In Southern California, Blacks Beach enjoys an offshore submarine canyon as well. On a swell from the right direction, the waves will be bigger there than anywhere nearby. Not only are the waves at G-Land bigger than on Bali but sometimes certain waves in a set will be quite a bit larger than the average of a particular day.

There was a new swell during the morning of a particularly good day and the boys were stoked. Not that the surf before had been bad, but a new swell is always a cause for rejoicing wherever surfers gather. This new energy, reinforcing and re-intensifying the surf energy already in abundance there, put a giddy feeling into the pit of every surfer's stomach. The present surf camp at G-Land has become very comfortable and accessible. Often surfers without the skills really to match the surf are there to fill the line-up. No longer the hardcore surf camp it was when it began, G-Land is now a regular stopping point on the all-Indo surf tour circuit. There can be over a hundred people out on a crowded day. A good size swell has the effect of tempering the enthusiasm of the less skilled, keeping some of them to watch from the safety of the beach. But for even the most adept, the paddle out is always preceded by a moment of mental preparation for ordeal ahead.

The ordeal is breaching the surf line, just to reach the line-up even before catching the first wave. Due to the lay of the land and the consistency of the surf, not penetrating through the surf line can have disastrous consequences. The long line-up and the strong sweep of the waves wrapping in can pound even the most skilled surfer all the way from Kong's through Moneytrees and finally down onto the Bar and Grill of Speed Reef almost before he can come up for air. The sets move down the line and if the timing is bad, the surfer won't be able to get away from them and will be dragged all the way down the unforgiving reef. To walk on the beach from Kong's past Moneytrees and down to the end of Speedies takes 15 or 20 minutes...it's a long distance. To ride that far on a wave is quick. To get beat the whole distance by pounding waves is even faster. The worst aspect of this experience is the further down inside a person gets swept, the shallower and more dangerous the whole situation becomes. Inside Speed Reef is not only shallow; in addition the reef is scarred by big outcroppings and jagged coral fissures, unlike the relatively flat reef inside Moneytrees and Kong's. On a low tide, inside Speedies can be sheer terror and lots of bloody cuts.

Even with some water on the reef, it's no picnic. The surf actually grows in size and power on that lower end of the reef. Those unfortunate enough to be stuck inside in that area better have their wallets open because they are going to pay in one form or another. To be caught in there after riding a wave is one thing, but to be dragged all the way down there while attempting to paddle out is a grim mistake. After riding a wave, there is always adrenaline in the system and some power to deal with the situation. To be caught under dozens of waves even before getting to the line-up zone is utterly demoralizing. The only hope is to somehow hang on and if lucky, get dragged down to the boat channel before getting ripped apart or hung up on a coral head. If this is a person's fate and he does end up in the channel, terrorized from the ordeal, out of breath, energy and probably everything else, two things will happen. First he will wish he had started from the boat channel in the first place, taking the longer but easier way out.

If the pounding was bad enough, in the future he likely always will paddle out from the channel and be safe rather than sorry. Or he will really study the paddle out and figure out how to do it correctly. Years and years of doing it with a few bad moments tossed in to keep us on our toes have taught us the value of doing it right. Patience is key because waves always come in sets with lulls between them. What not a one of us can count on is how long a lull will last, so it's all about making the move at the right moment. Sometimes it's a sweet paddle-out without any drama. Conversely, 20 feet behind a guy who's having it easy and I might be on the sheer edge of terror, skirting disaster by only inches. If and when there is a safe passage through the waves, we all breathe a sigh of relief. The next step is the tricky task of lining-up, trying to find a good position to start on this long and challenging wave, which appears to have no beginning place. And after that there is the most difficult part, paddling into the first wave of the day.

The very first time Peter McCabe and I went to G-Land was by boat from Bali, long before any surfers were camping onshore. We started out from outside, behind the waves and spent the entire week paddling up and down the surf line looking for something to line-up on. It was a frustrating experience because we never did find a good place to start. It wasn't until we started staying on the beach and watched the waves from the inside that we saw there were several spots where it looked like the wave had a good beginning. One spot was right in front of a small tree on the beach with leaves that were shiny and the same colors as the Indonesian currency. We called it the Moneytree and set up the mess hall there with a bright orange tarp for a roof. We could see the orange tarp from out in the surf so this really helped our positioning until we began to get familiar with the reef and wave and didn't need it anymore. The other spot was further inside; it was a definite peak that we named the Launching Pad because it would launch us right into the run at Speed Reef. There were several tall trees in the jungle that we could use to triangulate on the Launching Pad once we were able to recognize them at a glance. A definitive spot to line-up on is critical in any surf, but at G-Land it was paramount. To take off too far back and have to straighten out often meant a long trip around the horn. The whole set would peel off outside of where we were, helpless to do anything except watch, take the pounding and hang on until it was over, before finally paddling all the way back outside. It was a big bill to pay for only the most meager taste.

In the early days we never surfed at low tide because no one had booties to walk over the dry reef. In fact we timed all our trips to be there for the new and full moon tides only. We would wait until there was enough water to paddle out. Then we would have to come back in before the tide ran out too much. Of course we began to overstay our tide window and eventually discovered a soft, mostly sandy trail in over the reef. Here we could walk slowly without cutting up our feet after paddling in as far as we could on our boards turned upside down. Tom Parrish came with us one time and liked the solitude in the line-up at low tide when the rest of us were lying up on the beach. The second day he came back in completely cut to shreds by the reef. It took us hours to bandage all his wounds. No one went out at low tide again for the next several years until one time, Scott McClelland, a friend of mine from Maui and I were there in the camp by ourselves. He kept watching the waves at low tide. I guess I hardly looked out there until there was enough water to paddle. But the waves, indifferent to the tides, peeled perfectly. I was reading a book, not paying any attention when finally he looked at me in exasperation and said,

"You see how good those waves are, why the hell are we just sitting here?"

I looked up at the still dry reef and said,

"Relax, the tides still too low, just wait for the tide."

"What do you mean relax, the waves in Maui never get this good, I'm going out," says Scott. He put on his slippers, grabbed his board and started walking out over the reef.

"What are you going to do with your slippers?" I yelled after him.

"Stick them in the back of my shorts," he yelled back, already well out on the reef.

"You'll lose them," I said.

"So what," was all I heard and then he was gone.

I couldn't concentrate on my book anymore and got out the binoculars. Scott got to the edge of the reef, waited for a lull and slipped out more quickly than I'd ever seen it done. I watched him get tube ride after tube ride before I couldn't stand it anymore, got my slippers and surfboard and followed out after him. I remember watching him ride a good-sized wave not more than 50' from where I was standing on the edge of the reef. He gave me the sign as he went by, the middle finger extended. The whitewater from his wave dissipated down to a trickle as it got to where I was standing. I jumped off the reef and paddled out without getting my hair wet. It was the easiest paddle out I ever had. We discovered that the waves were breaking in about the same depth of water that they broke at high tide. The lesser amount of water inside made the waves seem thinner, cleaner and more definite – lining up was much easier.

All Scott kept saying was "I told you it was good."

He was right. We both lost our slippers but found there were little cracks in the reef that we could ride up into with the white water. It was high and dry on both sides. As long as we stayed in the crack, we could stay afloat until the whitewater stopped. Then we could climb up on the reef well inside of where the waves were bashing and not get cut. It was a startling discovery that refuted the low tide myth. We were both quite shocked by the discovery. It was a slow walk on bare feet over the dry reef back to the beach but we didn't mind.

DAN MERKELJA-FRAME

G-Land   LAT. -6.655053° LONG. 105.171153°

All arrivals for the G-Land surf camps hit the beach north of the point, allowing expectant newbies their first glimpse of the unfurling barrels from a side-on perspective. Not until you stand on the reef looking front-on does the scale of the wave become apparent. Furthest out to the far left is Kong's, which is often the messiest section of the reef, peaking up in a slightly haphazard way and capable of more shiftiness. West swell will see it slab and barrel while S will wall and shoulder more. It is the call when swell drops below headhigh (very rare) and the extra water depth makes it less sketchy than other sections. Still has enough power to snap boards on the smallest days, it's hard to stay lined-up and it's a long walk or endless paddle.Money Trees is the default setting for most G-Land sessions, attracting the bulk of the campers to what looks like perfect peeling barrels for 2-300m. Depending on the tide and swell direction, the tubes can undulate from cavernous pits to tight, high envelopes and getting caught behind is guaranteed, so time any cutbacks carefully. Getting in early and at the right spot is essential and shoulder

hopping is often punished, so fight the urge to spin and go and keep paddling. It's shallow at low, prompting many to wear helmets and there are a couple of holes in the featureless reef that ease the entry/exit scramble between sets. Money Trees gets better at size and is probably ideal at 12ft faces, but will handle up to triple overhead. Launching Pad is the least defined section because it only really appears on moderate to heavy swells and is rarely in the mood to transport surfers between Money's and Speedies. Wider rogue sets will hit the patch of reef beyond the normal whitewash line and look like tapering into nothing, but as the name suggests, it suddenly jumps up again and starts the pedal-to-the-metal section known as Speed Reef. Undoubtedly the champagne ride of them all, Speedies requires all the skills in spades. Just making the drop is an achievement, while drawing the right line and maintaining velocity are crucial as it doesn't let up or offer an easy escape for 200m of precision peeling. The reef whizzes by in clear menace, and is the sharpest, shallowest patch so surf it on the push from quarter tide.

We further discovered a tide cache of rubber slippers back on the beach. The high tide had swirled in and deposited a pile of lost slippers above the high water line. They must have come all the way from the ferry town of Banyuwangi and the Bali Strait because there were no people anywhere else. This was in the early years before plastic containers joined the flotsam, it was only the lost rubber footwear scrubbed clean by their journey in the sea. Here was a treasure trove of slippers that we could pick from everyday to walk out over the reef and discard as we paddled out to our new low tide spot. Later on we would bring booties that we could use to walk out to the surf. Once we were in deep enough water to paddle, we took them off and shoved them down in our wetsuits or Speedos to surf in our bare feet. Coming in was just the reverse. We surfed up into one of the cracks, which were smooth from centuries of surf washing through them at low tide, put the booties back on and walked in...easy. Over the years and countless sessions, we learned little things that make it all a little easier. The thing about surfing that is so stimulating and will keep us coming back is that this learning process never ends. Every time I go out, if I can stay open and aware, something I didn't know before or maybe I've forgotten will reveal itself to me. Often these lessons can be applied to life in general if we use our imaginations. They can have a profound effect when the light goes on, illuminating how much more these lessons apply to life even though they were learned in the surf. This is the process of Surf Realization and the more we become aware of it, the better our lives will be.

The surf was up at G-Land and we had successfully negotiated the treacherous paddle-out. We would always start out way up the beach to give ourselves plenty of room to be swept down in case we encountered a strong set because of poor timing. Outside we relaxed as the current caused by all the waves sweeping down the long point drifted us into our line-up.

We caught a few waves at Moneytrees. On one particularly good one, I got a ride right through the Launch Pad and all the way to the end of Speedies. I paddled back out to the crowd that was waiting at the Pad and pulled up to see what the sets were like there. Sometimes if Moneytrees is surfable, I assume that Speedies is not consistent or big enough. I have a hard time sitting down there, watching all those great waves break up the line at Moneytrees and nothing much coming down to Speedies. It was no different this day. Beautiful waves were pouring in at Moneytrees, but by the time they got down to the Launching Pad they were less than half as big and pretty much dissipated. Of course, the real wave at the Launch Pad is an entirely different set than what comes in at Moneytrees. This set swings far to the right and it is often missed because everyone is so used to watching up the line to the left. The wide arc of the set that peaks at the Launch Pad is what gives Speed Reef its formidable size and power.

I sat in the line-up talking to Betet, one of the great young surfers from Bali. He had come over with Rizal Tanjung, the first Balinese professional surfer, to visit and surf with us here in the surf camp. Like the rest of the crowd, we too were looking left when all of a sudden there came a big set at the Pad. As soon as we saw it everyone started paddling like mad to escape, but too late. The wave broke in front of us and we both had to duck-dive underneath it. Betet with his small board got down deep but with my bigger board, I couldn't penetrate enough. Underwater I felt the wave pulling me back in. I wasn't in any danger on this wave but I lost ground as the surge got a grip on my legs. I surfaced a good 20' or so inside of Betet but at a glance, I could see the next wave was smaller. I paddled furiously, got a good duck-dive this time and felt myself come cleanly through the other side even though this smaller wave was all frothy from the white water of the wave before. The sight that greeted me on the other side is not one I ever want to see.

Outside I saw what had to be the biggest wave that had come through all day. I saw at a glance that I was caught...cold turkey. I was way too far inside to attempt to paddle-out. I was dead center of the huge, wide Launch Pad peak; I was flanked on either side so there was no escape around it. I quickly looked in towards shore and saw that I was still in pretty deep water but was right on the edge of where it starts to get shallow. Meanwhile the wave moved in, gathering steam as it came. My mind was ticking like a time bomb as I ran through my options. I found no solace in any of them; there was no escape from this imminent pounding. Cold fear washed through me as I realized that I couldn't even abandon ship and dive underwater. It was just deep enough that this much white water was going to tumble me for a long distance down the point, longer than I could hold what little breath would be left in me after the first impact. For a moment I wondered from where this wave could have come. It was half again as big as anything that had come through at Moneytrees and easily twice as big as what had been hitting the Launch Pad. It was like a rogue wave, a one of a kind wonder of nature. As that thought crossed my mind, I also realized that it could be a rogue set with maybe more of the same behind it. I groaned with helplessness. I had no options. I was in the worst possible place anyone could be, and the thought of that made me weak. I was still sitting on my board, I hadn't moved at all since the first sight of this monster. And a monster it was, coming in to chew me to pieces. I knew that even trying to paddle further in was only going to make it worse because it got shallower and the hungry reef got closer. I was frozen in place, not doing anything, just sitting there dead in the water. My mind was on the edge of panic. I was seriously worried about surviving when this mountain of water slammed into me. And the whole time the wave just marched in toward me. I didn't even see anyone else; it was just me and the wave. Closer and closer it came and I still didn't have a plan. What do I do, what do I do was echoing through my mind, but no answer came to me. I watched the wave break, exploding with a detonation that I felt deep down inside me. The white water was a boiling cauldron headed right at me and it had death and destruction growling deep inside it. It was like the maelstrom of the ancient mariners, the whirlpool of death from which no one escapes.

The moment before impact, it seemed without any conscious thought, I turned my board towards shore, facing away from the monster behind. I sat there gripping the rails with hands and legs waiting for the impending collision that I could hear only too well as the wave approached. I took a deep breath and I think I even closed my eyes. Even expecting the crash, I was shocked by the power. It was like being hit from behind by a train traveling at full speed. The blast knocked me and my board up in the air and out ahead of the wave. Of course my surfboard was immediately gone from under me. I tumbled over and over like a scrap of lint. The thought came into my mind that I wasn't getting ground into the bottom. I could tell by the pressure on my ears that I was actually near the surface. Over, under, sideways, down I went until I felt the power easing up a little. I was down underwater so I grabbed my leash and started climbing up. My faithful surfboard was afloat and I pulled myself to the surface using it as a buoy. As I broke through, I quickly sucked in some air and looked behind to see what was next. As I feared, the wave behind was just as big and coming hard. I had time to climb up on my board.

I thought that sitting on the board, facing shore worked so well the first time, I might as well try it again. Again I turned away from the wave and hung on for dear life but I felt a little better than I had with the first wave. I'm pretty sure I closed my eyes too. The impact was as bad as the first time and the scenario was the same. I tumbled through space, climbed up the cord when it started to calm and before I knew it, I was back up above the surface breathing good, clean air. I looked outside as I climbed aboard my surfboard and realized that I was far enough inside that I could safely duck-dive the next wave. I duck-dived under the rest of the set and then I was down near the boat channel where I could easily paddle back out.

Once outside the surf, I stopped and started thinking about what just happened. At first I started giggling and then I was laughing out loud. Other guys paddled by me; they must have thought I was crazy laughing to myself. They didn't have any idea what I had just experienced.

As I thought about it, I understood how near the edge I had been. Total panic was just around the corner, but somehow I didn't go there. When there were no options available in the mind, when I absolutely didn't know what to do...I did what a total beginner would have done. I totally kooked out, but it certainly turned out to be the right thing. It made me think that maybe sometimes we have to go back to the beginning to find the answers to the questions we have at the end. The correct response may be so simple that it can be very easily overlooked. The truth is obviously What's So. Believing that the truth lies within, faith dictates that it will reveal itself when it is most needed. It's there, so keep paddling where it leads...

First published in Surf 1st magazine and subsequently in Gerry Lopez's autobiographical book *Surf is Where You Find It*, Patagonia Books, 2008

The Golden Armour

How I gate-crashed G-Land

DC GREEN

□

N 1992 I travelled with a very tolerant lady across the most populous island in the world: Java. It was a memorable east to west journey – watching the sunrise burst over Borobodur, listening enrapt to the Jogjakarta kraton gamelan and discovering a wide range of surf set-ups, with virtually zero other surfers. The only real negative was the continuing lack of swell, which hastened our journey as surely as a decent swell, while it lasts, can stall all forward momentum.

With 10 days remaining, we arrived in steaming Surabaya. My girlfriend planned to head on to Bali. Should I join her? I was running out of coastline to explore...until I remembered the last Javanese wave before Bali, arguably the most consistent and famous lefthander in Indonesia, if not the galaxy: the mind-boggling Plengkung, more popularly known as...g-land! Located deep inside Blambangan National Park, the only known way to surf the G-land reef machine was to pay out big US dollars to be boated into the exclusive surf camp. My problem was simple: my budget only allowed for being accommodated in local losmen. So I would have to find another way to penetrate the seemingly impregnable jungle...

I kissed my girlfriend goodbye and set off south toward the fishing village of Grajagan. My goal: to charter a fishing boat to Plengkung, some 40 kilometres away. Yet the men at the harbour simply laughed at me. The fishing boats had already departed at dawn, and besides, I needed a national park permit, and these were available only at the regional capital of Banyuwangi, a back-track of several hours. I sighed and turned around...

The pretty ladies at the National Parks office handed me a piece of paper that listed the expensive surf camp rates. I peered around desperately, until I noticed a map of Blambangan on the wall. I pointed at what looked like a village nearby to Plengkung and asked, 'Why can't I stay there instead?'

The head lady answered my question with a question: 'Why don't you want to stay at the surf camp with the other surfers?'

This was the tricky bit. I knew I couldn't admit that a week in the surf camp would exceed my entire trip budget, so instead I bluffed in my bad Indonesian, 'Er...but I don't like western food. I like *nasi campur* and *gado gado*, and staying with Indonesian people...so I can practice my Bahasa Indonesian!'

The ladies all smiled broadly at this answer. In the next half hour they convinced their boss out the back that I would be ideologically safe to stay at the village on the map, Pancur. Yet my problems were far from over. The ladies explained that Pancur was still a considerable 13 kilometres from Plengkung, and wasn't really a village as such. Only one old couple lived there, and they spoke no English. I would have to take in all my own food, and cook it. *Tidak apa apa* (no worries), I reasoned.

While my permit was being processed, I went shopping at the markets with the office ladies, who were equally keen to practice their *Bahasa Ingerris* (English). I slept in the office, having first copied down the big map on the wall. It listed by number where the various park fauna lived – including leopards, panthers, wild pigs and dogs. I was relieved to see that none of the potential man-eating numbers were listed over the jungle track I would have to negotiate each day to reach Plengkung. I only hoped the animals had seen the map too...

Getting to Pancur involved a long, bumpy bemo ride, followed by a warm-up 3km walk, lugging gear and food. My host, Mr Pancur, was a surly old fellow, who rolled gigantic tobacco cigarettes. Mrs Pancur, with her right-angled spine, preferred to chew huge wads of the stuff with her few remaining red-brown teeth. Their wooden hut, shared with chickens, had no electricity or western conveniences, but it would keep out the rain and Javanese tigers.

I was stoked to see the old couple had two ancient pushbikes – and they were prepared to rent them! A bike would make the journey to Plengkung much easier, I thought. One had metal rollers instead of pedals and a seat that would rise up to vertical at the slightest jolt. I elected to take the bike with no brakes, to tune up my G-Land surfing technique.

I quickly realised my mistake. The track to Plengkung is riddled with roots and rocks. It has narrow bamboo bridges, slippery waterfalls and countless suicidal gullies. Steering with one hand (my surfboard under the other arm), I flew down into these gullies, trying desperately to slow down by dragging one thonged foot. Soon my thongs were coated in blood, and my knees and ankles, with bruises. I discovered it's not easy pushing a heavy bike up a vertical gully with one hand. It was also bloody hot. By halfway there, both tyres were flat, the chain was choked with sand and the pedals would no longer engage, all of which at least took my mind off lurking leopards. Not that nature was in short supply. I passed monkeys who shrieked and threw sticks at me, heard several mysterious crashing noises in the jungle and witnessed two small crocodiles scuttle into a creek.

A few hours later I lurched into Plengkung. The surfers at the camp looked at me as if I was an alien visitation. I was sweaty, dirty, bleeding and bearded,

with a mangled pushbike and a seven foot gun. My brain was overdosing on adrenalin, but the surf was small, almost unsurfable. I was disappointed at this, but still buzzing to have completed my historic gatecrash. I sat out on the point and yarned with a surfer I knew from home.

I learnt the surf camp option provides: accommodation in basic huts that overlook the surf; all the food one can scoff; all the beer one can gurgle; plus facilities like ping-pong, TV and a rubber ducky lift to the line-up whenever the surf looks too big to risk jumping off the reef. At least this option keeps the crowds within some sort of limit – mainly because many surfer travellers simply can't afford a G-Land trip.

Low tide G-Land is both a thing of beauty and shop of horrors. Mind the reef on the way in and out and, by the way, don't stay out too late if you're a solo gatecrasher – the tiger-infested jungle can be even worse.

Almost imperceptibly, the waves were building, and I knew I would walk more in the next week than I had ever walked before. I returned next day to see the swell had indeed built. My first session at Indonesia's most famous wave was a delicious entree. Two days later, the swell peaked at nearly three metres, and I travelled faster on a surfboard than I had ever believed possible.

While the camp surfers regularly moseyed off to bloat themselves on pizza and doze in front of an Indiana Jones video, I would lurk out on the point and gobble down my daily packed lunch of fruit, rice and chillies. I had to rush, because I was the camp outsider. To get to the surf and back in daylight meant a minimum of six hours' walking each day, so I had to make the most of every minute at Plengkung, to get in as much surf time as my body would allow. Never before have I spent so much time alone with my thoughts or become so in tune with tides, the movement of the sun and the rhythms of nature. At Pancur, inspired by the great Lopez, I spent many hours stretching and meditating in a small cave. My dreams, ultra-vivid, hinted at strange and wonderful existences that transcended humanity.

A few camp surfers read my metamorphosis differently, flashing me the sort of worried sideways glances one normally reserves for the criminally insane. I was even asked in a hushed voice during a lull, 'Are you...the Jungle Man?' I didn't mind though, especially because I was allowed to claim virtually whichever wave I desired. However, I knew that if I'd been part of a group of gate-crashers, rather than just one person, the other surfers would have felt more resentment than respect. After all, they were being slugged what seemed an almost criminal amount of money to surf exactly the same waves – though admittedly they didn't have to leave the water mid-afternoon and trudge three hours through jungle for the privilege; a task I found increasingly difficult as the waves grew increasingly large. One afternoon I came in well beyond my deadline. I set off at a very brisk trot. Yet I didn't feel worried. I had that totally illogical feeling of invulnerable joy that comes from surf-stoke and exhaustion, as if I'd conquered all my fears of the jungle. After all, I reasoned, big cats are nocturnal beasts. In the daytime, man was king of the jungle!

I emerged from a gully, and there it was. A huge, hairy pig, tusked and ugly. It shrieked at me. I screamed back. It shrieked again and charged, but at an angle, off into the bush. I began to run, somewhat unsettled. The sun plunged lower. It became difficult to discern the track ahead. The jungle was a world of dark shadows. I ran into a tree and slammed backwards. Cursing, I knew I could advance no further this way. My only hope was to detour to the left, to the beach that ran roughly parallel to the track, which I would hopefully be able to follow to the Pancur turn-off. Everything bad that could then happen, did then happen. Pandanus and sharp vines clawed my legs, arms and face. Mosquitoes zoomed in, and I became paranoid about malarial doom, about how loud even my breathing must sound to all the hungry cats I feared were now listening to and laughing at the king of self-delusion.

As I drew closer to the beach, I heard a roaring. It grew louder and louder. I emerged onto sand, into a full-bore torrential downpour, and was saturated in seconds. Everything was black, apart from the dull luminescence of the sand (which also happened to be extremely soft and difficult to walk through). I followed this dull arc of sand, muscles twitching and burning, until the dull arc of sand ran out.

I'd come to a headland. The rock was jagged and scarred with crevasses. The intensity of the sheeting rain meant everything ahead was black, so I bound my T-shirt around my head to protect my face and eyes and set off like a B-grade movie mummy, my hands groping ahead. I had no choice but to negotiate every step, and climb, and wade, inch by laborious inch. In the daytime, this may have been an easy passage, but not now. I knew if I fell, I would knock myself out, and drown. Every step meant groping my leg ahead. If I could feel nothing, I would toss a stone, and listen. Sometimes the stone fell so far, I heard no sound at all, so I knew I was on a cliff edge, compelled to backtrack. Other times, there was nothing but sheer rock ahead of me, unclimbable. Backtrack. I became so exhausted I lay down beneath an overhang and began to cry. The surf camp option now seemed like such excellent value for money. Oh, for a single pizza slice!

One thought only goaded me back to my feet – if I slept here, I would be a completely vulnerable snack. So I forged on, and eventually reached the apex of the headland. In the distance, I could just discern a second arc of beach. I whooped with joy, though it took me hours to reach that beautiful sand.

Now I only had to worry about finding the Pancur turn-off. The single sign that marked this turn-off was a small waterfall. So I had to follow every tiny creek from the ocean to the jungle wall to listen, and hope – and there were many new waterfalls from the ceaseless rain. At around 3 am, I found the track, I hoped. The steep walkway was so sleek, I had to bore my fingers into the clay to crawl upwards. Atop the waterfall, I broke into a deranged jog – and ran right into the old couple's hut! I have never been so happy to see anyone as old Mr Pancur, still grumpy about his bike, when he opened the door of his hut. I hugged him with a mad intensity until he pushed me back and cackled at how drenched and pathetic I looked. Mrs Pancur hobbled over to fuss over my wounds and serve me up a mug of grey well-water and a bowl of cold rice and mystery lumps in chili sauce: the best meal I have ever devoured.

'You guys don't need Indiana Jones,' I laughed between mouthfuls, and was asleep on the floorboards five minutes later (and for most of the next day). Be it ever so humble, there's no place like hut.

No experience had left me feeling so exhausted on all levels. Yet in the aftermath, I attained levels of strength I did not believe possible – physically, mentally and spiritually. I returned to Australia with a self-confidence and inner calm that amazed the people who knew me. I could suddenly solve the most intractable of problems, seemingly with but a wave of my hand, as if my G-land experience had forged an impenetrable armour over my entire body, the colour of a Plengkung sunset. Anything was possible.

My mistake was to assume I would remain forever at this plateau. Work commitments slowly ground me down. I failed to adequately polish and maintain my armour. Gradually, over a period of weeks and months, my spiritual powers waned. I could feel my shining armour dropping from me, piece by piece. One frustrating morning, the final plate dropped from my body and clunked beneath my desk before disappearing. I was a naked fool, again.

Three years later, the opportunity arose for me to cover the first Quiksilver Pro at G-land, to return to the jungle in relatively decadent luxury at the surf camp, which had once shunned me. I leapt at the chance to ride that remarkable wave once more, and to perhaps rediscover even the chest-plate of my golden armour...

First published in *Australia's Surfing Life* magazine, December, 1992

Red Island

The Grajagan gold rush

BY LEO MAXAM

□

W E'RE GOING TO a funeral. Yesterday we were blissfully pulling into perfect 6ft Money Trees. Today we are walking through a steamy Javanese village wearing somber faces. We were invited here by our new friend, Adi, our favorite staff member at the G-Land camp we've been staying in. Gregarious and talkative, Adi has been our guide for the past week, schooling us on the ping-pong table and showing us how to keep our rooms monkey-proof. Over late-night beers he's regaled us with tales of jungle cats, Kelly Slater arriving at G-Land in a helicopter and the tsunami that hit this coast and his nearby village back in 1994.

Today Adi is unusually quiet. He's come home from G-Land for his uncle's funeral, and he's brought us – five surfers on a pleasure trip from Bali – with him. We're embarrassed, strangers showing up to such an intimate family gathering. But Adi's family greets us warmly. Men shake our hands and women bring us food. They seat us at the front of the ceremony. Adi's uncle died in a mining accident not far from this village. He was working in a tunnel below the earth when something went wrong and there was a cave-in. That's all Adi tells us. We don't ask for more.

The next day Adi takes us to the beach. "I want to show you where I started surfing," he says. "We're going to Pulau Merah." Adi told us about Pulau Merah countless times back in G-Land. It's just an hour's drive from his village, he said, insisting that we bring our boards with the promise of a fun rivermouth A-frame and no other surfers around for miles. "We call this place the Magic Wave," Adi says as we walk through a shady grove of jungle trees fronting the brilliant crashing surf. "There is always something to ride here, 365 days a year."

Unlike its neighbor at G-Land, the wave at Pulau Merah isn't world-class, but it's still damn fun. We go to town on the peaky sandbars, flying and flaring without an audience. It's a welcome break from the crowds and surf schools back in Bali. In fact, we only encounter one other surfer all afternoon, an amiable twenty-something local named Yogi. He's riding a tattered yellow twin fin and having a blast. He says he's been surfing every day since he was fired from his job with the mining company.

"That mountain there is one of the largest gold finds in the world today," says Yogi, motioning to the massive rock we've been surfing in front of all afternoon. He points to the next peak west. "They reckon that mountain over there has even more."

We're standing on the beach with our boards, watching the sun sink behind the misty islands that guard the bay at Pulau Merah. Yogi is telling us how he used to work as a drilling operator for an international mining exploration company here in Pulau Merah, until he was fired last month along with some 200 other employees. He explains that Pulau Merah, which means "Red Island" in English, is named after the towering rock in front of us. It looks like it dropped from the sky and landed in front of this picturesque white-sand beach. The island is covered in thick vegetation, but we can see gaps revealing the deep crimson rock below, the telltale sign of oxidized copper and gold. Yogi begins telling us about the Indonesian gold rush happening right here in Pulau Merah, a few bays west of G-Land.

"We may be in the middle of nowhere," he says, "but there are mountains of gold here."

Adi has to leave Pulau Merah early to take care of some business. Our plan is to meet him back in G-Land for the impending swell in one week. We say goodbye next to the beach road, as hard-hatted mining company employees zip by on shiny new motorbikes on their way to work.

"Nice bike," says Adi, then he buzzes off on his aging Yamaha.

We're staying at a simple surfer homestay recently built by an Aussie expat and his local partner in front of the beach at Pulau Merah. Every morning at 0700 the mining company's helicopter roars to life next door. We eat breakfast and watch the chopper run supplies and equipment to the base camp up on the mountain where the drilling takes place. The Australian company doing exploratory drilling into the mountain is investing millions of dollars a year to explore and map out the earth below Pulau Merah. Their research shows gold and copper deposits worth hundreds of millions. So far the company's operations have been limited to exploratory drilling, says Yogi, but if they get a permit to start a full-scale production mine, this quiet corner of paradise could see some drastic changes.

The company's drilling operations are located between two of the largest national parks in Java – Meru Betiri National Park, home to one of the most important sea turtle breeding sites in Indonesia, and Alas Purwo National Park, where G-Land is located. Many locals we talk to, including our hosts at Red Island Surf Camp, say that the foreign company has no business mining in a national park.

"One thing that caught us by surprise is how an Australian company got permission to mine in a national park, even if it's just exploratory drilling," says Mick McComas, part owner of our surfer homestay. "How did they get that exploratory permit in a protected forest? That's my main question."

One day Yogi takes us into an illegal mining camp adjacent to the company's drilling operation on the mountain. The mines can't be reached by car. A snaking motorbike trail into the protected forest is the only way to get there. We don't realize how rough it is until we're halfway there. It's essentially a dirtbike track, filled with logs and patches of mud. When we finally arrive we are met by a bustling tent city in the middle of the forest, everyone here searching for gold in the national park.

About three years ago, local prospectors started showing up at Pulau Merah with hand-made tools and gold pans looking to strike it rich. Today there are over 2,000 people from all over Indonesia working in the illegal mine, Yogi tells us. They work in teams of 10 to 15 people digging tunnels into the ground, some as deep as 100 metres. The tunnels snake through the earth and their walls are held together precariously with sticks and scrap lumber. The miners often stay down there working overnight. It's a risky living, but one with a higher payoff than working in the rice fields all day under a hot sun for a few bucks a day. It was a risk Adi's uncle decided to take, and many of the illegal miners we meet say they knew him. One wiry man, chain-smoking cigarettes, says Adi's uncle would often dig under the earth while at the same time pumping out groundwater from the tunnel with a foot-powered pump.

"He wasn't scared of staying down there for days at a time," he says.

Before gold was discovered in Pulau Merah, says Yogi, most of the locals worked as rice farmers or fishermen. Now, most of those workers have moved into mining, either in the illegal mine fields, or if they have a connection, for the mining company.

"Maybe mining isn't the best thing for Pulau Merah in the long run," says Yogi, "but people here have no option."

Back at our surfer homestay, Ari Zainal, a Banyuwangi local and McComas' partner at the surf camp, says that many people have died in the local mines from cave-ins and exposure to dangerous chemicals used to separate precious minerals from the rock. Ari believes that developing eco-tourism in Pulau Merah will serve the community better than mining in the long run.

"I'm trying to educate people in Pulau Merah about the benefits of tourism," he tells us. "We have all the green gold we need right here: the oceans, the mountains. If we can protect our green gold, then we can survive in the long term – not only for us, but for our children and grandchildren. If they mine here, eventually all the gold will be removed and we will have destroyed the mountains and the sea. Then what will we do?"

As we take our last look at Pulau Merah's flawless crescent bay and *Super Mario World* islands just offshore, it's hard not to agree with Ari. But a bombing swell is scheduled to hit and it's time to leave. We've decided to make the trek out to G-Land to catch the swell, and to see Adi one last time before we return to Bali. When we arrive, the staff at the G-Land camps seem more concerned about the latest swell forecast than the mining development at Pulau Merah.

Michael, a surf guide we meet at Bobby's Camp, says that even if the talk of a large-scale open-pit mine and a shipping port at Pulau Merah becomes a reality, it probably wouldn't have a noticeable impact this deep in the jungle.

"Straight line, it's about 45 kilometers from Red Island to G-Land," he says. "If you were to follow the coastline, you'd cover 250kms. If the proposed mine was on the other side of the bay at Grajagan, maybe it would be more of a concern, but it's three bays over from here. It's far enough away. If they're dumping toxic mercury, the rivermouth at Pulau Merah where people surf and the fishing village in the corner of that bay are going to feel the immediate impact."

Others, like Bobo, the manager at Joyo's Surf Camp who's been working there year-round since 1998, aren't so confident.

"We don't see anything from the mine here," he tells us, "but I have heard some rumors about a port being built if they open a big mine. Maybe that will bring pollution in the water to G-Land from the currents. Maybe, maybe not. I hope not."

Adi, meanwhile, is nowhere to be found at our camp. We want to tell him about our visit to the local mining camps, and the good things the people there had to say about his uncle. We want to thank him for letting us in on the beautiful secret of Pulau Merah. We look for Adi at his usual hangouts – cleaning the dining room, holding court at the ping-pong table – but we can't find him anywhere. When we ask the manager, he tells us that Adi quit a few days ago. The last anyone heard he was heading to the mining fields near Pulau Merah hoping to strike it rich.

This article was first published in *Surfing Life Magazine*, Issue 290, October, 2012

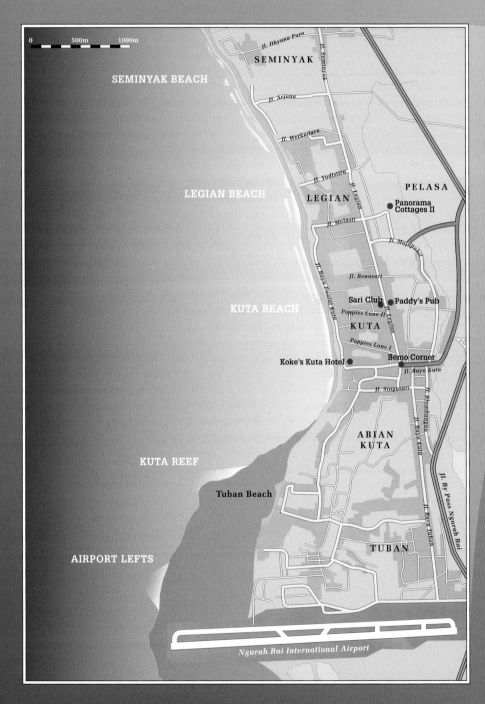

SEMINYAK BEACH

SEMINYAK

Jl. Dhyana Pura

Jl. Seminyak

0 500m 1000m

Jl. Arjuna

Jl. Werkudara

LEGIAN BEACH

Jl. Yudistira

LEGIAN

PELASA

Jl. Legian

Panorama
Cottages II

Jl. Melasti

Jl. Majapahit

Jl. Benasari

KUTA BEACH

Jl. Raya Pantai Kuta

Sari Club Paddy's Pub

Poppies Lane II

KUTA

Jl. Legian

Poppies Lane I

Koke's Kuta Hotel Bemo Corner

Jl. Raya Kuta

Jl. Singasari

ABIAN
KUTA

Jl. Blambangan

Jl. Raya Kuta

KUTA REEF

Tuban Beach

Jl. By Pass Ngurah Rai

Jl. Raya Tuban

TUBAN

AIRPORT LEFTS

Ngurah Rai International Airport

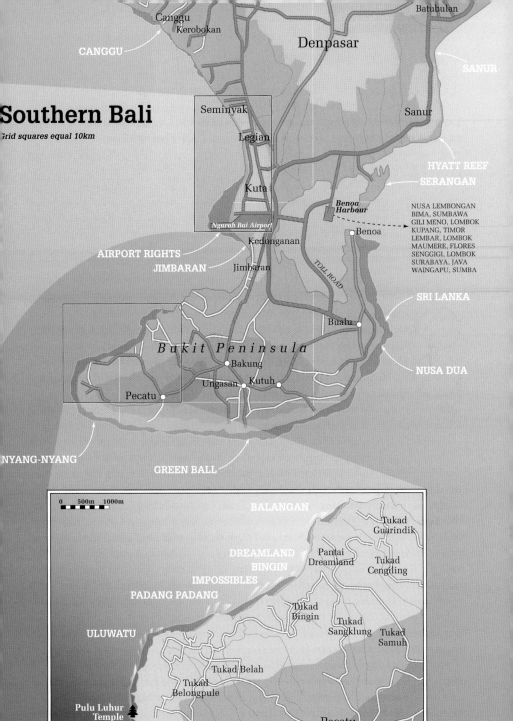

Bali's First Surfer

Long before *Morning of the Earth* the real Genesis moment happened on Kuta Beach in the 1930s

RICHARD E LEWIS

□

SOMETIME IN 1936, an American named Bob Koke took a break from building his hotel on the deserted shore of Kuta and strolled down to the breakers for a surf on his home-made Honolulu style surfboard. He'd learned to surf when he was in Hawaii, a sport he took with him to Bali, and that afternoon, he was the only surfer in the water for thousands of miles.

He soon had other boards, and his guests and his staff frolicked in the waves. Village kids also snuck off on the boards now and again.

On the Dutch maps of the time, the impoverished fishing village was spelled "Koeta" but according to Louise Garret, who travelled with Bob to Bali and would later marry him, most Western tourists pronounced the name like a hog call, "Ko-ee-ta", so when they put up the sign for their hotel, the sign read "Kuta".

Louise, in her fascinating memoir *Our Hotel in Bali* called Kuta the most beautiful beach in the world. Their hotel was located on the beachfront where the Hard Rock Hotel is now. But it wasn't the first hotel. Apparently, Bob and Louise initially went in a joint venture with another American, a Scottish-born woman named Muriel Walker, who'd taken the Balinese name of K'tut Tantri. This first establishment was across the dirt road, in what would later be the Natour Beach Hotel. But soon there arose disputes – one of the first of many, many expat squabbles to come – and by many accounts of expats and Balinese who knew her, K'tut Tantri was an unpleasant stump of a woman. So the Kokes leased property across the road, and not a mention of K'tut Tantri's establishment is to be found in Louise Koke's book.

In a passage reminiscent somewhat of today's surf schools, Louise provides an account of one guest, who was no doubt Bali's first Pommie surfer:

"Down from the hotel came Lady Hartelby, in a severe black bathing suit, her stern English features lit with determination. My heart sank. Only a few days before she would have drowned in a deep and turbulent spot had not Bob been there to grab her. She could not swim, she was nearing seventy, and now she wanted to go surfing. I tried to dissuade her, but the undaunted spirit of the British empire won.

I demonstrated how she must hold the board in front of her, how to wait and plunge as a wave approached, how she must fling herself flat and then crawl up the board as the current gripped it. Over and over I pushed Lady Hartelby off, until she was carried all the way to shore, more than enough for the first day.

But not enough for Lady Hartelby. Though she was worn out, she struggled back for more, falling under the impact of each wave. I picked her out of the foam, holding her with one hand and her board with the other. The next wave was a beauty. When I pushed her off she disappeared in the spray. A second wave was catching up to her, and I knew that she would not be able to keep her board's nose up. It would dive to the bottom.

My heart racing, I hurried after her. Her empty board was bouncing around but she was nowhere. Then, yards away, I saw her gray head, cap gone and hair streaming over her eyes.

She never complained about the ugly green and purple bruises along her thighs where the board had hit her... 'I don't mind,' she said [to a friend]. 'I had one jolly good ride. It was worth it. My only regret is I won't have time to try it again. How did you catch on so quickly? You're really topping'."

At the start of World War II, the Kokes had to leave Bali as the Japanese began their Asian invasions. Bob returned after the war, but the hotel was gone, nothing left but weed and daffodils. The next time an expatriate took up residence in Kuta was in the '50s, when Dr. Spenser Reed, an English doctor working with Balinese lepers, built a family bungalow on the former Koke hotel property. My family would visit, and we kids would swim and bodysurf, but after Bob Koke, there wouldn't be a board surfer surfing Bali's waves for another thirty years.

This story first appeared on Richard E Lewis' blog www.balisurfstories.wordpress.com

The First
Time to Bali

Sweet memories from when the Pipe Master found himself in the biggest candy store on Earth

BY GERRY LOPEZ

□

I GET A LOT of credit for being a pioneer of the surf in Indonesia. I really don't deserve it. If not for a good friend of mine, I would not have had the good fortune to arrive there as early as I did. Jack McCoy and I had grown up surfing together during the early 1960s on Oahu's eastern coast near Aina Haina, Niu Valley and Kuliouou. We travelled to Australia together for the 1971 World Surfing Championships as members of the Hawaii State surf team. We loved Australia. The place was spacious and inviting. The people were friendly and imbued with that particular essence of rugged individualism for which they've become justly famous. The surf exceeded our expectations. When it came time to leave, Jack calmly announced that he wasn't coming. He decided to stay "Down Under."

Well, I supposed, why not? It was a great place. We left and he stayed. Jack and I kept in touch. I began doing some business with my surfboard company in Australia, and we enjoyed catching up during those visits. Several years later, when professional surfing contests began to happen, Hawaii and Australia were the two main venues. Australia became a regular stop on the surf circuit and a very agreeable one at that. In Australia, surfers were regarded as legitimate professional athletes. That was a big step up for us. At home surfers were marginalized, regarded as outcasts who disdained the core values of the larger society and lacked any form of work ethic.

Jack perked my interest in going to Bali. He deserves most of the credit as one of the premier Indonesian surf pioneers. Jeff Hakman and I were staying with Jack down in Torquay for the annual Bells Beach Easter Surf Classic. The little beach town of Torquay is a cold, gloomy part of Victoria during Easter, but sometimes the surf can be pretty good. Jack had a great health food restaurant he owned with a couple of friends. On the wall there was a black and white photograph that intrigued me from the moment I first saw it. It was just a small 4 by 5 print of a water shot Jack had taken. Among his many talents, Jack is a first class surf photographer and a formidable water cameraman. The picture was of Wayne Lynch up high in the lip of a sweet looking left. In response to my eager questions, Jack revealed that the wave was indeed even better than the photo could show. It was at a place called Uluwatu on the exotic island of Bali. As a child I had a thing for Bali after seeing the movie South Pacific, where Bloody Mary sang a haunting song about a mysterious place called Bali Hai. I barely knew about the island, but as soon as Jack said Bali I was certain I was going.

Jack and I went to work on getting Hakman excited about it. Eventually we got him to agree that after the next contest, the Coca-Cola Surfabout in Sydney, we would all go check it out. Jeff was not wholeheartedly enthusiastic about the place because when Jack related the story behind the photograph, there were some reasons for concern.

The year before, Jack, Wayne and Nat Young went up there on the first Bali trip for all of them. The surf they found was great, but there were too many late nights, too much sunburn, a few hairy motorcycle crashes, and Wayne came down with malaria upon their return to Australia. Neither Wayne nor Nat wanted to go back again. Jack, however, was a Hawaii boy born and raised. He'd had no trouble acclimatising to the steamy equatorial weather. The surf there had something that he hadn't seen anywhere else. Jack broke out the Alby Falzon film *Morning of the Earth*, which had a section of Steve Cooney and Ted Spencer riding the long, winding left at Uluwatu. The waves looked terrific. Finally Jeff said OK.

The flight from Sydney to Denpasar is a relatively short one. With the long 12-hour haul from Honolulu to Australia still fresh in our minds, the five-hour Bali flight was a breeze. With Jack as our amiable and well-seasoned guide, we were headed toward great waves in a warm place where surfing was still new. We flew into our final approach to the island winging in from the south. Out the side windows we could see long lines of surf wrapping down a rocky headland. Even from that altitude the waves looked good. Later we learned that this headland was called the Bukit. The west side of it where we would find Uluwatu was all lefts. The other side had lots of rights, but the prevailing southeasterly winds blew onshore. That same wind was straight offshore on the Uluwatu side. Those wind-combed, beautifully peeling waves beckoned to us right from the start, while we were still flying in on the airplane. After landing on a runway – built directly on the reef and protruding out into the surf – we taxied to the small terminal. When the crew opened the door, a blast of hot, humid air hit us like a breaking wave. We filed out as if we were passing through the portal to a dream. Beyond the airport, everywhere we looked were coconut trees, thousands of tall, beautifully shaped trunks capped with fronds that swayed gently in the tropic breeze.

Bali in 1974 had a sleepy village atmosphere. Everyone and everything moved at a languid pace. The tourist trade, consisting mainly of European travellers, had been directed to the east side of the island, near Sanur. Two main hotels, the Bali Beach and the Bali Hyatt, handled most of the island's guests. There were excellent reefs in front of both hotels with fast, peeling rights, but they were always onshore by late morning.

We were headed for the side of the island where the winds blew straight offshore. It was not far from the airport. Our destination was Kuta Beach, where small *losmens* or bungalows were intended for tourists who wanted to rough it a little. Compared to the international hotels of Sanur, the Kuta Beach accommodations were a bit primitive. Jack had stayed at a place owned by a Mr. Kodja, who greeted him upon our arrival like a long lost relative. The unexpected friendliness of the Balinese people was completely genuine. After five minutes, we were treated as though all of us were family. Kodja's *losmens* were nestled in a coconut grove a short walk from the beach. It was an idyllic spot, cool in the shade, quiet and peaceful.

I was stoked. We dropped our bags inside and headed to the beach for a look at the ocean. Our first sight was a wave crashing in the shorebreak. It was a perfect wave, swept clean by offshore winds. Following behind it was a seemingly endless procession of more just like it. The water was a clear blue-green and was beckoning us to jump right in. Jack and I looked at each other, peeled off our shirts and raced down to the water's edge. We were like two kids loose in a candy store. We spent the next few minutes bodysurfing the thumping shorepound, pulling into spinning barrels and squealing in complete delight.

"I told you, didn't I?" Jack gloated.

"And I believed you too, didn't I?" I replied.

We slipped into another bodysurf where I slid up on Jack's back and rode the big man like a bodyboard. Giggling we popped up together from the close-out.

"Come on, let's get out, I've got to show you something better," Jack announced as we waded in. From higher up the beach he pointed out a wave breaking on an outer reef to our left.

"See that? That's a perfect left just like Ala Moana. I say we get our boards and paddle out, what do you think?"

The candy store was getting bigger all the time. We got our surfboards and walked about a half mile to where the crescent-shaped beach curved out toward the outer reefbreaks. There were a couple of hotels along the way, built just back from the beach; one called the Kartika Plaza looked like the biggest hotel in the area. Another smaller one that seemed to be about 10 bungalows built around a courtyard was the Sunset Beach hotel. This one was right in front of the end break on the outer reef. This outer reef ran for about a half mile before it intersected the airport's reef runway. It was a long paddle out to the surf, but with nothing better to do and all day to do it, we jumped right in. As we got closer to the waves, they got bigger and better, and we paddled harder. No one was out and Jack informed us that this break was called Kuta Reef. It was indeed very much like our home break of Ala Moana; a long, peeling left with a big, hollow bowl about midway, then another whole inside section that tapered down and finally ran out of gas into the deep water channel.

It was heavenly and Jack kept saying, "I told you guys. Didn't I tell you?"

He did and he was right. I was never so stoked to be anywhere in my life, and it was only the first afternoon. Our tickets were booked for a month's stay, but Jack had assured us that we could extend them if we wanted. The next day, Jack declared we would look for the real waves out toward the point we had flown over on our approach to the airport. Kuta Reef was just an appetizer. Uluwatu was the main spot, and the waves there were quite a bit bigger. The candy store seemed to be turning into a shopping mall and I couldn't wipe the grin off my face.

Uluwatu Unveiled

The first time to Uluwatu began with aspirations of a well-planned, precisely-executed Special Forces assault on the surf. It quickly deteriorated into a fool's mission right from the start. It was our second day in Bali and we had seen few other tourists where we stayed in the sleepy village of Kuta Beach. There were a couple of hippie backpacker types, some older Australian couples but no other surfers. Jack McCoy, who was a veteran of another trip here a year earlier, knew he could hire transport for us down on Bemo Corner.

He explained as I followed him on the dirt road fronting our losman accommodations that a *bemo* was a little Datsun or Toyota pick-up truck with a canopy built over the bed and bench seats. Private cars were scarce. The occasional taxi was a late 1950s or early 1960s Chevy, painstakingly maintained but most likely still running on the original factory parts. Engines wheezing, rods knocking, mufflers shot, shocks long worn away. The American vehicles were lovingly cared for and polished at every idle moment to a high gloss, but were much too big and overweight for the narrow, pot-holed, mostly dirt tracks and lanes.

Denpasar and the more built-up Sanur tourist areas might have been different, but in Kuta Beach time seemed to stand still. The few private vehicles we noticed were motorbikes of miniscule engine displacement, but also kept immaculately clean even after years and many miles of use. The consummate family ride featured father, sporting an antique motorcycle helmet offering little or no protection, doing the driving. Mother in traditional sarong, wearing a construction hard hat offering much less protection, sat side-saddle behind, with the youngster or sometimes two squeezed in between. It made quite a picture but the lack of traffic and the sedate pace of....well, everything, kept their world safe.

Bemo Corner was a busy place. Three *bemos*, their drivers and assistants plus a half dozen bystanders made for a huge crowd. Jack, towering over everyone by a foot or two, spread them apart by his immense presence and high volume talk show host voice.

"I want to hire *bemo* all day," he boomed.

His dad, Big Jack McCoy was a much-listened-to radio personality in Hawaii and young Jack had inherited 'The Voice'. Two of the drivers immediately found they were busy, but the third, with the oldest, most beat-up *bemo* perked up with interest. Jack and he put their heads together and exchanged a rapid fire dialogue with much sign language which I couldn't follow but soon realized was a spirited negotiation. Jack came back to me, all smiles and shaka signs.

"Yeah man, we got him to take us out to Ulu and wait for us all day for 4,000 rupes. He's going to get gas and will come by our place in half an hour." Jack informed me. At 400 rupiah to the U.S. dollar and 600 to the Aussie dollar, I guessed 10 bucks for a car all day was a pretty good deal. We went back to wake up Hakman, who was a late sleeper by nature, to tell him the good news and get our gear together. We loaded our surfboards, some food, water and ourselves into the back of our ride and off we went. It was early enough that most of the shops were still closed and the roads empty. The exhaust fumes blew directly into the back where we sat, but we were too stoked to care. We passed the turn-off to the airport and were into new territory. At one point, shifting down into low gear, our little truck strained up a fairly steep hill. Looking out the back, a veritable sea of coconut trees stretched as far as we could see. On the left we had a brief view of a beautiful bay of jade-green water, with the airport runway on the far side and a wave breaking off the end of it. Jack informed us it was Jimbaran Bay and the high ground we were now on was the southern tip of Bali called the Bukit. At the end was an ancient temple inhabited by monkeys. There we would find the surf of Uluwatu. We had surfboards, we had food and water, we had plenty of stoke, and the waves were stacked to a horizon yet unseen.

We rolled through several little villages where everyone smiled and waved. We smiled and waved back. We saw a couple of other *bemos* headed the other way, their backs crammed with people. A few times we slowed down or stopped to let a man, or sometimes a very young boy, herd beautiful looking cows across the road using a long stick. The cows were golden-brown and white, and looked more like beefy deer than bovines. No one seemed to be in a hurry except us.

Back then, there weren't many surfers around, and there were no signs or indications where we would find Uluwatu. We drove to the end of the road and walked out to the deserted temple perched on the sharp point. It was a sheer drop to the water below, maybe 800 to a 1,000 feet straight down. The temple must have been hundreds of years old and was deserted except for the occasional monkey flitting through the shrubbery. The surf looked great but disappeared out of sight around the point. Jack said he wanted to show us this place first, the southern-most tip of Bali, but that we needed to backtrack down the road to get to the surf spot of Uluwatu. An occasional track led off into the shrubs but they all looked the same. Jack had been here a year before but couldn't remember which was the right track. Our driver and his assistant were no help, as neither had any idea what we were looking for nor was there anyone around to ask.

Finally we came to a track leading off the road that looked good to Jack. Our driver wanted to know about when we would be back and we guessed at about four to five hours. Except for us, the chirping of the birds and bugs, there wasn't anything else. We looked at Jack, shrugged our shoulders, grabbed our gear and started down the track. The terrain was rugged limestone full of hills and gullies and the track was steep, crooked and rough. It was a single track bordered with a thorny cactus-like plant that grew like a vine. We just followed where the track led. Up and down it went, back and forth, never in a straight line for very long if ever. The thick walls of thorns didn't allow much view but the track seemed to be going somewhere. We came to an intersection and debated which turn to take. Figuring the main road we came in on was more or less parallel to the coastline, we decided we needed to move at right angles to that. But the trail had twisted so much before the intersection it was hard to tell which way that was. We chose one and moved off. Soon we came to another trail crossing; again neither way seemed headed towards the ocean. We took another guess and continued on. Before long it became apparent that we were headed back towards the road so we backtracked to the intersection and took the other way. After following this track for a while, it didn't seem to be going where we wanted either. Jeff climbed a nearby tree to get his bearings. It was a small tree, but I climbed up behind him. From this elevated view we could see the ocean in the distance and clambered back down with enthusiasm. Suddenly Jeff let out a screech, lifted up his shirt, searched himself and plucked off a tiny, black ant. Then one bit me rather painfully, I peeled off my tee shirt and Jack jumped in to help us brush the ants off. Jeff held one of the tiny creatures up between his fingers, exclaiming, "How can such a small ant have such a large bite?"

This was our introduction to the insect life of Indonesia, a study that would fascinate us, over the next 25 years of discovering and marveling at the many strange types.

Knowing which way the ocean was didn't seem to be much help as the trail wouldn't head that direction. I had the idea that we should breach the thorny trail boundary and cross-country it. This met with the approval of both Jack and Jeff, since we sure weren't getting any closer the way we were going. We walked along until we found a light place in the thorns, moved some aside and slipped through. The other side was a huge, open space like a pasture except without much grass. It was an empty field, so the going was easy and we happily headed the way we wanted to go. This didn't last long as we soon came to the end of the open area and met with another thorn wall. Finding an opening to get through was more difficult, but after breaking our way past the thorns, we were on another track headed somewhere, but not towards the ocean. We had been walking for over an hour and a half, were hot, sweaty, ant-bitten and out of patience. Going back wasn't an option either as we had to admit we were lost. Just when it seemed like we might start going for each other's throats, we heard someone coming. Around the corner came three surfers who looked like they knew where they were going. Introductions made, we found ourselves with three Maui boys, brothers Mike and Bill Boyum and Fred Haywood. It was a chance beginning to a life-long friendship and many shared adventures.

Finally with the new leadership we arrived at the cliff overlooking the waves. It was as magnificent a sight as any surfer could behold. Perfect lines, swept by clean offshore winds, rolled in, peaked up and peeled off, occasionally hollowing out, spitting spray and continuing to peel off further. Jeff, Jack and I blinked our eyes, blinked again, looked back and realized we weren't seeing things. This was real and except for Mike, Bill and Fred, there wasn't another soul around. We had just walked up to the gateway of Paradise. We followed the Maui boys down a makeshift ladder into a sea-cave. In contrast to the searing temperature up above, it was refreshingly cool. The sand was coarse and clean. Mike had a Balinese boy who worked for him, carrying an Igloo cooler jug. He brought it down the ladder and handed it over to Mike who beckoned us over to take a swig.

"Fresh pressed cane juice with lime," he explained.

It was ice cold and delicious. There were some white things floating in the juice that he said were mangosteen. They were even tastier. We left our shoes and gear with his boy whose name was Ketut, followed Mike's lead and paddled out of the

cave entrance. When we burst out into the sunlight, a sight right out of the best wet dream greeted us. As great as the waves looked from up above, they were even better up close. The surf was awesome. Punching through the inside whitewater, we timed our paddle out and slipped through the surf line. Outside we could see a wedging peak that looked like a nice beginning to a long, fast peeling wall. Bubbling with barely contained excitement, I stroked out towards the peak, saw one swinging wide, paddled to intersect it and dropped in. It was a steep take-off, but the wave face was so clean and beautifully textured by the light offshore winds that I could have made it with my eyes closed. I stalled my turn, timing it to slip under the pitching lip, and tucked into my first tube at Uluwatu. A feeling of complete satisfaction washed over me as the wave curled around me. A smile spread across my face and I let out an unrestrained hoot. I knew this was some kind of surf heaven – and I was only on the first part of my first wave here. We surfed hard for the next several hours. The sets were consistent with more than plenty waves for everyone. It was a steady 5 to 6 feet with an 8-foot set steaming in on a regular basis every third or fourth set. The peak shifted around but bowled nicely, allowing a perfect backdoor set-up right off the take-off then it was a race down the line as far as we wanted to paddle back out. Eventually the tide began to go out and the waves went into a transition mode, still good, but not as defined at the peak take-off. The Maui boys suggested we go into the beach and rest a little, let the tide go out and come back out later. Ketut had brought our gear around to the front beach where there were some little caves at the base of the tall cliff offering cool shade. We crawled in, drank more of Mike's cane juice and tried to close our eyes. They wouldn't close, or if they did, images of perfectly peeling waves reeled off behind our eyelids.

An hour later the tide had dropped dramatically, exposing the reef all the way out to where we had been surfing. Some local villagers in their bare feet walked out and began poking around the dry reef. It seemed the lower the tide got, the better the waves became. The take-off seemed to be farther down the line from where we had surfed at the higher tide. It was an unusual wave that started small and then grew as it peeled down the line. We picked our way over the dry reef carefully so as not to slice up our bare feet. Not far from the edge, the wave stood up, crashed over then quickly died down to a gurgle where we stood not 30 feet away. It was the most amazing thing; the wave was powerful and hollow where it broke, but dissipated down to nothing in a short distance. Although getting to it was going to be tricky without getting our bare feet all cut up on the reef. I noticed some cracks in the reef that seemed to lead out and were deeper. I put my surfboard in one with the fin up, carefully lay on it, keeping my full weight off by pressing down on the reef with my hands. When the surge washed in underneath, it floated my board and I was able to ride back out with it. As soon as it was deep enough to paddle, I could make better speed and left the others behind doing their rock dance. Eventually there was deep enough water below me that I could roll my board over the right way and paddle full stroke. The rollover was a maneuver that I had down pat, having practiced many times during long waits in the line-up. I could do it in a flash without even getting off the board. Before long, I was in position to catch a wave while the others were still inching their way on dry reef.

A wave about 4-feet came towards me and looked good. The take-off was easy and I flicked a turn up onto the wall. The wave stretched out ahead of me as I raced it down the line. It seemed to grow not only in height, but also in girth. I could see a section looming ahead of me that was twice as big as where I had first caught the wave. With good speed and a good line, I flew into the backdoor of the section and found myself deep inside a serious tunnel. A few more pumps and I shot out the other end, easing over the top as yet another even bigger section loomed ahead. My heart was pounding, my breathing rapid, with both increasing when I saw the next wave. I put my head down and paddled hard to get out of the way of a full-on 8-foot, top-to-bottom, thick barrel. Angling for the shoulder with a good head of steam, I slipped around the wave, but not before I had a chance to look deep within its bowels. I saw that it was hollow and clean enough to ride 30-feet back in the barrel. I was shaking like I had a fever, realizing how lightly I had taken my first wave. I had to be careful pulling into these thick inside waves, as they broke very hard in very shallow water.

Fred Haywood was on the third wave. He had made it out pretty quick, maybe his feet were toughened by the sharp, low tide Shark Pit reef in Lahaina, Maui. Riding backside, he approached the heavy inside section I had backdoored a few waves earlier. His wave was much bigger than mine. As I sat up to watch how he planned to negotiate this difficult section, he hit his turn perfectly and projected high on the wall just as the whole wave threw out over his head. Bent over at the waist, he eased a turn back down, somehow held his edge and blew out of a tunnel big enough for our *bemo* to fit inside. We named the inside section the Racetrack that day because it was exactly that – high-speed, full-throttle runs that you raced to win or die on the razor-like reef waiting below. To this day, I remember pulling into a backdoor that I was watching break three sections ahead, ducking late into the first one as the second one was already pitching over and seeing the third section in the distance getting ready to throw. Somehow I slipped through all of them and squirted out safe and sound.

The surfboards we brought to Bali that first trip were our contest boards for Australian events at Bells Beach and the North Sydney breaks. I had a 7'8" diamond tail, a 7'4" wing swallowtail and a 6'8" that I only remember as wide, thick and fat. The 7'8" was too long and didn't get much use. The 7'4" was the best size for what we were riding, but not one of my boards worked as well as I wanted. I got so frustrated with the 7'4" I brought it back to Kuta one day, took a Surform tool, shaved off the wings and reglassed over the bare foam. At the end of our trip, I gave it to Kim "The Fly" Bradley of Avalon who was with us in Bali. I never wanted to see that piece of crap again. Kim hung on to the board and recently Jack acquired it, showing it to me last winter on the North Shore.

Jeff's boards didn't work any better and he ended up riding a board I had made for Jack in Torquay right before we left on the trip. Jack is a big man so the 7'4" I built was a big board. But Jeff liked it and rode it every day. Able to knee paddle because of all the flotation, he had the added advantage of seeing the sets first. One time he also spotted something swimming towards us. As I looked where he was pointing, we both realized at the same time that it was a huge sea snake. We both turned and bolted for shore, paddling right through the Maui boys sitting further inside. They didn't bother to ask what we were running away from, they just turned and joined our flight, all of us knocking each other over trying to get away. Of course, the commotion we made trying to escape chased the snake away but we didn't know that.

This trip was the first time that Jeff and I had worn surf leashes; they took some getting used to. They had been around for several years, but I guess we were old school and felt we didn't need them. The rocky shoreline of Uluwatu at high tide was death on lost surfboards. Every one else used a leash so Jeff and I gave it a go. The leashes of the day were black surgical tubing with a length of nylon inside. The theory was that the tubing would stretch out until it reached the length of the nylon, stopping the board from going any further, then rebounding it back to the surfer. The only trouble was that the waves at Ulu didn't stop pulling when they reached the end of the cord inside, and easily snapped the nylon. The wave kept pulling, stretching the rubber tubing to the thickness of a rubber band, at which point the rubber broke or worse, it recoiled the board back like a rocket. Unless the surfer was aware of this and ready for it when it happened, he would surface after getting tumbled by the wave to find his board flying back at his head. If he was lucky he might get his hand up in time to stop it. If not, he could get nailed right in the face. I fell off my board a lot so I had to put up with all the crap that went with using a leash. Jeff, on the other hand, gave up on the leash and concentrated on never losing his board. The only time he lost it was one time when Mike Boyum bailed off right in front of him and it was either let go or get nailed by Mike's board. The attitude was different back then. When someone lost his surfboard, the guy riding the next wave surfed in and retrieved it.

I loved everything about Bali – the surf most of all – but the people were special too. I think the Dutch realized that when they colonized the region because they left Bali much as they found it while exploiting the heck out of Java and Sumatra. Uluwatu was a world-class surf spot. Jeff and I would go out there four or five days in a row until its intensity just wore us out, then we would stay in Kuta for a few days surfing a much tamer Kuta Reef. A day or two of that and we would long for the power, the size and the sheer magnitude of Ulu. We got a little motorbike; I would drive while Jeff held both boards behind me. Often we would be the only ones there. Boyum lived right across the street from where we stayed, and we would try to get him to go out too, but Ulu was a heavy place. Nobody wanted it too much. The days we wouldn't go out there weren't because of a lack of surf, it was just a lack of motivation on our part. We were weary from all that surf. Jeff would sleep all day long on those days. It seemed the surf never stopped. Ulu was never less than 6 feet that first trip for the entire six weeks. It was utterly relentless. We would give it a miss just to come down from the high energy. By contrast, the people and the pace of life in Bali were languid.

There was a period in my life – the previous six or seven years – when I had no desire to be anywhere else than the Ala Moana parking lot during the summer season. Missing a south swell at the Bowl was anathema to me until I went to Bali. Then all I wanted to do was go home, work, make some money and new surfboards and get back to that idyllic island as quick as I could. Life is quite a journey, we find something we like and immediately build a fence around it to keep it the same. Then something else comes along and we are over that fence in a flash with out hardly a look back, chasing off after some other pipe dream.

First published in Gerry Lopez's autobiographical book *Surf is Where You Find It*, Patagonia Books, 2008

Instant Karma

Headlong into battle against the forces of evil

BY DC GREEN

□

> Instant karma's gonna get you, Gonna hit you right in the face...
> JOHN LENNON.

EVERY DAY IN Bali, beautiful, simple offerings are placed at millions of key points around the island to appease evil spirits, amongst other functions. These offerings of rice, flowers and incense on a woven banana leaf base are often gobbled down by scowling street dogs. Yet the Balinese Hindus remain unperturbed. After all, dogs – or *anjing* – are but incarnations of evil spirits, so all is as it should be. Only in the last decade has the western concept of keeping dogs as pets become popular. But the rabid, skulking, snarling, unloved street hounds with more scabs than fur, still outnumber the dogs with collars.

At the end of a big night out, I clambered onto my pushbike and veered back to my *losmen* in Poppies Lane 1. I felt at peace with the world as I paused to hand out 500 rupiah notes to beggar mothers ... until a shrill blast from the shadows almost scared me from my saddle. A barking dog! Mangy *anjing* (dog), I cursed, as I steered my bike toward the darkness. I chuckled, Have a taste of your own foul *obat* (medicine)! The *anjing* yiped and scurried into the blackness of a covered walkway. I gave chase, as if I had become the living, riding embodiment of instant karma ...

Of course I didn't see the solid wooden cross-beam lined with rusty nails. But I sure felt the several holes it drove into my forehead. My spectacles smashed. I crashed from my bike. Babbling and concussed, I somehow made it back to my room, where I passed out in front of my door, unable to operate the key. I awoke, baking in the sun, terrified I'd gone blind, though dried blood had merely fused my eyelids together.

Over the next week, many people enquired of the scabs across my head: 'Coral reef cuts?'

Embarrassed, I replied, 'Ah... yeah.'

First published in *Australia's Surfing Life*, Volume 71, August 1994

Hell in Paradise

Surviving the Bali bomb

HANABETH LUKE

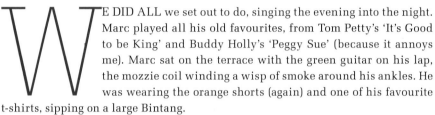

W E DID ALL we set out to do, singing the evening into the night. Marc played all his old favourites, from Tom Petty's 'It's Good to be King' and Buddy Holly's 'Peggy Sue' (because it annoys me). Marc sat on the terrace with the green guitar on his lap, the mozzie coil winding a wisp of smoke around his ankles. He was wearing the orange shorts (again) and one of his favourite t-shirts, sipping on a large Bintang.

"Bintang!" He tried a poor imitation of a Balinese accent as he held up his beer in a salute to us all before taking a swig (he sounded more like Speedy Gonzales). Bobby cackled as he wandered up to join us, reading Marc's shirt out loud:

"Your village called, they want their idiot back...nice." He nodded his head with a smile, swigging on his own Bintang.

Marc glanced at me with a cheeky smile as he started to sing:

"Oh Peggy Sue, Peggy Sue, pretty, pretty, pretty, Peggy Sue ..."

"Rah! I hate this song!" I protested, laughing, before singing along. Next, as Marc started to sing our song I closed my eyes and listened to his beautiful voice.

"Sail away with me honey, I put my heart in your hands, Sail away with me honey, now ..." I still loved to hear that song, especially hearing it this time. I was dreaming of the fresh start we were set to make in Australia, now that we'd grown together through our hard times.

I wasn't originally going to go out. Bobby and the boys had decided they were getting up at 5am for an early Sunday surf sesh at Canggu, and I committed to the early start, but Mel and Marc were so keen to party, being Saturday night n' all. I went into our room and closed the swing-doors, considering my choices. It made sense to leave them to it and get an early night ... however, it was only a few days ago I'd said how I would love to have a girlfriend to party with. I rifled through my bag and picked out some funky suede shorts with tassels down the sides that had been my birthday present from Marc, pulling on a black singlet my sister Mellie had sent from Italy, together making up my 'Lara Croft' outfit. When I pushed open the green doors dressed in my party gear both Mel and Marc cheered.

"Lara can do both! Why not dance and then surf too?" I joked. I swapped my hard boots for sandals because of the heat - which was lucky for Mel. I kept treading on her poor flip-flopped feet as we walked down the busy lane to the Sari Club. A group of children followed us, holding up their open palms with tired, wide, dark chocolate stares. I had long-since learned to ignore them. You give to one and ten more will follow you the whole way, calling out to you: "Please miss, one dollar..."

Mel wanted to go to Paddy's but it was dead so we ended up at the Sari Club, of course. It was about 10:30 pm and I decided that I'd be out of there by 11 and tucked up in bed after a dance or two. A line of sellers bustled outside offering cigarettes, marijuana and jiggy-jig to all those entering and leaving the club. We wound our way past the bouncers in to the busy club, hanging by the bar as the dance floor filled up. Marc and I shared a jungle juice, which was so strong I couldn't even drink it.

You never know quite what you're getting with jungle juice. The mix is never the same and as *arak* is cheaper than orange juice, well, that's just asking for trouble! I decided to do the familiar rounds, popping across the road to Paddy's a couple of times looking for Blaine. Of course, then a song came on that I had to dance to and I dragged everybody onto the dance floor.

My memory is hazy. There was laughter and silly moves and cheesy tunes and ...just...general silliness. There was a group of very young, very pretty girls with their hair in tiny braids (a sure sign of it being their first trip to Bali). A pissed-up Aussie guy with no shirt and lots of mates cleared the dance floor to make way for a running jump onto his belly, sliding through the spilt beer to the whooping amusement of his mates. It was pretty funny but the floor was filthy. I thought he was lucky there was no broken glass on the ground. I looked around, remembering what Oka had told me, noticing that the only Balinese in there were working behind the bar. I couldn't really relax into it, but I've always tried to make the most of every situation. I love the saying: "go hard, or go home." My personal variation was "dance hard, don't drink, then go home and get up for the early surf."

I got into the groove, dancing to all sorts of cheesy shit, shaking our heads in mock embarrassment as we grooved to "I'm Too Sexy". The Sari, at the very least, is a place where you just dance as if no one is watching. As I lost myself in the groove, I recalled years of Bali trips between Paddy's and the Sari.

"Do you believe in life after love," started to play; a song Marc particularly hated, as he couldn't stand Cher's electronic voice. He raised his eyebrows at me as it came on, and indicated his jungle juice was getting low, shaking the bottle.

"Sorry guys, I have some pride!" he laughed as he walked off, disappearing into the crowd.

"See you in a bit!" I chirped and turned to face Mel. It was my Bali song, but of course Marc didn't know that. When that song first came out I was eighteen years old and out at Paddy's on my first solo trip. I'd recently experienced my first break-up back in Australia, so I'd danced harder than ever to that tune when it came on. Whenever it played, in whatever country I happened to be in, it always took me straight back to that filthy, steamy dance floor in Bali, under the flashing lights, watching Cher on the big screen. They played it every night in those bars. I always chuckled at how the music lineup would never change each night: the same stuck record in both bars. You could hear 'Land Down Under' downstairs at Paddy's and wander straight across the road to Sari only to hear it again. By the time you'd had a dance and wandered back to Paddy's to see who you could find, it'd be playing again, upstairs this time.

From the speakers, 'Murder on the Dance Floor' started to play. I looked around, wondering where Marc was, as we loved to play up to that song. I couldn't see him, but instead two drunk and creepy young guys sidled up to Mel and I. We tried the subtle brush-off manoeuvres, but they didn't work, and neither did the turned back, or even the elbow in the ribs. I was thinking how ironic the song was, as I wanted to kill these guys! Rather than resorting to stomping on their toes, I danced Mel away to the back of the dance floor, further from Marc who was watching us from the sunken bar at the front of the club. We now danced in the corner of the L-shaped bar which spanned two sides of the dance floor. The Balinese guy behind the bar was swaying to the music as he served the next jungle juice with a smile.

We reveled in our new space with plenty of room to boogie. 'Without Me' came on. As we watched Eminem dressed as a superhero flashing on the big screens above the dance floor there was a loud bang over the music. It was not a familiar sound, but no one paid much attention until the electricity flashed off, and we stopped for a moment, glancing about as the music took a few seconds to come back on. I tried hard to place the sound. Was it a shotgun? Surely, not in Bali. Was it a party banger? A car back-firing? Maybe...must be, surely. A chill rippled up my spine. The air in the club shifted as if a wave had passed through. The lights flashed on and off. Something wasn't right, but despite the uneasy feeling in my gut I took the decision to go and check it out when the song was finished. If anything was wrong there was no point in running straight into it, I thought.

That momentary decision was to save my life. Unbeknown to me, the inquisitive Marc wandered towards the door, jungle juice in hand.

The music started playing again, the screens flicked back on. On the chorus the beat was thick and Mel and I were getting low, bending our knees, wiggling our hips as we grinned at each other.

"Last song for me," I muttered below the music, as I imagined the crystal sunrise waves at Canggu.

The noise which came next I will never forget. It was an empty sound that did not resonate. It was a thud, like the slam of a car door but multiplied to a volume I simply cannot describe.

THE SOUND IS all around, blasting through my ears, my body, my soul. It feels like someone has burst a hot air balloon on my face. My hair is streaming and my ears are screaming.

All the air in the club is sucked out, replaced with a gust of hot pressure, which picks up the dancers and the whole club like a dumping wave or an angry child throwing dolls and pencils with a frustrated shriek. I'm being hit by the biggest, most powerful wave I have ever known, except it is hot.

In slow motion I see the club around me explode, ribbons of fire tearing through poles and people flying through the air as my mind captures this moment in a three dimensional photo. As time slows I am picked up and suspended in mid-air, twisting to face down as I slam to the ground.

As everything hits the floor I find myself in eerie blackness. I lay amongst the rubble as I feel the roof collapsing around me, stopping close above my head. After the impact comes the silence, stretching out for an eternity as the music of the Sari Club stops forever. No one knows what has happened, and the living have not yet realised they can still scream.

And as I lie here I can feel the pressure of rubble on my back. Am I still alive? I think that this silence is the end, and that this simply must be my time. I feel a peace floating over me, and I can accept that what will be, will be.

But, oh no, all the things I want to do, but can never do, all my dreams, hopes… gone.

Another voice comes into my mind screaming a clear message: "NO!" As I snap from my daze, the voice speaks clearly: "What are you thinking? Get out of here, NOW!"

Right. If there is any way out of here I am going to find it. I try to move my aching body, and to my amazement it responds. I throw off the wood, tiles and whatever is covering me to crawl out on my belly. Thank God. In the darkness I can hear Mel's voice close by.

"Hanabeth! Are you OK?"

"Yes! Are you?"

"Yes. Don't panic, we'll get out of here."

Where is Marc? He'd been standing too far away to know now. We're on our hands and knees with several others crawling under the collapsed roof, away from the amber glow at the front of the club. If we don't move quickly we might be trampled as there are people moving behind us too, pushing in the darkness. A hot and putrid stench burns at my mouth and nostrils and thick smoke is gathering all around as we crawl, trapped under the rubble. I notice the ground is soft, and in horror realise that there are people under my feet, alive or dead I do not know, but I can't stop. I kick off my sandals … I know that every split second counts. I can see the ominous amber glow growing from the front of the club. I know I'm very far from safety, and every sense is on overdrive as I feel my way through. We find a hole in the collapsed roof through which we can see the stars, and people immediately start to surge upwards onto the roof. I stretch my hands up the rubble to pull myself through, pushed from behind. Everything is hot to touch, like the stones of a fireplace. The part of my mind still stuck in the world of thirty seconds ago curses at the loss of a good pair of shoes.

"Oh, it's okay, I'll probably be able to come and pick them up tomorrow," I think momentarily, just as another voice in my head screams: "What!! Fucking shoes, what about Marc?" It is like my brain has split in two as it struggles to comprehend this reality. My heart thuds as I think of Marc. There is no way back, but where is he?

"Marc!" I scream out loud, but no answer comes. Again I can hear Mel's sweet reassuring tone:

"Don't panic, keep calm."

But the girl behind her screams: "Run! RUN!" I think that is a more appropriate approach right now.

I find myself on the thatch of the roof. Around me I see the fallen roof broken up into so many segments and different levels, trying to make sense between what I can see now and what was supposed to be here before. Everywhere I look I see patches of flames in the straw lighting up silhouettes of those coming out behind me...Where is Marc? No, I decide, it's hopeless. To turn back will be death. Now is the time to run, now is the time to panic. My blood runs cold as I see that we are amongst the kindling of a massive bonfire, well on its way to catching alight. I can't see Marc so I can only hope beyond hope that he is close behind, or is finding his own way out (of course he is).

I use both hands and feet to scramble up the roof like a monkey, moving as fast as I can as the adrenalin surges into my veins, jumping across gaps between the roofs. The fire is getting louder and the flames are starting to create a dull roar as they advance across (and under) the roof. I try to push through what seems like a window between tiers of the roof, but a man and I jam shoulders and as we both pull back to surge forwards, it happens again, yet neither can fit through unless we take our turn. We pause:

"After you," I say.

"No, after you," he pushes me through and follows. We jump down to the ground, safe and free. On second thoughts, no, we are not. As I look up my heart sinks and then rises to my dry mouth in fear. In front of me rises a towering wall, and I realise that we are still in the club. I don't remember this wall. Where am I? My eyes scan up and down the tall, grey wall to see no steps, no way forwards, no way out. To my right are flickering flames and to my left a couple of guys are boosting girls up the wall. Should I ask for help? No (that voice again): I am able bodied, I'll let them help others and themselves. There must be a way to do this by myself. Searching the darkness, the only light is the flickering, growing wall of flames behind me, casting my tiny shadow on the grey wall. The thick power lines that had been hung along the front of the club now lay severed and hanging down the wall. Could they be live? I hope not, but what is my alternative? Without hesitating I grab the rubber casing firmly and run up the wall, hauling myself about four metres up in seconds.

"Argh!" I yell as I rip some skin off my knee while pulling myself onto the top of the wall. It could be worse. The rough top of the brick wall is only four inches wide, and on the other side, far below there is nothing but rubble…it's funny, I can't remember there being a building site here. It's a short distance to crawl along to where the flimsy framework of a roof remains, as long as I don't look down. The roof is little stronger than a pile of matchsticks, so I choose my steps carefully as each hand and foot finds its place to manoeuvre slowly, following behind a Balinese man.

As I reach the other side, my heart sinks again as I am met by a large drop, the size of the one I've just climbed. I can see piles of debris; broken tiles, wood, shrapnel and glass littering the ground. People are down there staring up at us as we appear over the rooftop. One man yells out to me:

"I'll catch you, you can jump!" (Bless him) I yell back for him to help others first, as I would probably just injure him if I land on him, anyway. I'm able bodied enough. I climb carefully down to the edge and ease myself down until I am hanging from my hands. I can only pray as I release my grip, dropping like a stone.

I feel the full impact of the drop, with my knees bent as I fall back on to my hands. I turn to look back over the roof I've climbed over. There aren't many people coming over the same way; I think I must have been one of the first out of there. Maybe I can help others down, but my size and height make it seem pointless. I'll just hurt myself. I scan the people on the roof, searching for Marc coming out behind me. Maybe he got out first? I run across the road, stopping in the middle, taking in the scene of fire and panic around me. The whole street seems to be in flames. The sound of a car horn stuck down makes an eerie background noise to the cries of human panic and suffering. I feel a huge rush of blood to my head as I remember this place. I've been here before, in the dream of four nights ago. This was the exact same scene. What has happened?

The gravity of what is occurring finally hits me as I see a body being dragged away from the flames by a Balinese man; it is the body of a young man, with only skin flapping where a skull used to be. My heart goes cold as I take in the orange shorts he is wearing. The blood rushes to my head and my heart thumps in my chest. But no, these are plain shorts and it is the body of a teenager. I see the pale skin and freckles, maybe European. They are orange boardshorts: not Marc's, not Marc, yet still that image burns in my brain. I can't see Marc around me so I run between the burning cars to try to get to the south side of the street towards the front of the club, and maybe back in to get Marc. If not, I want to get to Cempaka to see whether Marc has gone there, and to see Bobby and Blaine. The flames are thick, so I brace myself to try to run along the narrow blackened pavement, between burning buildings and cars. As I run forwards I can see several blood splattered bodies on the pavement to my right. There is someone moving in the orange glow of the flames. I crouch down to see a young male, alive.

"Oh my god," I mutter, as I crouch down and grab his hand. "Can you move?" I shout above the roar of the flames and the chaos.

"No, I can't," he replies in an Aussie accent. He can't be more than eighteen years old. I glance up at the flames ripping from the car only a few feet away. I try to haul him up, but he is much bigger than me. I have to shout: "Look, I don't give a damn if your legs are broken, you have to get up now otherwise you're not going to make it! I can't carry you but I'll help you all I can." Thank God, he is trying to get to his feet. It's all I need, so I use his own momentum to pull him up, holding on to his left hand and locking it over my left shoulder. It's wet, and as I look down I notice it is completely red, sodden with blood. I feel sick – I'm not good with blood at the best of times. I put my right arm round his waist, taking on as much of his weight as I can. When we are clear of the flames two men approach us to help the young man, freeing me from his weight. I immediately turn a full circle: Where is Marc? Where is he? I can't stop so I just keep on running and searching. Finally I find Mel standing wide-eyed on the corner of the alleyway. We rush towards each other and embrace. Mel speaks first:

"I'm so glad you're okay. Where's Marc?"

"I don't know Mel, I didn't see him come out. I can't find him." I can hear the fear and thickness in my own words, and they scare me.

"It was a car bomb. They fucking bombed us," Mel says.

"No way!" I reply firmly, shaking my head. There's no way there could be a car bomb here. "It must have been an accident…" My words seem naïve, even stupid.

"Maybe it was a gas explosion?" I mutter. I cannot believe this is a human, deliberate action. Who would, who could, do this on purpose? We look back towards the club we were dancing in five minutes before. Red and orange flames stretch up high above the roofs, eating into the blackness. Suddenly it dawns on me, and my internal organs feel like exploding from my body.

"Oh my God, there are people still in there. No-one's coming out! Mel, are there people still in there?" I ask hysterically.

"No," she says, "I think everybody got out." Is she just trying to calm me?

"Look at the people around! They didn't, Mel! We have to go back!" I start to run back towards the front of the club, my heart ready to burst out of my chest. I feel a hand reach out as Mel grabs my arm and pulls me back, stopping me from running back into the flames. But I have to get back. I have to do everything I can to get those people out. I struggle with Mel, trying to pull away, but she cries out:

"Hanabeth, NO! There are still petrol tanks and gas bottles that are yet to explode. Stop! You will get yourself killed. Marc will be fine. He'll be looking for you on the other side. It's not as bad as it seems." As she locks me in her arms her tone is soothing, and she is speaking all the words I want to hear, but I know she is only trying to comfort me. As much as I want to, I just can't believe her. My body goes limp as powerlessness engulfs me. I stare at the enormous tower of flames and something in my heart turns cold and still. This time I speak in a quiet tone, half calm yet half a whimper.

"He's dead, Mel. He's gone, I can feel it." Somehow I feel quite sure and I speak as if it were a matter of fact.

"Don't be silly. Don't give up yet! Think how many places he could be. He will turn up soon," she reasons. I want nothing more than to believe her, and have no intention to stop looking, but I have a deadly feeling deep down that is difficult to ignore. How can you love someone that much and be that close to them and not know the moment they leave this planet?

Suddenly there is renewed panic – everyone around us starts to scream, running up the street, sprinting away from the flames. They are yelling something about another bomb. Maybe another petrol tank has exploded. Before I know it I too am running amongst all the others, sprinting up the street until eventually I come to a halt, as many sprint on. It seems a little crazy, and I don't know what started it. So I wait for a very short while before I jog back down the blackened road, calling out to the injured lying on the side of the street.

"I know CPR, can I help anyone?' My voice rings out with a question I quickly realise is ridiculous. It's hardly any help to those lying under the column of smoke feeling their skin burn as their lifeblood runs from them. What can I do? How can I help? How can I find Marc?

"We need water!" someone yells, as they attend to an injured man lying on a makeshift stretcher.

"Hanabeth, we have to get water." It's Mel's' voice. She grabs my hand and leads me across the street. At the mention of water I become aware that my mouth is very, very dry, and a choking, thick horrid flavour sticks inside my mouth. I have never known such thirst. We duck into a restaurant and walk up to the bar, pleading for water. Between us we have no money. Mine was in my 'handbag' (Marcs' pocket). The barmaid kindly hands over two small bottles of water. In our frantic thirst we forget what the water is for as we rip off the lids and throw our heads back, glugging down the life-giving liquid. Suddenly it occurs to me, there must be a mirror here. I pull Mel into the bathroom where there is a little light and we can see ourselves in the mirror for the first time. I take a step back in shock to see my face smeared with blood, my whole body grey-black from the smoke and the explosion. Our hair is thick with dust, dirt and blood. I turn around on the balls of my feet, examining my limbs, my skin, checking myself for injury. I know enough about the effects of shock to know that either of us could be running around with serious injuries. Mel turns on the tap and we rub at the blood, finding nothing more than mere scratches underneath. The blood is not from our veins. We stare at each other, astonished that we are unharmed. But still, Mel is unsure. She holds out her arms:

"My arms hurt. Could you look at them?" I examine the backs of her arms where she has indicated, but can see nothing. I feel the bones in her arm gently.

"You seem okay, Mel. Everything seems in tact." In my shock and naivety I do not stop to consider the possibility of burns.

We shout our thanks to the bar staff as we rush outside back into the chaos. Mel takes the water to the young man and once more every scrap of my energy is focused on finding Marc. I cross the street, pushing through the crowd, turning people around, looking for his face somewhere amongst the chaos. The silly boy (it's almost funny) had dyed his hair jet black a few days before, to cover the three faded blue spots left over from his mushroom outfit for the SAS Ball. Looking for his dark skin, I turn around a hundred men that could be him, only to reveal unfamiliar Balinese faces. Never before have I longed so much to see his wide grin, his gangly arms, feel his warm embrace. Once again I remember my dream, as I had pushed through the crowds searching the faces...and, yes, in the dream I'd found him. This renews my hope to keep going. I must be running around in circles because I keep finding the same young man lying on a stretcher made from a large shop sign. His jet blackjet-black hair is sticky with blood. How many times already have I stopped in my tracks to stare at his face? I gently stroke his head and tell him he is just fine, although I doubt it.

"I don't want to die here. Please don't let me die," he begs of me and Mel, who is staying by his side holding his hand. Her soothing voice and kind words must mean the world to this young man.

"It's okay darling, you are going to be just fine. Don't you worry," I hear her say, over and over.

My heart breaks a thousand times tonight. I want to stay with him, but I must find Marc. I cross the street again to climb up on a white jeep, standing on tiptoes trying to see past the flames to the south side of the Sari Club. There lies my hope that Marc is alive, and I hear myself screaming his name:

"MARC!! MARC!!" I cry out over and over, until my voice is hoarse, then I just keep screaming his name anyway. If only a weak reply were to meet me through the chaos. Again I recollect my dream from the week before and the moment when I found Marc in the darkness, but this is beyond any nightmare that has ever crept into my sleep. I run back to Mel still screaming his name, frantic now.

"Have you seen Marc? Where is he? Mel, I have to find him one way or another." She stares at me through scared but kind eyes.

"Marc will be fine, darlin'," she reassures me, as she looks down at my feet. "Hanabeth! You are standing on broken glass! I look down at the floor to see the remains of a shop window piled under my bare feet. Suddenly I become aware of a dull ache in the soles of my feet. I grab my ankle and balance on one leg, pulling several thick shards from deep in my flesh. Once I'm free of the glass I am running again, weaving through the crowd, this time more conscious of trying to avoid the worst of the glass.

Time is passing, so surreal and twisted that I have no idea of the speed or the sequence of its passing. We have helped to move some injured people into taxis. After an agonising wait, fire engines and ambulances start to turn up. I'm guessing it must be more than forty minutes since the explosion. This is too little too late. I've been running in circles in the dark for such a long time. It is Mel who finally instigates the move.

"Hanabeth, my arms are really sore." She now has my full attention and I examine her upper arms under the fire light, seeing bubbles starting to form on her skin.

"Oh shit." Finally, I realise my stupidity in not recognising that she has been burnt. Someone produces a wet rag that we press on the burns. I look around, scanning the crowd again. I have to have just one more try.

"Just wait thirty seconds. Wait right here." I run off once more to look through the crowd one last time. I slow to a walk, coming to a stop back next to Mel, finally deciding that my chances of finding him at the hospital are greater by this point. I grab Mel and virtually pounce on a motorcyclist.

"Will you please take us to the hospital?" Suddenly my voice is clear and urgent. The Balinese teenager nods and we jump on the back of his bike, Mel in front of me so I can keep holding the wet rag on the back of her arms and shoulders. A man comes up to take a photo of us and we scream at him in anger.

"How dare you take photos at a time like this! Fuck off!" As the camera flashes I give the photographer the finger and we speed off through the seething crowd, away from the flames into the black night.

[On the 12th October 2002, the terrorist bombings on Jalan Legian caused the deaths of 202 people, including Hanabeth's boyfriend, Mark Gajardo.]

This is an extract from *Shock Waves - Finding peace after the Bali bomb*, by Hanabeth Luke. See www.facebook.com/shock.waves.hanabeth.

Mourning of the Earth

The Bali bombings aftermath

DC GREEN

□

I CLIMB OFF MY push bike at Bemo Corner and stare down Jalan Legian. For the first time in the 15 years I've been stumbling to Indonesia, before the full moon rave parties and sealed roads to every wave on the Bukit Peninsula, doubtless since Jim Banks was a wide-eyed teen Bronzed Aussie, there are to be seen no cheeky grommets keen to imitate my accent, no conspiratorially whispering ganja salesmen, no laughing Gudang Garam or Mentos hawkers, no Maduran whores beckoning in shadow, no mothers clasping babies and silently reaching out for coins, no *bakso* carts with ringing bells, no lurching drunks, or traffic snarls, or honking bikes, or familiar movements of any kind.

It is midnight, the beginning of the seventh day since two terrorist bombs tore a chasm, literally and spiritually, in the heart of this surf-spawned metropolis by the sea. Asia's most famous street, walled shoulder to shoulder with shops, restaurants and bars stretching north through Legian and Seminyak as far as the eye can peer, is desolate. Inconceivably desolate. I close my eyes. Yet the only sound is the near imperceptible breeze whispering through the *tiga kancuh* trees that line the empty footpaths. In more ways than can be measured, Kuta is this night a ghost town.

I begin to walk. The slap of thongs on bitumen echoes back harshly. I bend, and catch movement in my periphery. Beneath a shop awning, several figures sit facing the road, watching me. Some nod, or attempt to smile. By their distinctive front-knotted headpieces and chequered sarongs, I can tell these men are members of the local *banjar* (council). They are sentinels, armed with walkie-talkies and a grimness that such an outrage will not happen again, not on their watch. I nod back, like the *banjar*, not wishing to disturb the strangely beautiful stillness of this night with the ugly pettiness of words.

Barefoot, I walk on, past the narrow entrance to Poppies Lane I, and more groups of squatting *banjar*, all discreetly, strategically placed, often alternating with similar sized groups of armed *polisi*. Despite the arse-protective political and media hysteria urging westerners to bunker in their hotels and flee Bali post haste, I have never felt safer in Indonesia than I do now. Or more...loved. Or such stillness.

I walk on, passing boarded windows and ever more buckled roller doors. Glass fragments sparkle in the street and waxing moon light. To my right, *polisi* and news trucks clog the car park of the New Bounty, all lit up, yet still closed like most of Bali's major nightspots. Wreaths weaved with brilliant flowers, handmade and natural, line the gutters and sealed-up storefronts in increasing density. Yellow police tape and 20 metre linen sheets dangle along both footpaths, scrawled with messages of support and condolence. And anger: "Fuck you terroris cunts!" Ahead, the very road itself appears to blaze.

Yet as I pass Poppies Lane II, still clogged high with debris, I realise the fire is no more than several hundred orange candle flowers speckling the road. Several locals kneel and pray in ceremonial garb, or stand with bowed heads before the hill of wreaths and single flowers piled several feet high outside the gutted remnants of The Aloha Shop. Beyond this point, the road is taped off and guarded by an even larger throng of *polisi*. Ground zero.

The English language contains several hundred thousand words, every one utterly incapable of describing the heinous magnitude of the carnage wrought by the 150kg ammonium nitrate bomb loaded with fuel oil and packed into a road-blocking *bemo* amongst such a crush of people. I struggle to reconcile this rubble-strewn vision of Hell with the image of mates' beaming faces psyching for 'a huge Saturday night' at legendary Aussie bar, the Sari Club, or perhaps across the road, at the more cosmopolitan Paddies: Asia's social twin towers. They will never be rebuilt; not on this island of spirits.

Two middle-aged westerners approach the *polisi* line, clutching each other for support. Their eyes roam across the floodlit rubble that was the Sari, across the obscene crater in the road to the melted black skeleton that was Paddies, searching for meaning where there is no meaning. Tears slowly blossom in their eyes, burst, and wend down well-worn lines; and not for the first time, well up in mine as well. From the small crowd, even from the *polisi*, palpable empathy flows. Emotion in the eyes cannot be faked, nor tears from the soul. Whatever trace of resentment the Balinese Hindus and the local Muslim minority who eke out an existence on the streets may have felt towards Australians over East Timor is now as much rubble as our national fantasies of immune isolation. The tolerant, beautiful Balinese especially, are as much victims of this atrocity as the Aussies, Javanese and partying citizens from a dozen other countries who were torn to shreds, burnt beyond recognition or 'fortunate' to survive with injuries that will scar or disable for life. They will never forget; nor must we.

JASON CHILDS

Next morning, local superstars Riz and Betet pick me up for a run to Canggu, Bali's most rippable right reef. Escaping Kuta is a guilty pleasure, but surfers are ever-opportunistic dogs. The Left is pumping, while Canggu itself pulses with four to six feet sets. I stay in the water until my shoulders ache, until my soul and sinuses have been at least partially cleansed. The crowd maxes at around ten, remarkable for Canggu. Yet more remarkable is the vibe. Despite the presence of surfers from several different nations, I am snaked only once, and the offending Balinese guy paddles straight back to me and apologises as if he has committed a great crime. When I hoot a Brazilian who pulls in backside, he paddles back out and...hugs me! For this day, at least, the facade falls from all our constructions of race, rivalry and nationhood, and we are left but brothers and sisters, with the same naked human fears and passions.

The Sari Club in the aftermath of the October 2002 bombing.

Though the rains are yet to arrive, the *Angin Tenggara* trade wind shifted ninety degrees around late September to a wet season southwesterly, meaning wave action had also swung to Bali's east side. The week before the bombing, there were at least 40 surfers at Nusa Dua every day. The day after, there were four, including a big tattooed guy who'd narrowly escaped Paddies by climbing over the back fence to avoid the stampede to the front entrance, and who sat on his board sobbing and shaking like a little girl. As for Ulu's, according to Betet, only a few locals were onto the early morning sessions. More than anything else, Indonesia's surf remains the same. It is immaterial to the waves that roll across the Indian Ocean whether there are humans to celebrate their reef climax or not.

Australian surfers dug the foundations for tourism in Indonesia, for all the Sari Clubs. Once certain developmental points were passed, the motel chains came, and the budget travelers, and the celebrating footballers, and the Japanese and Taiwanese package tourists, both of whom outnumbered Aussies in the first half of 2002 for the first time ever. Yet these latter waves of arrivals have the least reason to return now, and surfers the most. If there are only handfuls of tourists, there need be no nightclubs. And though the huge night out in Bali has become an institution, even a rite of passage for many young Aussies, do surfers really need all that? Dancing and drinking are fine and fun expressions of individual freedom, but is that why Jim Banks, or Alby Falzon, or Steve Cooney first came to Bali?

I believe if we flee, if surfers jettison moral responsibility, if we tear the baby from our breast, abandon Bali to economic ruin, and Megawati's moderate Indonesia to the extremists who didn't even have the guts to die themselves while smashing every tenet in their sacred Koran, if we allow these epitomes of evil to violate our hearts and reforge our decisions against our will, then shall we have lost, and terror won?

Fuck you terrorists. I know whose hearts are stronger.

[There were further bomb attacks at Jimbaran and Kuta on October 1st 2005, where suicide bombers were responsible for the deaths of 20 people.]

First published in *Waves* magazine, December 2002

Infinite Games

The final days of Peter Crawford

DC GREEN

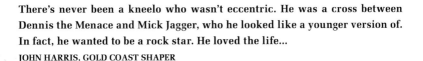

□

There's never been a kneelo who wasn't eccentric. He was a cross between Dennis the Menace and Mick Jagger, who he looked like a younger version of. In fact, he wanted to be a rock star. He loved the life...
JOHN HARRIS, GOLD COAST SHAPER

We went to Sumba in 1977. The king cursed him because he took pictures. He went crazy for a month, not know himself. We took him to a *balian*, a witch doctor. That fixed him. – KETUT PITUR, ONE OF THE ORIGINAL ULUWATU BOARD CARRIERS, NOW HEAD LIFEGUARD AT THE LEGENDARY LEFT.

He was like an educated, intelligent three year old. He'd approach people and talk without any barriers. The people who were most spun out by him were those with the most barriers, those with the most to lose with the removal of the mask. – STEVE PALMER, FORMER QUIKSILVER BALI BOSS.

He was a cosmic prankster, beyond this planet in many respects. At the end he was like Elvis ... No matter how completely fucked up he'd get, he could still go out there and be a complete professional, shooting stuff no-one else could dream of. – DAVE WYLIE, LONG-TERM INDONESIAN RESIDENT.

The Man

ONE MAN, SO many truths, so many half-truths and untruths, including my own...

1995 (1). The first Quiksilver G-Land contest. Pro surfers filled the cabins at Bobby's, while the media bunkered down two by two in the Jungle camp. There was much sniping interest in the appearance of Peter Crawford, then shooting for one of his own, ill-fated surf publications. Bent over with a back injury, he mostly hung with his gorgeous, Zen-calm lady. One morning I emerged from the bush toilet and there he was. Crawford

JEFF DIVINE

approached me with a mischievous look in his eye. "DC..." He smiled, and rolled his eyes back to introduce himself... "PC..." The eyes rolled up and on, with the intonations of his voice, framed with a smirk. "DC...PC...DC, PC..." As if the combination of our initials was the most amusing thing in all of East Java.

Peter Crawford's odd fins were just the tip of the iceberg. This was a man of unusual metabolism, otherworldly perception and unstoppable creative talent who kept people guessing throughout his life.

Next, he opened his clenched hand to reveal a palmful of colourful pills, which he ostentatiously gobbled down without water, cackled, waved a farewell and was gone. That was our first ever conversation. I'd said nothing, though I wondered much. Were the pills a wondrous conduit to realms few even knew existed? Were they just fancy vitamins? Were they a prop, to be spat out? Or was he in that much pain? At first his actions and words seemed affected, even deranged, though I have since thought of more than a dozen interpretations of that coded conversation.

Later at the meal tables, Crawford told me about his 36 second tube ride somewhere on Lombok, a wave that so altered his perceptions he did not surf for six months afterwards, as if it took this long to digest the magnitude of the spiritual insights the wave had force-fed him. Then he shot me a quizzical look, and I wasn't sure if he was testing, playing, fibbing, bemused, deluded, earnestly revealing the path to enlightenment or simply out somewhere beyond the asteroid belt.

And now he's gone.

I have often been described as a gonzo journalist (gonzo being the act of actively participating in a story rather than passively reporting) frequently with the aid of mind-altering substances (especially as popularised by Hunter S. Thompson). Yet when Crawford's final lady friend allowed me to read through the journals of his last two years, I realised how little I understood, how I am J. Alfred Prufrock wading in the gonzo shallows compared to PC hurtling into the deep end, naked and screaming. For his journal pages bulge with brilliance and diversity, with quotes from songs, Woody Allen and Omar Khayam, photos and poems of his father and children, cartoons like his hand-drawn sketch of a marlin thinking *Bloody humans!*, weather maps, newspaper clippings, dried four leaf clovers, mini film reviews, ever-growing lists of things to do and people to contact that represented a who's who of pro surfing and the world surf media. All this is interspersed with family birthdays and events, details (with sketches) of dreams such as this gem: "Dreamt the most incredible tube ride ever – the cannonball tube ride – patent on water parks". Cosmic equations, such as "Positive over (a word I can't quite figure out, possibly enchantment) = Buddha x Tibet x the square root of infinity over the square root of the square root of God over Teacher = the flame (with illustration), the time (infinity) and the number (7)", plus an assortment of brilliant one-liners:

"Cats in Bali are cockroaches with fur."

"Sometimes in Indonesia I feel like toilet paper – roll me out and rip me off!"

"Pamela – all we can give is each other's soul"

"The brain is the current day appendix, it can blow up on any day."

Now I am supposed to write the truth (whatever the Hell that is) about the last days of a man who was not only a groundbreaking photographer in the thick of surfing from the formative years of professionalism, but was also himself one of the best surfers in the world, besides being a publisher, writer, poet-philosopher, designer of fins and the archetypal kneeboard shape, a bonsai gardener, insomniac, husband, lover ('wonderful' I was assured), father of three sons, the tightest of mates, tortured, unique, unknowable, a man who cried at sad movies, could sleep under tables at parties, read auras like morning newspapers and learned his limits by regularly voyaging beyond them. Print-worthy Crawford stories could bloat a volume of magazines, so I apologise to the many whose names and stories I have omitted or brutally culled, for chapters becoming sentences, for being the poor surfer's Sherlock Clone (the blundering Watson, more like).

The Mystery

Peter Crawford died one week before the year 2000 dawned, stunning the surfing world. Yet in the many published eulogies, curiously few even mentioned the people who were with him at the time of his death, and then only cursorily. The official story is simple. Death by snakebite on Bali. Yet the pre-loaded symbolism is daunting. The descendant of dinosaurs is the Chinese sign of beauty and intelligence; the Devil's representative in Eden's Garden; the star of nightmares and phobias; a treacherous act or person on land and in the line-up; an act of deception; the creature who devours it's own tail; the beast that sheds its skin to grow; who can hibernate, spit poison, hypnotize, strangle... It is said the poison from a *lerlipi gadang*, or green pit viper, never leaves the system. If bitten on a finger, the hand must be chopped off within five minutes, for there is no anti-venom... And still, the prime murder suspect has never been found.

Others say he died by spider bite. While for some, any sort of death by wildlife just seems too... mundane. Especially for Crawford. So rumour suspects have multiplied like buzzards since his death became the surfing world equivalent of Jim Morrison's mystery shrouded demise, with conspiracy theories to rival JFK. Was it karma, for his running down an old Indonesian three years earlier? Was the snake a cover-up for a drug overdose, for as envious rival photographers were only too eager to point out, Crawford certainly knew the sights along the road of self-abuse. Was his bizarre passing a defiant rock star piss-in-the-face of old age? A radical divorce from his convoluted marriage with convoluted Indonesia, so he didn't have to witness the Sari Club rubble of the new millennium? He was a kneeboarder too, and by the time of his death, kneelos were like dinosaurs after the big meteor smote Earth, existing in ever dwindling pockets, seemingly destined for extinction. Was his death somehow symbolic of the corporatisation of surfing, the demise of surfing's truly weird and innovative, the extinction of pure gonzo? Or was his ending merely that which we all fear the most, a random, stupid act of horror? None of which explains all the crazy psycho-spiritual (and just plain crazy) stories that circle in Chinese whispers, or my feeling that even now Crawford's eyes are sparkling like that morning at G-Land, delighted at all this confusion, about his enigma in an afterlife riddle status.

1999: The Last Days 1

Extracts from the pages of Crawford's 1999 journal:

Nov. 14: (written exactly 39 days before he died.) "Sunrise on the New Moon. Jesus Christ's calendar. 39 revolutions early. I want to travel to space. Put sperm donation in."

Nov. 26: Crawford exultantly lists the birth details of Chris "Critta" Byrne's newborn daughter, Milla, concluding with a quote from the Brian Cadd song: "A little ray of sunshine has come into my life in the shape of a girl..."

Dec. 2: "Chromosome 22 cracked. The most densely packed of genes."

Dec. 6: "Australia wins Davis Cup. Wake up for last shot – Scud. Drive south for Critta and Milla."

Though it is four years later when I visit the ex-Aggronaut, ex-pro surfer in his home north of Wollongong, Critta clearly remembers that Crawford visit. For that was the last day Critta saw his best mate alive...

Critta: "We've been sound soul buddies since 1974. We both knew if something was wrong with the other. That time he seemed a bit... distant, a bit sad and agitated, like he had a one-way ticket or something. He mentioned he had something wrong with the valves in his ticker ... and kept telling me to take really good care of that beautiful kid..." Like virtually everyone I spoke to about Crawford, Critta struggled for a moment with emotion. "Before he left, he went all serious. He said, 'When I'm gone, look after my legacy. Make sure they don't make a mockery of me'."

And Critta looked at me.

The Clues in Life

1951. Peter Crawford was born on Mick Jagger's birthday, July 29. At age one, his family moved to the hard Sydney beach suburb of Dee Why. The PC-sized holes in the walls of his home were testament to the violence of his youth. Remembers John Harris, a few years younger: "Dee Why then was another world. It was tough. The separation (from the rest of Sydney) wasn't just in kilometres. We had the best, the heaviest wave, and no one else was having it. You couldn't hide from the point." Indeed. This was the brutal barrel that shaped first Crawford's brilliant kneeboarding and later his fearless, ultra-close brand of water photography.

Both activities, of course, paralleled expatriate American George Greenough, who was pulling full bore roundhouse cutbacks before such a move existed and peering out from behind the curtain with insane regularity before Lopez had even grown pubes: a fact most people managed to ignore in the 1960s (and since) simply because GG was a kneeboarder. PC inherited this mantle in the '70s, becoming the antipodal eccentric. Critta: "He loved Greenough, that barefooted, outrageous innovator with a rope around his waist, still doing amazing stuff. Crawford was the same, with his own dress code – socks with plastic coloured sandals and a groovy shirt..." Yet for both, surfing spoke louder than fashion. It took two decades for the stand-ups to catch up with the kneeboarders roundhouses, deep tube riding, carve 360's, barrel rolls (like the one Crawford pulled at the '76 Aussie Titles) and sheer ability to take on the heaviest of breaks.

Critta: "He did my gardens, and knew all the scientific names of the plants. He built his own housings. He was a talented writer who could lay out and produce a whole magazine on his own. Basically, he was good at everything." PC and Critta first met at the NSW and Oz Titles when PC was in the middle of his extraordinary domination of Australian kneeboarding, winning a hatful of consecutive titles (even beating MP in one final). The two regularly absconded to surf secret South Coast reefs together. PC helped Critta mend his broken back and later when Critta almost lost an eye in Indonesia. "He'd had so many illnesses himself, being a tall skinny cunt always carrying heavy tripods, cameras and housings. So he was a book of information about living. He could sleep for days, then wake like a baby, full of energy."

Critta agreed there was an air of mystery around PC's death, that it was possible other substances could have been involved. "His life was... moving toward an end. He was brilliant early in his career. Then came his divorce, his magazines went down and every year there were another 30 new photographers with auto-focus... The industry should take better care of their legends. Instead, they let them wash up on the shore...Fuck I miss him. Every day."

The Dreamland

Of Crawford's last two years, roughly one was spent in Indonesia, on and off, and much of that time with a core group of people who I'll get to, including Critta (though not on the final trip). The archipelago, Bali especially, was Crawford's work and pleasure paradise retreat where he truly lived, and the Dreaming land of magic, karma, ritual and demons where he would die. Critta: "When Lopez and company stumbled onto Ulus in the early '70s, PC wasn't far behind. He didn't like how Kuta evolved into such a rat race, but he always liked hanging out with the local surfing crew. His favourite eateries included the fish market for noodles, soups and fish, Aroma's for vegetarian food, Tubes for surf movies, the Sari Club, like all Aussies and ex-pats and (Club) 66 for a bit of a laugh." Added Pamela Peel, Crawford's ultimate lady: "He also loved Strawberries, Warung Kopi for Indian feasts, Glory Restaurant for big steaks and Sandy Parla for watching the sunset over Kuta Reef."

The influence was two-way. Indonesian surf photographer, Piping, 45: "Peter was my teacher, my father, my friend. He gave me many tips – how to play with current, protect your energy when you swim, shoot manually and play with camera. I try to become more relaxed and patient, more underground, like Peter. He one westerner who support me, who say the feedback will be more strong if I give to the people than if I just surf for myself. Now I have good life, teach two young photographers. I want to help like PC."

1995 (2). President Soeharto's infamously corrupt son Tommy wanted to develop the land around Dreamland on the Bukit Peninsula. Yet the old man who owned the land wouldn't sell, despite the urgings of his son. According to Pamela: "They needed a western person to run him over, famous even better. And so the old man was shoved in front of Peter's speeding car. Peter stopped and was amazed to see that the car following him contained a foreign doctor and nurse, ready to pronounce the old man dead. But everyone was mad because he was only injured..."

Added Critta: "They all wanted to kill PC."

Steve Palmer helped Crawford and his girlfriend evacuate and arranged cash to placate the old man's family. Steve doesn't think the old man was pushed onto the road, and remembers him only breaking his leg, which disproves somewhat the karma suspect. Yet Steve was sure PC would have been "driving at a good pace and chatting at the time, even if to some imaginary passenger..."

Three years later, Crawford returned after his passport had expired, with a new number. Tommy Soeharto owned Dreamland. That was the trip Crawford re-met David Smith and discovered Pamela Peel, both of whom would be with him on his final days. It was also the trip PC shot Crumplecar and entered into one of the most prolific periods of his career.

The Witnesses

David Smith first met Peter Crawford on a surf trip to virginal Papua New Guinea in 1986. A dozen years later, the two met up again, inside the Uluwatu cave. David, now 35, was (and still is) a team rider and rep for Indo Dreams in Bali. For the last two years of Crawford's life, or at least his slabs of time in Indo, including the final week, the two had 'amazing conversations' and plotted clandestine photographic missions, 'thick as thieves.' Best of all was Crumplecar, the supposedly secret wave barreling down a shipwrecked hull that few realised was virtually in Kuta's back yard, photos of which fast became myth and marked so dramatically the beginning of PC's renaissance.

David: "We were getting up at 4.00am every day for two weeks, Peter was so excited. He had a zest for life like a mad scientist, with his genius level IQ and unrelenting energy. We'd hide the bike with the seaweed fishermen and sneak out, sometimes with me towing Peter because he had broken ribs. But he had a heart of gold. The fishermen were dirt poor, so Peter would always give them money and presents. Every so often Quiksilver would deck him out with new gear, but if he didn't like it, he'd just give it all away. The photos that resulted were amazing, especially considering he had hardly anything, just second-hand cameras, old flippers and his girlfriend's ancient bodyboard.'

That was the same trip Crawford met Pamela Peel. David: "She was already friends with guys like Dick Hoole and Jack McCoy. They were a classic couple – the Hawaiian princess doubling PC around with his '70s hairstyle flying everywhere. Money came and went very quickly for PC, so Pamela was very good for him. She really inspired and pushed him. And funded a lot of his projects, going through rolls of Velvia like ice cream. PC was in the wilderness there for a few years before he met her. Unfortunately, not everyone sees her like that."

I met Pamela, an exotic English-Irish-Polynesian-Chinese-French blend, at her NSW Central Coast family property. Shifty, her hulking 11-month-old bull terrier/pit bull bounded out and slobbered his welcome. I was even more floored when

Pamela announced, "You're the first journalist to ever visit me about Peter. But I knew you'd come." Pamela almost died in a car crash six months after Crawford's death. She lost her mother too, and her health and finances have fallen apart. Yet the return of high times seems inevitable for this lady who has lived a life so varied and determined that Crawford considered her "his amazing female equal..."

The two met at the Sari Club on April 24, 1998 (though the two had actually been neighbours at Sunset Point, way back in 1976, when Pamela was living with Felipe Pomar). She remembers hearing a voice behind her: "I finally found you. I've been looking for you all my life..." Pamela whispered to her friend, "Who's he talking to?" Her friend smiled and replied, "You!" So a somewhat stunned Pamela turned and replied, "Well, come and introduce yourself."

And PC smiled, "My name is Peter Crawford. And I'm famous!"

Pamela: "Lovely to meet you. I'm Pamela Peel and I'm infamous... But I'm sorry, I've never heard of you!"

'He laughed, threw his arms up and cried, "Perfect!" And we were together from that day on until I left him in the morgue, 20 months to the day later.'

In that short time, Crawford contracted dengue fever; spent a week in Wyong Hospital after tangling in another surfer's leg rope at Bonzai, Forresters Beach, NSW; and was presciently bitten by an assortment of miniature wildlife. At the Noosa Longboard contest, he was savaged by sandflies. A month later he went to hospital with a sling on his arm. Doctors discovered live sandfly eggs inside the remaining bites. He was also stung by a scorpion in Indonesia. Again, infection followed, and a trip to the hospital, where half a scorpion was unearthed inside the swelling. Crawford's weird hyper-metabolism, which was actually tested by fascinated scientists at Sydney University when he was seven, seemed a magnet to the invertebrate world.

Pamela: "I miss him terribly. Most people are so borrring, but Peter's mind was always buzzing with endless ideas. We had a great relationship, the same friends and the same interests, from I Ching, to Supernature, to film... We were sitting in Aroma's and a mist appeared beside us. 'Hello, mother,' Peter smiled, like it was the most natural thing to talk to a dead relative."

1999: The Last Days 2 – Return to Bali

Dec. 12: Crawford made an offering to Duke Kahanamoku comprising a piece of a palm tree that resembled a surfboard, a giant Queensland orchid, angel hair and a big cloth poster of the Duke.

Dec. 16: Packing day. Peter's sons, Justin and Scott (now 33 and 26), dropped around in the afternoon to share a few chuckles and wish him a happy Christmas and a safe trip. On his final night in Australia, he was struck down with a fever.

Remembers Pamela: "We almost didn't go, but being holiday time, Garuda wouldn't change the tickets. Still, I was glad to leave Dee Why. Peter always fell back into old, bad habits there."

Dec. 17: At Sydney Airport, Peter and Pamela bought litre bottles of Duty Free Tequila and Scotch. On the plane, Pamela remembers Peter peering out the window: "He had his glasses on and his binoculars out, looking like a mad professor, searching for Crumplecar, his baby. Then he slumped forward and said, 'I can't see it.'." Around 4pm the two were picked up (along with a consignment of new Byrne boards) at Tuban Airport by Made Lana's girlfriend, who then dropped them at Panorama Cottages II, where they had stayed so often before. Pamela: "The doors to Number 18 were wide open. It was like, 'Welcome to your destiny'." Late that evening, I asked Peter if he was coming to bed. "Oh Pamela," he replied. "Let me enjoy our beautiful garden and get drunk the first night of our holiday. I deserve that at least." Standing beneath the giant heliconia tree, wearing only his boardshorts, glass of Cuervo in one hand, he looked up at the moon and said, "We're finally home." As he reached up to touch a flower, a *lerlipi gadang* (green pit viper) uncurled, bit him on the left arm above the elbow and moved on to drink water." Crawford joined Pamela in bed soon after, unaware of the magnitude of what had just happened.

Dec. 18: In the morning, Pamela remembers being scared when "Peter's eyes clanged open like a robot, or an alien, in a cold way I'd never seen before. There were strange silver spots in his eye pupils." When Pamela asked if Peter was OK, he snapped angrily, "Nothing's wrong! You're stupid!" He leapt up. "It was then that I noticed the lump on his arm, the size of half a navel orange. Seeing

ANNA MILLAIS

The Green/Bamboo pit viper
*(*Trimeresurus albolabris *or* insularis*)*
lives in trees, bamboo or bushes and is
the unconfirmed cause of PC's death.

Peter was in such an unusually foul mood, I went to the beach and visited friends." Later in the day she returned to be greeted by a message from a surgeon: "Peter has had an operation. Please come to Sanglah Hospital." At the hospital, Pamela found her boyfriend "asleep in bed, out to anaesthetic, his arm bandaged. Beside him was a metal kidney dish and a giant metal syringe full of greeny yellow mustard coloured pus. So I wrote him a big note, saying I'd be back at 9am in the morning, and left him some rupiah, snacks and water."

Dec. 19: Pamela: "Next morning, Peter was ready to be checked out. The doctor asked if he wanted the pus tested. But besides costing US $50, the tests would take 14 days, and we weren't even sure if we'd still be in Bali then, so Peter said, 'Forget it. I feel fine.' That afternoon, he rested at home"

Dec. 20: Journal entry: "I'm guided by a signal. In the Heavens. First we take Manhattan. Then we take the millennium. Is it Sydney?"

Pamela: "Every morning we went to the Legian Medical Clinic to have the dressing changed. Later that morning, David Smith came over, so I went to the hairdresser, while Peter rested and chatted about Crumplecar. In the afternoon we decided to go to the movies. David's girlfriend wanted to watch Deep Blue Sea, so we did. Then Peter wanted to watch Inspector Gadget to 'neutralise the first movie'."

Dec. 22: Final journal entry: "David Smith and I voyage back to Crumplecar to see the..." (unfinished).

At the former site of Crumplecar, Peter put up a big 'Save the Turtles' sticker on a post where he used to hide his motorbike. The two couples continued on in their rented *bemo* to Benoa Harbour to see where Crumplecar had been towed.

Dec. 23: The full moon was the closest to the earth in 285 years, and the last of the millennium. After dusk, Peter, Pamela, David and girlfriend went next door to Paul King's bungee tower. Pamela: "Peter raced up first, like the roadrunner, to shoot the moon," as Tim Baker eulogised, "chasing thrills beyond the endurance of his legendary constitution until the end."

Pamela: "Later, PC was sitting up in bed, selecting photos for Alby Falzon's forthcoming book. He started to shake and fit. A pale bluish colour crept across the skin of his neck like a shadow, which I later realised was his lymph gland releasing dormant poison, which had multiplied, into his body. Then it was gone and he went back to normal. Seeing how worried I was, Peter said, 'I'm OK. You know my crazy metabolism.' So I got him the takeaway spring rolls he wanted for dinner and he went to sleep, his cure for everything... Around midnight, he woke and said he was hungry again. I asked if he wanted to drive to get some food, but he said no, he wanted some exercise. He returned at 4am."

The Last Day

Dec. 24: Pamela: "Next morning, Peter seemed alright. We went to Warung 96 for breakfast with David's girlfriend and her architect friend. It was Christmas Eve, so I went to book us a table for four at the Aussie Smorgasbord lunch at the Gardenview in Legian. My motorbike had a puncture, so I was gone two hours. It was very hot, so when I returned, I was sweating like crazy. Peter didn't look well. We'd moved the mattress downstairs onto the cool tiles, and he just wanted to give me a hug and sleep there with the fan on. I went and told David and returned to the room to read magazines while Peter slept. Late in the afternoon I gave Peter a kiss on the forehead and went out to the supermarket, just across the road, to buy juice, water and supplies. I picked up a bag of sugar, and it exploded outward, not down with gravity. The Balinese girls packing shelves looked at me and went, "Ohhh!" In retrospect, that must have been the exact moment..."

During the short time I was out, a huge storm rolled in. Thunder crashed and rain bucketed down, so I ran across the road with the shopping bags. "I'm back!" I cried, and went over to PC to give him some juice. He was limp, his forehead cool. "What?" I cried, and started shaking him. I couldn't believe it. I'd only been gone 15 minutes. "Peter! Peter!" I felt for a pulse. There was none. Lightning flashed. I started giving him CPR and screaming out to the Balinese workers out the back. I knew I couldn't stop. The workers came in and called for help. I refused to stop giving Peter CPR. I was in total shock and couldn't do anything else. Brown liquid dribbled out of his mouth and nostrils. Finally a Javanese doctor and nurse arrived, Doctor A.H. Herman Anggawisata, who'd been on a call at Kuta. He gave Peter three adrenaline shots, while I kept crying, "Look up! Wake up! This isn't funny anymore!" I was going mad. My soul was screaming. The garden flooded. Finally, the doctor said, "He's gone." I went with Peter to the hospital, where they said the same thing, then to the morgue, where I had to fill out all the paperwork. I kept expecting him to sit up and laugh. The doctor said the bungee run had released the poison, but it would have been released in the next two weeks and killed him either way. The whole thing lasted from 8pm to 11.30pm. Back at Panorama, the police came and I had to go with one of the boys to the station in the rain. It was surreal, like a movie. All the police wanted, when they finally drove me home at 4am, was a *Playboy* magazine."

The Afterlife

Dec. 25: Pamela: "I lay there shattered, maybe slept for one hour. When it started to get light I talked to Peter in my mind, remembered my Tibetan teachings and planned an offering. Then I went to David's. Thank God he was there. I would have died of grief and shock. I was so shattered, I just couldn't think at all, or function. He was a great help. We made an offering of flowers and personal items and blessed

Peter. Late in the afternoon David returned from the big lunch I'd booked, but couldn't go to."

David's girlfriend beamed, "Pamela, you won't believe it! PC is already doing stuff!" This poor couple, living on a tight budget, had won a first class return trip to Lombok as soon as they entered the luncheon. They'd brought back little mince pies and a piece of Christmas cake, which we added to the middle of the offering. Not one ant touched the food.'

David: "Mate, I've never won anything in my life. Pink Floyd's "Wish You Were Here" was playing. I really felt him there... It was so weird and strange going in there to console Pamela. The crazy man wasn't there anymore. That day was horrifying. So many heavy decisions..."

Pamela: "I had Peter's last roll of film developed. One of the shots from the Dee Why Sun Festival had a lit-up Ferris wheel appearing like a perfectly placed frangipani behind Peter's ear. I called Critta, Mick Mock, the boys, as many people as I could, but telling the story over and over was just too hard. At that point, I wasn't sure exactly what had happened, if it had been a spider bite, or what. I couldn't sleep there, so I moved to another room and we returned every day to visit, take photos and be a part of the energy. I talked to the manager and made sure no-one touched Peter's room for three days, so he could get used to being in a spirit body."

Dec. 27: Pamela: "On the third morning, I noticed a piece missing from the corner of the Christmas cake, like a rat nibble. David opened the cupboard, as the door had slammed inward, and there was a big dead rat in there. We were all blown away. You tell me how that happened?'

Dec. 31: Pamela: "PC's embalmed body flew back to Australia at 1am so he could see in the new millennium at home. I flew back two days later.'

The New Millennium.

Jan. 7: PC was cremated at the Northern Suburbs Memorial Gardens and Crematorium in his favourite clothes: brown Quiksilver shorts, sarong and the Outer Island shirt with a hibiscus motif and Egyptian eyes. At the request of Scott and Justin Crawford, no autopsy was performed.

Jan. 8: At his beloved Dee Why Point, hundreds paddled-out to say farewell, including perhaps the last great gathering of the kneeboard clan. A double circle was formed, representing PC's favourite number, infinity, and his ashes were thrown into the air from film canisters. On the return to shore, a seemingly endless set of three feet waves rose up from a flat ocean...

Afterlife stories abound. Andrew McKinnon was sure PC sent him a remarkable tube when he entered the final of the Australian kneeboard titles for a lark. A gardener friend of Crawford's remembered a conversation two weeks before the end in which he was told, "I think I'm going to be bitten by a snake and go to my mother's arms this Christmas." Another friend reportedly heard PC bashing on his door just 24 hours after he'd passed away. Pamela regularly does 'I Ching' readings and talks in symbolic language to her dead lover. "I asked him to do something from the other side. 'If you can do something, do it.' I walked to my post box. On the way, I looked for four-leaf clovers, which is something we always did together. I found a little patch with 40. Two days later, I found 80. The four and the eight on its side equals "for eternity', the zeroes for emphasis, a very Peter equation. I've never found another four-leaf clover in that spot. In fact, clover doesn't even grow there anymore.'

The Ends

In Bali, I sniffed around Crawford's favourite hangouts. The manager of Panorama Cottages II, Wayan Tirta, showed me through the rooms of Number 18. I found no easy answers or clues, physical or psychic. Wayan: "Of course I not forget Peter. He lovely man, always funny, but sometimes very nervous, and rushing. He always chew the side of his sunglasses until he destroy. He give to me the chewed glasses, but I lose." We went into the garden, where Wayan named all the plants in the garden. I checked them all, but from a respectful distance, in case whatever fanged creature within had developed a taste for surf media. Wayan's name for the big tree with many colourful flowers and upright purple leaves, was a *kamboja*. "In Java, they have these in cemeteries."

Wayan mostly remembers Pamela crying on the fateful evening. "I must report to *polisi*, because Peter is my guest." He seemed dubious about the cause of death. "I never hear of people die from snake in Bali. If green snake bite, it burn. People go, "OHH!" Peter little sick, but later he go up bungee tower. From that, I not believe in snake or spider." So what then? "I think he sick already inside." Wayan taps his chest. "He cough like he have flu. He have often. I wonder why he not have health report."

Piping was even more blunt: "I think snake bullshit, because snake live in bush. Whatever happen, he just go. Hopefully, PC have a good place, because I know he have good karma."

For others, the snake makes perfect sense. Kim "Fly" Bradley, long-time Bali denizen, spent many nights partying with Crawford at the Sari Club. "I knew a guy who died one month after being bitten by a snake. And PC was very allergic. When we were in Sumbawa, he got bitten by something and his arse blew up like a football. He was so sick, he couldn't eat the one good meal we were served. So

I don't believe the other stories... His mental state in his final months was really positive. He'd met Pamela, he was loving life and really focused on his work." Drugs? Fly shook his head. "Just beers by the pool, maybe a few big nights a week. He wasn't doing anything else, at least not in front of me."

According to Pamela and Davids Smith and Wylie, not to mention his own journal, Crawford's future was solidly booked: the Philippines for January, a Paul King Indo project for April, more Indo, more books, plus Crawford's gonzo goal to film himself kneeboarding Chicama for several kilometres, and much more besides. None of which supports the rumour of a man planning to end his own life.

Yet still the rumours swirl, though no one would put their name to any for this story. Yet for any of the rumours to be true, there would have to be a cover-up, a conspiracy, plus a compelling reason to do so. Given the love for Crawford of those around him, the only reason I can conceive would be born of the best intentions: to protect his name.

More interesting is the place the conjecture emerges from. Certainly, conjecture make the story more intriguing, like the *Sydney Sun Herald*'s headline, 'Star's Mystery Death'. Rumours create an air of ambiguity, rendering Crawford's death not unlike his life. But they also tarnish. As David Smith said: "He always called a spade a spade and didn't care about the repercussions." Yet there were always repercussions, and thin-skinned editors. Critta: "Some of his bad situations resulted from the envy of his peers. Sometimes he was too brilliant for his own good. As for his death, no one will ever really know."

Beyond all the bullshit, Peter Crawford's death was but a minuscule fraction of a remarkable life. His legacy, his work, will endure beyond the life-span of mere memory: portraits of unequalled intimacy with the world's best surfers, both on land and deep inside the barrel, from Dee Why Point to Pipe, from cliff-top to helicopter; his art a portal into life on the edge, into the unique, insightful, dangerous, transgressional and majestic CrawfordWorld.

In Bali, a friend lent me a book by James P. Carse, *Finite and Infinite Games*, about the two game types people play. The object of the more common finite game is to establish a winner and loser according to set rules, and thus end the play; whereas infinite games, played by more advanced souls, continually open up and expand, even beyond death, for the object is to continue play. At every turn, the book reminded me of PC, perhaps surfing's ultimate infinite game player, laughing even now at my feeble attempts to unravel the unravel-able.

First Published in *The Surfer's Journal* Volume 13, No. 3 (2004)

Searching for the Dreamland...

First impressions of the Bali myth

ALEX DICK-READ

◻

> "The mind is its own place, and in itself
> Can make a heav'n of hell, a hell of heav'n."
> JOHN MILTON, *PARADISE LOST BK 1*. 1667

> "Travel no further in search of your goal, it's under your feet."
> LAURIE MCGINNESS ON BALI, *SURFING WORLD* MAGAZINE, 1978.

BALI – WHAT'S a surfer supposed to make of it these days? The signals are confusing. From what I can pick up, two radically different reputations mask its realities and if, like me, you've never even been there, it's hard to know what to expect. On the one hand there's the Bali cliché: the 'Island of the Gods', a land of exotic scents and magical ceremonies. Its people are gentle, welcoming, guided by karma and always seeking harmony and balance. And its shores are so well endowed with groomed, perfectly barrelling waves that, for a surfer, Bali is as close to an Earthly paradise as you'll ever find. In short, it's a place that any sensible surfer should have a relationship with. And most do.

Then there's the other angle: Bali is a has-been, overrun, sold-out, tourist trap. It developed too fast and is crowded out with surfers, backpackers, smug expats living the dream and regulars too cool for school. Its mellow spiritualism is tainted by loud western hedonism, many of its people are being exploited or infected with greed while at government level, corruption and criminality are rife and operating on a vast, uncontrollable scale. Don't even mention terrorism. In terms of surf, it has good waves, yes, but not as good as its neighbours', and these days they're crowded to the point of comedy, or for many, tragedy. It ain't what it used to be, and all that. In short, any sensible surfer will avoid Bali these days and look elsewhere for their Earthly paradise, because it sure as hell isn't there anymore.

Here's my friend Sparrow, a long-term, hard-core, ground-level Kiwi traveller, who echoes the thoughts of many I know:

"Bali has become hideous in my eyes – not just for surfing, it's also all the associated mainstreamers who've bought into the whole idea of that lifestyle and actually bought apartments, pet dogs, bars and all the other crap that goes with.

I've seen the ongoing progress about every two years for the past two decades and I think there's been more development in the last four or five than in the previous 15...and it's really just the beginning. It amazes me that people would actually want to live in Bali, unless they're either a sheep or a developer, which are what many people there seem to be.

This view is cynical, I know, but a month or two ago I saw the polar opposite end of the spectrum – two weeks of perfect waves with just me and a mate. It was actually the least crowded Indo I've ever come across for such high quality waves over a prolonged period. It's not the only place like that either.

I could, of course, just harden the f--k up and go hop in the water every day and deal with the crowds. Of course, I'd get plenty of waves by doing my time, being in the right place in the right conditions etc. etc. But why bother, when there's so many empty places on the planet?"

Before I leave for Bali, this is one of my problems. I've never even been there and already I know too much. As the trip approached the two opposing visions battled it out in my mind.

"Aw, it's going to be shit," I'm thinking. "A crowded theme park," versus the blessed-out view: "mmm Bali...I can smell the incense already...massages, mangos and sweet coffee...barrels, as far as the eye can see."

In reality, I wasn't that fazed by the bad rep. In fact, I was thrilled by the fantasy take on Bali and absolutely over the moon to be going there, surfwise. I couldn't wait to surf Uluwatu; I had cold sweats about Padang Padang; I'd become intrigued by Bingin's short, sharp barrels, frothing for Impossibles (looks makeable to me), tripping on Dreamland and hungry to check Airport Rights, Canggu's reefs, Keramas and anything else on the east coast that offered a windless window. Surf thoughts alone had me dribbling over the guidebook. Of course, this actually makes me a total kook. Everyone has been to Bali and here am I, a surfer of some 25-plus years, a surf mag editor for 14 years and I'm so late for a party that, word is, it's hardly worth turning up to at all. But here's me, pissing my pants with excitement about going to Bali for the very first time. Mea kooka.

We finally arrive and my friend JC Pierce and I find ourselves standing at the carousel in Denpasar airport late one night in June, tired, curious and expectant. The excitement has only grown. My mixed-up mind has hardened. I've made a decision to ignore all negative press, take whatever comes and look at the positives. So the garish surf-hostel posters and surf-school posters and surf-everything posters that greeted us in the arrivals hall were mere amusement, and the fact that

I was perhaps the 10 millionth surfer ever to stand at the carousel waiting for my surfboards was neither here nor there. JC, of course, had been here before – twice actually, but not since 1984 when he was a sponsored pro based out of Florida. Back then pros didn't just rock up at Denpasar and get chauffeured to the Quik mansion like I assume they do now. Those were the days of unpaved roads along Kuta Beach, home-stays with families, and long walks down to the ladder at Uluwatu. Like me, JC was curious about what we'd find here, but unlike me, he knew what was coming.

Uloooos!

The forecast promised an 8ft swell in two days time. Until then we'd have to make do with whatever the Indian Ocean threw at us, which suited me fine. We'd landed on our feet with a spacious room in Puri Uluwatu, a hotel on the hill above Uluwatu's main peak. The room had a small lawn out back with a stone shrine of carved gods and ornate monsters. Offerings made of banana leaf and filled with flowers and spicy incense were scattered all around. From the shrine we could see paradise, or that's how it seemed on that first dawn as we stared down the valley at The Peak.

We could see trails of whitewater wisping across wave faces in the semi dark, so we grabbed boards and headed down the valley via steep steps through trees filled with silent monkeys giving us surly looks. At the foot of the stairs we reached the *warungs*, little businesses with open decks out front that overlook the break. This is where the world congregates and a hierarchy of Balinese entrepreneurs slice some of it off while its here. The bamboo and wood structures that JC remembers are made of concrete now and they've multiplied and diversified into t-shirt stalls, kitchens, bars, massage areas, ding-repair dens and photo shops. And the famous wooden ladder that descends into Uluwatu's cave is now a cast concrete stairway, though it's no less dramatic, especially for a first-time kook like me.

Apart from the guidebook guidance I didn't really know much about Uluwatu's waves. I knew there were several of them along the stretch of coast that marks the tip of the Bukit Peninsula, one being Temples, further up towards the tip from where we were, but the rest were all a kind of blur of lefthanders. Beyond that most of my knowledge of the place came from two classic films, *Morning of The Earth* by Albe Falzon and David Elfick, and *Tubular Swells*, by Jack McCoy and Dick Hoole.

These are timeless films, beautifully made, but both are from an era long, long passed. The best I could glean was that Ulus had good waves, yes, but they were somehow not that noteworthy anymore.

Surfing in Bali started in Kuta around 1936, but it wasn't until the late sixties that American servicemen started sniffing the coast out and finding new places, maybe even Uluwatu. The break's genesis moment comes with *Morning of the Earth* in 1971, which shows young Australian Steve Cooney and older Hawaiian guy, Rusty Miller, riding the first waves at Ulus. Albe Falzon describes the discovery thus:

MICK CURLEY

Uluwatu   LAT. -8.816372° LONG. 115.085626°

Ultra-consistent "Ulu's" is the focal point of Balinese surfing thanks to its ability to handle any size swell from small to large and spread the biggest of crowds across a wide playing field of reef. Its sectioning, hollow walls always produce great waves, starting with faster, high tide, occasional tuck-ins up at Temples that lead down to the muscular, steep drops of The Peak that offers open faces with hollow pockets directly in front of the famous cave. It can sometimes jump the deadspot and barrel through to the start of the Racetrack, which twists and bends the wailing walls in an ever increasing race against the falling curtain. When swells exceed the 8-10ft mark, Outside Corner will rumble into life, with heavy, thick-lipped sections at low tide for experts on sturdy pintails. Main hazard is the crowd, followed by the reef and the constant higher tide sweep that requires aiming for a spot well south of the cave to come in. Blow it and you'll paddle another 15min circuit.

"We stayed in Kuta on arrival. It was just a small coastal village at the time. Dirt roads, topless old women leading pigs around on a lead, chickens everywhere, very few losmens, no tourists – just a few German hippies hanging out on the beach.

"As far as we know, we were the first surfers to venture out on the Bukit. When the surf was flat at Kuta one day, we went out to the temple overlooking Uluwatu – not exactly overlooking the break – up the reef a bit. It was pretty flat on the reef so we walked along the headland to the corner of Uluwatu and to our amazement there was small, 2-3ft surf wrapping around the headland. It looked perfect. The water was really clear – it just looked like a dream place to surf. A few days later when the surf kicked in at Kuta, we thought maybe there'd be some good surf out at Ulus. To our surprise, when we arrived it was around 8ft and pumping."

Falzon and crew were followed by others of the underground, like Gerry Lopez, Jeff Hakman, Jack McCoy and Dick Hoole, who in turn were followed by a few more of their ilk, and then others of their ilk, and so it slowly spread. Gradually, Bali, and Uluwatu in particular, became known among the small global brotherhood, as a tangible paradise, not a mythical island like Santosha, but a real life surf nirvana with a backdrop of exotica that defied belief or comprehension.

"For the first few years Ulu was all I could imagine perfect surf could be," says Gerry Lopez who, come summer when the Pipeline shut off, had eyes for no other … even after Grajagan was discovered. "Bill Boyum yelled down from the cliff when he got back from the first time to G-Land, 'This isn't even a surf spot!' He's lucky we were down on the beach because we would have stoned him.

"But later, even once we got set up to comfortably campaign G-Land – that's where we'd be during the full and new moon tide periods – but we'd still return and surf Ulu on the in-between tides." Bali offered the likes of Lopez a new universe of waves, culture and spirituality to explore and an everyday existence beyond compare.

Here's Australian writer Laurie McGinness again, talking about the later '70s, when Ulus was already widely known among the surfing fraternity:

"At the time Bali really was the end of the search for many of us. We knew that better waves like G-Land and Nias existed, but we also knew that, for variety, lack of crowds and consistency, Bali at that time was as good as it was ever going to get. If you can imagine arriving at Uluwatu on a perfect morning, looking down the length of the Bukit and knowing that you were the only surfers in the whole area, or riding an outrigger out to perfect empty Nusa Dua; they were our everyday experiences."

Stepping down into the cave that first morning, it felt like I was tasting the magic. I'd only been in Bali for 10 hours but so far it felt like the dream come true. I waded in and paddled-out on an exiting surge, noting how sharp the cave's walls look and not to mess with this place at higher tides. I paddled for the light and soon rounded a big rock at the entrance then found myself rushing down coast in a current that totally owned me. A few metres away, just across a shallow shelf, deep blue walls hurled over themselves and throttled down the reef, growing all the way. As I paddled and drifted and duck-dived, waiting for a lull, I saw sights that gave me shivers of joy, and fear. No one told me it was this good. I slid out back and wandered across a broad plain of water, watching peaks rear up, arc and race along ruler-straight zip lines in the near, the middle and the far, far distance.

A crew of guys was scattered widely and peaks rose up outside and in on the ledge. The outside waves heaped themselves into deep blue mountaintops, rolled and thundered in, while inside, the slightly smaller swells held off until the last moment, chucking when they hit the shelf. All the waves looked thick and fast, and as they ran down the line, they grew.

"It's a proper wave," I thought to myself. "And if the 8ft swell is coming in two days time, what's this?"

In all the pep talks about Bali I'd had, everyone said Uluwatu was "a great wave", but none went much further than that. People rarely rave about it, so while I'd read the guidebooks and got the gist, I wasn't really ready for all this…detail. The thickness – the volume of water in every wave – was more than I'd imagined. My 6'4" Wade Tokoro barrel-chaser felt small. I felt small.

It's hard to imagine how Steve Cooney must have felt in 1971, 15 years-old paddling-out here for the first time and taking-off backhand on one of those growers, before anyone had ever even tried it. Even Lopez and his Hawaiian crew couldn't ignore the power.

"Ulu was intense," Lopez says. "We were all alone out there. Except for a few fishermen and reef gatherers, it was just us...me, Jeff and Jack. Sometimes some of the few other surfers in Bali would come and that was very welcome because the energy, isolation and relentlessness of the place was pretty overwhelming."

Forty-odd years later, in a time when the whole surfing world has been there and done that, a time when teams of lifeguards watch from the cliff, bars pump music and photographers with 600mm lenses capture high-speed sequences of every wave ridden, the place still feels big and full of power. Whatever else has changed, the reef and the waves and the brutal currents and the magnificent setting haven't.

We surf until the water is greeny turquoise and the sun is high. It is an exhilarating first surf. Speed is the main sensation – speed and wonder at its beauty and power. As the blood sugar levels deplete, I enter a state of blissed-out delight. My board's a little thin for the occasion, but aside from that, there's not a thing wrong with the world. I'm living the Bali fantasy. I'm fresh off the plane and I've woken up in the dream I was told didn't exist anymore.

The line-up had started off virtually empty but gradually fills. The crowd ranges from kids to old boys, mostly Australian and none of them looking too impressed with the magnificence around them. The crowd tightens as the tide changes, and wedging peaks appear (really wedging. I never knew Ulus had such kick-ass little bounce). I surf on, even enjoying the range of characters, and the skills of some of these Aussie tube-hounds. But the energy's changing.

Soon little flashes of negative electricity start sizzling through the crowd. There's some scowling and muttering going on, and some drop-ins and snaking. I pull back from a wave again to make way for a Brazilian guy who'd snaked me, again, and who I knew was too deep, again. I turned and faced a set, the first wave already rearing further out than me, then paddled for the edge of the whitewater. Just as I got there an Aussie guy who'd been getting more than his share of barrels swung late to drop in, right above me. He saw me, bailed and his board met mine somewhere in the soup. His was dinged pretty badly, but mine was fine. I felt for the guy – forced to paddle in when the Peak was on fire. Then he paddled up and showed me the damage and it turned out he wanted to blame me, though he clearly knew he'd screwed up and caused the whole thing. He huffed and puffed and paddled off cursing.

Suddenly I felt angry. I looked around and realised I was surrounded by maybe 50 people, all waiting for the same thing I was. It was a magic, beautiful, powerful thing we were waiting for, a little hit of the magic wave-bong. But at that moment it felt sordid. I felt more like a junky queuing for a methadone prescription, somewhere in Australia.

This may have been the blood sugar reaching dangerously low levels and shorting out my positive chi or something, but whatever it was I suddenly wanted out. I didn't love it anymore. I wasn't in the Bali Uluwatu surf nirvana fantasy anymore. I was sensing the flipside. Retreat and recuperation seemed like the best thing to do.

This was the right move, and the right tactic for our week at Ulus. Ignore all negatives. Seek only the positives. We surfed Uluwatu every day from then on, usually several times, always returning in a state of bliss. Turned out the 8ft swell had arrived two days early, so it dropped from Day Two onwards, but not by much. All week we gorged on thick, fast barrels, and for most of that time stayed firmly planted on the upside of the Bali dream. The bullshit was out there, but we wilfully ignored it and just surfed the wave. She is an interesting, many-mooded beauty, easy to fall in love with if you can block out the 50-plus other blokes she's flirting with at the same time.

I asked Lopez what happened to his relationship with Uluwatu, when and why it lost its lustre. Interestingly he didn't say, "Aw it just got too crowded". He said that, but with a twist, touching on the role of the beholder in the equation:

"Uluwatu was, is and always will be a world-class surf break. [But] as the years went by and the crowds increased, something changed. Later on when I thought about it, I reckoned it had to do with a loss of freedom. The high tide peak at Ulu is a shifty devil and when I had the line-up to myself, I was free to roam and chase down those scattered peaks. The low tide inside Racetrack had one easy take-off and with more than a couple of people there, it became congested. Each time I returned, I found the wave less satisfying as my movement in the line-up was increasingly restricted by more and more people. Somehow, it seemed, the magic was gone. I've often thought about what it was that changed and the only answer I could come up with...was me, and something in my mind. The place hasn't lost any of its magic, I just lost the ability to feel it."

Mega's World

Mega Semahdi reckons he'll be a priest by the time he's 50, but until then he's happy being a pro surfer. "Varuna is our god of the sea," says the diminutive 21-year-old Rusty rider as he sits in his Bingin heartland surrounded by his posse, empty beer bottles on the table, in-jokes flying, a guitar and a couple of adopted foreigners who've joined this friendly, but high-end inner circle of the Bingin beachboy brotherhood. "Varuna is a good god, but he also gets angry," says Mega. "As surfers we know all about that." Sounds like he'll make a good preacher, I think.

In all respects the scene resembles any similar brotherhood of locals anywhere in the surfing world, except that among this group there's one red-hot, highly paid sponsored rider and a number of others soon-to-be. Also, because they're Balinese, talking seriously about being a priest later in life and discussing the moods of the gods that surround you while downing some beers and boisterously shit-talking the afternoon away, isn't unusual. These days it's entirely normal.

Mega is a Bukit Peninsula kid turned pro and as such he's the direct descendent, in the family tree of surfing in Bali, of Steve Cooney, Rusty Miller, Gerry Lopez, Jeff Hakman et al. He's the inevitable outcome, if such a thing can exist, of the influx of surf into his island home back in the early '70s. Between then and now, two generations of Balinese kids have grown sea legs and become surfers. The first generation is made up of the few who dared join the foreigners playing in Varuna's domain. After them came more brave souls, and talent borne of unlimited daily perfection. Eventually Indonesian surfing started appearing on the global surf radar with the exploits of the half-Chinese, half-Balinese goofy-foot, Rizal Tanjung. Rizal became a household name and part of the inner-sanctum of Hawaiian and top pro surfers. As his fame and wealth grew he always offered a helping hand to young Indonesian up-and-comers, so that they too might lift themselves out of poverty and into the healthy funding stream of the ever-growing Balinese surf industry.

Mega takes home a good cheque from his sponsors every month – as much for his everyday surfing as for contest wins, although over the years he's won a Pro Junior at Kuta Reef, Rookie of the Year award in the Indonesian Surfing Circuit tour and taken a 3rd at the big annual Rip Curl Padang Padang contest. He's a slim, featherweight guy, but he's no slouch in the big barrels of the Bukit. "I think there may be a god of big barrels, too," he tells me.

Mega looks at his future as being entirely bound up with surfing, at least until he's 50 and he becomes a priest. "As long as I can surf every day," he says of his next couple of decades, "I'll be happy." His father, once a farmer and then a self-educated lawyer, has always supported his son's surfing even though for him such a life seems strange, culturally. For Mega's grandparents, it's virtually impossible to get their heads around. In their lifetimes, Bali has transformed beyond imagination, although like true balance-seeking Balinese, they do not judge Mega. He tells me he feels he has the support of everyone important in his life.

I offer Mega a beer and he says, "No, thanks." His uncle, who taught him how to surf when he was about 10 years-old and hangs with the crew and gently watches over his 21 year-old nephew, sidles up to me and asks, "Please, don't buy another round. He doesn't really drink and I don't want him to get tempted."

Mega doesn't look like he needs a drink, dipping into the banter with familiar ease, chucking in one-liners that crack the crew up, strumming on the guitar a little and looking out over his beloved Bingin. This is his domain. Their domain – backpackers, surf tourists, sea gods and all. His smile never fades. Right now, in my mind, Mega is Balinese surfing. Young, strong, comfortably part of the global surf culture, but still culturally distinct, cashed-up, taboo-breaking, but respectful of the elders and the spirits and oh yes, surfing as good as the best of the avant garde aerial generation of today.

Jaded travellers may be 'over' Bali, but these Balinese surfers seem to be living in some other version of Bali and loving their life. Who can argue with that?

Detourism

We surfed Ulus every day, but made a couple of instructive day trips. Not far, mind you – with our tiny mopeds and so little time, it seemed that Keramas – a couple of hours of hard, dangerous driving up to the northeast coast – was off the menu. So was Canggu and anywhere much further afield than Kuta. But we had to hit Kuta.

By the time we arrived in the late afternoon, the golden sun was dipping towards the emerald waves of Kuta's seemingly limitless Halfway beach. The day felt nearly done but people, mopeds, cars, buses and bemos buzzed at swarming speed along the main road behind the beach. JC and I wandered onto the sand, glanced admiringly at the miles and miles of emerald walls and bright white manes with an offshore wind pulling them back. It wasn't like checking a surf spot. This didn't feel like somewhere I wanted to paddle out, though plenty of the waves looked plenty hollow and plenty makeable. It felt like a holiday beach, a really, really crowded mass tourism vacation beach, with semi-close-out barrels as a backdrop.

We were drawn to the street chaos so we found a cool drink and a perch where we could watch the world go by. It was enough to remind me that it's not just surfing that has changed Bali. Of course, surfing's just a sideshow, albeit one of the key attractions that makes this place marketably 'cool'. Kuta is everything touristic. It's backpacker, package tour, mainstream tourist heaven. A major world attraction. A place that every just-out-of-school kid will inevitably go to, like Phuket or Goa, but also a headline holiday for Chinese, Japanese, Korean, Taiwanese, Malaysian and other oriental group tours, and of course the mainstream Australian cheap getaway crowd. Oh, and don't forget the Indonesians from all over the archipelago who also come as tourists.

In amongst the crowd are the Balinese and Javanese hustlers who rent bikes, boards and cheap accommodation, sell sweets, beer, t-shirts, drugs, "dick bongs" and cigarettes, and organise parties, full-moon raves and girls that may be guys for guys too drunk to spot the difference. Here they all were. Like the *warungs* at Ulus, multiplied to a mass-market level.

We sat and sipped our beers. The traffic – human, two-wheeled and four-wheeled – was thick, the noise a continuous cacophony of horns and tingling Asian dance tunes. The swarms of mopeds never abated. Busloads of Chinese tourists passed by, rental cars, delivery vans, surf tour wagons and local buses with bored Balinese commuters heading home from school or work. In amongst them, occasionally, sat old men on mopeds in traditional dress, sedately abiding the traffic jam and lunatic crowds of beachified youth. They looked like they've been coming down this road forever, since back when it was a dirt track through the trees.

A group of teenagers dressed in black and all with bleached hair, lounged on the wall nearby looking semi-menacing but not, because you could see they all had the same logo on their shirts and were obviously not scary biker punks, but were actually just the Asian teenage pop version of biker punks, leafleting for a club. Fat white girls in slim bikinis and stumbling young Australian scamps wobbled past with beer cans and sloping grins. In the time it took to down a slow beer and a pack of peanuts, we saw a million people pass by, most of them semi-naked and sunburnt. We heard French, German, English, American, Spanish, Portuguese, Australian ('mayte, mayte, mayte, mayte') and all kinds of unknown Asian languages. We were the only still creatures in a hurricane of holiday fun. And then we were done. We'd seen enough. Kuta, in all its beautiful vulgarity. Done that.

We laughed in wonder and pulled out, back to Ulus, which felt like a quiet, lazy oasis.

On another afternoon we wandered down the Bukit Peninsular by bike determined to surf somewhere else. Bingin was small and crowded, Impossibles looked fun, but a long walk for a bunch of waves that always end up nailing you. It seemed like an unnecessary way to bait the sea god or the god of reef cuts.

We snooped over at Dreamland, which looked dreamy, but still too full, tide-wise. So we killed time and explored some more, but pretty soon ended up back at Dreamland, tempted by the clifftop view of its magnificent walls wafting in across the green-gold sea. We decided to get in, sure that as the tide pulled out it would start sucking on the reef and barrelling off in both directions. We paddled out and surfed with patience and expectant joy, making the best of the flat surfaces and lips that never quite threw. After an hour or so the doubts had well and truly set in. JC was chatting with an older Australian guy, a regular, it seemed. "Does it get hollow out here on the lower tide?" he asked.

"Nah, mayte, this is as good as it gets. It's just a shit wave."

We made our way in through hundreds of Chinese holidaymakers nearly drowning in the shorebreak. They were staying in the nuclear bunker of a hotel building, owned by one of Suharto's sons, concreted into the cliff above.

We left feeling foolish. With the whole Bukit and beyond available and accessible to us, and barrels as far as the eye could see – literally – we'd chosen just about the only shit wave on Bali.

But at least we had Uluwatu to retreat to, and these diversions confirmed our journey's most valuable lesson: the surfer's dreamland doesn't exist, and yet it is a real place.

First published in *The Surfer's Path* Issue 81 December, 2010

The Bali You Remember

Where dreams become realty

MATT GEORGE

□

Uluwatu – 10ᵗʰ Jan, 2012, 11:30

I T IS YOUR birthday. You are fifty-three years old. You still surf the world. Today you find yourself eight degrees below the equator, standing on a cliff's edge at the rich people's villas at Uluwatu overlooking the break at the Temple. The 100 metre sheer cliff makes your knees oily. You have your surfboard under your arm and a waterproof backpack on your back. You are going to climb down the cliff's secret south path and you are going to walk, surf and paddle the entire Bukit Peninsula over the next three days. You will be dusting off memories, looking at it again. Your first visit here was 28 years ago, when things were different.

It's low tide. You start to walk. You are living in Bali now. Three years under your belt.

An expat. Drawn to this far-off place, far from home, because of the bizarre freedom it offers. And because you have never been able to shake her call. Like a glorious courtesan, she calls you, makes you feel special, makes you feel like you are the only one on earth that can love her. Even though millions of others can have her too. And they do. Any time they like.

You are drawn to Bali and the Bukit Peninsula because there are no rules here. Watch your back, make the right friends, keep under the radar, don't make a fuss, let it be, get along, smile, make friends, but keep the locals at a certain distance. And forget the golden rule.

Nobody treats anybody the way they would like to be treated here. Get that straight, mate.

And you know that there is a strange beauty in that. It's every man, woman and child for themselves. Survival, but with unlimited fun, perfect waves, spiritualism, outrageousness and the freedom of taking care of ones self, without anyone sticking their nose in your business. Unless, of course, you fuck-up. Then it's all over. As sure as a popped balloon. Complete with the noise. If not the Kerobokan jail, then surely the airport. Never to return.

But you love the risk. Bali is Dodge City with palm trees. And you, the Gambler. You know you can be anyone you want to be here. You can re-invent yourself. Or just be who you always were with no trouble from nobody. No government, no cops, no hassles. All smiles. As long as you are aware that here the smiles are like icebergs, where unimaginable dangers lurk below. Romantically, philosophically, physically. Good luck. As long as you keep your nose clean, don't misstep, and thank the spirits everyday whether you believe in them or not...you just might make it. Watch your back. Ain't no rights. Plenty of wrongs.

Only savvy will see you through. From the booze-addled, sex brutalized carnival of the construction site formerly known as Kuta Beach, to the eat, pray, love of the creaking bamboo forests filled with monkeys and birds and spirits of the past that you can actually see from time to time. It has been 28 years since your first visit. Bali has been intertwined with your fate, your place in life. Your station in life. You are here.

You reach the bottom of the cliff, barely; the swinging rope section was a little hairy. You walk. Crunching along in the seashell sand. Your feet covered in mittens of the stuff. That has never changed. You can see the hooptydoodle of modern Uluwatu up ahead. The cliff sagging under the weight of the astonishingly irresponsible real estate development. The beer soaked *warungs*, the beer soaked bars, the beer soaked resorts, the beer soaked infinity pools, the beer soaked sewage, the beer soaked litter and the paper money that drives it all. Scads of paper money.

You can remember a time when there was only three warungs. So it goes. Surf Colonialism.

Surfers. Such shallow, selfish thinkers. Short of slaughtering people, as bad as the Dutch. The surf's not bad, only thirty-five guys out. It is off-season after all. You'll put in at the cave. Grab a wave and make your way to Padang Padang for the night. You can see the Bukit white kids are out. Their white skin standing out amongst the brown. There is always brown skin in the line-ups now. That is one thing that has changed for the better. The locals have taken this place back from the invaders. Not the Dutch, the English nor the Japanese could take this place forever. Why should it be any different for the western surfers? We could only hold the place so long. Too much treasure.

You see the great Jim Banks take off with his boy, Harley, on the same wave. You guess Harley would be about thirteen years old. Just like his other white mates out there. Luca Carlisle, Luan Huberman, Dyou Worawong and Max Desantis. They live here too. Growing up with their expat parents. Most of them single parents. Bali is not a place you go to live as a white person, it's a place you end up. The kids are growing up in the shadow of the temples. You know that much. Like the Lost Boys of *Peter Pan* they live on an enchanted island shrouded in magic, steeped in the mystical at every turn. And danger, yes, there is danger on land and sea for them. Massive swells their Captain Hook. Uluwatu their Wendy. Little Bingin their Tinkerbell. Their lives a melange of languages, mixed blood, exotic scents, monsoons, brown skin, bigotry, jealousy and phantasmic surfscapes. Their playground the best waves in the world. They breathe in the belonging to a place that will never belong to them. Never belonging, but always owning up to it. Paddling out day after day into international line-ups of every creed and color on earth. Rubbing shoulders with their heroes, the Indonesian greats and the silly international surf movie stars. They have backstage passes to every party, every contest, every happening. Thirteen years old and already familiar with the taste of the beer and lipstick. Kuta sees to that. They are growing up as a man-child cadre, they stick together, stay close, relate, compete now and then. They want to be champions all. That's the ticket here. Then you don't have to be a real estate agent. Champions of the world they want to be. An almost impossible dream on an island where the local surf brands don't sponsor little white kids. White pegs trying to fit into a brown hole. Still, they live in a dream that takes guts. Carving out their place while delicately balanced on the tightropes of mixed culture. Carving out their place. Carving.

You put in at the Uluwatu cave. You look back inside its cavernous walls. It breathes back at you. It always has. No matter what, no matter what anyone says, still the most exotic entry point into any line-up in the world. This mysterious cave, a surf star itself, held in your imagination for twenty-eight years now. You've paddled out through her when she was a maelstrom of tangling sea snakes with your heart in your throat. And you have swum in her crystal clear pools with exotic topless beauties. And your heart was in your throat then too.

You have honored her. Entered her like you would a church. The hush of the place is something you always remember. Everyone talks in whispers in the Uluwatu cave. Japanese, Indonesian, Korean, Russian, Aussie and American. Hushed. You have never heard so much as a shriek from a child inside her dripping, bat-laden overhangs. From her old wooden ladder days to her modern Dr. Seuss cement stairs you have loved her.

Just the other day you paddled out from within her into the crowded line-up with twenty other fellas. White and brown alike. You all paddled out and sat beyond the line-up and held hands in a big circle. Here, with the hapless Eco Surf Rescue Uluwatu non-profit guy, you promised to keep the place clean. To honor the water. You remember everyone, once the circle broke up, skipped the ceremony up in the Edge Bar on the cliff where Rip Curl's USD5000.00 check was presented. Everyone instead just tore into the line-up where a clean four-foot swell was running. A mad, hungry line-up. After all, you had all just spent fifteen precious minutes away from the waves, holding hands in a big circle with a bunch of other men promising to keep things clean around the place. A guy sure could use a barrel after all that time spent like that.

The thought makes you smile and you huff a laugh to yourself as you jump off the edge of the green reef and stroke as hard as you can to miss the oncoming set over the racetrack reef section. You feel the weight of the backpack for the first time. The trouble it's going to cause you. You make it out and sit up and watch Jim Banks swoop by you, front hand cupped like an offering, eyes as intense as when he was a boy. And you knew him as a boy.

You look at the young kids in the line-up and hope they realize some kind of shit. Knowing that if they realize some shit, then maybe the Bukit stands an even chance.

And you think, if only everybody realized that it was all about water. If only everybody realized that the sea is the home of all water. Every drop of it. That all water is simply off on a journey unless it is in the sea. That it is homesick and that it fights with all its will to get home. Water, whose memory is perfect and who is forever trying to get back to where it was. The sea. Life-giving water. Evaporated from the sea, kidnapped, up into the pregnant clouds, sailing inland to the hills and mountains, disgorging their magnificent bounty, falling upon the riches of the earth, and then moving, racing, running, following her secret paths of least resistance, roiling, running, flowing, always headed home. A raindrop becomes a rivulet, a creek, a stream, a river and then, finally, the sea and home.

And then us. Waiting for her. Floating on the edge of water's home, playing in her sea waters. When just below our feet it is her returning, filtered fresh water that carves our reefs into magnificent, crescent sculptures, refracting the sea's power, allowing us to ride within the sea's hollows. Providing to the end.

You hope at least these white kids out at Uluwatu realise this. That they realise that they ask everything from her. Everything. And that she asks nothing of them. And you hope these kids realize how all the grown-ups on earth, with all their great advice and rules and truths, have treated the ocean: like a global garbage can. And you hope these white kids figure out how to change things. Make it worth money to someone to clean up the water.

Because the only way things ever change in this fucked up world is to make it worth money to someone. Anyone. Because there is only one real problem in this world. We think we have time.

And you think, thousands have lived without love, but none without water. And you think, must these kid's world never know the worth of water until the well runs dry? And you hope the next generation you are looking at realizes that the cure for anything is salt water.

Be it sweat, tears or the sea. Every drop they drink, every breath they take, they are connected to the sea. No matter where they are on Earth.

The Ocean. A body of water occupying two thirds of a planet that these we are told was made for man...who has no gills. No water, no life. No green. No blue. You hope these kids realize this.

Because your fucking generation has fucking failed to.

Padang Padang – 11ᵗʰ Jan, 2012, 09:30

Yesterday, you had made it into the small cove of Padang Padang on dusk. Past the roaring reef, hollow as usual, about three foot. The tattooed Russian bodyboarders just lording over the place. Spending more time in the tube than any conventional surfer could ever imagine. The wave just a Flowrider to them. You smiled at one of the Russians after his outrageous tube ride. Across the cultures. He flopped back out. He saluted. You saluted back. Connection. This place was anyone's game these days. Da.

You had made shore and walked up to your favorite *warung*. The one with the ninety-year-old Ibu that has served *nasi goreng* to the greatest surfers in the world. Since 1969.

You had negotiated a small price and you had pitched your tent on the rattan covered massage table next to the dripping cliff wall. You had bought three warm beers and then you had filled your thermos with the water dripping from the limestone cliffs an arm's reach away. Ibu hadn't bat an eye. She knew of your eccentric behavior. Her thirty-five year old granddaughter had told her all about it a long time ago. You had drank deeply of the warm beer and of the water. Both had tasted as earthy and fresh as your own blood. At midnight the hissing lanterns had been turned down, the darkness had been complete. Walking waist deep in the ocean, you had urinated. Returning the water to the endless cycle. You had rinsed off the sand on your feet at the *warung* with the ice water long melted in the cooler full of clinking beers. You had

Some days, no wave in the world is breaking better than Padang Padang.

slipped into your tent to sleep. The thirty-five year old granddaughter had slipped into your tent as well. As she had done before, long ago, in 1996, when you were making a Hollywood film here at Padang Padang.

This was before her two kids and the deadbeat Norwegian husband and all her troubles. Before she was forced to return from the land of snow and sell sarongs again on the beach to sweaty Germans. Her kids scrabbling it out with the rest of the urchins. A cycle as endless as water itself in this place.

You had asked her why, why, after all this time, she had returned to you this night. And she had whispered into the night, into your face, onto your lips, that there were no mosquitoes in your tent and that it had been cold lately. And that had seemed enough. As natural as a heartbeat you had held her close and dozed through the rainy night. The smell of her skin a dark, roasted coconut. Dawn. Different than anywhere else on the island. No roosters on the beach. She is gone. Her coconut scent a floating apparition. A ghost. Or maybe proof. Old Ibu has more *nasi goreng* waiting for you in her spitting, battered iron skillet. Philosophical, Old Ibu rests her hand on the back of your neck for a long moment, looking out to sea. Remembering the big generator you secretly had given her family when the Hollywood movie cleared out back in 1996. The generator that had given her family a small fortune. A better *warung*. A life here. A gentle pat on the neck and Ibu is gone too. You pack up and grab your board like a lance. A little ashamed of what you had done during the night, but a little proud too. Like all men.

Now you shoulder your waterproof backpack, take to the water. The surf has dropped.

Still absolutely perfect at 24 inches. You paddle out through the channel, remembering how different it was the last time you were here. And about that 6 o'clock set that had become Bukit Lore. You remember. At first it was thought to be a cloud. But then it was moving too fast. It was 17th October, 2011 around 18:00. And the Bukit was about to be slammed by the biggest set of waves in living memory. All that day the Bukit was as big and as good as it gets. And no place on the planet was better than Padang Padang. Not everyone wanted a piece of it, but the luminaries were all there. Made Bol Winada Adi Putra, standing tall, Mustofa Jeksen at play in his Spiderman mask, Rizal Tanjung, the whole damn world was there. Jason Childs tear-assing around on his ski with his faithful Man-Friday, Made, snapping photos like mad. The Balawista lifeguards at the ready, oiled tourists gawking and set after perfect set pouring over the reef under a blistering hot sky. By noon most had howled themselves hoarse. By 17:00, most had gone in, not able to lift their arms for one more. But by 18:00 those that remained witnessed the unforgettable.

Made Lana, at outside corner Uluwatu was the first to deal with the great waves. He dropped into history. At Padang Padang, three minutes later, no one was prepared. The only guys that stood a chance were Jason Childs and Made on the ski. They had just cleared the top of the first giant when it roared and shut down the entire bay behind them, bypassing the Padang Padang reef and channel and roiling into one long serpentine hydraulic monster to Impossibles. Bingin became no more than a shorebreak. Dreamland was non-existent, Balangan dismissed. Jimbaran bay awash. Surfers no more than tsunami victims at this point. And Jason Childs and Made and the Balawistas were out until dark, effecting rescues. It was estimated at 13 broken leashes. And it was said that even an airplane taking off at the airport had its wings soaked with the offshore spume of the great waves that washed ashore and expired at the end of runway 284.

So you paddle out, remembering, through the innocent Padang Padang channel, past the reef, out into deep water. You sit up on your board. Looking back at the white sands of Padang Padang, the beauty of the cove, the perfection of it, you wish it well. Knowing that for the rest of your life, for all your life, it will remain the most Goddamned romantic place on your earth. As it has been since 1996. And you wonder if you need to thank Hollywood for that. Then you belly down, adjust the backpack, hang a right and start making your way north, down through the Impossibles line-up. North. Toward a place you were personally responsible for destroying.

Bingin – 11ᵗʰ Jan, 2012, 22:40

You pitch your tent on the beach in exactly the same spot that you photographed from 26 years ago. You had to hike in then. The place only a rumor. It was a hot hour and fifteen minutes down a limestone path through a dry jungle back then. You had followed a little boy who carried you and your mate's boards on his head. An impossible load. You couldn't have done it. You had come out onto the beach at what would become Dreamland. Not a thing there. Not a soul. A sparkling creek, inviting, emptying into a turquoise sea.

In the distance, the prize. The most perfectly shaped short lefthand wave on the planet.

You were working for *Surfer* magazine then. You shot three photos and then you and your mate started running for it. The little boy keeping pace easily with your boards. You built a small shelter on the beach and for the next 8 days surfed Bingin with no more than four white guys at a time. When you filed your story two weeks later with *Surfer* magazine, the exodus began. The best shaped, most friendly wave on the Bukit. Uncrowded perfection. The dream.

Later that year you had found yourself at the Action Sports Retailer show in Long Beach, California. You had sold one of the photos to the Prolite Surfboard luggage company.

It was one of the first three shots you took that day that depicted the little boy, surfboard Prolite bags piled on his head, perfect empty surf peeling in the distance against an impossibly exotic background. Prolite had turned it into a billboard on the front of the Long Beach Convention Center. Inside the great hall another giant light box, as tall as a canoe, shone through the masses. Crowds were gathered before the photo. Dreaming. Planning.

You remember being proud at the time.

You are tired now from the day. You slip into your tent up on the rocks at Bingin. It is 22:40. A local cliffside hotel owner with a hard looking armed security guard rousts you like a roadside bum. They tell you that you either have to stay at one of their cliffside hotel and spa's for two hundred bucks a night, or you have to clear out. You pack up and paddle out into the night. Karma.

Balangan – 12th Jan, 2012, 19:59

Dreamland had just been too hard to look at as you paddled into the beach under the cover of night. That giant, grey, shoddy cement edifice gouged clumsily into the north cliff. A real honest to God hatchet job of a big fuck-off ugly hotel and bar. Crassly re-named "The new Kuta Beach: The Bali you remember." Good God, you thought, meaning the Bali we live in now is gone? Who in the fuck could have possibly thought that that was the right thing to say?

You pitch your tent near the creek mouth, up against the south hill. Composing yourself to sleep for the second time that night. You fall asleep remembering the days of yore. The cool little *warungs* of Dreamland beach, cleaner than anywhere else on the island. All gossamer, swaying mosquito nets over cool, crisp, bleach scented sheets. The open *warungs*, the open beds, the cool green surf, the icy Coca Cola's. The talcum sand. The photographers from around the world that would come to shoot fashion magazine covers. The light reflecting off the limestone cliffs unique in all the world. Nothing like it. Life on a beach through a filtered light. All forever young. Now a bruised monstrosity of grey cement, varicose veined, ten-dollar margaritas. Rattling, giant tour buses waiting like a sad herd of pachyderms in the parking lot, chugging exhaust into the atmosphere for hours. Machines and drivers both hopeless beasts of burden. And you. Bastard. You helped start it all with your ego photographs.

And now here you lie on the Balangan point. Having paddled down mid-day. You had left an offering at Dalan Pura, Balangan's powerful temple, dug into the cliff. Trying to make sense of something. Complete with her swooping bats and a single, eternal light bulb illuminating the Hanuman Monkey God deity back in the recesses of the cave. Mystery had filled you.

Wonder. What must the spirits think? What do you think?

You had a few waves, a little crumbly, while an Italian photographer was doing a photo shoot on the beach with the two most famous fashion models in the world. No one seemed to notice. The natural barefoot beauty of the Balinese women in the *warungs* eclipsing the fashion model's gross, painted, commercial facade. Their false smiles. Tittering, insincere. Beauty as greed. As money. Paper money. Now in your tent. Early evening. On the north headland of Balangan cove. Bali's most forgotten beauty. A stunning crescent beach. You didn't even bring a camera this time. Instead, you deliberately chose the most exposed site you could. Facing the twinkling lights of Kuta and the roaring Airport runway a mile away.

The great modern terminus of the Bukit Peninsula. One-hundred-and-six flights a day.

You watch for a while, rain dripping through your eyelashes and onto your lips. Thinking about how peaceful Kuta looked from a distance. Of course, you think, a herd of rhinoceros would appear the same.

You had to peg your tent down. Not like you. Not a smart camp. Exposed as you are to the sky, a driving rain, monsoon winds and the spirits. A penance. You tried to drift off to sleep on the hard, volcanic ground. Another penance. The farmer of this land gives you a wide berth. So do the cows. As they would any crazy demon. Tomorrow you plan to paddle around the corner, with your waterproof backpack, to Jimbaran Bay. Past the Five Seasons resort carved into the south cliff. Past the last remaining beach *warungs*. You plan to make shore and stand upon the exact spot in the sand where the main blast of the 2005 Bali bombings erupted within the beachside restaurants and where 21 innocent human beings had become bloody rags. Though 23 died, no one really wants to count the terrorists.

And you stare at the sky from your tent and you plan to pray for forgiveness when you get there. Because you know that wherever you live is your temple, if you treat it like one.

Because you know there is still hope for this place called the Bukit. Because the eyes of the surfing world are watching Bali now in a whole new light. Because though the outside world may be able to blow out a candle, it cannot blow out a fire. Which is why here in Bali, you think, you must continue to fan the dreams into flame and care for this place as the precious gem it is. You must try. You have no choice. In many ways you created this place.

You are a western surfer. And like all western surfers, you have been an asshole to this place. You plan to take the dream seriously again. You must. After all, like the sound of the *gamelan*, you can't unring a bell.

First published in *Tracks* magazine in March, 2012.

Snowing in Bali

An excerpt from Kathryn Bonella's book about surfers and drug smuggling in Bali. It follows the stories of several surfers she interviewed while researching the Bali drug underworld and foreign inmates in the island's notorious jail, Kerobokan – dubbed Hotel K. Their radical tales cover the crazy highs that come with putting it all on the line and living large in the island of endless parties and perfect waves. Alberto's story offers a glimpse of the lows.

KATHRYN BONELLA

The Busts

"Bali can be heaven one minute and hell the next." – ALBERTO

AFTER BEING BUSTED selling a small amount to a Balinese snitch, Alberto was blindfolded and driven crouched in the back of a car to a remote house.

Tipping his head back slightly, he glimpsed unpainted walls, raw brick and a bare concrete floor – an unfinished house. He saw five pairs of feet in leather sandals – each slightly different; soon the trait that he would use to distinguish his captors. The air was full of tension; the cops were angry and for Alberto, standing impotently blindfolded, cuffed and vulnerable, every sound and touch was magnified by fear and blindness.

Alberto flinched as the cops grabbed his arms and shoved him into a room, pushing him to sit down on the edge of a bed.

A door slammed shut, then boom, it was on, fists raining brutal blows into his stomach, ribs and back, a hand slapping his face, as someone else used a plank of wood to slam into his head. He was helpless, the handcuffs preventing him from even lifting his arms to shield his face. It was against every human instinct, but he had to just surrender his body to the blows. Even gritting his teeth, he could not stop crying out in pain.

JASON CHILDS

After an hour or so, the cops slammed the door behind them, leaving him slumped on the bed, hurting badly and trembling. He knew that was only round one; that they would be back to hurt him again, until they broke him down into helping them set someone else up. Right now Andre, who owned the pills, and Rafael, whose name the

Perfect surf – how bad do you want it? Kerobokan, home to generations of foreign surfers in Indo.

cops had already tossed out, were blissfully unaware of his predicament, oblivious to how close they might be to falling into the same dark hole if their friend broke.

As Alberto sat there, trying to slow his ragged breathing and pounding heart, he was praying that he had the grit to take whatever was coming without capitulating.

The worst thing was the hits on the head with a wooden stick.

"They have this big piece of wood, solid, heavy. They hit like on the side of the ear, on the top of the head, close to my forehead, on the back of my head. One guy hitting and another guy punching on the ribs or slapping the face, together, two guys, at the same time. My hands handcuffed behind my back. They hit me for one hour, two hours, then they go out of the room, and lumps come up on my head, and then they come again two hours later, and hit the lumps. That's fucking painful...You want to cry; they make you see stars. That was heavy. That's the real pain, the real pain."

Whenever they left the room, Alberto slumped on the edge of the bed, feeling fainter and sicker, but his mind was trying to figure a way out. So far offering cash hadn't worked. They wanted to create a domino effect because it meant far more cash in the end, as well as a bunch of high-profile arrests.

He knew these brutal bashings would eventually end, but if he turned rat he knew his soul would never recover. So he kept stoically denying and absorbing the pain, trying to figure out a way to end the torture as fast as possible.

"All the time I was sitting on the bed, handcuffed and blindfolded, just sitting thinking, 'How am I going to get out of this?' I would hear the door opening again, I would go, 'Here we go again.' I could see through the bottom of the blindfold the feet arriving, the leather sandals, so I knew if the same guys came back."

"Then they would start all over again, bang, hit me on the head, bam, slap on the face, bam punch in the ribs, saying, 'Come on, use your tongue, say some names, help us to help you, come on,' and just hit hit hit. Sometimes, they put a piece of wood on top of my bare toes, and one guy comes with a real strong kick, bam, and you see stars and always like screaming, 'Ahhh fuck.' 'Come on, talk,' and just keep on going and going like this."

"So in the end, after two days, they realised I wasn't going to talk or set anyone up – I was already a fucking zombie – and they finally came in, saying, 'Okay, let's go. You're not going to help us so you're going to go to jail for 10, 15 years, is that what you want?' I was like, 'Okay, if that's it, that's it, but please take me to the police station. I wish I could help you, but I can't.' 'Bullshit.'"

Finally, he was piled into the car, his blindfold removed, and was driven to the police station to start the next phase of hell. He was in a bad state, but said nothing of the torture as he was processed. As he walked into the crowded cell, 30 or so pairs of eyes turned to look at him.

The concrete floor exacerbated his pain, but during the interminable days there was no choice but to sit in the cramped cell, usually playing cards, unable to even stretch out his legs. He nicknamed this hellish hot concrete cage 'the freezer' – because here life froze, with nothing to do but wait to learn your fate.

NUSA

TENGGARA

View to a thrill – somewhere east of the Wallace line.

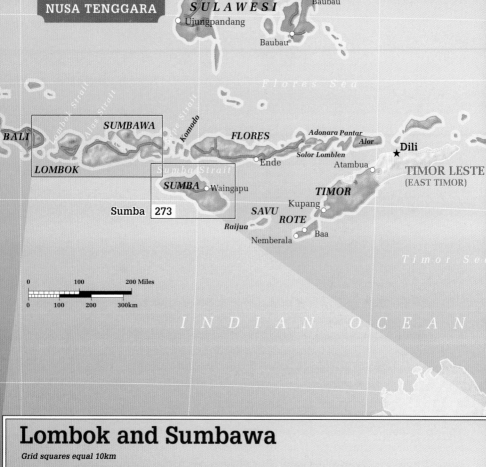

SULAWESI
Baubau
Ujungpandang

Baubau

Flores Sea

SUMBAWA

Komodo

BALI
FLORES
Adonara Pantar
Alor
★Dili

LOMBOK
Ende
Solor Lomblen
Atambua
TIMOR LESTE
(EAST TIMOR)

Sumba Strait

SUMBA
Waingapu
TIMOR

Sumba 273
SAVU
ROTE
Kupang

Raijua
Nemberala
Baa

0   100   200 Miles

0   100   200   300km

INDIAN OCEAN

Lombok and Sumbawa

Grid squares equal 10km

BALI

Gili Trawangan Gili Meno
Bayan
Gili Lawang
Pulau Moyo
Gunung Tambora
2821m

Gili Air Tanjung
Sambelia
Balebrang
Doro Mbolo
1180m
Orumboho
1576m
Suromandi
1181m

Senggigi
L O M B O K
Mt Rinjani
3726m
Gili Pentangan Mapin
Utan
Sumbawabesar
Rohu
1128m
Bima
Sila
Raba
Kute
1340m

Bangko
Mataram
Mantang
Selong
Seteluk
Brangbiji
Serading
Pulau Ngali
Daa
Dompu
Cenggu

Bangko
Praya
Labuhan
Haji
S   U   M   B   A   W   A
Lape
Mafaka
1260m
Bangkulia

Taliwang
Jaranpusang
1203m
Santong
Bangkulia
Waworada

DESERT
POINT
Kuta Ekas
Labuhanbalat
Batulanteh
Mt Bersanak
1132m
Mt Tukan
1400m
Ampang
Huu Parado
Wawotolodongo
1254m

SCAR REEF
Mt Sepekat
1147m
Mt Dinding
1349m
Plampang
LAKEY PEAK

SUPERSUCK

A U S T R A L I A

The Whirlpool

Power struggle in the Lombok Strait

DC GREEN

THE STRAIT BETWEEN Lombok and Bali is one of the most treacherous on Earth. This is the famous Wallace Line that divides Asia from Australasia, the line beyond which the rhinoceros, elephant and tiger could not penetrate. For even in the deepest Ice Age, the South China Sea to the north drained into the Sunda Trench.

Today this water still drains at several knots, right into the teeth of big Indian Ocean swells, often with a gale force trade wind howling in from a third angle. Little wonder then when eight feet swells suddenly desist, when stationary tidal waves rear up in the middle of the strait, when massive whirlpools open wide their hungry throats and bloated ferries go down without a survivor.

A strait crossing is at best an interesting experience for surfers who rent fishing boats with patched-up engines and captains who cannot swim five metres. On one such charter, and the guy in Paddy's assured me this was a true story for he was the third swimmer...the single engine broke down, and the *perahu* (local boat) began to drift towards a whirlpool big enough to consume 10,000 such vessels. The three surfers on board decided to abandon ship and paddle for help on their surfboards towards Lombok – a bold plan, for they too were unable to escape the suck-back force of the vortex behind. So they paddled, and paddled, and finally cheered when their boat shuddered to life. Yet rather than picking up the surfers, the captain motored towards his own guaranteed safety! Lombok!

Tight muscled Bruce shouted to his mates: 'I'll be back!' He put his head down and sprinted toward the fleeing boat until he was able to get in close enough to grab a thrown rope. He was wheezing and livid, especially when the skipper refused to return to rescue his friends. So Bruce pushed the skipper from the wheel and assumed command.

Having worked on enough tuna boats to know that a direct rescue charge would leave insufficient time to turn and escape, Bruce instead steered wide and approached at an angle. He ignored the screaming captain. The two swimmers had separated, so the more alert crew members were only able to rope in one. Undaunted, Bruce punched free and looped in for a second pick-up 20 minutes later.

The Indonesian skipper was so impressed, he let Bruce steer all the way to the harbour in Lembar. The last of the fuel spluttered out at the harbour breakwall. Bruce steered the silent boat towards the wharf.

That night, he didn't have to buy a single Bintang (beer).

First published in *Surf Europe*, Number 2, 1999

PETE FRIEDEN

Desert Point   LAT. -8.749826° LONG. 115.824170°

When it's on, Desert Point is indeed one of the longest, makeable lefthand barrels on the planet with over 20secs tube time possible on one wave. The take-off area can shift around a little but generally rewards a deep attack. High speed is the key as it quickly winds up and starts peeling mercilessly across the shallow reef, cutting a trench in the coral where the mechanical lips have been slamming for centuries. The caverns get larger and faster as the inside section commits the tube rider to a lock-in that usually ends on dry reef. Only surfers good enough to deal with the tricky exit, the shallow reef, evil out-going currents and plenty of wave-starved rippers should apply. Desert's has a reputation for inconsistency, with only the biggest groundswells igniting it and high tides making it disappear as fast as it came. Surf charters keep flocking from Bali and dedicated hardcore surfers wait for weeks in basic beach shacks, forming a frenzied, barrel-hungry pack on those rare classic days. Boats have access to the sheltered bay of islands behind Bangko Bangko where there are some big swell, high tide options for intermediates around the other Gili islands like Ringgit.

Desert Drifting

Paddle struggle in the Lombok Strait

MATT PRUETT

ESERT POINT IS one hell of a surf spot. Many claim that when it's on, it's the best wave in Indonesia – which pretty much means the best wave in the world.

I didn't quite see it to be that exactly. At least not for long.

We chartered the *Dream Weaver* out of Bali – your basic, ghetto Sumbawa/Lombok/Lembongan run – and Desert Point was #1 on our list. Once there, we found shimmering, high tide flatness, and dipped in immediately. Sure enough, within 30 minutes of a tidal shift – two, four, six-foot... For an hour, we exchanged flawless, multi-section pits. Before long, the most proficient of our bunch bagged a sweet, deep one from further up the point, so a couple of us paddled over in hopes of getting one for ourselves. My buddy spun on the first, and what would be the only wave of the set, taking the plunge mere inches away from me. With nothing else approaching, I turned to head back to where we originally sat, but wasn't making any progress. I was going backwards, *fast*, delivered out to sea by a nightmarish current showing no boils, discoloration, or surface fissures.

I punched and punched, furious with the irony that ten minutes before I could've touched my buddy on the shoulder. Now he was nothing but a speck on the horizon to me, and me to him. I thrashed violently forward, backward, sideways ... anything I could do to escape becoming a Lombok Strait pinball to oblivion, the intense physical turmoil the only thing overpowering panic mode. My upper body burned with lactic acid. My lower body quaked with trepidation. My mind raced a million miles a minute: "Why am I moving so fast?"..."Can't anyone see me?"..."What on earth is swimming beneath me right now?"..."Who's going to explain this to my mom? The last thought concerned me the most, as she had already lost a child before me.

A little under an hour, I couldn't hear the waves anymore. I stopped struggling and hung my head down in defeat, my eyes tightly sealed. I was too tired to cry, too horrified to look how far gone I was. But then, I was delivered by an unlikely hero in the form of a dinghy driver dangling an Ardat from his lips. "What boat, boss?" he asked, referring to which charter I was a part of.

"*Dream Weaver,*" I choked with eternal gratitude.

"Not boat," he replied, and then puttered away. I could feel my stomach turn inside out, my face go white before resigning myself once again to death's certain clutches. Considering all the dangers present in this region – ginsu reefs, malaria, stonefish, marauders – I felt this was a comparatively weak way to go out. But seeing as I was wearing a green rash vest, maybe I deserved such an ending. Balinese mythology speaks of Nyai Loro Hidul, "the Indonesian Queen of the Southern Sea," and how she's attracted to the color green and been know to take as lovers those seafarers who dared wear it. Somewhere between recollecting that tale and being retrieved by my own dinghy, the thought literally made me vomit. Later on the boat, flushed with exhaustion, I didn't know what to believe concerning the Nyai Loro Hidul superstition, but threw the shirt overboard nonetheless.

The remainder of that trip, I didn't feel quite right. The joy of riding waves had been tainted for me, yet oddly, it wasn't a wave that made me feel so low and alone, but something far creepier – that which surrounds the waves.

Today, a full five years later, I find it almost inconceivable that the thing that scared me most in life was something completely invisible to me.

First published in *Surfing* magazine March 2006

Robbed at Desert Point

Bandits, blood and a heroic effort to save a life

LEO MAXAM

AST YEAR (2013) there were several reports of surfers being robbed on their way to and from Desert Point. There was a couple from Hawaii who got shaken down at gunpoint inside their hotel room in Bangko Bangko. Then there was a carload of Brazilian surfers who were robbed by a group of armed men who had blockaded the road at night. Armed robbery is nothing new in these parts. Just ask Pablo, aka "Mr. Deserts", who sports a large scar near his collarbone courtesy of some knife-wielding pirates who tried to jump him and his buddies on the beach years ago. Pablo has been surfing Deserts longer than anyone, back when there was no road in to the beach and you could surf a swell with just you and a couple of friends. According to Pablo, even back when the place was still a secret, the danger of pirates was always very present.

"Back in the day there was no road out to the beach. You had to wait for low tide and hike around from the cliff (past the end section of the wave). There was a regular crew that used to come out there – a few Aussies, Kiwi guys – and we'd just camp on the beach. There was no one out there back then and we were pretty vulnerable. You could come and rob us and leave without anyone knowing about it.

The first time we got robbed was in August during a full moon. Some guys came out with full balaclavas (face masks) and knives. I was in my tent and I always used to sleep with my spear gun. The guys came in and started smashing shit and they had those big parangs (machetes). This guy Johno, a big Australian guy from South Oz, they had him down on his hands and knees and they had a knife right on his neck. They were like, "Money! Money! Give us money!" Johno was the biggest guy out of us all, so I guess they were scared of him and they had him down like a hostage. Luckily, they just took the money and split.

So after that incident, there were enough of us that we hired this Indo friend of ours, Bun, from the village back over the hill to be our night watchman. He would come every night and stay up at night and walk the beach and keep watch. One of the surfers, Chris, had a whistle with him, and he gave Bun the whistle and said, if anything happens, blow this whistle to warn us. So one night around 2 or 3 in the morning, sure enough, that whistle started blowing like crazy. So we all got up and it surprised the robbers, because they thought they were going to sneak up on us.

I got up with my spear gun and ran out of my tent and the scene was like a punch-up. There was probably 10 or 12 robbers, but the whistle and us waking up spooked them, and they ran down towards the riverbed. There was one surfer camping in the riverbed and he was by himself, this guy Blair from Australia. He heard the commotion and got up, and I guess he just saw one of the Indo guys and grabbed a stick and started fighting him – they had big ol' knives. Well the rest of the robbers ran into Blair when they got down to the riverbed, and that's when we heard yelling and screaming.

When I got to the riverbed, Blair was on his hands and knees and they were just hacking him up. If I had got there a minute later, he would have been done. It was a full moon, and at Deserts it's like daylight on a full moon, you can see clear as day. So I started screaming, and I had a big old spear gun. They saw that and immediately ran off. Blair tried to get up and didn't know what was going on. All I could see was his arm was hanging by a thread. I was yelling for something to plug him up with and put the thing back together. One of my buddies had a sarong and I kinda wrapped his arm and shoulder together. I didn't see until later that Blair had cuts all over his back. We laid him down and put pressure on his arm to keep the bleeding down and tried to think of how the heck we were going to get him out of there.

If we stayed there he was going to bleed to death, there was no question. The road that you drive in on now was just a little footpath back then. And the robbers had ran that way, so there was only one way we could get Blair out of there – we had to go around that cliff. And if you've ever seen that cliff at high tide and on a big swell, it's a nightmare to get around. It was night. The tide was high. And to make things worse, the swell was pumping.

We had made all kinds of furniture when we camped at the beach. We had chairs and shit made out of bamboo. I had a table I had made, and we put Blair on the table and carried him down to the point. We had a guy climb up on the big rock and watch for sets. When there was good a lull he said, 'Go! Go! Go!' We were scared we were gonna get washed by a wave and lose Blair. You have to go with the current. It sucks you around the point and down.

It took hours. We had to get around the cliff and then get him to the village where the blacktop ends. Once we made it to the road, we found a car and took him to the hospital in Mataram. He made it. They sewed him up in Mataram, then flew him to Bali. When he got back to Oz he had all kinds of infections because they didn't do a great job at the hospital in Mataram.

Blair did end up coming back years later. He still surfs well. He almost lost his arm, and it could have been worse. If those guys had got any arteries with their knives it would have been over real quick. He was pretty fortunate not to have died."

This is an extract from a longer interview with Pablo entitled, "The Most Barrelled Man on Earth" in issue 3 of Bali Belly magazine and on www.BaliBelly.com

Surreal Sumbawa

An unscratched itch in ultra perfect Indo (2009)

LEO MAXAM

STRUGGLING TO FIND satisfaction? Ever feel like a junkie who can't get the buzz you used to? Don't worry, it's a common symptom of addiction and it happens to us all, even to the best surfers in the best waves in the world.

With each stroke he took, Takayuki Wakita felt the sting of the fresh reef cuts across his shoulder blades. He had covered them in bandages and duct tape, but the tropical saltwater still managed to seep its way through to the torn flesh. Add to that the constant chaffing of the wounds from his wetsuit top, and the 100-yard paddle out to the tip of the bay was beginning to seem unbearable. Well, almost unbearable – until a set would come thundering down the reef straight at him, making his adrenaline surge enough to forget about anything else.

Wakita had received his new tattoos the previous afternoon courtesy of this wave, a freakishly hollow freight train that broke well below sea level. The sun was sinking low on the barren, Mars-like landscape of remote Sumbawa and the biggest swell of the Indo season was hitting its peak. Wakita had already snagged a few solid pits, but for the most part he was playing it safe on his first time out at the spot. The waves were easily 6-8ft Hawaiian and throwing out lips several feet thick on tubes as wide as they were tall. It was similar to Teahupoo, Wakita had thought, but with less water moving.

This wave was just as hollow, for sure, but at Pipe and Teahupoo there was more mass to the waves. Here there was less water per square inch, but the shape was more perfect, like a machine. The length of the ride at this spot was also much longer than both of the more famous left tubes Wakita knew so well. Here, the barrel actually grew as it moved along the reef, with each section more hollow than the next.

"If I knew about this wave, I would have come over here a long time ago," Wakita thought as he paddled into position for a smaller wave in the fading daylight.

At most surf spots the smaller waves are less dangerous. Here, when the tide was low, the inside waves broke too fast and dangerously shallow. Wakita learned this the hard way. As he took off on the four-footer another surfer was scratching frantically for the shoulder, forcing Wakita to bottom turn into the flats to avoid running him over. He pulled into the tube off his bottom turn but quickly saw that he was too late. He tried to punch out the back of the wave and was relieved when he popped up on the other side. But then he felt the pull of the wave again and was sucked back down over the falls, directly onto the reef. He hit on his back and was dragged across the sharp coral for several seconds.

"I guess that's why they call this place Super Suck," he joked later that night as his good friend, legendary Balinese surfer Pepen Hendrik prepared to squirt lime juice over the searing wounds. The reef rash wasn't so bad when compared to other injuries Wakita had sustained in the past at spots like Teahupoo and Pipe. But a strange thing happened this time around. As he paddled in to shore, blood clouding the water around him, Wakita began to feel a chill run through his body. His muscles tightened throughout his body and soon he could barely paddle. By the time he finally reached the beach, he was shivering.

"It's the poison from the animals in the reef," Pepen told him. "The lime will kill it."

Now, less than 24 hours later, Wakita was back out sitting on the bowl, along with a hungry pack of professional tube hunters that included Jamie O'Brien, Mikala Jones, Danny Fuller and Kekoa Bacalso. In spite of his injury and the crowd, Wakita was determined to make it out of a good set wave this afternoon. After all, he had been dreaming of surfing this wave for months – ever since Pepen let him in on the secret.

"It's like three Padang Padangs," Pepen had told him. "Wave so long and barrel the whole way."

Then, at the trials for the Teahupoo contest in May, Australian charger Anthony Walsh showed Wakita some jaw-dropping photos of the wave at eight feet, taken from a trip a year earlier. The images burned themselves into Wakita's brain, playing over and over every night.

During the Teahupoo trials Wakita hit the reef and was in the hospital for a week, unable to move. The doctors pumped him full of morphine and Wakita spent most of the time drifting in and out of sleep. However it wasn't nightmares about the throttling he received from the Tahitian beast that filled Wakita's dreams. It was the images of those cartoon-like, green tunnels funnelling down a reef somewhere in Sumbawa, and he slept with a smile on his face.

More than a month later, on a warm night in Chiba, there came a phone call. It was Pepen. "This is it," he said. "This is the swell. We're going to Sumbawa."

Wakita was already planning to fly to Bali later that month, the same annual migration he's made for the past 18 years. Now he quickly switched to an earlier flight, packed his boards and was out the door. Wakita had known Pepen for many years and trusted his advice. Every time he came to Bali it was Pepen who would play host, take him to all the spots and remove all the guesswork of where and when to find the best waves. Wakita would return the favour during the North Pacific winter, when Pepen would come to stay with him on the North Shore of Oahu, and on occasion Japan. When Pepen made a call about the surf in Indo, Wakita had supreme confidence in it.

Pepen picked him up at the Denpasar airport around 5pm. After a warm reunion and a brief cruise around Bali to pick up Garut Widiarta, Pepen's heir to the throne at Padang, they headed for the port to catch the midnight ferry to Sumbawa.

The journey was the kind you only make for a world-class wave – long, uncomfortable and arduous: Drive to the eastern tip of Bali; cross the Lombok Strait overnight on a smelly ferry; drive across Lombok in the early morning; take an even dirtier ferry over to Sumbawa, then head south. The ferries were old, dilapidated and mind-numbingly slow. People huddled and slept in all corners of the filthy craft. There were no emergency lifeboats to speak of, even though it looked as though the ferry might sink at any moment.

But Wakita didn't mind any of this. He was used to long road trips. Back home in Chiba it was normal to drive for hours in search of good waves. Plus, taking the overnight ferry allowed one to get some sleep under the stars, which meant Wakita could once again fantasize about his first encounter with the wave.

They arrived at the bay two days later and were met by the Hawaiians, who had also been tracking the swell and organized a mission to the reef. Kekoa Bacalso, Mikala Jones and Danny Fuller all arrived together. Right behind them was Jamie O'Brien, with an entourage of two photographers, two videographers and three tattooed, mohawked punk rockers on vacation from Moscow. All together they were quite the travelling surfing circus.

You know a wave is heavy when the Hawaiians don't go out and immediately dominate. Such was the case during the opening session at this wave, which was new to many of the visiting pros. Kekoa surfed conservatively and only took off on two or three waves. Mikala snapped his board. Even O'Brien, the youngest Pipe Master in history, seemed to struggle to make it out of the endless drainers. Early on he snapped his leash and had to swim 200 meters in to the beach to get a new board. The vengeful waves appeared intent on running down and swallowing any surfer who made the drop.

"Brah, how heavy was that wave?" said O'Brien later that night while watching a particularly nasty one from the day's footage.

"That wave was fucked up today, it was so shallow," agreed another surfer in O'Brien's entourage. "I need a wave I can at least duck-dive."

The next day dawned just as big. Wakita, Pepen and Garut slept in and missed the early morning high tide. They were forced to surf as the tide sucked out to a deep low and the wave went dry in certain sections. There weren't many makeable ones coming through and a couple of the boys paddled in without even going on a wave.

That evening it would be a different story. Garut scored probably the two heaviest waves of the day and Pepen surfed masterfully on his backhand. O'Brien was his usual freakish self, scoring a 10-second backside barrel and later hanging five off the tip of his 6'0" while slotted deep in the belly of a heaving cave. With half the guys in the water regulars at Pipeline or Padang, and the big sets coming through less consistently, getting the good ones was a challenge. On more than one occasion, Wakita found himself in the right spot for an A or B+ set wave, but let one of the other guys take it, hoping to get the next one.

Finally a good one came with his name on it. He paddled furiously to claw his way down the face and get in early, but as the three-foot-thick lip began to pitch Wakita was still suspended near the top not quite to his feet. Time slowed and all eyes in the water focused on the drama about to unfold. Wakita air-dropped down the face and set a rail. As he peered up and the acceleration kicked in, it was clear he was locked into a spinning vortex that stretched ahead for as far as he could see...

Wakita came in at dark, happy about finally making his first trip to this super-hollow left. It was undoubtedly a world-class wave and he already considered it one of his favourites. But he couldn't shake the feeling of not quite being satisfied. He had caught some good barrels, but never really felt like he got a truly sick one, the kind of wave that stood out from the rest in his vast memory bank of heavy tube rides. It wasn't that he didn't see them on this trip, he just never snagged a truly perfect one from the crowd.

"If I could rewind, maybe I would change that," he thought to himself as he, Pepen and Garut motored down the dusty track towards Lombok. He would think about some of the waves that got away for many days afterwards. He already ached to return. "Next time," he thought.

Until then, he would just have to dream.

First published in *The Surfer's Path* magazine Issue 75 December, 2009

The Road to Lakeys

Alternative transportation therapy for the Indo-wise

FABIAN HAEGELE

I
T WAS JUST another Kuta Beach afternoon: hawkers selling anything and everything, overweight tourists frying in the sun while getting their feet massaged, and local beach boys chilling in the shade, joking beside beat-up mini-mals and a cardboard sign reading: "For Rent". The dropping sun painted the whole scene in warm, golden colours and silhouetted the outlines of groms boosting airs in the shorebreak.

I'd come to drink a few beers with my friend Tim from NSW, before heading off to catch the 26-hour bus ride to Dompu in East Sumbawa. I only had five weeks in Indonesia this time. This was just a stopover on my way back to Europe after a year spent in Western Australia, a chaotic road trip across the Nullabor and a disastrous mission to Samoa. I had too much stuff with me to do any serious travelling and was kind of worn out, so had decided just to go and surf my brains out and enjoy the easy lifestyle in Lakey Peak, East Sumbawa. Being on a tight budget, I planned to take the bus to save money, instead of flying which most travellers do. The bus is a mission, but I've done it before – it's uncomfortable, but bearable.

My mate Tim has been living the dream for the past few years, working the charter boats in the islands off Sumatra in dry season and enjoying the Bali lifestyle in wet season. He and I were about halfway through our second Bintang when his friend Red Dog joined us. He's an Indo veteran with 30 years of experience around here. Red Dog just laughed when he heard I was taking the bus. "Why the hell would you wanna do that to yourself? Why don't you just go by bike?"

That, to be honest, hadn't even crossed my mind. I've always been wary of motorbikes, the Indonesian people's favourite means of transport. That's because I've seen too many guys out of the water – for days and even weeks – with ugly injuries not from shallow reefs but from motorbike disasters.

Red Dog, however, started telling us stories about his earliest Indonesian explorations, most of them by bike, and suddenly, with every tale he told and every Bintang consumed, it all made more sense. Going by bike is cheap and it gives you almost unlimited independence. And besides all that, it's a great way to see the

ROGER SHARP

Lakey Peak LAT. -8.80479° LONG. 118.378°

Perfect Lakey Peak peels off short, 30-40m lefts and rights into channels either side. The right will often throw up backdoor tube rides but gets too shallow at low tide, when the left is churning out predictable, ideal-speed barrel rides. Mid-tide lip-smacking sessions will appeal to intermediates and the flattish reef is user-friendly, except during full or new moon phases. Getting out to the Peak is easy with only a short 450m paddle or take the Zodiac for around $2 return. Lakey Peak can hold juicy sized waves, but the optimum time to hit it is when it's in that perfect headhigh plus range.

country from a different perspective. The longer I thought about it, the more I liked the idea. That's why, when the time came to leave for the bus terminal, I ordered another round of Bintangs instead. "Tell me more, Red Dog!"

Everything's Fine

The next morning I got up early, organised somewhere to stash my stuff, found a good bike to rent and bought a few things for the trip. Before lunchtime I was on the road with two boards in the rack on the side of my trusty 125cc scooter, and a small day-pack on my back. What I didn't have was a valid driver's licence. Red Dog had warned me this could get me into trouble in Padang Bai, where I had to catch the ferry to Lombok. But, having got through the mayhem of Denpasar's traffic in one piece, my confidence was high. I wasn't scared of corrupt cops. Besides, dealing with Indonesian police can be like dealing with wild dogs: If you show them any fear, they'll tear you to shreds. As long as you're confident but respectful, you'll be fine.

The cop I dealt with was actually pretty cool. He motioned for me to sit down with him and have a chat. I just smiled a lot, told him what I was up to, pretended that I'd already done it a thousand times and laughed at his jokes. "I know we can work this out, boss." And we sure did. I gave him 50,000 rupiahs and he let me off. Imagine getting caught without a driver's licence anywhere else in the world, paying less than five bucks and getting sent off with a wave and a smile. No worries.

It was already dark when the ferry arrived in Lembar and I was tired so I took a little detour to a friendly home-stay in a back alley in Senggigi that I'd stayed at on a previous trip. I set my alarm for 5am and went to bed early in preparation for a long day on the road. First I'd have to drive across Lombok to catch the ferry to Sumbawa. Then, from Labuhan Tano, there were still several hundred kilometres of country roads separating me from my final destination.

I hit the road before sun up. Traffic was quiet but villagers were already busy working many of the roadside rice fields, and the market in Mataram was bustling with activity. Smoke and the smells of fried bananas, horse dung and a thousand other things hung in the air as a rising sun slowly lit up the horizon and the countless vendors and farmers delivering their produce to feed the island's main city. During the three-hour drive through Lombok, it never really felt like I'd left the city. There was a constant flow of traffic and houses and people along the way, but it was an easy enough drive and before I knew it I was on the ferry to Sumbawa, enjoying a leaf of *nasi campur* (mixed rice) for breakfast.

Streets of Sumbawa

The one road in Sumbawa turned out to be the complete opposite of the crowded, hectic arteries of Bali and Lombok. After a short while there were no other vehicles in sight and I found myself cruising solo through a sparsely populated picturesque countryside of rice fields and pastures with a prominent chain of mountains always to my right. The sky was blue, the sun was shining and I was thoroughly enjoying the drive ... until a roadblock a few kilometres before Sumbawa Besar.

This time I wasn't so lucky. The cop who pulled me over sent me straight to his boss who had dollar signs flashing in his eyes the moment he saw me. He was a tough customer, this one, and he kept me on the spot negotiating for probably 45 minutes. The official fine for driving without a licence, he showed me in writing, is 6 million rupiahs or up to 6 months in jail. That's what he threatened me with. He was bluffing of course but no matter what I tried he just wouldn't budge. After half an hour he was still demanding 2 million rupes. I kept telling him I didn't have that much on me. Eyes bulging, he pressed on. "I want all your money!" He asked to see my wallet because I was trying to pay him off with money from my pockets. Fortunately it only contained a stack of small change that I'd gathered in Bali. The real cash was safely stashed away in a pair of smelly old socks.

I was over it by the time he finally let me go. It wasn't so much the 120 grand that he ended up stinging me for, but the hassle I had to go through to get there. And I was on a pretty tight schedule if I wanted to make it to Lakeys by nightfall. What's more, the clouds in the mountain chain, which at some point I would have to cut across, were now starting to stack up and darkening fast. This was definitely a matter of concern considering it was only mid-March, still well within the rainy season. To make things worse, I took a wrong turn in Sumbawa Besar and ended up on a side road that took me straight up into the mountains. I hadn't been able to find a map of Sumbawa in Bali, so had no idea that I was way off course. After following the increasingly steep and winding road for approximately 45 minutes I came through a tiny village just as it started drizzling. The few people I saw all stared at me like they'd seen a ghost. Then, only a couple hundred metres further, the road turned into an impassable mud track. I was literally in the middle of nowhere. When I asked for directions back in the village, half of the people were just gaping at me, jaws dropped. They didn't even speak Bahasa. But I already knew the answer anyway, so I just got on my way.

The rest of the afternoon was kind of tense. The sun had disappeared and thick, black rain clouds concealed the peaks of the mountain chain. Every time the road cut to the right I thought I was doomed. By now, my behind was sore and my shoulders aching. Plus, the long stretches of bumpy potholed roads were slowing me down. I was losing hope that I'd be able to make it. Only my strong desire to wake up and go for a paddle at the Peak first thing next morning kept me pushing on.

But it wasn't going to be. Darkness had just about fallen and it was drizzling again as I drove into Dompu, still another hour or so from Lakeys. Frequent flashes of lightening, each one followed by cracking thunder, illuminated the sinister-looking blackness beyond the region's major town, revealing heavy curtains of rain. Against my better judgement I decided to keep going, maybe hoping that the thunderstorm was moving away.

Progress was very slow. The countless potholes were now filled with water, so their depth was impossible to judge, which made it risky to go any faster than 30mph.

In the end, the potholes didn't matter. After only 20 minutes, all hell broke loose and I found myself in what felt like the centre of the maelstrom. I pulled over at a little shack at the side of the road out of which the owners were selling the usual stuff – cigarettes, water, junk food, Extra Joss, mosquito coils, etc. – and asked for shelter. The lady was just preparing dinner and they immediately invited me to join them. After a hearty meal of rice, fish and vegetables Omnor, the man of the house, offered me a cigarette and a cup of *kopi susu* (white coffee). Legions of mosquitoes buzzed around us as we sat there chatting in the dim light cross-legged on the floor of his tiny home. Soon Omnor even asked me if I'd like to spend the night in the little windowless hut they had out the back. I gratefully accepted.

By the time I finally went to bed my head was spinning from the sweet *kretek* (clove) cigarettes. And right there, right then I could have not been more appreciative of the wooden bunk with only straw for a mattress. The unconditional hospitality of some people who have so little never ceases to amaze me. That evening with Omnor and his wife was without doubt a highlight of my trip. It's those experiences that, apart from scoring great waves, make an overland trip so special and so rewarding and that are not included in your average package-deal holiday. I slept like a baby that night and woke up feeling as fresh as ever. Omnor made me sit and drink a cup of coffee and a sugary pastry out of a plastic wrapper for breakfast before he let me get on my way. He never asked me for any money.

Making it

Lakeys was just like I remembered it. There were a couple of new makeshift buildings on the beach and a brand new bridge across the creek at the south end of 'town', which would get washed away in a heavy storm only a week later. But it felt like nothing had really changed in the two years since my last visit. Astma at Puma Bungalows hooked me up with a good deal and so did Gerry and Onki from my favourite restaurant, Fathma's Hand. The peak was 2-3ft and as perfect as ever and there were only a handful of guys out, so I went for a paddle to wash off the dust and the dirt and the grease and the grime from the road.

And, although everybody else in the line-up had taken the comfortable 50-minute flight to get there from Bali, it felt that much sweeter being out in the water having worked for it just a little.

For the next four weeks I surfed every day. Some days the waves were better than others. I scored some of the lesser-known breaks in the vicinity – uncrowded and firing – thanks to the mobility offered by my bike. I drank a lot of coconuts, ate a lot of *nasi campur* and *gado-gado* and huge plates of yellow-fin sashimi. I did a bit of yoga and tore through a few books. And of course I had the odd icy cold and refreshing Bintang here and there. It was, in essence, for a surf traveller in Indo, nothing out of the ordinary.

But one thing is for sure – on my next visit to surfing's wonderland I'm going exploring. And unless I end up on a boat of some description, I know what my transport of choice will be. A hint: it's got two wheels, sounds like a lawnmower and it's the one thing that Indonesia has even more of than perfect waves.

First published in *The Surfer's Path* magazine Issue 70 Jan/Feb, 2009.

What Becomes A Dream

A Sumba saga of warriors, waves and awareness

KEVIN LOVETT

M
ANY INDIGENOUS SOCIETIES on this planet believe that not only does the dream state occupy our periods of sleep (nearly one-third of our entire lifetime), but also that our waking moments are experienced as a dream-like reality from which we are yet to truly awaken. Time is a relative perception that we process in a variety of manners especially through our senses and the deep conditioning accumulated through lifetimes of experience.

The Buddha said, "We are what we think, all that we are, arises with our thoughts, with our thoughts we make our world...think with a pure mind and happiness will follow you..."

Could it really be this simple, that we just make it all up as we go along? Karma and interdependence, however, reign supreme in our dream world; they make our universal ball of wax shiver and shake. Take a trip down memory lane and delve into the illusory domain of the past, ruminate on those fragmented moments in time that we once perceived of being the present. These snapshots of one's life in retrospect can be viewed with a degree of objectivity that was once missing when the living was being done. Of course it's not all just smoke and mirrors, we are responsible and we remain accountable for our every action.

In every moment we are different yet the same, a spec of subtle awareness on a continuum whose end has no beginning and whose beginning is without end. It therefore gives me a chuckle to not only contemplate my own past, but also the past of others that I've been closely associated with. We all have the opportunity to dream ourselves a beautiful life, and for Claude Graves, he's been working on his *pièce de résistance* for a long time.

Born a baby boomer and raised in Brigantine, New Jersey, across the channel from Atlantic City, Claude grew up in a small white population of nearly 3,500 people; on a surf-blessed island that was actually a sand spit six miles long and less than a mile wide. The early years centred on school and hanging with his dad from whom he "learnt a little bit about a lot of stuff", principally by helping his father build the family home. They were easy days; by 1960 there were about 15 surfers on the island split up into two groups.

"My first boards were plywood made by a local carpenter who had been to California. The next year the first surf shop opened in Ocean City and my father drove me there to buy a 9' 6" Daytona Beach Surfboard. It was a ripper compared to the others. However, I still thought the board was too long so the next season I cut off a foot and a half and made it an eight-footer with a spooned nose. I wish I still had that board; it was a great nose rider. It was an absolute magic time; I was hanging out with the older guys, great guys, but all a little twisted in a Jersey kind of way. We did regular trips down the coast to Florida and Hatteras chasing surf, in fact that's what got me into surf travel. We were soul surfing, 100%."

Life changing events often occur when least anticipated, poking through fresh deposits at the local rubbish tip one day brought the inquisitive 9-year-old an unexpected bonanza. A complete collection of *National Geographic* magazines in mint condition lay inside one box like a treasure beyond measure, and in another box lay a collection of '50s nudie shots that would make more than your hair stand up. His dad, of course, claimed the 'nudies' whilst Claude discovered a world that challenged his imagination. The textured photography and detailed prose ignited a sense of destiny within the young boy, which he sought to fulfill in his dreamworld. Sun-drenched Tahitian images of palm trees and crystal blue water became indelibly imprinted on Claude's mind. Africa was also a major attraction to the youngster as the family had a close connection with Kenya. Claude's uncle, Ladislaus Von Menyhart, was the proverbial great white hunter, guiding the rich and famous on safari from his base in Nairobi. A larger than life character, he became an object of hero-worship and a source of aspiration to the young boy.

The island's surfing conditions impacted heavily on his adolescent development, too, of course.

"In those days Brigantine had icy cold winters, snow on the beaches and some years the bay would freeze. Salt water freezes at 28°F; we had shitty stinkin' old dive suits with flaps in the crotch. By the end of a session you would be pushing your balls back into place from somewhere up in your chest. We surfed and lived a life with a hormone-driven fantasy as our dream. We never talked about just going to California and doing all that shit. Hawaii was our Holy Grail 'cause back then no one knew about surf in Tahiti or Indonesia, but through it all, I never thought I would ever realize my fantasy"

And just what was that fantasy, Claude?

"The dream for me was real clear; it was an absolute pristine beach with a great wave, palm trees hanging over the sand, a beautiful girl and me! I was still a virgin, so you can imagine how wild that fantasy is – you're dreamin' about getting laid as well as surfing a perfect wave without a wetsuit, checking out palm trees that you've only ever seen before in a magazine or a postcard."

A month after he turned 18, he got drafted and life changed dramatically.

"It was a disaster. I thought my life was over, it was a ridiculous war, which I opposed and it scared the shit out of me."

What did the army teach him?

"Well I learnt how to shoot, throw grenades and drive tanks, but maybe most importantly, how to take orders from loud obnoxious people without worrying about it".

Vietnam was patiently waiting in the wings as Claude set about doing his utmost to not make it onto the plane.

"Good fortune shined on me when I found out that a high school buddy was working in Fort Dix administration and with a bit of file shuffling he could get me stationed to Europe, I think he saved my life. The German posting, however, was not what I thought it would be. Without knowing what was up, I was sent to "guard" an American military base. I thought it was the posting of a lifetime. Within the first hour of arrival, before I could even unpack my gear, I saw a Sergeant with a sort of crazed gleam in his eyes standing in the doorway of the room I would share with eight others. He watched us fire up a chillum before casually tossing a grenade into the room; it ended up rolling under my bunk that we were all sitting on. I thought it was a joke until everyone started moving. As we charged for the door the grenade went off and caught the three guys running behind me. I didn't get to know them or see them again because they got hit badly and they ended their careers in a hospital somewhere. My bunk was mangled and the room was destroyed beyond repair. I soon found out what this place was about. It was a holding pen where the mental cases from the war were sent to chill-out before being returned to the States. Out of 5,000 troops at this post 4,000 should have been in insane asylums. They where suffering all kinds of battlefield stress syndromes and were looked upon by the military as a potential political embarrassment for the Government, who kept telling the public that all was well on the war front. I witnessed all kinds of bad things going on, everyone was fully armed, crazy and very dangerous; this was not a safe place to be. I did what was needed to get through it in one piece and took my Army discharge in Germany. After this experience I was in no hurry to go home, the country's politics and policies were too far out there for me. So I travelled all over Europe and spent time in Kenya. It was a return to the good times."

Nevertheless, he returned to New Jersey (when his time was done), broke and disillusioned. Borrowing his father's '62 Pontiac Catalina he set out on his own voyage of personal discovery through the heartland of Americana. South of Houston he pumped his last ten bucks into the tank just as fate served up a chance meeting with a southern gentleman who introduced Claude to the oil industry.

This connection developed further through on-the-job work experience and was to eventually transport Claude halfway around the world. Before the departure to foreign shores, only one thing remained to be completed; the West Coast road trip.

San Francisco beckoned like a kaleidoscopic beacon of light. Jimi Hendrix's Sky Church music wailed from the speakers as the desert melted into the rear view mirror; Claude in the fully fuelled 'Catalina', with Kerouac in the glove box and girlfriend in tow, cruised the byways headed for 'The Haight'.

"Man, in '71 San Francisco was too much fun. Great food, plus it was still all sex, drugs and rock 'n' roll. Although it was towards the end of its peak it remained very exciting and inspiring – it changed my life".

Circumstances shape life and direct the movie that becomes our lives; in the end we're all just actors and all that we do is just acting. For any travelling 21-year-old the early seventies was a magic carpet ride that delivered wide-eyed wonderment at every footfall. Claude's journey with Brown & Root the international oil conglomerate initially wound through the Middle-East incorporating work stints as a supervisor in the field in Saudi Arabia and down time in Beirut and Baalbek up in the Bequaa Valley.

"Beirut was a beautiful city in 1972, incredible food, lovely people, I was totally fascinated by the history of the country and the evidence of ancient times."

Claude found himself captivated for the first time by an ancient culture with a fascinating history.

The Acropolis of Baalbek is one of architecture's greatest achievements. The other main claim to fame of the Bequaa Valley was its status as the hashish capital of the Middle East. The local 'Lebanese red' and 'Baalbek blonde' had been blowing minds and fuelling fantasies long before Alexander the Great whose boys trudged through the valley in 325BC sampling its finest wares along the road to Damascus. In early '72, during a ten day layover in Beirut, the shit hit the fan.

"I was hanging out at a bar with 5-6 other kids my age drinkin' beers munching on falafel rolls. This rocket came out of nowhere and just shattered the Intercontinental Hotel across the street from us. I had a first class room up there fully paid for, it was totally destroyed"

The Middle East boiled over with America, Israel and the Arabs becoming intricately entangled in a scene where Politics, Oil and War all fitted together hand in glove. It all had a minimal effect on Claude, but nevertheless, when the contract ran out at the end of that year he seized the opportunity to make a move.

It was simple, Alaska or Indonesia. His superior explained that Brown & Root had a contract with the Indonesian government oil company and if he accepted it he would also gain a further promotion. "A return to the States was just not on as I had seen too much, but where the fuck was Indonesia?"

He literally had to pull out an atlas to discover the location of the world's largest archipelago. Staring at the countless islands scattered either side of the equator, images of the tropics, palm trees and waves saturated his mind stream.

"It was a no-brainer. I immediately dusted the cobwebs off my two surfboards and packed a bag. The deal was that Brown & Root were putting together offshore drilling platforms and their main site was Anyer Beach in West Java. I flew over with 2 other guys both in their 40s; one guy wouldn't leave the airport, the other one lasted a month. I, however, hung in for the duration. They had me staying at the Pertamina Hotel, 5 stars, on the beach. I would walk out of my bungalow across the sand to left and right beachbreaks forming off a small point. It was just beautiful."

To say Claude was in his element was an understatement.

"I was catching a lot of surf, principally because the company had a huge boat that could cruise at upwards of 40km/h. The first few times I took the boat around Anak Krakatau we couldn't get near it as it was spewing out lava bombs".

He quickly appraised himself of the local history. Anyer was once the largest Dutch port in the Sunda Strait, but all that changed around 10am on the 27th August, 1883. Lying some 50km from the site of Krakatau, Anyer, copped the full impact when the great mother volcano generated the equivalent energy of 2000 Hiroshima bombs. A feast of data remains from the biggest bang of modern times, however, on Anyer Beach nothing remained as the resulting tsunamis threw up walls of water up to 40 metres in height. Blocks of coral weighing 100 tonnes peppered the coast; a Dutch freighter was reportedly shifted 80km inland. Anak Krakatau, the bastard child reared its smouldering cone-shaped head in 1928 and ever since has continued to remind us of the power and impermanence of our natural world.

Making full use of the floating gin palace, Claude cruised the west coast of Java surfing the rights at Panaitan and around to the east as far as Ombak Tujuh. After doing a couple of Singapore trips on the one-week-off rotations he finally ran into a Sulawesi girl on Bugis St of all places, who told him that he should head to Bali instead. His only connection with the island at this stage was via the Rogers and Hammerstein classic *Bali Hai*, so on his next free week, in the middle of '73, he flew into Bali.

"I got off the plane and spent three hours at Kuta Reef. Almost immediately I met Zenik (a local Balinese woman who later founded 'Poppies Restaurant' and became a life-long friend). I instantly recognized that this was the place for me"

I quietly posed the question, "Why?"

"Well, it was obvious: the surf was perfect. There was nobody out. Kuta Beach at that time was just pristine. This was my dream from when I lifeguarded as a 14-16-year-old at Brigantine. I realized that I had been distracted. I got drafted and then went to work. There was a period of four years when I never saw water. The dream kinda disappeared."

The late afternoon glass-off and dramatic sunset tones on a beach fringed by shady palm trees brought it all back home.

"Wham, it just hit me, the surf dream was alive in me again. It didn't take me long to get out to Uluwatu, and as you can imagine it was just magnificent."

The Balinese shared a reality that was like a wish-fulfilling jewel to the eclectic and eccentric westerners that were drawn by the island's mesmerizing power. These people had departed their own shores from all points of the compass on a journey without end. Their goal lay wrapped in the presence of the search itself and this was clearly reflected by life on the island in its myriad manifestations of magic. Even though the concept of a 'golden age' remains empty of an inherent existence for those that were present in Bali through the early to late '70's, it remains a watershed experience in their lives, beautifully encapsulated in Alby Falzon's movie, *Morning of the Earth*.

Today almost everybody has heard of Bali. To some it means a smart place to go, one of the many ports on a round-the-world cruise; to others it brings mental images of brown girls with beautiful breasts, palm trees, rolling waves and all the romantic notions that go to make a south sea island paradise.

Miguel Covarubias, the self-taught anthropologist, wrote these words in the introduction to his much celebrated book *Island of Bali*, shortly after arriving on a steamer from New York late in 1930. The dream burned brightly for many. In the chapter titled 'Rites and Festivals', Covarubias gave us a bird's eye view of Balinese life and culture.

Placed between two poles from which emanate opposing forces (the positive from the mountains and the negative from the underworld), the entire life of the calm and sensitive Balinese, their daily routine, social organization, their entire ethics, manners, art; in short the total culture of the island is moulded by a system of traditional rules subordinated to religious beliefs. By this system they regulate every act of their lives so that it shall be in harmony with the natural forces, which they divide externally into pairs, male and female the creative principle; right and left, high and low, the principles of place direction and rank; strong and weak, or healthy and sick, clean and unclean; sacred and powerful or unholy and dangerous in general: Good and Evil, Life and Death.

None of us could have chosen a better playing field upon which to take part in the great experiment, although it remains arguable whether any of us quite understood the vagaries and subtle intricacies that were woven into the experience of Kuta in the '70s. From the artist communities situated in the jungles of Ubud and the beachside communities in Sanur to the old slave market fishing villages of Kuta and Legian, diverse tribes of 'Lotus Eaters' interfaced with the Balinese on a hallucinogenic level of orgasmic rapture. The juice flowed through the painters and sculptors, the writers and practicing psycho-anthropologists, the cinematographers and surfers, the smugglers and born again *sadhus* from India, the intergalactic space pilots, war correspondents and CIA rejects.

Into this cosmic soup of humanity was ladled liberal lashings of 'spice' in the form of local psilocybin-packed mushrooms, Oswald Oswley's lysergic varieties of 'window pane' and 'clear light', Nepalese 'temple balls', Manali hash, sinsemelia sticks of awakened perception more commonly known as 'buddha', opium from the 'Golden Triangle', Sumatran bullets from Aceh and dare I say it, the double-dragon brand of 'Hammer' from Burma and Laos. The instructions were simple; stir the soup gently, bring it slowly to the boil, then let it bubble and squeak. Life in Kuta wasn't all psychotropic states of altered consciousness, although it seems for the most part in retrospect to have been exactly like that. The elemental five coloured light dawned in the expansive minds of many, but for many more as the neuro-biochemical pathways opened they found themselves stuck between fear and self-deception, the proverbial rock and a hard place.

> **"We are always acting on what has just finished happening. It happened at least 1/30th of a second ago. We think we're in the present, but we aren't. The present we know is only a movie of the past."**
> TOM WOLFE ON KEN KESEY'S PHILOSOPHY.

No such additives were required by the local people who were mostly already in the know. Animistic beliefs overlaid with ancient Hindu and tantric Buddhist practice deeply rooted the Balinese into a shamanic culture with an elaborately sophisticated worldview. Their exposure to other cultures and influences had traditionally been handled by absorbing what was on offer and, with relevance, shaping it into their own kind. Surfing was summarily assimilated by the island culture under the influence and assistance of some of its luminaries from Hawaii and Australia.

"I met Gerry Lopez at Kuta Reef in '74 with Mike Boyum," said Claude, recalling that they stayed in the middle of a coconut field towards the airport.

" We surfed Uluwatu together – it was a challenge and still quite a daring thing to do. Lopez and his Hawaiian friends like Rory Russell, his brother Victor and guys like Roy Mesker were the only ones surfing it regularly during the season. I also met Jack McCoy around this time and we became firm friends".

By late '75, Claude had completed construction on his own house, which was substantial and very comfortable by any standard. Upon the walls hung indigenous artefacts and classic Indonesian textiles. Looking like something out of a *Tropical House and Garden* collectors issue, the pad lacked only one thing, electricity.

JASON CHILDS

Claude Graves, adventurer, explorer, founder of Nihiwatu Resort and the Sumba Foundation and, controversially, protector of the waves out front.

I had the good fortune of being introduced to Claude in early '76 by the lovely Marie Pollard, girlfriend of Peter Shearer, who was the elder of the Shearer clan, which also included Jan, Judy and Bugs. We were holed up in Komala Indah 2; Legian Kelod (south), just a few rice paddies away from Claude's house tucked in behind the sand dunes halfway to Legian.

The absence of electricity meant that either the moonlight or the ubiquitous kerosene lamps guided our nocturnal movements. Mystery, magic and myth naturally abounded in such creative conditions. All of that changed a little when Claude brought light to Kuta.

"I had this massive sound system that I had brought down from the condo in West Java, but it needed real power to crank it up. The closest sub-station was at the harbour in Benoa so I bought enough poles and cable and had the line run into Kuta. 'Poppies' and my house were the only places in town with light." That was until some light-fingered locals began tapping in to the source draining it to the point that the music died from lack of juice.

"I had to patrol the poles regularly in order for the music to flow," laughed Claude, and flow it did. The fusion of Afro-American rhythms by world music originators 'Osibisa in their '76 anthem 'Sunshine Day' will forever evoke these classic times in Kuta. The lyrics "Everybody, do what you're doing, your smile will bring a sunshine day," constantly blared from the cassette shops, it seemed to be repeated by everyone from *warung* attendants, to sellers on the beach and of course the cheeky board carriers out on the Bukit.

Hanging out at Claude's pad was heavenly, Jack McCoy related recently; "Gerry and I would sometimes call by in the afternoon after a big day out at Ulu just to chill in Claude's green room. He had the big sound system and an air conditioner. His whole scene was very cool because we were just used to hanging out in funky little *losmens* (local accommodation). Claude would entertain us with these amazing stories about Africa and his uncle in Kenya. We heard about his uncle being gored by a rhino, attacks by leopard, and elephants stamping on people who mistreated them. It was larger than life stuff so we nicknamed him 'Claude of Africa'."

The man knew exactly where he should be in his life. He was living the dream. When it all got too much and he needed peace of mind, he headed for Shipwrecks on Lembongan, which at the time was totally deserted.

"I gave some money to Pak Putu, a local guy who built me a great little house right on the beach in front of the break. This suited me fine. I had done the Grajagan thing with Boyum earlier on, before they built the tree houses, and I wanted somewhere closer than G-Land to hang with my friends away from the crowds that had already started to invade Bali. We had outrageous full moon parties over there 'cause there was no one around and I was very particular about who I invited. Not many surfers made it, though Jack McCoy and Terry Fitzgerald were two that did."

Jack remembers it all fondly. "Some of the best times I've spent in Indonesia over the years were those early trips I did over to Lembongan with Claude before it all got too weird. He was an adventurer, a real pioneer, a visionary, you could say. The locals loved him because he treated them fairly; a case of mutual love and respect."

Life is an evolving series of moments that segue together into a fluidity of causes and conditions, once a set of conditions have expired then another set will arise and so the flow continues; nothing lasts forever. Intuition takes on more importance as we evaluate and interpret the inner signposts appearing in our travels; the trick is not to get stuck on the stepping-stones. By '79 Claude saw it all coming and wanted to make a break. The numbers were stacking up. Lembongan's sleepy-hollow cover had been blown and Bali was fast becoming a regular tourist destination; it was time to move.

He chose the Dark Continent. Kenya was his destination. He was still seeking adventure in his life. Our paths diverged and I wouldn't meet with him again for 10 long years, when the dream led him on into the wilds of Sumba, the fabled 'Island of the Warriors'.

I want to be present to the Dream, so that it knows I am listening. I want reverence for the Dream, as you would the wilderness, for the Dream is the wilderness. There, we connect with the world, the world speaks to us. It is our connection to the wild, the soul of the world. We must conserve our capacity to Dream. It is the reminder that once we were wild, and underneath, still are.
JAMES DOLAN

awn breaks through the lowland evergreen rainforest radiating warmth and light across an ancient land. The subtle gold rays illuminate the *imperata* fronds of the savannah grasslands as they wave excitedly like pony tails in the cool mountain wind. The spirit of renewal embodied in the light from a star 98 million miles away caresses and revitalizes all that is seen and unseen along the shimmering river of life. From high up in an areca tree by the floodlit river, an apricot-breasted sunbird alights from its nest in the canopy, pumping its wings it swoops low down the valley heading for the coast. As it glides, it emits the mesmeric whistling sound 'Sooomba'. The land has spoken; the island of Sumba materializes out of a mist-filled darkness to greet another day.

In a time before the beginning, from the sacred space of unified awareness (Mother Moon and Father Sun) a separation occurred that clearly defined a non-dual upperworld and an underworld inhabited by spirits and deities concerned primarily with fertility, death and productivity. Existing impermanently in between the two was the world of mankind. Out of the unified awareness, also known as Mother Binder of the Forelock and Father Creator of the Crown, appeared the *Marapu*. The *Marapu* clans descended to earth to transcend the duality or two-fold nature of the universe. They would transmit the law through time, space and form, dissolving the polarity of male-female, heat and cool, highland versus lowland, east and west, the worldly opposing the spiritual and, finally, communicating the relative to the absolute.

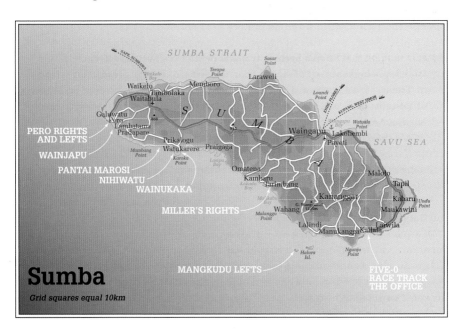

Sumba

Grid squares equal 10km

Their gyroscopic descent from the Heavens hit turbulence, landing them initially somewhere near India and their subsequent trials and tribulations became the basis of the orally recorded heroic 'journeys of the ancestors'. The sixteen founders of the seven original clans arrived in Sumba by crossing over the mythical 'bridge of time' in the north of the island. Shortly after they separated to explore the new homeland, one such *Marapu* clan stepped ashore on the southwest coast, having become shipwrecked on the deserted beach between present day Rua and Lamboya. The surrounding area was declared *keramat* – a location of magical or holy significance. Before travelling inland to establish their first village they consecrated two rocks on the fine-grained beach; one was called *batu perahu* (rock boat) in honour of the vessel that had overturned. The second rock was called the *Ngihi* stone or *Ngihiwatu*. It was seen as a fertility symbol shaped in the form of a *lesung*, the receptacle used for the pounding of grain.

The Nihiwatu Resort, founded by Claude and Petra Graves, lies elevated some 300 metres away, overlooking these *Marapu* roots that naturally ornament the pandanus-lined bay and a beach that drips serenity.

In the time before even the appearance of the *Marapu*, Sumba was tethered umbilically to the supercontinent of Gondwanaland. The great southern landmass comprised South America, Africa, Antarctica as well as India and Australia. Attached to the northwest shelf of Australia on the edge of the Tethys Sea lay Sumba. Sometime, nearly 100 million years ago, it detached itself and over the proceeding 50 million years the microcontinent inched higher towards the equator through the Tethys' primordial laboratory of creation.

It is thought that Sumba became trapped behind the East Java Trench as that island was squeezed out of the sea floor somewhere near the present day island of Timor. Java's westward march dragged Sumba into its present position of latitude 10º S and longitude 120º E, aided and abetted by the northward moving Australian tectonic plate.
WHERE WORLDS COLLIDE **BY PENNY VAN OOSTERZEE**

Geologically consisting of uplifted limestone and sedimentary rock, Sumba is one of the few non volcanic islands in an archipelago that stretches some 6400km. Lying east of the Wallace line, which differentiates the fauna and flora of Asia from Australasia, the island remains forever a unique study in timelessness.

Marapu spirits are immanent in all aspects of Sumbanese life both in the apparent and the non-apparent. Every clan, forest, water source, cave, beach as well as certain objects and animals have their own *Marapu*. The ancestors essentially created the ritualized framework by which mankind could communicate with both the spirit world and the upperworld. Ritual art was elaborately carved into massive tombs, which symbolized a person's status and his journey into the afterlife. These great tombs could weigh 30 tons; take 40 men two years to prepare and 1000 men to drag it from the quarry to its site. These Megalithic sentinels represent the first stone given by the 'Creator' to the *Marapu* to use as a compass to find their way to Sumba from India.

The *ratu* (shaman or priest) invokes the *Marapu* spirits during any ceremony concerning marriage, birth, death or the establishment of a house, in fact every important act of everyday life. The *ratu* operated in a restricted zone of power, however humility and self-deprecation appear to be their greatest attributes as the most revered shamans maintain that they were only, "...like small children grasping at the rope of a spinning top."

They fulfilled their duty to their people by engaging the cosmic system in ritual procedures where the sacred mysteries of the universe would become apparent.

"We are just the lips told to pronounce, we are only the mouths told to speak."

Although the *ratu* was an authentic ruler of the clan Kasibu, at some point in the murky past, temporal power was ceded to another related family member who assumed the role of the noble raja or feudal lord. In East Sumba the role of the *rajas* and their lines of descent flourished, whereas in the West the division of power was more evenly shared. Over time this megalithic culture was nurtured by waves of influence from both the Middle East and India to adapt and evolve into a unique indigenous society.

I remember flicking through encyclopaedias as a boy and reading about the famed Sandalwood Island. Two thousand years ago, traders from the Middle East and China pursued the source of this precious essential oil in Timor and Sumba. In India, sandal was said to promote the awakening of the kundalini (latent female energy), as well as being a muscle relaxant, an antiseptic and a treatment for diarrhoea. It was also valued as a reliever of nervous tension, stress and anxiety. In mute contrast to the effects it promoted, the sandalwood forests of Sumba were decimated to the point of extinction in the relentless quest for this natural commodity. All that remained to trade then was buffalo and horses, plus the only other valuable chattels in abundance; people!

By the middle of the 15th century, people smuggling became big business in the archipelago as the Chinese and Portuguese moved large quantities of slaves from Timor and Flores for sale in Kuta on the island of Bali. Throughout this time, Sumba was left alone as its reputation as an island of war-mongering warriors and magical headhunters was the stuff of legend. Headhunting has always captured man's imagination; whilst killing one's enemies meant victory, acquiring the heads conferred the mystical benefits, and then performing ceremonies for the victims head would enable its spirit to become a friend, guardian, and benefactor.

Headhunting is not solely about violence; it is part of a sophisticated mythological, ritual and cosmological worldview. – ROBERT MCKINLEY

The ratu katoda was the war leader who communed with the *Marapu* and transformed his community's grief and anger into spiritual anger; in the language used in divinations before a raid, the andung skull tree was said to 'boil with heat', the stone circle surrounding it to 'steam with anger'. In East Sumba headhunting dominated the warring factions of the rajas or noble clans; it also symbolized their defiance against the colonial Dutch outsiders. The rites and rituals of headhunting in West Sumba, however, displayed an 'ideology of vendetta' that characterized acts of revenge between equals.
THE HERITAGE OF HEADHUNTING, JANET HOSKINS, 1996.

The colloquial term 'loss of face' which assumes such importance in Asia, stems perhaps from this age-old ritual. Taking heads, it seemed, caused a loss of face in another tribe, an action that was to be avoided at all costs.

It took the Dutch East India Company a further 200 years to successfully develop trade links with the Sumbanese nobility and persevere with their ulterior motive; control of the island. It was not until the early part of the twentieth century that this was achieved, although the Dutch regarded the island as being bereft of any economic value once slaving had died. Christianity, the Japanese war machine, and a benevolent dictatorship based in Jakarta, all impacted heavily upon the island as the second millennium drew to a close.

Journeying in Sumba always involves taking a walk on the wild side; one's conceptual framework is always challenged by the Sumbanese, who seem to be stuck in the past and separated from our own ingrained notions of time and existence. Seeing through this illusory veil is what brings adventure alive in Sumba; for these people dance to a different beat, and somehow they evoke within us a subtle reconnection to that primeval energy we call the rhythm of life.

David and Janine Thomas together with David Wyllie arrived in Sumba in '74 on a quest. They had formulated a plan six months earlier in Terrigal, north of Sydney, to explore the island in search for one of its most valuable treasures, the fabled Sumba *ikat* blanket. As Dave Thomas recalls,

"Trading in antiquities was in its infancy at the time; Michael Palmeri was in Borneo, Kent Waters was in Flores, Zac Saklofsky together with Perry Kessner were sussing Bali and Jogya John was in Java. We gave each other space to explore. Most importantly, we had a spiritual search happening in our lives. Living with our Balinese family in the heart of Kuta, we lived life as a ceremony, however, when we got to East Sumba it was like stepping into a Stone Age spirit world."

The two Daves were foreigners in a land that had been stripped of that playful quality of innocence which so freely existed in Bali. They explored with an open mind and relied heavily on intuition and, after a succession of back-to-back trips, they found themselves on the inner circle of the Kings of East Sumba.

"We arrived during an interesting transition in Sumbanese history when the kings or *rajas'* power was being systematically eroded by the central government in Jakarta and by non-Sumbanese traders looking to free up the local economy. As the kings died, their replacements were not recognized by the powers that be. This was essentially a feudal society where the various *rajas* would still have their own slave villages. It was fascinating watching how the hierarchy functioned around the kings, and consequently we were a little in awe of what we were witnessing."

The kings were cashing in their treasures as they realized that their all-powerful cultural dynasties were coming to an end. As their fledgling trading business between Sumba and Kuta took off, the boys found more time to unravel the complexities of this mystifying land. Stocked up on anti-malarials and Admiralty charts, the two Daves talked Jack Rife, the retired Air America pilot of Zamrud Airlines, into flying a couple of motor bikes down to Waingapu in his DC-3 so that they could explore the forgotten SE coastline of the island. Bypassing the one truck per week to Melolo meant the intrepid duo gained increased mobility through the use of the bikes; however, they also ended up in places they weren't supposed to. As DT (Dave Thomas) points out,

"You have to remember that prior to us, the previous white people in SE Sumba were the Australian commandos who hid out down there from the Japs in WW2".

Roads were non-existent and the terrain exacted an unrelenting toll on both the riders and machines. It was a scene far removed from the celluloid imagery of *Easy Rider*, although the soundtrack of *Born to be Wild* was completely appropriate.

"Getting through to the deep south in the district of Waijello was very tough, but from about 200 feet above the coast on an exposed tableland we suddenly caught sight of surf breaking on the offshore reefs. We stood there completely stunned by the view. It was already late in the afternoon, but we decided to head for the beach that we could see inside the enormous bay to try and find shelter for the night. Eventually we found ourselves on a beach that was just so idyllic. Actually the virginal white sand beach stretched for miles around a deep blue azure bay to the south, inside of which was a lagoon with a fringing reef and rideable waves firing off along it. Majestically tall lontar palms lined the bay and the remains of turtle eggs and large seashells were scattered everywhere. We found a little lean-to and laid out our blankets to kick back and catch the last rays of what was an unforgettable sunset. We then decided to celebrate the occasion by consuming our remaining tabs of acid." In the '70s one explored on every level possible, however, the boys' priceless commemoration of life on one plane invited the demons to hatch on another.

"We were soaking up the vibes in the afterglow of the sunset as the first stars started to pop out of an inky black sky. I said to DW (Dave Wyllie), 'did you see that?' I'd been catching sight of these little flickers of light in my peripheral vision. He dismissed it as being the lysergic kicking in. However, these little lights flicked on and off in the darkness of the surrounding bush until with an ear piercing shout we looked up totally astonished to see this mass of angry locals screaming in a full charge towards us. We became immediately surrounded by these frothing beetle-nut stained faces that were just ranting and lunging at us with their spears. The little lights were in fact these guys signaling each other with torches. There was this one old white haired guy who taunted and provoked the mob as they would back off and then charge to within a metre of us waving machetes and swords in our faces."

It was a bit like Davey Crockett and Jim Bowie at the Alamo as our hallucinogenic heroes stood back to back remaining calm, but internally struggling with the immensity of the experience. DT recalls,

"During the madness of it all, I momentarily glanced upwards into a twinkling star-filled Milky Way and said to Dave, 'well, if we are going to die, then it sure is a beautiful night for it'. He quickly replied saying, 'Fuck that Dave, I didn't come to Sumba to die!'. Next thing a young guy started imploring them not to kill us; apparently he had seen us days earlier at the headman's house in the village of Melolo. He saved our lives. As the intensity started to wane we realized that they weren't going to kill us there and then. They insisted on tying us up, but through broken Bahasa we agreed to accompany them to their village about one mile away for an interrogation."

Indonesia was already engaged in a civil war that was brewing with the Fretlin in East Timor. Unbeknownst to the boys, an Indonesian Intelligence unit had alerted all village heads along the SE Sumbanese coast to detain all suspicious looking persons. The likely lads fitted the bill perfectly. DT continued,

"The mob were still pretty jumpy as they kept fueling up on the beetle nut, however, after we were introduced to Amahaho (the village head) and showed him our passports and permits things started to settle down. Amahaho had recently crashed the district's one and only motorbike and had a lacerated knee that we immediately attended to. It was all a case of just being natural and letting the events flow; needless to say, we stayed up all night talking, and of course became lifelong friends. In fact DW is still down there married to one of Amahaho's daughters."

The world of the two Daves expanded dramatically that day and night. Suddenly their stay on the island became multi-purpose as the discovery of significant surf meant that they could combine their trading and textile research together with their passion for riding waves. All they had to do was keep it secret. They returned soon after with a truck full of building supplies, boards and loved ones. They set about 'living the dream' that thousands dreamed of. Yet, as is so often the case in the dream of life, the way things appear is different to the way we perceive them. DT again:

"On one level it was just bliss, a real paradise, but then on another, when you lifted the reality veil, you saw the locals struggling to eke out a day-to-day existence. We had come from Bali where food was abundant, but in SE Sumba life was just brutal. Sickness was widespread, infant mortality was incredibly high, so we had to plan meticulously to cover our own possibilities of a serious injury and illness. It was a view as far removed as possible from the glamour of the movies and magazines. We balanced living with death and suffering by experiencing the mystical, the spiritual and the occult."

Claude and I crossed paths again on the beach at Kuta Reef in '89. His subsequent tales of pounding surf, the scent of the West Sumba savannah, and the enriched culture of the local people of Nihiwatu set my heart racing. There was only one question, when would I receive an invitation? Good things come to those that wait, and wait I did. When I couldn't go immediately I decided to read about the island. The two Daves were legends in their own lounge rooms, but they kept details of their adventures in Sumba to a minimum. So it was by chance that I happened upon a diary written by Jim Banks of his initial journey to Nihiwatu with Claude, Petra and Jack McCoy that really kept the embers burning. Jim's diary evoked the awe-struck innocence of a stranger in a strange land.

The country here is beautiful, steep grassy hills drop down onto raised plains that are carved up by rice-paddy lined valleys. It looks like parts of Hawaii and feels like Africa. My mind drifts back to those old Tarzan movies as we form a long train of people carrying surfboards, bags, eskies, tents and cameras heading for the surf. As we meander through the paddies we pass some enormous water buffalo and marvel at the unique roof structures of the local architecture.

We end up sliding down an incredibly steep track through a sweet potato field and then, over the edge of a small cliff, we finally see it, Ubi Jalar Point! (Sweet Potato Point). It's only small, but the potential is obvious. It's a long reef that freight trains down from the point; about three quarters of the way down there is a giant coral head that sticks about a foot out of the water, momentarily interrupting the wave before it wraps through the final bowls to finish in a deepwater channel... I'm straight out there.

The feeling of paddling out into a virgin break in the middle of a tropical paradise is one of the best feelings in the world. I'm buzzing even before I take-off. It's deceptively bigger than I thought. The first wave jacks very quickly and I get swallowed up in the pit, I look up and what seemed a little four-footer is now well and truly overhead and charging down the reef like a wounded bull! This place has grunt and much more than Bali. The wave twists, jumps and pushes like inside Sunset, a comparison that is confirmed over and over again. Within an hour there are some very solid sets pouring through, some producing a good 12ft of vertical face. Almost every take-off is a free-fall out of the lip. My seven-footer is feeling right at home and I can't

imagine tackling this wave with anything less. Claude appears from nowhere and picks off some real clean ones. There is plenty of variety in the sets, from the fun peelers to the jacking, heaving, spitting mothers.

Just before midday a mega set has Claude and I scratching for the horizon. We actually get sucked into paddling too far out and even with my 7'0" I can't paddle into it. The big sets here contain a lot of water and they create the impression that the whole ocean is coming at you. It gets a bit hairy as the tide drops so we head in while we're still in one piece – well, almost, as I've torqued my shoulder getting blasted inside one of the barrels and it's getting too sore to paddle.

Jim's diary, together with Claude and Petra's stories, kept me fuelled for two more years. Petra, in her inimitable style, grasped a unique view of Sumbanese life from a woman's perspective.

The women enter one door of the uma or home and the men another. The men sleep on one side of the house, the women on another and there is a bed in the middle for lovemaking. The Sumbanese have a great connectedness and exhibit a real simplicity towards life; I think this is something that we (as a people) are also searching for. The women in Sumbanese society are the nurturers of life, whether it be for the men, the children, their animals or the land; this is their ultimate role. You can imagine how surprised we were when we entered a village on one occasion to see a big chubby woman all bare breasted and smiling; she nursed her baby on one breast, and something grey and hairy on the other. On closer examination, the something grey and hairy was in fact her piglet! We were shocked, of course, but then it just seemed so natural, the energetic smile on this woman's face displayed her true happiness; we were the ones confronted by our inhibitions, not her. Life is a delicate matter when it is lived in extreme conditions. You just do what you have to do; the women in Sumba exude an inner strength, and durability just like their textiles.

Tales of intrigue and drama get spun out of circumstances of uncertainty and over time are woven into fabrics that symbolize the life of a people. In her book *Between the Folds*, Jill Forshee describes the renowned Sumba *ikat*:

"Cloth in Sumba excites elusive realms of the imagination. Designs in fabrics reveal profound shifts in the perspectives of those who create them. As a social, economic an aesthetic medium – an art-cloth is a channel for the passions that underlie people's endeavours."

The warp and weft threads of the Sumba blanket are the fibres that hold this authentic people together. What is interesting about the tradition of weaving cloth is that it forms the basis of several different indigenous cosmologies.

Upon a mountain of pure Awareness the ancient Navajo Spider Woman set up her loom to weave the web of life. In the 'Dreaming', she cast out strings as she weaved her magic and where these strings intersected a living being appeared. Herman Melville, the humble American Universalist, saw the whole of life in an empty thread when he wrote, "We cannot live only for ourselves. A thousand fibres connect us, and among those fibres, as sympathetic threads, our actions run as causes, and they come back to us as effects. On a daily basis, we affect the web of all existence, just as we are affected by it."

Our thoughts are like strings that we cast about, weaving the fabric of our own lives moment to moment. The women of the district of Lamboya, in West Sumba adjoining the Nihiwatu Resort, believe that the surrounding country was woven out of the dreams of a mythical python.

"The python motif dominates the Lamboya textiles and symbolizes the vitality in the earth," writes Danniel Giernaet-Martin in her book, *The Woven Land of Lamboya.*

One could envisage a python as a big piece of string, maybe even a bundle of strings woven together in a constricting mass of energy. When I finally showed up at Nihiwatu in '91 together with Claude and Richard Flax, funnily enough it was not the groundswell wrapping down the reef that grabbed my attention, nor even the exotic feeling of being on safari in the land of the headhunters; but it was the python stories, mythical and true, that Claude told after dark in the eerie half light of the gas-fired lantern, that really got my adrenalin flowing.

Jim Banks off the bottom. Over decades of surf exploration in Indonesia, Banks has clocked more time on this wave than almost anyone except Graves.

He remembers once driving across to Waingapu around four in the morning when he was jerked awake by the driver slamming on the brakes, there, stretched out across the three-metre wide bitumen road, warming itself was a massively thick snake. A closer examination with a torch revealed that at least 2 metres of the reticulated python had already disappeared into the scrub, but importantly there were still 2 metres of undulating muscle that hadn't yet made it onto the road. That makes it 7 metres or over 20 feet. They say there are eight metre-plus giants hibernating in the hollows of the limestone caves that dot West Sumba.

Petra also remembers one brave staff member who had to jump into a well, Johnny Weissmuller style to hand-wrestle a beast that had been blocking up the six-inch intake valve with its tail. It's a bitch down there when your pipes are blocked. Richard and Judy Flax had to deal with a five-metre constrictor that had curled up under their bungalow on another occasion.

"There was no way in the world that Judy and the kids would sleep the night in that room even though it was completely sealed," said Richard. The locals threw a bucket of crushed raw onions over it to try and move it; apparently this had worked for them in the past. But it only made the snake rear and bolt deeper into the foundations. Seizing the opportunity, Dato, a trusted and fearless employee, grabbed it by the tail and ran in the opposite direction, in fact right up the hill, eventually letting it go.

Time conjures up different feelings within different people; mostly in the West, 'time is money'; in Sumba, time is measured in terms of its value and the Sumbanese invest their time "in sacred objects, textiles, animals and events." (Hoskins).

For surfers, however, in the *Free Ride* gospel according to Shaun Tomson "time expands in the tube", and by the October of '94, my time had also come.

From the moment that I arose that morning I knew this was the day I had been waiting for; I practically created it with my own incessant thoughts over the previous three years. In my three previous journeys to Nihiwatu I had come away empty handed, surf wise. I was yet to taste the bountiful fruits of what this unique location could deliver. Instead I had feasted upon Claude's tales full of derring-do and bravado and re-read Jim's diary when I needed a fix. On smaller days, generally the swells are straighter and the rides shorter, consequently, when Claude laid down the law on what constituted a real wave i.e. "when you take-off beside, in front of, or beyond the rock" I felt maybe riding real waves here may be beyond my ability.

This day completely fulfilled the Big Fella's criteria for real waves; there was no doubting it. The tide was now coming off high at about 2.30pm, the trades were light, the walls were glassy and the swell was pumping. It was time to go. I stepped off the beach and slipped silently into the maelstrom. The rip was performing a very good imitation of stand-up rapids – hell on wheels. Departing the beach, there was an ever-present risk of being swept across the channel to face the music. Copping a pounding on the rocks at the aptly named 'Suicidals' was to be avoided at all costs.

Earlier in the morning, I had been hideously caught inside by the largest wave I had ever seen. At the big righthander off the Marosi headland the whole ocean seemed to rise up and completely engulf me. Jim's diary was eerily coming alive. Death's warm, furry feeling was certainly attractive; one breath it seems can last a lifetime whilst one exhalation will end it. Tennessee Williams said "Life is so many moments, death is only one", recognizing the moment bought humility and renewed vigour; I needed it, for the following three waves pulverized me into putty. My day of destiny was nearly killing me. I had somehow survived the agony, but now what I needed was some ecstasy. Taking my time in an extended paddle into the line-up, I quietly imbibed the energy that was on display. My normal line-up markers were redundant. I quickly realized that the rock was not only the focus, but it was also the locus point of entry onto the wave. Six-wave sets with minor lulls in between breaking in the 6-10' range, meant that I had plenty of choice; there was, after all, no one else out.

I patiently waited till it felt right. The trick was all in the choice. The waves peaking beyond the rock with the tapering shoulders were the go; their direction was more from the south which meant they would go all the way through the inside, a ride of some 100-150 metres. It was 'Goodnight Irene', though, if you chose badly. The wave appeared out of nowhere, all dream-like just as it always is. Crawling over the ledge took extra effort, but having done so the drop became the moment of unparalleled ecstasy. When I had commenced paddling for the wave it looked like a solid six-footer, perhaps a bit bigger, but now as I was free-falling down the face it had seemed to grow by at least 50% in size and volume. The bottom to the wave was non-existent. The drawing action of the water off the reef and up the face meant that the only option was to slide sideways left in a real hurry. Whilst this choice was obvious, it presented some difficulty, as I had yet to catch an edge. Somewhere, two-thirds of the way down, board, knees and wave all came together as I pulled into a substantial chamber of excellence.

I only comment upon its generous proportion as the view from inside looking out was at once stunning and awe-inspiring. Hitting the mid-section of the reef, however, the wave elongated before bending into the bowls; the womb became claustrophobic as I closed my eyes and hung on. When the light did re-appear it was in the form of a bolt from above, refracted magnificently in the crystalline clear curvature of the tube. I momentarily caught sight of the thatched roofed bungalows blending into the hillside; what seemed extraordinary now all looked so ordinary. The intensity abated, the speed slowed, then, just like a rollercoaster designed to thrill, the tunnel opened again, and the dynamic energy that becomes the second bowl kicked in.

I remember shedding a few tears of joy on the paddle back out. The session lasted maybe two hours. I caught about five waves. The delirious after-effects of my first wave quickly evaporated as I fell out of the face on my second and copped a beating by an unrelenting set. This wave demanded that you be at the top of your game or else pay the consequences. Propped up later at the bar I drank in the exceptional view with my family and the eclectic bunch of friends who had come together to share another priceless Sumba sojourn. The bay was cloaked in layers of gold from the electrifying sunset tones; plumes of spray rising from the pounding swell backlit by the sinking orb created a surreal effect. Markus, the island's most congenial barman, quietly ripped the top off another cold one (the first hadn't even touched the sides), handing it to me he gently enquired,

"Did you have a good day today, Mr. Kevin"?

"Markus", I replied expansively, "today I think I've seen it all." In his soft dulcet tones he then pleaded, "Please, Mr. Kevin, make me a promise that you will come to a Pasola, then you will see everything!"

The real power in West Sumba lies in the hands of the *Ratu Nale* or 'Lord of the Year'. He is the sea worm priest who, being the custodian of the sacred objects, duly sets in motion the calendrical wheel of his clan. The essential well-being of the clan and its villages lay in his ability to read the complex interplay of forces involved in the cycle and the rhythm of the seasons. The nale is a multihued-segmented worm of the *Eunicid* family (*Leodice viridis*). Basically once a year, from somewhere on the ocean floor, these worms are released and though affected by rainfall, tides and current they appear at dawn under the watchful eyes of the *Ratu Nale* at four different locations along the West Sumba coast during February and March. They represent the supreme gift of the Sea Goddess's body. As the supreme controller of Time the *Rato Nale* is the eye of the storm, so to speak, in the Nale festival, which begins a new year and heralds the commencement of the Pasola.

Lawrence Blair, in the book based on his ten-year Indonesian odyssey, *Ring of Fire*, vividly describes a Pasola in West Sumba.

"With a growing sense of excitement we joined the throng now climbing up to the Pasola ground. Several hundred magnificently bedecked horsemen were already cantering around in tight circles working themselves and their mounts into a preliminary frenzy. This sweeping battlefield overlooking the Indian Ocean was edged with scattered burial megaliths, but these were now mainly hidden by a milling swarm of enthusiastic spectators who had gathered from miles around. As we waited, a great hush descended and even the horses stood still. All we could hear were a few birdcalls and the surf breaking below. Suddenly, the two high priests of the Upper and Lower Worlds broke their ranks and galloped their horses at full speed towards each other into the centre of the field, waving their spears and invoking the energies they represented to come and join battle. Then, with unexpected violence they hurled their javelins from a distance of about fifteen feet; intentionally missing each other by a hair's breadth. This was the signal for the battle to begin, and as they withdrew from the centre stage they were engulfed as the first thunderous onslaught of spearsmen charged each other at the gallop, their vivid orange, red and green turbans and ribbons streaming in the breeze. The sandalwood horses, small, but heroically proportioned like the Arabian horses to which they are believed to be related, were ridden bareback, and stirrupless, their riders gripping far forward with their knees while maneuvering expertly at full speed in unbelievably tight curves. The warriors rode in two great circles reflecting, it was explained to us, the orbits of celestial bodies."

At the intersection point of the circles the spears flew. Documentary filmmaking brothers Lorne and Lawrence Blair had been trying to film a Pasola for years; they were joined this time by the remarkable Zac Saklofsky as assistant cameraman. Lawrence continues:

"Lorne was satisfied with the wide shots and was eager for more detail; he suggested we set up his tripod in the centre of the field, with Zac on the second camera beside him, and myself reluctantly wielding the tape recorder and still cameras. We were barely installed, when a wall of howling spearsmen charged towards us. While Zac and I blanched and fumbled with the wrong buttons, Lorne contentedly glued his eye to the viewfinder and began shooting. Once the riders had passed, he was surprised to see three spears, closely grouped, protruding from between his camera's tripod. They had been hurled with such force that, despite their blunted ends, they protruded from the earth like well-grouped darts in a dartboard".

Lawrence poignantly describes his companions island adventure, "We had come to Sumba for a glimpse of our earliest beginnings, of megaliths and the origins of war, where a warrior still looked his opponent in the eyes, but we found something more. It seemed there is no animosity here, but rather, a recognition that we are all participants in the interplay of light and darkness, order and chaos, reflected in the life-giving seasons of the planet itself, if we but knew how to interpret them like the *Ratu*."

JASON CHILDS

Pasola warrior. Of all the rich cultural traditions still thriving in Sumba, this event encapsulates the island's powerful connections with the ocean and the land, the forces of light and darkness.

The recognition that we are all a part of the presence is what keeps drawing Michael McHugh back to Sumba. Michael is a longtime Indonesian surf adventurer and extreme snowboarder; he remains one of Claude and Petra's closest friends.

"The place has an intensity and a calmness; you get confronted by your own presence in a natural space. Life is stripped of all distractions so that you can just be. Of course the dream now includes hot water and A/C in refined comfort, but nothing beats those early days when it was all so raw. On my first trip, Claude's horror surf stories and the thundering swell kept me awake all night; he woke Richard and I up by banging on a pot yelling out 'come and get it boys'. I looked out of the tent and there was all this mist on the water lit by a soft golden light with lines of massive waves breaking all the way through the channel. It was a bit like Valdez in Alaska where there are no distractions, just pure focus."

My own last journey to Nihiwatu coincided with the commencement of the bombing of Afghanistan. The instability rocking the planet provided a wonderful opportunity for a diverse collection of people and their children to come together at this unique resort, which overlooks the edge of the world. The camaraderie of our group experience, the interaction with a devoted staff and the genuine nature of the local people touched us deeply. Michelle, wife of photographer Jason Childs intimately relates her personal journey,

"Sumba touched my heart and left me humble; I feel as though I've been cleansed and have been given so much more awareness from a people who seemingly have so little. Can you imagine walking into a village that has no water or First World amenities to be greeted only by smiling faces, offerings of beetlenut and kids who want to play high-five?"

I've always respected Claude and Petra for their fearlessness in facing the challenges that have arisen during their time in Sumba, whether it be in the solitary testing of Claude's own ability in a variety of extreme surfing conditions, or absorbing the repercussions of the earthquake that shattered more than just their reality. Through it all they have remained resilient and true to their dream. I'd be kidding, though, to say I have always agreed with the way 'Claudius' has gone about meeting some of the more contentious issues. Certain dreams contain negative nightmarish aspects which confront the dreamer when they are least expected, such was the case in the distant past when Claude strapped on his diver's knife and paddled out the back to scare off several surfer trespassers. From the ensuing argument he sliced through a couple of their legropes and wrote himself into the traveling surfer's hall of infamy. The word on the jungle grapevine was something like "there's some crazy bastard down there in Sumba that would pull a knife on you if you surfed his wave uninvited". Nothing can condone such action, but I had to also chuckle knowing full well that 'Claudius' would have tackled the uninvited guest problem like he would a charging rhino; head on! He describes them as his Mosquito Coast years and unreservedly apologizes for his actions.

Exclusivity of ocean frontage and denied access to waves has been a troubling issue for myself and also many others in the surfing tribe. It is an issue that runs deep and releases strong emotions. Like many, I was once a backpacker surfer before the term even existed, together with my mate John Geisel we camped in the magnificent coastal jungle of Lagundri on Nias and lived the pure perfection of 'the Surfers' Dream'. In retrospect, it's easy to see why concepts of freedom can be confusing; because the way life appears, is not always the way life is. Alas, the Lagundri dream 27 years on encompasses a ghost town of funky huts alongside a degraded reef. Janis used to sing that, "Freedom's just another word for nothing left to lose" but it seems that in acts of subtle deception, we end up destroying that which we seek solace in; the search for freedom leads to understanding, it generates compassion and promotes equanimity.

Always recognize the dreamlike qualities and reduce attachment and aversion. Practice good heartedness toward all beings. Be loving and compassionate, no matter what others do to you. What they will do will not matter so much if you see it as a dream. The trick is to have positive intention during the dream. This is the essential point. This is true spirituality.
CHAGDUD TULKU RINPOCHE

Claude calls it as he sees it.

"We knew that once we settled here others would follow and that if we were not careful we would be responsible for having created another surf slum. We felt very strongly that it was our responsibility to protect this pristine environment. To do so meant investing many years educating and training the local villagers and a lot of money in acquiring the land to close the area to outsiders. I know this has not gone down well with some of the surfing community, but times are changing. Developers of surfing destinations should step up and take responsibility for the long-term effect of their actions. In general, the surf travel industry does not positively impact the remote destinations it feeds off of. The sorry truth is that wherever a "new discovery" is made the end result is often overdevelopment and pollution of not only the environment, but also the cultures of the local people."

The swell was inconsistent and I patiently awaited the arrival of a set of five-footers that would make my day. Looking back I saw Claude paddling out to join me. We got to talking about life, the war and the ageing process, and for the first time ever I heard him really sing the blues. He had momentarily succumbed to the grind of the constant obstacles that lay in the path of the resort's financial success and out it flowed. Then, just as suddenly, the wind shifted offshore to gust from the northeast, causing the temperature and barometric pressure to drop dramatically as a change kicked in. We both spied the set finally looming out the back, as we paddled for position he said to me,

"You know, Kevin, I've got this idea I've been working on for three years called the Sumba Foundation. It will be ready in another month and it will do the aid work that has been a major part of the Nihiwatu concept. We're making it a non-profit organization registered in Delaware to directly benefit the locals here. I'm gonna dedicate my life to it."

I was stunned by his statement. He was first into position, but he graciously offered me the wave of the day. After I kicked out and paddled in, I had only one thing on my mind; the Sumba Foundation and it felt like the start of a beautiful relationship.

Nearly half of the world's population exists on less than $2 per day and half of that total exist on less than $1 per day. According to Jim Wolfhenson of the World Bank, "The fight against poverty and inequity is the fight for peace."

The Sumbanese are arguably some of the poorest people in Indonesia. The country's economic crisis has left Sumba a complete basketcase. The basics that we take for granted in the west such as clean water, healthy living conditions, medicines and medical facilities, education for their children and employment facilities is what the Sumba Foundation is striving to provide the Sumbanese.

Michael McHugh, however, wonders whether we have the right to make the judgment calls on other peoples' behalf. He explains his view,

"The ignorance of many 'do-gooder' aid organizations is seen through a tunnel vision and it remains illusory, the aid given often creates more problems as is the case in places like Somalia and Ethiopia where starving people are fed and then forgotten until the next generation of the survivors' children are again starving. The cycle has proven to repeat itself every 20 years or so. We need to tread carefully in our approach in giving aid; the rights and freedoms of individuals must be seriously considered and enshrined in antiquity, as this is what I believe, is most precious. Giving handouts is not the solution. But at the same time, it is important to deliver basic improvements to peoples' lives, and help them create and sustain an economy, so they can retain such freedoms; ultimately, I think this would be more beneficial than allowing cheap-end tourism to develop. The Sumbanese culture is very precious and must be preserved at all cost."

Our responsibility for each other is unchanging; when we care for the other, we are caring for ourselves. We are no longer, as the advertising catch cry once read, 'Surfers of Fortune'. We are and should always be surfers of conscience. The adoption of a more altruistic attitude by a surf industry that has long profited from selling 'the dream', could, I believe, effectively benefit thousands of marginalised people that live adjacent to surf travel destinations. Untold potential is lying dormant in the industry's bottom line surpluses as only a fraction of these profits has to be freed up to significantly assist those in most need. The unity of surfer and ocean contains within it a complete path of personal transformation and inner disarmament. 'Soul surfing' is not a concept; it has no use-by date, attempting to define it would only devalue the very essence of what it is that we recognize deep within ourselves. Our greatest challenge as surfers is to integrate this wisdom more fully into our daily lives; by changing the way we see ourselves, we can change the way the world appears.

If my heart could do my thinking, and my head began to feel,
I would look upon the world anew, and know what's truly real.
VAN MORRISON

Nihiwatu has not only a physical basis but it also manifests on an aspirational level in our mindstream. It remains symbolic of the natural simplicity of a life where every being has the right to enjoy a happiness devoid of suffering, and where we as a collective can display the compassionate means to achieve this noble end.

First published in *The Surfer's Journal* Volume 11 No. 4 Fall 2002

Epilogue

The Nihiwatu Resort continues to operate, offering exclusive access to the lefts made famous by Occy in the '92 cult classic *The Green Iguana*. Claude Graves recently sold the resort to retail billionaire Chris Burch, but Claude will continue to be the driving force of the Sumba Foundation. The surf break is protected and limited to only 10 surfers per day. Exclusive is the buzz-word as prices start from $1250 a night and further price hikes are likely as the resort gets enlarged and refurbished.

The Sumba Foundation was registered as an NGO in the USA in 2001. Their aim is to provide humanitarian aid by fostering village-based projects that impact health (including access and malaria control), education, water and income-generation, while preserving and respecting the fragile culture and traditions of the Sumbanese people. Notable acheivements include:

- Five health clinics built and staffed by the Foundation
- Malaria infection rates reduced by 85%
- More than 60 water wells and 240 water stations developed
- 16 primary schools supplied with water, toilets, tables, chairs, library books and supplies
- Sumba Foundation Clinics provide reliable healthcare to over 20,000 people
- In 2014 the Sumba Foundation Australia arm have joined forces with SurfAid to continue its commitment to the improvement of mother and child health, an increase in access to clean water and the reduction of malaria.

Nihiwatu: A Rude Awakening

A snapshot in time from 2001 chronicling the Sumba experience for a few feral surfers

PAUL KENNEDY

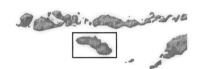

YOU JUDGE BY the amount of boardbags being loaded onto the ferry how many other surfers you will be sharing waves with. If you're heading to Sumba you look for tags labelled Waingapu. Less than ten boardbags and everything is cool because only one ferry stops there from Bali each week, while another stops in every ten days. Most surfers disembark an island earlier in Sumbawa, to surf the mechanical yet ridiculously crowded waves at Hu'u. Sumba harbours no such blessed surf locations and is isolated in its southern location. Throw in misinformation in a main surf guidebook as well as unconventional surf camps, and it all becomes a bit hazy for surf-starved travellers looking for safer odds. Even the official tourist brochure of West Sumba, with enticements such as, "there is a shore with one of the longest waves in the world for surfing, and for people who like to have fishing adventure, the sea is offering blue and black marvin games", doesn't seem to have opened the tourist floodgates.

My first trip to Sumba was in 1997. There were six of us to be exact; an instant crowd, not that it made any difference. On arrival in the port town of Waingapu, we opted to charter a bemo straight to the wave known as Occy's Left, made famous in the film *The Green Iguana*. We stayed for ten days at the small village of Watukarere, which overlooks the surf break from high in the hills. As is custom in Sumba, we made an offering of betel nut and cigarettes to the village head. Chief Metebulu and his wife Maria were used to catering for a slow trickle of surfers, who were housed in a traditional peak-roofed house.

On the way in, we had passed a solitary surfer walking to the main road to catch a lift out. But he was the only surfer we saw. For ten days it was just the six of us.

Each day we'd trudge down the hillside through the forest, out onto the rice paddies below and then half a mile along the beach to the wave. It was a peaceful walk, a kind of pre-surf meditation, and on the hot walk back up to the village, there was a spring in the forest to cool off at. The waves were 4ft for the whole 10 days. Fun, but not exactly what you visit Indo for. Was the break a fickle hoax? It was too hard to tell. The woodwork inside the house was carved with moans and bitches from visiting surfers about the wave. The jury was out and we left Sumba having only visited Nihiwatu.

Four years later I returned with two friends, John and Adam. Our first destination was the expansive horseshoe bay at Tarimbang. Its righthand point attracts most surfers who visit Sumba. The wave is an odd mixture of hollow intensity and faceless fat sections. To get out to this wave requires a paddle about 800 metres each way, an exercise that becomes a bit of a chore. After three days the swell dropped and we'd had enough of paddling. It's not easy finding transport down Sumba's rugged dead end roads. But at least anything that moves is transport – trucks, jeeps, bemos – they'd all take our money.

We left in a battered Land Cruiser, eight surfers and backpackers squashed inside. The four Sumbanese sat on the bonnet, able to jump clear should the jeep falter on the steep roads out of Tarimbang.

Our next stop was Watukarere and Nihiwatu Beach, and we were unsure of what to expect. In front of the wave at Nihiwatu is the Sumba Reef Lodge aka Nihiwatu Resort. When we were

Nihiwatu lineup looking tempting but now off limits if you're not a local living within a mile of the beach, or a guest at the five-star resort.

there in 1997, its only occupant was a caretaker. But it was now open for business with guests paying US$200 per night. In the *Surfing Indonesia* guidebook, the wave described as being the subject of some publicity in the past was now said to be 'off limits to all tourists, including surfers'. It described the area as an eco-tourism project exclusive to Nihiwatu guests – enough to stop most people from going. Claude Graves, the American owner of Nihiwatu Resort, was also the author of the Sumba chapter of this guidebook, and everything seemed a little strange.

Chief Metebulu and Maria greeted Adam, John and I when we arrived at Watukarare late one night. We offered betel nut and cigarettes and were housed in a new concrete building, which Metebulu must have decided visiting surfers would prefer. This was disappointing because staying in the old peak-roofed house was part of the Sumba vibe, but at least we were welcome thus far, much to our relief. An American named Randy was the only surfer staying at Watukarare. He'd been travelling continuously for nineteen years, working as a fisherman when he had to. He had numerous hilarious stories to tell. The one about the police-raping gay Mexican *bandito* born out of incest, with three fingers on each hand was disturbing, making us thankful to be in Sumba. To a lone warrior like Randy, four must have been a crowd, and before long he set off to an unknown location.

The walk down through the forest, over the rice paddies and along the beach hadn't changed. The wave however was totally different from the one of four years ago. It had turned into a solid beast, glassy and hollow, enticing but worthy of initial caution and respect. For 10 days, the swell pumped and only the mood of the wave changed, subtle yet significant changes demanding alertness and concentration.

Strangely, the Nihiwatu Lodge was all but empty during most of this time. An American navy diver named Paul was its only guest. Owner Claude Graves was away and if the beach was off limits then we weren't aware of it. Paul seemed happy to share the waves with what were now four other surfers. Steve, an Australian who had a long-time desire to surf Nihiwatu, had joined us at Watukarare. One morning we headed down the track for one of our last surfs at Nihiwatu. Steve got down to the beach way before us and when we came down he wasn't sitting in our usual spot. Claude Graves was back with some guests and had asked him to move along the beach where he wouldn't be noticed. It hardly mattered because we were ready to leave, but question marks still remained.

In the meantime John flew home, and Adam, Steve and I went west to Pero in a bemo called Tragedy. It had a flat when the driver picked us up, and Sumba bemos carry no spares so he forced Tragedy 20km to Waikabubak on the flat tyre before the rim and axle began to overheat. Problem fixed, we made it out west, and ended up staying in the village of Ratan Garo, right in front of a beach covered in huge megalith tombstones. Unfortunately a flat spell was upon us. We lived in our host's peak-roofed house; our every move scrutinised by dozens of staring eyes. Out here we were a novelty. This region was remarkably poorer than east and central Sumba, money was almost non-existent and we were constantly asked for cigarettes. The overbearing attention and lack of waves ground us down, forcing us to retreat to the town of Waikabubak for our final few days in Sumba.

But doubt over Nihiwatu still remained. Would it be open to surfers in years to come? It was well known that Metebulu and Graves had had many disputes over the years and at certain times Graves had tried to keep people from surfing the wave. Weeks before John, Adam and I had visited Nihiwatu, Graves had issued two surfers with trespass notices.

I had to make contact with Claude Graves to clarify his position in respect to the wave. In 2002 we made contact. He told me that the track from Watukarare, down to the beach is owned by Nihiwatu Resort. Apparently there is no way to access the beach without crossing the resorts land. Up until now an issue had not been made of trespassing across the resort's property because so few people stay at Watukarare. But the resort had recently employed marketing reps in the USA, Europe and Australia who sell Nihiwatu as an up-market hideaway for divers, bird watchers and Europeans interested in culture. Because these guests will be expecting an exclusive property, the resort invokes its rights to keep non-Nihiwatu guests off its land, which includes the beach. Graves went on to say that the government authorities are aware of this problem and supportive of the decision to keep access through the property restricted.

"They know that 12 high-end accommodation units will bring in more tax income than 150 *losmen* rooms selling at $15 per room. It's important to note that less people equates to less pollution and cultural conflict. We are the largest single employer and taxpayer on the island. We provide aid to the people where the government cannot. Through our marketing we are providing a worldwide awareness of Sumba. We initiated the expansion of the Tambolaka airport. We funded and built the 12 kilometres of land accessing Rua and Lamboya. We are building a new clinic at Hobawawi. We are purchasing our own drilling rig so that drinking water wells can be provided to the local villages. All local people from up to 1km outside the property boundary can access the reef and beach, tourists not staying at Nihiwatu cannot. All of this is clearly stated in the contract".

When asked why he became involved in the Periplus *Surfing Indonesia* guidebook, when there was clear conflict of interests, he replied,

"I didn't want to be involved with the Periplus or any other guide for that matter. But I was convinced to and my reasoning at the time was that by writing the article I could write Nihiwatu out of it".

This was good for a few of us because it kept the crowds down, but was it what people should expect from an objective guidebook? The majority of surfers, who travel on a limited budget are now to be denied. We stay in the village, living simply like the locals, enjoying the culture and surf. What about the money the surfers bring to Watukarere?

"The financial contribution of surfers at Watukarare is negligible. I know the amount for the last two years and it amounts to only about two weeks of Nihiwatu's contribution" said Graves.

"We have established a non-profit organisation called the Sumba Foundation. The purpose is to turn the resort over to the foundation and all of the resort's profits will be used for aid projects in Sumba.

"The waves will never stop at Nihiwatu, Tarimbang, Kodi, and Kalala or at the other great places you don't yet know about. Regrettably the only difference is that the other places will become, yet again, additional surf slums on the map of Indonesia. Like G-Land, Rote, Sumbawa and Sumatra. Sumba, once publicised, will be inundated with too many surfers, *losmen* and the bad vibes that go with it all.

"The problem is not really with the surfers. It's with the surf industry, the surf magazines, guides and product sellers who create the awareness of the new locations. Remember 'The Search' is what it's all about."

But Graves was the one who had given Nihiwatu its profile. He invited Occy and Jack McCoy to come and make *The Green Iguana*, which created the awareness of this new location. And now he's trying to hush it up, claiming exclusive ownership to the beach accessing this five-star wave. What's worse is that most of Nihiwatu's guests don't come for the surf, which leaves the wave predominantly unutilised.

Most locals we talked to said that the beach was government property, and open to everyone. Graves states that ownership of the beach is the jurisdiction of the local government.

"As far as I know Indonesians have the right to access beaches in most but not all places. In some areas designated for tourism, even locals don't have the right to access a hotel's beach. I don't agree with that, but that's the way it is" he says.

When asked how he would stop surfers from walking across the beach he said,

"I'll let the government decide the best way to sort access out. So far they've suggested us building a barbed wire fence and having access gates for the local people to use. Police support has also been offered. I will be planting a 'living' border fence this rainy season. This fence will consist of trees closely planted together and will be 6km long".

I put it to him that if the beach can be owned, then at least the ocean can't. What would he do when people started turning up in boats?

"I would leave that to the local government to decide. My immediate concern is trespass on private property."

It's amazing what money can buy, especially in a cash-strapped area. Unless you have $US200 per night to spare, Nihiwatu will soon be off-limits. That's unless you own a boat, or can find any other way to run the gauntlet and get out to the wave, to surf what belongs to everyone or no one at all.

This story was first published in *The Surfer's Path* magazine in 2002 ...

Peruvian Cheetah of Nemberala

Stalking the Rote line-ups with the 1965 World Champ, Felipe Pomar

SUSAN CHAPLIN

ELIPE POMAR BECAME World Surfing Champion in 1965 when the contest was held in Peru, and he was just 21. I first met him in July of 1994, on Rote, the most southerly island in Indonesia. He was 50 and I was 49. We were out surfing perfect headhigh waves in a small, mellow crowd at an unnamed left-breaking wave near a village called Nemberala.

The green waves, as beautifully and painfully transparent as the memory of first love, were fronted by a long, white beach and a regal, rustling forest of coconut palms. Catching the waves one after another (his 10 to my one), it was obvious that Felipe was a predator. I felt nervous about chatting up this powerful, focused surf legend, as if my presence might sully him – like walking across a plush white carpet in muddy boots. Though not overly tall, he looked to me, even astride his board, like a giant. His short brown hair was sleek with seawater; his strong nose pointed at a small mouth taut in concentration. I paddled up as close to him as I dared. He rode a shiny blue 7'4 thruster and I a mass-shaped 8'6" covered in sandy wax and healed with duct tape. Felipe on his thoroughbred and me on my draught horse, sat between sets and baked under the noon tropical sun. We floated amid odours of surf wax, sunscreen and brine. Finally, I said hello. Felipe, lithe in a blue rash vest, turned toward me and delivered a lecture designed to improve my surfing.

"The sport of surfing," he said, his voice smooth with Latin accent, "is about riding waves."

He had noticed how instead of paddling out to the line-up by launching like most surfers from a rocky point, I paddled a quarter mile out through a rip-torn-channel between the lefthander and a less-ridden right known as the Bommie. I always returned to shore the same way.

"You shouldn't waste energy in the channel," Felipe said. "Save your strength for catching and riding waves."

I have always felt (a fact that still haunts me) that Felipe saw me as his equal. He was convinced that if I could acquire his focus and passion I could ride waves as skilfully as he did. During the first weeks that I shared Nemberala with Felipe, neither of us knew about the other. He was a renowned big-wave rider and a surfing champion. I was a middle-aged woman who had started surfing late in life. I was intrigued with surf travel and was on my 12th stop on a worldwide surf trip. I had been travelling for two years. Other than being the same age and owning surfboards, Felipe and I had little in common. He stuck to his corner and I to mine. Felipe enjoyed comfort and routine. He stayed in a comfortable *losmen* that faced the waves and followed a daily regimen of callisthenics and stretching. Felipe had his own crowd, mostly accomplished surfers. He schmoozed with Hawaiian big-wave riders who dropped in on Rote's surf season. Most of all, Felipe enjoyed the company of his longtime friend and compadre, Tony 'Tarzan' Maldi, with whom he had once shared a house at Sunset Beach. Maldi had helped Felipe start a surf camp in Kon Tiki, Peru. Felipe was well connected and well traveled.

In Nemberala, I followed the advice of a traveling Aussie surfer whom I had met in the urban jungles of Kuta: "Take the hard road as a traveler." I was convinced that the heart of a foreign culture, whose inner workings I loved to plumb, could only be found beating in its lowest substratum. I lived in a basic *losmen*. The bathroom required the abstemious use of water and the liberal use of the left hand. Pigs, goats, dogs, chickens, and stick-thin brown children roughhoused throughout the premises. Twice a day, the losmen turned these creatures (minus the children) into meals served with a mound of rancid steamed rice. I slept on a board bag and a straw mat side-by-side with penny-pinching Australians: Stumpy, Rowan, Simon and Banana. Square of body, young, blondish, and eight-hour-a-day surfers, they reminded me of schooling bait fish. One would change direction (usually the frequency and creativity in his use of the F-word) and the impulse was felt at the core of the group. In a flash, they pulled tightly together and swore (or surfed) in perfect unison. They called me "Seppo," a nickname for Americans, and short for septic tank (Yank). Simon, the youngest, stuck up for me: "If anyone out in the surf gives you trouble, mate," he said, "jus' look 'em in the eye and tell 'em you aren't out there to fuck spiders."

The Aussies taught me Indonesian. *Tidak apa apa* meant no worries, mate. *Tidak (bercakap) bahasa Indonesia* meant I don't (speak) Indonesian and was a good thing to know. *Besok* meant tomorrow, which was when most things happened in Nemberala. The Aussies showed me that one US dollar was worth 2,000 Indo rupiah and could buy *satu bir bintang besar dingin*, a large cold beer at Franz's. Franz, a small man of indistinguishable nationality and race, owned the only refrigerator in town, and thus the only cold beer.

My paddle-outs through the channel (unnecessary according to Felipe) acquainted me with the Yacht Club, a nickname for the flotilla of boats that anchored for months in the channel between the lefthander and Bommie. Among the surfing yachties were Mike Miller, his companion Betty, and a dog named Iris. When he wasn't surfing, Mike basked on his giant, resplendent catamaran, the *Humuhumunukunukukuapua'a*, named after Hawaii's state fish. Mike was silver-blond, tall, regal and not young. It was said that he owned a house on the North Shore of Oahu and that Quiksilver subsidized his travels. In tiny trunks, holding a golf club over his shoulder, I saw him strutting on the beach in Nemberala. It was said that he paid local kids to fetch his lost golf balls.

Other yacht clubbers were the compact red-haired Gary Burns, his strong wife, Elaine, and a tow-headed tiny daughter. Gary and Elaine, aboard a small modest yacht, were from San Diego. I talked to the Burnses as I passed their boat on my way out to the surf. Elaine, tanned and enduring, offered me a warm smile. Like Felipe, Gary took me under his wing. If I did not appear to spend long enough in the water, he accused as I paddled in, "You're not dedicated enough." If I went out when he thought conditions were too tough for me he said,

"You really think you can surf waves like that?"

The Yacht Club had its transients. Surf charterer Mark Coleman parked his motor yacht, the *Perkasa*, with his clients aboard in the channel. Gossip said that, as *Playgirl*'s original centerfold, Mark was a pioneer. Paddling past the Yacht Club, I heard screams of rage and lust. Boyfriend/girlfriend swapping was common in the Yacht Club. Some people got so fed up that they jumped ship to live in Nemberala.

When there were no waves, Felipe visited me in my *losmen*. To Felipe, the next best thing to surfing was getting stronger so that he could surf better. Felipe heard that I worked out every day, so he came over one day to see for himself. Using the *losmen*'s disintegrating furniture and rafters for gym props, I showed him my stuff. After that, we worked out together regularly. Felipe appeared for workouts neatly dressed in spotless shorts and a clean T-shirt. We swapped exercises; he taught me more than I taught him. We did pushups with our hands on two chairs, feet on a bench. We dropped our chins low to the floor and pushed up to failure, five sets. We did painful ab work lying on our backs, we described tight circles with feet held an inch from the floor: 60 to the right, 60 to the left, several sets. Felipe and I went running, a three-mile round trip on the beach to a triangular stone we named Mexican Hat Rock. Felipe liked to sprint on the dirt road through Nemberala. My knees were not up to it.

"As we get older," Felipe said, before setting off on a sprint, "we must work on our explosive strength."

Ragged barefoot children, old men, and women in tattered *pareus*, lips red with betel nut juice, lined up to watch Felipe sprint. He ran in a dusty canyon bordered by walls of humanity. Like rock canyon walls might gaze down in amazement at a tumbling river, the residents of Nemberala gazed in awe and disbelief as Felipe sprinted past.

Post-workout, if there was still no surf, Felipe told stories. He lounged in the cool breeze and shade on the silky sand under a palm tree lean-to that he and his Hawaiian friends had built on the beach facing the surf. Surfers sprawled next to him like a pride of big cats resting from the hunt. In the early days, Felipe told us, he traveled to G-land with his buddy Tony 'Tarzan' Maldi:

"I called my mother in Peru and told her I was going to this camp in the middle of an Indonesian jungle to go surfing. My mother asked, 'Are there any wild animals in that jungle?'

I said I believed there were snakes and rhinos, and even tigers.

She said, 'Oh, you must be very careful. Who are you traveling with?'

I said, Tarzan. There was a moment of silence on the line. Then she said;

'I guess you will be OK.'"

He shared with us about how in the summers between 1964 and 1966 he was a Waikiki beach boy: He gave surfing lessons at George Downing's Waikiki Beach Center.

"Among my notable lessons were Hugh Hefner and his then girlfriend Barbie Benton. In the end she went on with the lesson while Heff stayed smoking his pipe on the beach. Barbie loved it and wanted to come back the next morning for another lesson. Heff nixed it."

Felipe mentioned that, in 1974, he and a friend, Piti Block, possibly rode tsunami waves to shore at Kon Tiki, Peru. He and Piti were swept out to sea as the tsunami waves prepared to assault the shore. The two surfers caught a couple of large waves that later smashed boats.

"I felt totally insignificant," Felipe described his experience, "smaller than a grain of sand. We were caught in the midst of a huge struggle between the continent and the ocean."

Of his '65 championship win, Felipe modestly said, "There were very few surfers in Peru then."

After the contest, he told us the clothing company that sponsored him arranged an interview with a vice president at Metro-Goldwyn-Mayer.

"I sat there in the office amid large pictures of Elvis and Frank Sinatra. When the meeting was over the vice president said, 'You will want to move to LA and start taking acting lessons.' After thinking about it for a minute, I responded that I was happy surfing in Hawaii. The vice president said, 'This is unusual. I have never had anybody turn me down.' I thanked him and suggested he keep me in mind for any surfing movie filmed in Oahu. Then I walked out."

The surf in Nemberala could get huge. Waves rolled in like boxcars on the train named Ocean Freight. Simon always woke me, but I rolled over. Triple-overhead waves shaped my decision to remain on land. One big day, I saw that local fishing boats still sailed out through the channel. Their triangular sails carved between the two surf breaks' maelstrom of foam like blue sharks' fins. For ballast, sailors

RILEY COONEY

attached themselves to a line hung from the top of the mast and leaned out from the side of the boat. The Yacht Club remained safely anchored in any swell. I paddled out through the channel with my Nikonos in a waist pack to take pictures. I had no intention of surfing. I rode a rip current past the *Humuhumu*, Gary's boat, and the *Perkasa*. The wide Indonesian faces of the *Perkasa*'s crew stared at me in disbelief as I headed for the waves. Everyone was out surfing. Once out between Bommie and the lefthander, I felt the power of the situation: I would soon be trampled by a thundering herd of green and silver buffalo. I took pictures, but the action was too far away. It took all my strength to maintain my position in the channel. A lull convinced me that the swell was dying. I paddled over to visit the surfers. Gary was grim-faced and determined. Mike looked calm and in his element. Felipe in his trademark orange trunks on his big red board sat alone and focused on the horizon. Stumpy, Rowan, Simon and Banana sat close together and for once did not compete in their use of the F-word. I did not recognize a few of the surfers.

Peruvian veteran Felipe Pomar in synch with majestic Rote.

Gary glared at me and said to Mike, "Hope she cops one on the head. That'll teach her some respect for what's out here."

The horizon swelled like a giant green balloon. Surfers scrambled for position. I barely paddled over the top of a big incoming wave. I wondered who of the surfers had caught it. When a surfer took off next to me, I realized that I'd drifted back into the line-up. A wave unfurled toward me. Smooth and not too big, it invited me to join it, as a green hillside invites a stroll. No one was on it. As the wave picked me up, I saw a surfer dredging along its base. He carved up on his rail to my level. I turned turtle and bonded to my board like wax. With my limbs – my soul – around it, the board went over-the-falls and hit the water nose first like an elite diver. I heard applause in the thunder of the water around us. I felt pain in my ears and opened my eyes; it was dark. Something held me against the reef like a giant foot. I struggled. Gold spots and silver comets danced before my eyes: I was running out of oxygen. I wasn't conscious when the next wave set me free. I came up gasping for air. My board bobbed beside me. The Yacht Club was not far away. Weak and dizzy, I paddled to the *Humuhumu*. Mike and Betty, Gary and Elaine, and Mark smiled down at me. I heard music. Surfers hefted bottles of Bintang in celebration of epic surf. Gary said, "We were worried about you. Your board was bobbing and jerking like there was a body at the end of the line."

Mike spoke to me, and I felt I had joined a club. Maybe a good wipeout was as good as a good ride. "Quite a show," he said. "That guy you dropped in on has a story."

I was bloated with seawater. The current was strong, so I rode the Bommie's whitewater in to the beach. If I hadn't seen Felipe sitting with his board across his lap in the shade of the palm frond lean-to, I would have sat down on the beach and cried.

"Catch any waves?" Felipe said. As usual, he gave me the option to have surfed as well as he did. I resisted the urge to empty myself from both ends. I smiled and said, "It's big out there."

A surfer plummeted down a set wave and caught Felipe's eye. I sprinted for the bushes where I rid myself of perhaps the lining of my digestive tract.

Trudging back to my *losmen* I felt weary and crestfallen. I had lost my camera in the surf; I had disgraced myself in big waves. I drank bottled water and took a nap. I woke almost at dusk and hiked to the point with my land camera. There was still size and consistency to the swell. Like a round, gold ingot, the setting sun challenged me to steal its 14-carat-gold light. Perfectly accenting the waves, the surfers showed me that the gilded overhead waves, not them, were the things for me to honor with my camera. Going for his last surf of the day, Felipe carried his red board along the point. He danced barefoot over the coral, floated his board, and melted into the darkening ocean.

Rote's hunter-gatherers, the tide-pool foragers, young and old in rags, were out. Silhouetted black against a livid sunset, they wielded plastic buckets, little shovels, and small homemade wire spears. Hunting small fish and octopus, they mock-fought for the ownership of the most fecund tide pools like an army of childish gladiators. The great waves huddled closely around Rote. As Holland protects its land from the sea with a strong network of dykes, Rote's magnificent Indian Ocean protected itself from the land by corralling it with mighty waves.

I felt deeply sad. Two years ago I had set out on a solo worldwide surf trip. I was intoxicated by the adventure of surfing. I had no doubt that I would become a good surfer. Yet, looking out at the vast collective skill of these elite surfers, I knew

I could never match them. I felt great respect and envy. I fell into the chasm of Felipe's fanatical patronage of me, and the hole I'd dug for myself by starting the sport too late to get good. I had lost my sense of purpose.

Lit by a last paroxysm of the sunset, a lone rider slipped by high on the wave. As he smoothly dropped into the dark abyss of the trough, I saw a flash of red and knew it was Felipe. He extended himself across the face of the wave in the 80-mile-an-hour race of the cheetah. He was of higher consciousness; he used his prey to nourish him, and then released it unharmed. Like the seawater that still dripped out of me, a smile seeped across my face. If anything summed up the life of the surfer, it was intimacy with waves. My wipeout had been a love affair with a big beautiful wave. In a few days, I would travel to the Philippines in search of waves.

Walking back to my *losmen* under a full moon, I saw my shadow stretch itself out flat, as if in a dead run. As I ran faster, a sense of purpose and joy coursed though my veins. Like Felipe, I was the cheetah: I was a surfer.

Felipe Pomar has returned to Rote every year for 20 years. He and a friend, Diego Arrarte, built a surf lodge facing the waves. The Malole Surf House started accepting guests in 2007. Our lives have put distance between us, but I know that in each of my surf sessions, if I remain passionate and focused on riding waves, I honor Felipe Pomar. He currently lives in Hanalei, Kauai. He and his girlfriend, Devaki, offer fitness and anti-aging counseling.

"Our mission," Felipe recently told me, "is to help others in extending their health. For a surfer this means adding 10 good surfing years to your life."

First published in *The Surfer's Journal* Vol 18 No. 6.

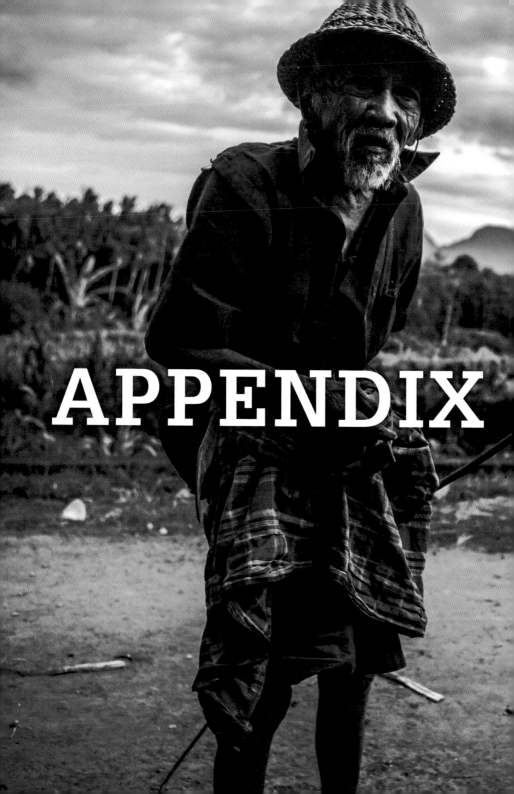

APPENDIX

Stormrider Surf Stories

- **Have you got any amazing stories of your life spent chasing waves?**

- **Have you witnessed any seminal moments of discovery, danger or death?**

- **How about some compelling cultural commentary, or insights into love 'n' hate and good versus evil?**

We're looking for the most incredible, bizarre, jaw-dropping, beautiful, spine chilling, hilarious, unusual, unexpected and downright stoke-inducing tales for a new *Stormrider Surf Stories* collection. If you have read and enjoyed this book, then you know what we are looking for, and that might just be your surf story.

We want your surf stories from all corners of the Earth, to ride shotgun with your *Stormrider Guides*, so when you head off into the unknown, you will be well armed with facts, fables and engrossing background stories about the waves and places you are actually visiting.
   If your story makes the grade, not only will you earn some cash towards your next surfari, but it will become part of an upcoming title list that includes: **Stormrider Surf Stories Central America and the Caribbean; Africa; South America; Europe; Pacific Ocean; Australia; North America; Asia**

So what are you waiting for? Get writing and send all submissions to surfstories@lowpressure.co.uk or contact us at **www.stormriderguides.com**

THE **STORMRIDER** SURF GUIDES
Indo travel essentials

INDONESIA
AND THE INDIAN OCEAN

Stormrider Surf Guide | Surf Journal | Playing Cards

INDONESIA   Java and Bali   Nusa Tenggara   Sumatra

Stormrider Indonesia eBook collection